UNIVERSITY OF MINNESOTA   *Twin Cities Campus*

David Pearce Demers, Ph.D.
Visiting Professor
School of Journalism and Mass Communication
31 Murphy Hall, 206 Church Street, S.E.
Minneapolis, Minneosta 55455-0418

University Office: 612/626-1514   Fax: 612/483-8681
Home Office: 612/490-5829   E-mail: DPDemers@aol.com

The Menace of the Corporate Newspaper

The Menace of the
CORPORATE

NEWSPAPER

Fact or Fiction?

David Pearce Demers

Iowa State University Press / Ames

For the Minnesota Team:
Phillip J. Tichenor, George A. Donohue and Clarice N. Olien

David Pearce Demers is a visiting professor in the School of Journalism and Mass Communication at the University of Minnesota. He is on leave from the University of Wisconsin–River Falls, where he is assistant professor of journalism.

© 1996 Iowa State University Press, Ames, Iowa 50014

♾ Printed on acid-free paper in the United States of America

First edition, 1996

Library of Congress Cataloging-in-Publication Data

Demers, David P.
    The menace of the corporate newspaper: fact or fiction? / David Pearce Demers.
        p.   cm.
    Includes bibliographical references and index.
    ISBN 0-8138-2269-6 (acid-free paper)
    1. American newspapers—Ownership. 2. Press monopolies—United States. I. Title.
PN4888.O85D46   1996
071'.3—dc20   95-41462

Contents

Part 3: Origins, 127

Part 4: Effects, 203

Part 5: Conclusion, 305

Preface

This book brings together and synthesizes in one place many of my writings on the corporate newspaper and related topics that have appeared since 1987 in *Journalism and Mass Communication Quarterly* (formerly *Journalism Quarterly*), *Journalism and Mass Communication Monographs* (formerly *Journalism Monographs*), *Journal of Media Economics, Newspaper Research Journal,* and *Communication Research.* A substantial proportion of the book also contains unpublished material from my Ph.D. dissertation[1] and my most recent national survey of daily newspapers in the United States. In particular, most of the data that examines the effect of organizational (corporate) structure on organizational goals, advertising rates, and editorial-page content (editorials and letters to the editor) — data that is critical for testing the main theory of this book — is being published here for the first time (see Chapters 7 and 10).

This book is a scholarly work and, as such, is intended primarily for an academic audience, especially scholars and graduate students in mass communication, history, sociology and political science. However, it is hoped that journalists, policy makers and concerned citizens also will find it useful, since the findings have implications for the newsroom as well as for public policy. Each chapter contains a summary, and the final chapter includes a summary of the entire book. An effort has been made to keep scientific jargon to a minimum in these sections.

As pointed out in Chapter 1, it is my belief that the rise of the corporate form of organization in the newspaper industry has been greatly misunderstood. For nearly a century, many scholars, journalists and citizens have mourned the demise of the small, family-owned entrepreneurial newspaper and criticized the growth of the corporate form of organization. They believe the corporate newspaper — which is characterized by absentee ownership, a complex division of labor, emphasis on written rules, and efficiency in decision-making — is destroying good journalism and democratic principles. The corporate newspaper, they argue, is a menace.

But this perspective, I will argue, is based more on nostalgic myth than on historical fact. The entrepreneurial newspaper — which is characterized by local ownership, a simple division of labor, emphasis on informal rules, and tradition in decision-making — has fallen far short of the journalistic ideal, for at least four major reasons. First, the entrepreneurial newspaper is, historically, a vestige of smaller, less complex communities, where a diversity of opinion and social conflict are rarely appreciated. Second, entrepreneurial publishers and their families traditionally have had strong ties to the local community power structure, which decreases the probability that the newspaper will challenge or criticize dominant groups and their ideas and values. Third, the entrepreneurial newspaper operates on a smaller profit margin, which reduces the probability that it will be critical of any single advertiser or the groups they represent, albeit no newspaper can afford to alienate large segments of its advertising base. And fourth, the entrepreneurial newspaper has fewer human and capital resources. The corporate newspaper is structurally organized to maximize profits as well as product quality.

Many previous studies and analyses have failed to identify these social and structural constraints because they have relied heavily on intuition and personal experience rather than systematic research methods. Much of the literature, in fact, is literally devoid of formal theory and is based on personal anecdotes or case studies rather than comparative analysis. What makes the analysis in this book different from others before it is that it relies heavily on formal sociological theory, rather than intuition, to generate propositions about processes and effects, and it relies more heavily on data from probability surveys, as opposed to anecdotes or case studies, to test those propositions. The major advantage of probability surveys is that they allow generalizations to large populations of cases.

The central theme of this book is that the corporate newspaper should be viewed largely as the outcome of increasing complexity in a social system (or what some researchers call structural pluralism[2]), and that even though the corporate newspaper is more profitable than the traditional family-owned entrepreneurial newspaper, this does not necessarily mean the end of diversity of ideas or democratic ideals. Corporate newspapers, it will be shown, actually publish more editorials and letters to the editor that are critical of established power groups. This gives the corporate newspaper a greater capacity than the traditional entrepreneurial newspaper to promote or accelerate social conflict and social change. The rise of the corporate newspaper helps to explain, in fact, many of the social and political reforms that have been implemented during the 20th century.

Although I will argue that the corporate newspaper is more critical of established power groups than traditional forms — and in this sense a more potent force for social change — this perspective should not be interpreted as an apology for the corporate form of organization. The corporate newspaper is no messiah. It often publishes news and information that has adverse consequences for disadvantaged, challenging or alternative groups and for society as a whole. Corporate newspapers, like their entrepreneurial counterparts, provide broad-based support for dominant institutions and value systems; rarely do they promote radical social change. Like schools and police, they are agents of social control.[3]

The reader of the sociological literature will recognize that many elements of the theoretical model presented in this book are not new. This analysis draws heavily from and is indebted to the writings of classical scholars such as Adam Smith, Karl Marx, Emile Durkheim and Max Weber, and contemporary scholars such as Daniel Bell, John Kenneth Galbraith, Phillip J. Tichenor, George A. Donohue and Clarice N. Olien. More specifically, Herbert Gans has argued that the media are not so much liberal or conservative as reformist.[4] And sociologist Morris Janowitz, who studied the weekly newspaper in an urban environment during the late 1940s and early 1950s, also noted that

> the social scientific view must reject the notion that the growth of the mass media necessarily produces an undifferentiated society with a general lack of articulation and an inability to make collective decisions. Researchers must see the mass media as instruments of social control and social change that may have either positive or negative consequences, depending upon their organization and content.[5]

Yet, despite this intellectual expropriation, the theory of the corporate newspaper presented and tested in this book cannot be attributed solely to any of these authors. The theory represents a new synthesis — a synthesis that is, I believe, much greater than the sum of its parts. My hope is that some day this theory will become a footnote in a more advanced and sophisticated conceptualization of the corporate newspaper or media. Of course, my claim to originality also means that I alone am responsible for any shortcomings and errors contained herein.

Some readers also may believe that my theoretical model, which is neither clearly critical nor supportive of the structural changes occurring in the newspaper industry, is an accommodation or a "copout" — that I am attempting to please both the critics and the supporters of the corporate form of organization. I wish, indeed, that I could satisfy both groups. This has not been my experience when I have presented the findings of my research. But popularity has never been a good measure of the quality of a social theory. My hope is that the skeptical reader, especially those with a neo-Marxist or post-modern orientation, will keep an open mind.

This book is composed of 11 chapters. The first chapter defines the problem and provides a brief overview of the theoretical model. Crucial here is an understanding of the term corporate newspaper. In everyday conversation, the term corporate newspaper is often used synonymously with one or more of the following: a legally incorporated business, a newspaper owned by chain, a newspaper managed by professionally trained and educated experts rather than the owners, and a large bureaucratic organization. All of these dimensions and others, it is argued in Chapter 1, characterize or reflect some feature of the corporate newspaper, but none used alone is sufficient. Heavy reliance on one of these characteristics, in fact, is responsible in part for the widely mixed findings in the field. An entrepreneurial newspaper, in contrast, is the ideal-type antithesis of the corporate newspaper. It is unincorporated (sole proprietorship or partnership), owned independently, managed by the owners, and small.[6] Although this book will often use the terms "corporate" and "entrepreneurial" when discussing the origins and consequences of organizational structure, for the empirical analyses newspapers are rank-ordered on a continuum composed of multiple indicators and anchored by these ideal-type adjectives.

The next three chapters provide a historical and theoretical background for understanding the theory and data that are presented in later chapters. Chapter 2 briefly traces the history of organizational structure in the U.S. daily newspaper industry. The focus is primarily on how newspapers as organizations developed and changed from the early 1700s to the present. Social and economic theories that attempt to explain the origins and consequences of organizational growth and change are presented in the next two chapters. More specifically, classical theories are presented in Chapter

3. The focus is on the ideas of Smith, Marx, Spencer, Durkheim, Weber and Schumpeter. In Chapter 4, these ideas and others are synthesized in a discussion of social system theory, the overarching theoretical framework for the theory of the corporate newspaper presented and tested in this book. The review traces system theory from the 19th century to the present, focusing heavily on how criticism through the years has changed the theory.

The origins and growth of corporate form of organization in the daily newspaper industry are examined in Chapters 5 through 7. Contemporary theories and empirical research are reviewed in Chapter 5. My theory of origins and development is presented in Chapter 6 and is tested in Chapter 7. Multiple sources of data are used, including two studies of aggregate-level data collected at the national level in the 20th century and one cross-sectional national probability survey.

The effects or consequences of the corporate newspaper are discussed in Chapters 8 through 10. The existing literature on consequences or effects of corporate structure is presented in Chapter 8, which is followed in Chapter 9 with my theory of corporate newspaper effects. That theory is tested in Chapter 10; again, multiple sources of data are used, including several national probability surveys and content analyses. The 11th and final chapter summarizes the previous 10 chapters, draws conclusions and discusses the implications of the findings. A bibliography and index are also included.

The debt I bear to others for this work is heavy. I am extremely grateful to my wife, Mona, who has supported and encouraged my scholarly pursuits and has mastered the role of devil's advocate. University of Wisconsin-River Falls students Tami Jech, Emily Rollings, Terri Boyer, David Anderson, Kristin Webb and Jennifer A. Sellmeyer helped collect or code much of the data, freeing me to concentrate on other matters. Patrice Peterson put her exquisite copyediting skills to bear on the entire manuscript. Her friendship also has been a source of strength. I wish them all the best in their careers in the communication field. And I wish to thank Marvel Allen, whose administrative efficiency is exceeded only by the warmth and charm of her personality.

The Ohio State University Professor Kasisomayajula "Vish" Viswanath, North Dakota State University Professor Douglas Blanks Hindman, and University of Minnesota Professor John Busterna took time from their busy schedules to critique the entire manuscript. Their sage advice greatly improved the book, and I am deeply grateful for their professional support and friendship. A major intellectual debt also is owed to the members of my dissertation committee at the University of Minnesota: David Cooperman, Hazel Dicken-Garcia, George A. Donohue, Donald M. Gillmor, Daniel Wackman, and Phillip J. Tichenor. Other colleagues who have read portions of the book or past papers include University of Utah Professor Julia Corbett and University of Minnesota professors Jeylan Mortimer and Ronald Aminzade. The UW-RF Institutional Studies, Research and Grants Committee funded part of the 1993 national survey of journalists and the content analysis study (Faculty Research Grants #1493-9-93, #1450-5-94, and #1450-5-95). I thank the committee as well as William Campbell, director of Grants and Research at UW-RF, who provided assistance and advice in seeking those funds. Gretchen Van Houten, editor-in-chief at Iowa State University Press, and her staff provided much needed technical assistance and support.

A special note of gratitude goes to Suzanne Nichols, professor emerita of Central Michigan University, Dick Carson, editorial editor at the *Columbus* (Ohio) *Dispatch*, and Phil Tichenor, my Ph.D. dissertation adviser. Sue's enthusiasm for teaching, Dick's devotion to journalistic ideals, and Phil's intellectual perspicuity have been major sources of inspiration for me through the years. I have dedicated this book to Phil, George and Clarice, a. k. a. the Minnesota Team, whose 30-year program of research comprises the substructure for many of the ideas contained in this book. I wish them health and happiness in their retirement years.

Notes

1. David Pearce Demers, *Structural Pluralism, Competition and the Growth of the Corporate Newspaper in the United States* (Ph.D. Diss., University of Minnesota, 1992).

2. Structural pluralism may be defined as the number and variety of groups in a social system. A more systematic treatment of this concept is provided in Chapters 1, 4, 5 and 6.

3. One rare exception is the colonial press during the American Revolution.

4. Herbert J. Gans, *Deciding What's News* (New York: Vintage, 1979).

5. Morris Janowitz, "Communication, Mass: The Study of Mass Communication," pp. 41-53 in David L. Sills (ed.), *International Encyclopedia of the Social Sciences,* vol. 3 (New York: Macmillan, 1968), p. 41.

6. An ideal-type is a conceptualization that represents a phenomenon only in its abstract or pure form. Ideal-types are heuristic devices that researchers use to help them understand some phenomena or concept, even though they do not exist in reality. Max Weber originated the term.

Part 1

INTRODUCTION

Chapter 1

The "Problem" of the Corporate Newspaper

One of the most controversial trends in the U.S. newspaper industry during the 20th century has been the growth of the corporate newspaper.[1] Figure 1.1 shows that in 1900 the typical daily had a circulation of 7,500, and only 1.4 percent, or 27 of the 1,967 dailies, were owned by a group or chain.[2] Most were owned and operated by individuals and families who lived in the community their newspaper served, and only a handful of workers were needed to produce the newspaper. Decision-making at these entrepreneurial newspapers tended to be informal, and the publisher often performed many roles, including that of advertising manager, editor and circulation manager.

But by 1990 the typical daily was seven times larger (circulation 38,000) and was managed by professionals rather than the owners. About 75 percent of the 1,626 dailies, or 1,217, were part of a chain or group, which in turn owned eight other dailies that had a combined circulation of 342,000 and employed hundreds of workers.[3] In contrast to the entrepreneurial newspaper, decision-making at today's corporate newspaper tends to be hierarchical, guided by various rules and procedures, and delegated to specialists or experts in various departments who depend heavily on each other to do their jobs. There is increased emphasis on rationality in decision-making, or finding the most efficient way to accomplish a task. Many rely heavily on marketing research to understand readers' needs. And the publisher, who was once involved in nearly every

Figure 1.1
Mean Circulation and Percent of Daily
Newspapers Owned by Chains (by Year)

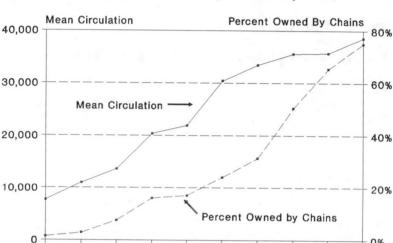

Sources: Mean circulation data obtained from *Editor & Publisher International Yearbook* (various volumes) and U.S. Bureau of Census, *Statistical Abstract of the United States* (Washington, D.C.: U.S. Government Printing Office, various years). Chain data obtained from a number of sources: for 1900 data, Michael Emery and Edwin Emery, *The Press and America* (Englewood Cliffs, N.J.: Prentice-Hall, 1988), p. 335, and Frank Luther Mott, *American Journalism* (New York: Macmillan, 1962), p. 648; for 1910 and 1920 data, Raymond B. Nixon and Jean Ward, "Trends in Newspaper Ownership and Inter-Media Competition," *Journalism Quarterly* 38:3-24 (1961); 1930 to 1960 data, Benjamin M. Compaine, "Newspapers," pp. 27-93 in Benjamin M. Compaine, Christopher H. Sterling, Thomas Guback and J. Kendrick Noble, Jr., *Who Owns the Media: Concentration of Ownership in the Mass Communications Industry* (White Plains, N.Y.: Knowledge Industry, 1982), pp. 30 and 39; and for 1990 data, *Editor & Publisher International Yearbook.*

major decision, now focuses more on long-term matters and problems than on day-to-day operations.

The shift from the entrepreneurial to the corporate form of organization has been controversial because many scholars, journalists and citizens believe the corporate newspaper is destroying good journalism and democratic principles. More specifically, the corporate newspaper is accused of placing more emphasis on the profits than on product quality, of restricting journalists' autonomy, of alienating employees, of failing to meet the informational needs of the community, and of failing to provide a diversity of ideas crucial for maintaining a political democracy. As Ben Burns, former executive editor of *The Detroit News*, puts it:

> Modern corporation management and packaging theories are sapping the vitality of creative editors and reporters. It's the General Motors syndrome. In order to survive, newspapers try to look like everybody else. People who stand out from the crowd are at risk. And what you breed out of editors is the willingness to take risks with their careers. Now we think we can create good editors by management training. You end up with a CPA mentality among mid-level editors.[4]

James D. Squires, former editor of the *Chicago Tribune,* and William L. Winter, director of the American Press Institute, agree. Says Squires:

> ... The new corporate owners of the press have taken the responsibility for "news" content out of the hands of trained, experienced professional journalists whose goal was peer recognition for quality journalism, and put it into the hands of trained, experienced professional business managers whose goal is peer recognition for successful business management.[5]

According to Winter:

> There's no question that most newspapers have become much more bottom-line oriented, even ones we think of as quality newspapers. We hear a lot of editors talking about staffs being cut back, and how difficult it is to do. Editors are having to fight harder to get any kind of increase. All of this is the direct result of the corporatization of American journalism.[6]

The emphasis on "rational market journalism," says mass communication researcher John H. McManus, means that newspapers and media

> ... must serve the market for investors, advertisers, and powerful sources before — and often at the expense of — the public market for readers and viewers. To think of it as truly reader- or viewer-driven is naive. ... Most of the time, market journalism is an oxymoron, a contradiction in terms.[7]

Media critic and scholar Ben H. Bagdikian argues that

> the antidemocratic potential of this emerging corporate control is a black hole in the mainstream media universe. Though the social problems are immense

and compacted, in the media they emit no discernible light. For me, it is a compelling illustration of what is wrong with excessively tight control: it has real consequences for what the public learns. What the public learns is heavily weighted by what serves the economic and political interests of the corporations that own the media. Since media owners are now so large and deeply involved in the highest levels of the economy, the news and other public information become heavily weighted in favor of all corporate values.[8]

And philosophy professor Douglas Kellner warns that

if we do not radically transform our media system, matters will only get worse. The rule by media managers and political handlers will continue, and democracy in the United States will be further imperiled.[9]

These and other criticisms, which are discussed in more depth later in this chapter, are widely shared.[10] In fact, the condemnation is so pervasive that to the knowledge of this scholar not one major book or journal article provides a substantial defense of the corporate newspaper. To be sure, not every scholar or professional holds a critical view. Stone's review of the empirical literature on chain ownership is widely respected:

Chain ownership has the potential of either improving or decreasing the journalistic product, but certainly there is no consistent documentation that group ownership of newspapers is inherently bad. The chief changes likely to occur with chain ownership are related to economic considerations, primarily: Chains have a distinct economic advantage derived from their experience and expertise in management, marketing and use of the economies of scale. Evidence is that this financial planning sophistication can make newspapers more profitable businesses without debasing the journalistic product.[11]

But this conclusion cannot be called a fervent endorsement of the corporate form of organization. The only enthusiastic supporters appear to be the owners, some corporate executives and a handful of economists, all of whom appear to be relatively indifferent to the critics' charges.

Yet, despite all the complaints, there is little evidence to suggest that the actions of the corporate newspaper will be significantly regulated or controlled in the foreseeable future. The corporate newspaper continues to operate with virtual impunity, presumably growing more powerful every day. The irony of this situation seems to have been overlooked by most critics. If the corporate newspaper is such a menace, then why does it continue to be the dominant form of organization in the newspaper industry? Are the critics, who include some of the most powerful and prominent individuals and organizations in professional and academic circles, politically impotent? Or, alternatively, is the corporate newspaper so powerful that it can simply ignore the criticisms? Will society merely stand by as the corporate newspaper destroys a political system that many believe is free and democratic?[12] Or are the critics wrong? Have they overstated the dysfunctional effects of corporate structure and misunderstood the origins and consequences of the corporate newspaper in society? Indeed, is the corporate form of organization incompatible with democratic processes and institutions, or can it, under certain circumstances, expose injustices, lessen inequalities and promote social change? Could it even play the role of a messiah, helping society to cope with social, economic and political changes in years to come?

The purpose of this book is to answer these and other questions surrounding the origins and consequences of the corporate form of organization in the U.S. daily newspaper industry. In contrast to the conventional wisdom, this book will argue that most of the criticism against the corporate newspaper is more myth than fact. This critique and analysis, which is framed by a macro-sociological perspective and supported by empirical data, does not conclude that the corporate newspaper is a messiah, as no single organizational form can meet all of the needs of social actors in a social system. But the position here is that most critics have misunderstood changes in newspaper organizational structure, in large part because few have taken into account the socio-historical origins of the corporate form of organization. More details about this alternative theory will be presented later. First it is necessary to define more precisely what is meant by the term "corporate newspaper" and to explore the charges against it in more depth.

What Is the Corporate Newspaper?

Although the term "corporate newspaper" is widely used in professional and scholarly circles, its meaning often varies. Journalists and economists frequently see it as a legal entity that, in contrast to a sole proprietorship or partnership, gives owners limited liability and other privileges under the law. Sociologists often equate it with a large, complex organization, like a bureaucracy, which has a hierarchy of authority, a division of labor, a multiplicity of rules and procedures, and rationality in decision-making. And from time to time both professionals and scholars have used the term as a synonym for a chain or group — i.e., an organization that owns two or more newspapers in different cities and is managed by professionals rather than the owners.

The assumption in this book is that all of these characteristics may be seen as capturing some aspect or feature of the modern corporate form of organization, or what the German sociologist Max Weber referred to as a "bureaucracy."[13] Weber defined a corporate organization as "an associative social relationship characterized by an administrative staff devoted to such continuous purposive activity." Corporate organizations may or may not pursue economic profits,[14] but they all establish and maintain boundaries for admission and continued membership. In other words, one must be hired or be allowed to join the group to become a member, and one is expected to abide by its rules. The rules are enforced either by the chief or head (*Leiter*) or by an administrative staff.[15]

According to Weber, a bureaucracy is a specific type of corporate organization — one in which behavior is goal-directed and decision-making is rational. By rational he means that bureaucratic organizations try to reduce the production and distribution of goods or services into routines so as to find the most efficient and effective way to reach a goal.[16]

> The fully developed bureaucratic mechanism compares with other organizations exactly as does the machine with non-mechanical modes of production. Precision, speed, ambiguity, knowledge of the files, continuity, discretion, unity, strict subordination, reduction of friction and of material and personal costs — these are raised to the optimum point in the strictly bureaucratic administration, and especially in its monocratic form. As compared with all collegiate, honorific, and avocational forms of administration, trained bureaucracy is superior on all these points. And as far as complicated tasks are concerned, paid bureaucratic work is not only more precise but, in the last analysis, it is often cheaper than formally unremunerated honorific service.[17]

In addition to rationality, Weber says bureaucracies are characterized by a hierarchy of authority, employment and promotion based on technical qualifications, a set of rules and procedures that define job responsibilities and show how tasks are accomplished, formalistic impersonality, and a division of labor and role specialization.[18] Authority in a bureaucracy is vested in the position rather than in the individual. This minimizes the disruption that occurs when an individual leaves the organization. Selection for employment or promotion is based on technical competence or expertise rather than patronage or social position, and loyalties are given to the organization and its set of rules and procedures, not individuals. In exchange, employees are given monetary compensation, promotions or other rewards. Interpersonal relations in bureaucracies are more impersonal than those in nonbureaucratic organizations,[19] but this was perceived as being necessary to efficiently accomplish the goals of the organization. Tasks in a bureaucracy are highly specialized and delegated to individuals who are ultimately accountable for their performance. Rules and regulations control and standardize behavior, enabling managers to control the actions of a large number of workers. And the division of labor and role specialization generate economies of scale and increase the productive capacity of the organization far beyond that of small, less diversified organizations. Weber writes:

> Bureaucratization offers above all the optimum possibility for carrying through the principle of specializing administrative functions according to purely objective considerations. Individual performances are allocated to functionaries who have specialized training and who by constant practice learn more and more. The "objective" discharge of business primarily means a discharge of business according to calculable rules and "without regard for person."[20]

Sociologist Roger Mansfield argues that the most important measure of bureaucracy is the presence of rules.[21] The bureaucratic system of administration, Weber said, is legitimized primarily by reference to a system of laws or rules. He called this authority rational-legal, and he contrasted it with two other forms of authority: traditional and charismatic. Traditional authority is legitimized by claiming identity with some group of persons that has always had authority, such as elders, high priests, chiefs or heads of household. Loyalties in traditional forms of organization, such as a patriarchy, matriarchy or gerontocracy, are given to individuals who obtain status through ascription or custom.[22] Tradition and the rule of authorities, rather than rationality and written rules, guide decision-making and behavior. Charismatic authority, unlike the rational-legal and traditional forms, is legitimized by reference to personality, expertise or the use of sacred symbols.[23] The Roman Catholic Church with its pope at the head is a good example, although it is important to point out that this organization and most modern organizations have elements of all three types of authority in varying degrees.

Although Weber believed bureaucratic organizations are very efficient, he did not believe they are utopian. One problem is that they tend to monopolize information. "Every bureaucracy seeks to increase the superiority of the professionally informed by keeping their knowledge and intentions secret. ... "[24] Bureaucracies also resist change. "Once it is fully established, bureaucracy is among those social institutions which are hardest to destroy."[25] A third problem, according to Weber, is that bureaucracies are powerful social entities whose actions sometimes are incompatible with democratic principles. He was, in fact, very pessimistic about the long-term consequences that bureaucracies had for individual freedom and autonomy and democratic decision-making.[26]

A number of empirical studies also have questioned the extent to which bureaucracies or corporations are rational or efficient. Sociologist Robert K. Merton has argued, for example, that employees of bureaucracies often place more importance on following the rules than on achieving the goals of the organization.[27] Others even argue that bureaucracies are self-destructive.[28] Many of these criticisms have some merit. However, time has demonstrated that, despite these problems or shortcomings, bureaucratic organizations often are capable of adapting to changes in the environment, and they still remain the most effective and efficient way to coordinate the work of large numbers of people. In fact, no other form of organization has displaced the bureaucratic or corporate form of organization,[29] and nearly all aspects of modern life are interpenetrated by it — including the newspaper industry.

Conceptually, then, under a Weberian model, the corporate newspaper may be seen as an organization that is characterized by a complex hierarchy of authority, a highly developed division of labor and role specialization, formalized rules and procedures, employment and promotion based on technical qualifications, formalistic impersonality, and greater rationality in decision-making. Although Weber talks about bureaucracies and other organizational forms in terms of dichotomies (bureaucratic vs. patrimonial, etc.) — and heuristically this is useful when discussing changes in organizational structure in the newspaper industry (i.e., corporate vs. entrepreneurial newspapers) — for greater precision, organizational structure should be conceptualized as a continuum. That is, any particular newspaper may be classified as occupying a space on a continuous scale from low to high in terms of degree of "corporatization."

The historical development of the newspaper industry, which is discussed in Chapter 2, follows a trend that can be described as a gradual shift from the entrepreneurial to the corporate form of organization.[30] Many newspapers began as small, family-owned enterprises during the 18th or 19th centuries and over time grew in complexity and began increasingly to take on the characteristics of the corporate form of organization — in other words, they have become more "corporatized" or "bureaucratized." For example, most are now managed on a day-to-day basis by highly skilled and educated professionals as opposed to the owners.[31]

Nevertheless, in the empirical world it is important to point out that all newspapers exhibit a mixture of the characteristics associated with entrepreneurial and corporate organizational forms — none are fully corporatized (or entrepreneurial) nor will they ever be. The transition from the entrepreneurial to the corporate form of organization should be seen as a process, not as a static or event. Thus, it is not unusual to find a family-owned newspaper employing a high degree of rationality in the completion of various tasks (e.g., efficiency) or to find a publicly owned corporation that is inefficient. Exceptions to the rule abound, partly because the actions and decisions of individuals and groups are not determined by invariant laws of the universe but, rather, are constrained or enabled by cultural, social, and psychological phenomena.[32] However, despite exceptions to the rule, the expectation under Weber's theory is that family-owned newspapers are less rational than corporate organizations, because efficiency in such organizations often conflicts with traditional practices or other organizational values (e.g., maintaining close, interpersonal relationships). Empirically, then, one would expect that rationality will be positively correlated with public ownership (as compared with family ownership),[33] and that the other dimensions of corporate structure will be correlated with rationality as well.

Operationally, chain or group ownership and circulation have been the two most frequently used measures of corporate structure.[34] Chain organizations and bigger newspapers can be expected to have a more complex hierarchy of authority and division of labor and greater rationality in decision-making than newspapers without these characteristics. Thus, a newspaper need not be legally incorporated to fit the definition of a corporation espoused here, but newspapers that are incorporated typically are more complex organizations than those that are organized as sole proprietorships or partnerships.[35]

Although chain ownership and circulation are frequently used measures of corporate structure, they are not the only possible measures, nor are they necessarily the best ones. Circulation is strongly correlated with organizational size,[36] which is the most frequently used measure of organizational complexity (i.e., division of labor, hierarchy of authority).[37] However, circulation also is a measure of consumer demand and may vary (however slightly) as demand varies. Using chain ownership as a measure of organizational complexity is even more problematic. Before the 1980s, chain ownership and circulation were positively correlated; that is, chain newspapers tended to be larger newspapers. They were larger because chain organizations were purchasing newspapers that were more profitable,[38] and larger newspapers are generally more profitable because they benefit from economies of scale.[39] However, recent research shows chain ownership and circulation are no longer correlated,[40] partly because chain ownership has become so diffused through the system that it no longer effectively discriminates between complex and non-complex organizations.[41] Measurement errors like this account in part for the inconsistent findings in many studies of chain newspapers. In this book, ownership and circulation will be used as empirical measures of corporate structure, but the analysis also widens the operational framework to include many other measures (division of labor, rationality, staff expertise) as well.

Criticisms of the Corporate Newspaper

After defining the corporate newspaper, it is easier to see why it is so widely criticized. As Weber pointed out, corporate or bureaucratic organizations tend to be impersonal. They place more emphasis on rationality, or finding the most efficient way to accomplish a task, than on developing deep interpersonal relationships as a basis for making decisions or for determining organizational goals and policies. They also develop formalized rules and procedures to control behavior, rather than relying solely on interpersonal communication. This is often perceived as being impersonal and anti-humanistic.

Criticisms like these are not new. At the turn of the century, Frank A. Munsey, a magazine and newspaper publisher, was widely despised for buying, merging and selling newspapers to make a profit and for proposing a national chain of newspapers.[42] He believed that many cities had too many newspapers and that this was inefficient. When Munsey died in 1925, William Allen White wrote:

> Frank A. Munsey, the great publisher, is dead. Munsey contributed to the journalism of his day the great talent of a meat packer, the morals of a money changer and the manners of an undertaker. He and his kind have about succeeded in transforming a once noble profession into an eight per cent security. May he rest in trust.[43]

During the 1930s, magazine editor Oswald Garrison Villard and radical journalist George Seldes also wrote about the dangers of chain ownership. Said Villard:

> It cannot be maintained that the chain development is a healthy one from the point of view of the general public. Any tendency which makes toward restriction, standardization, or concentration of editorial power in one hand is to be watched with concern.[44]

Seldes was much more critical. He accused 21 members of the American Newspaper Publishers Association, which he called "the house of lords," of using their papers mainly to advance the commercial and political interests of themselves and big business.[45]

During the 1940s, the Commission on Freedom of the Press continued this line of criticism, questioning whether freedom and democracy could survive in a system where the communication channels are concentrated in the hands of a few. "Have the units of the press, by becoming big business, lost their representative character and developed a common bias — the bias of the large investor and employer?"[46] Later, the commission added:

> Our society needs an accurate, truthful account of the day's events. ... These needs are not being met. The news is twisted by the emphasis on firstness, on the novel and sensational; by the personal interests of the owners; and by pressure groups. Too much of the regular output of the press consists of a miscellaneous succession of stories and images which have no relation to the typical lives of real people anywhere. Too often the result is meaninglessness, flatness, distortion, and the perpetuation of misunderstanding among widely scattered groups whose only contact is through these media.[47]

The growth of chain ownership during the 1950s, 1960s and 1970s ensured that "the problem of the corporate newspaper" would remain on the front burner. Bagdikian, a former newspaper editor, emerged as the leading critic. He even predicted in the 1980s that, "If mergers and acquisitions continue at the present rate, one massive firm will be in virtual control of all major media by the 1990s."[48]   While this degree of centralization has not occurred, large conglomerates like Time Warner do control a substantial amount of the total assets in the mass media industry.[49]

Reduction in Diversity

From a public policy perspective, the most significant criticism of the corporate newspaper is that it allegedly reduces the diversity of ideas in the marketplace. As Bagdikian puts it:

> If all major media in the United States ... were controlled by one 'czar,' the American public would have reason to fear for its democracy. ... Modern democracies need a choice of politics and ideas, and that choice requires access to truly diverse and competing sources of news, literature, entertainment, and popular culture.[50]

More formally, Herman argues that diversity may be defined as being composed of two parts: (1) All of the issues selected for attention by the news media should encompass all of the issues that are of substantial interest to the population; and (2) When there is a range of plausible facts and frameworks of interpretation on an issue, all facts and frameworks should be available for public inspection.[51]

Two major reasons are often advanced to justify the concept of diversity. First, diversity is seen as important for discovering truth and reaching sound public policy decisions. Second, diversity is perceived to be a prerequisite for and a measure of personal freedom.[52]

As a strategy for uncovering the truth and reaching sound decisions, the concept of diversity can be traced to the writings of Socrates and Plato, who argued that truth is best reached through rigorous discussion from which no fact or argument is withheld.[53] This line of thought is continued in John Milton's famous essay, *Areopagitica*, which espoused that government should not license or censor the press and that truth would defeat falsehood.

> And though all the winds of doctrine were let loose to play upon the earth, so Truth be in the field, we do injuriously by licensing and prohibiting to misdoubt her strength. Let her and Falsehood grapple; who ever knew truth put to the worse, in a free and open encounter?[54]

A more contemporary version of Milton's idea is embodied in Supreme Court Justice Oliver Wendall Holmes' "marketplace of ideas" metaphor, in which "the ultimate good desired is better reached by free trade in ideas — that the best test of truth is the power of the thought to get itself accepted in the competition of the market ... ."[55]

As a prerequisite for and a measure of personal freedom, the concept of diversity is seen as a means of assuring individual self-fulfillment. This idea stems from the writings of John Locke and others during the Enlightenment who emphasized the individual and "natural rights."[56] Several Supreme Court decisions also draw on the principle that "freedom of speech" is a natural right.[57] Although this view tends to focus on freedom of speech as an individual benefit, mass communication scholar William F. Griswold points out that freedom of speech also has implications for conflict management. Allowing dissident individuals or groups the opportunity to speak out, regardless of whether it leads to truth, may ease tensions and contribute to social integration and stability.[58]

Critics of the corporate newspaper often cite two major trends or factors as contributing to a loss of diversity: concentration of ownership and increased emphasis on profits.

Concentration of Ownership. Researchers generally agree that ownership in the newspaper industry has become more concentrated. Figure 1.2 shows that in 1900, there were about 26 daily newspaper owners per million residents, compared with only about three per million in 1990. By the year 2000, the figure is expected to drop to less than 2 per million.[59]

For Bagdikian and many other critics, this decline is prima facia evidence of a loss of diversity in the "marketplace of ideas." This very well could be true. However, it is important to point out that in terms of sheer numbers, the total number of newspaper owners actually has increased, not declined, over time, because of two other trends. The first is the growth of publicly owned newspapers. At the turn of the century, only a handful of newspaper companies allowed public ownership, whereas today about a third of all dailies are public. The stock of many of these newspapers is held by pension and mutual funds, which represent the investments of many middle- and working-class Americans. The second factor contributing to more owners is dispersion of ownership; that is, ownership tends to become dispersed as entrepreneurial owners die and bequeath their holdings to multiple heirs.[60] To support the notion that ownership in the newspaper industry has become more concentrated, the

Figure 1.2
Number of Newspaper Owners by Year
Per Million U.S. Residents

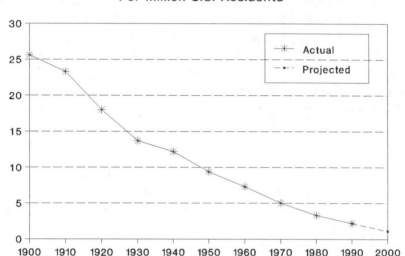

Sources: Resident population data from U.S. Bureau of Census, *Statistical Abstract of the United States, 1991* (Washington, D.C.: U.S. Government Printing Office, 1992). Number of owners compiled from several sources: for 1900 data, Michael Emery and Edwin Emery, *The Press and America* (Englewood Cliffs, N.J.: Prentice-Hall, 1988), p. 335 and Frank Luther Mott, *American Journalism* (New York: Macmillan, 1962), p. 648; for 1910 and 1920 data, Raymond B. Nixon and Jean Ward, "Trends in Newspaper Ownership and Inter-Media Competition," *Journalism Quarterly*, 38:3-24 (1961); 1930 to 1960 data, Benjamin M. Compaine, "Newspapers," pp. 27-93 in Benjamin M. Compaine, Christopher H. Sterling, Thomas Guback and J. Kendrick Noble, Jr., *Who Owns the Media: Concentration of Ownership in the Mass Communications Industry* (White Plains, N.Y.: Knowledge Industry, 1982), pp. 30 and 39; and for 1990 data, *Editor & Publisher International Yearbook.*

assumption Bagdikian and other critics make is that control of the large, public corporation is largely in the hands of a few individuals — i.e., the board of directors and/or top management — who are interested in serving their own interests before the readers' or the public's interests.

Emphasis on Profits. The second factor allegedly contributing to the loss of diversity in the marketplace is based on the belief that the corporate newspapers place more emphasis on profits than entrepreneurial newspapers.   The assumption is a zero-sum formula: If a newspaper maximizes profits, it has less to spend on collecting news, improving the product or serving the public.   Although this argument has a certain amount of intuitive appeal, the paradox is that newspapers which make more money theoretically have more money to spend on improving the operation. Thus, the question is not just one of maximizing profits but also one of how much and what proportion of profits are spent on improving the news product.

Three arguments are often put forth to support the argument that corporate newspapers are more profit-oriented. The first is that they have more market power; that is, they are less constrained by competition. The assumption here is that self-interest is the driving force behind human behavior and that competition prevents any individual capitalist from holding the community hostage. Corporate newspapers also are expected to be more oriented to the bottom line because they are more likely to be publicly owned, which means they must maintain profits to keep stockholders happy and to keep investment dollars flowing in. And the third argument is that profit-making at corporate newspapers is less constrained by the local community, because those newspapers are often owned or managed by people who do not live in the community their newspaper serves or have lived there only a short time. This also is seen as having a detrimental impact on community solidarity (discussion to follow subsequently).

The emphasis on profits means that corporate newspapers, in addition to spending less money on news gathering, are expected to cater more to the interests of advertisers and to be less vigorous editorially (i.e., less likely to criticize dominant institutions and elites) than entrepreneurial newspapers.   Corporate newspapers are expected to be less vigorous editorially because critical commentary could alienate advertisers, readers or sources, who may pull their advertising, stop buying the newspaper, or quit talking to reporters.

Worker Alienation

A second major criticism of corporate newspapers is that they alienate workers.[61]   This can be viewed as having an adverse impact on the diversity of ideas because reporters may feel less motivated to work and do a good job. But having satisfied, self-fulfilled employees may also be an end in itself.

The logic behind this criticism can be traced in part to the writings of Adam Smith and Karl Marx, who argued that the division of labor created work that is dissatisfying and alienating because it involves breaking down

complex tasks into a number of simpler, more discrete steps or tasks —
tasks that can often be performed by machines and deskilled labor.[62]
Routinization of the production process, they argued, makes work more
mundane and monotonous.

In addition to the division of labor, corporate organizations are
believed to alienate workers because they have a more complex set of rules
and regulations and because they place more emphasis on rationality, or
efficiency in decision-making, than on cultivating close, interpersonal
relationships among employees.

Loss of Community Solidarity

A third major criticism is that the corporate newspaper is destroying
community identity and solidarity. This complaint stems in part from the
observation that most major stockholders and top-level executives of chain-
owned newspapers do not live or grow up in the cities their newspapers
serve and, consequently, are not perceived to identify as strongly with the
local community as owners and executives of locally owned newspapers.
The local community, in fact, often views such individuals as "outsiders."
In the absence of strong ties to the local community, the corporate
organization is perceived as being more interested in pursuing its own goals
(e.g., growth, profits) rather than the goals of the community (e.g., access
to information, moral development). In fact, John C. Busterna, a
University of Minnesota mass communication professor, speculates that

> the passing of owner-managed, locally controlled newspapers to chain and
> corporate-managed newspapers will result in a greater concern for profits,
> perhaps with less concern for local issues.[63]

Critiquing the Critical Model

The conventional wisdom holds that the corporate form of organization is inimical to good journalism and democratic principles — that it
is a menace. This book does not dispute the notion that the corporate
newspaper wields a great deal of power and it, like other bureaucratic
institutions, often misuses that power. The corporate newspaper is no
messiah. But the "critical model" suffers from two major shortcomings.

First, most of the empirical research, which is reviewed in depth in
later chapters, fails to support it. Although the empirical evidence strongly

suggests that corporate newspapers are more profitable, there is relatively little evidence to suggest that corporate newspapers place more emphasis on profits and less on product quality as an organizational goal — in fact, the evidence points to the opposite conclusion. Contrary to the critical model, the empirical evidence also strongly suggests that corporate newspapers are more vigorous editorially than entrepreneurial newspapers. Although job satisfaction among journalists has declined since the 1970s, the empirical evidence shows that journalists at corporate newspapers are much more satisfied and that editors at corporate newspapers have more autonomy. And even though corporate newspapers may destroy traditional sources of social integration, there is little evidence to support claims that social order is breaking down. In fact, corporate newspapers, which appear to place more emphasis on nonlocal news, may help integrate local communities into larger, more interdependent or global social systems.

The second problem with the critical model is that it fails to account for social change and the role that newspapers have played historically as agents or promoters of change. The critical model assumes that the corporate newspaper promotes the interests of economic and political elites, dominant institutions and value systems with little or no capacity to promote challenging or alternative views. In fact, as media become more corporatized, their messages are expected to become more, not less, hegemonic, reducing even further the prospects for social change. When social changes occur, the critical model typically sees them as anomalies or as accommodations that have virtually no impact on changing the power structure, even in the long run. The problem with this perspective is that it is inconsistent with a large body of historical and empirical research. During the last century in particular, newspapers have played an important role in promoting (though rarely initiating) the goals of many social movements which have, in turn, succeeded in producing a number of social changes, including the expansion of rights and opportunities for women, minorities, the working class, homosexuals, and the poor. Such changes have not eliminated inequalities, discrimination or injustices, but they have changed the power structure.

An Alternative Theory of Effects

The alternative theory of effects presented and tested in this book does not challenge the notion that the corporate newspaper is an agent of social control. Like the entrepreneurial newspaper, the corporate newspaper provides broad-based support for economic and political elites and dominant values and social institutions. However, the crucial research question is not whether the corporate newspaper is a mechanism of social control — since all mainstream newspapers perform that function[64] — but, rather, how control under the corporate form of organization differs from control under alternative or traditional organizational forms (e.g., entrepreneurial newspapers), and the consequences that these different forms have for individuals, groups and society as a whole.

The alternative model posits that as a newspaper becomes more "corporatized," power and control over day-to-day operations within the organization shifts from the owners to the professional managers. The managerial revolution, as this shift of power has been called, occurs in part because the division of labor increases the complexity of the operation, forcing owners to rely more heavily on highly skilled and knowledgeable experts. Individual owners also tend to lose control over day-to-day operations because the increasing capital required to operate large-scale organizations reduces over time the proportion owned by any single owner. At any rate, the managerial revolution has substantial consequences for organizational behavior and content — for one, it means that the corporate newspaper has a greater capacity than the entrepreneurial newspaper to criticize the status quo and, thus, to promote social change.

Theory and empirical data will show, in fact, that corporate newspapers publish a greater number and proportion of editorials and letters to the editor that are critical of mainstream groups and ideas. Corporate newspapers are more critical of mainstream groups because they are more insulated from parochial political pressures and because those newspapers are more likely to be located in pluralistic communities. Corporate newspapers are more insulated because their owners, managers and journalists are less likely to grow up in the community their newspaper serves, are usually employed at the newspaper for a shorter period of time, are more oriented to the larger corporation and their profession, and are working in an environment where professional norms and values play a more prominent role in day-to-day decision-making. Professional norms and codes of ethics are designed to control the behavior of professionals, but they also help to insulate the news production process from manipulation by special interest groups, advertisers, governmental officials, and even the owners. Professionals are expected to report the news irrespective of the owners' interpersonal relationships or ties to the local community power structure. Corporate newspapers also publish more news and editorial content that is critical of the status quo because they are more likely to be located in pluralistic communities, which contain a larger number of groups competing for limited resources. This competition increases social conflict and generates more criticism of the status quo.

The alternative model will not challenge the widely held view that corporate newspapers are more profitable. They are, and this is one of the reasons for their persistence and dominance. Corporate newspapers are structurally organized to maximize profits. They benefit from economies of scale and superior human and capital resources. But contrary to the critical model, the alternative model will hold that corporate newspapers place less emphasis on profits as an organizational goal and more emphasis on producing a high quality product and other nonprofit goals (e.g., innovation, maximizing growth). The managerial revolution also explains this process. Corporate newspapers are more heavily controlled by professional managers, who are less concerned about profits than owners because they do not benefit directly from them; rather, managers obtain most of their income through a fixed salary. But even if professionals earned all of their income through profits, they still would place greater value on product quality, knowledge and expertise than the owners, because performance criteria (e.g., "doing the job well") are highly valued in professional circles and are deemed to be crucial for long term survival of the organization.

Contrary to the critical model, the shift from entrepreneurial to corporate structure does not reduce job satisfaction among journalists. Although satisfaction has declined since the 1970s, partly because of increasing competition and financial stress on the newspaper industry, journalists at corporate newspapers are more satisfied with their jobs. Role specialization explains part of this. Journalists at corporate newspapers are more likely to specialize and become "experts," which in professional circles accords them more prestige and status. Corporate newspapers also pay higher salaries. Role specialization also accounts for the fact that editors at corporate newspapers have more job autonomy. And although the managers and owners of corporate newspapers may place less emphasis on serving the interests of local elites, the greater autonomy they have from local power structures enables them to be more critical of established authorities. While corporate newspapers are more critical of the status quo, they also are much more tolerant of different points of view than entrepreneurial newspapers.

In sum, the alternative "structural" model being proposed here views the corporate newspaper as an agent of control, but one which has a much greater capacity than the entrepreneurial newspaper to promote social change. More precisely, *the corporate newspaper may be characterized as an organizational form that promotes change with control* — change that from time to time accommodates the needs of alternative or challenging groups without radically altering the power structure in the short term.

A Theory of Origins

The alternative theory of effects presented above represents a substantial departure from the conventional wisdom. One of the major reasons the corporate newspaper has been so misunderstood is that few researchers have studied its social origins and development. Most studies have focused on effects or consequences. This research is important for understanding the role and function of the corporate form of organization in society, but no theory of organization can be complete without taking into account the origins and development of a social form. The study of the origins and development of the corporate newspaper also provides important clues as to its effects.

The roots of the corporate newspaper can be traced to the early guild groups and the joint-stock company, the latter of which was created in the 16th and 17th centuries to fund large public works projects and overseas expeditions. One of the key advantages of the joint-stock company was that it enabled companies to raise large amounts of capital in a short period of time, which in turn stimulated organizational growth and role specialization. The corporatization of the newspaper industry came relatively slowly in comparison to other industries, partly because of problems of national distribution. But during the 20th century, the typical daily grew in size and complexity, and the proportion of newspapers under chain ownership grew steadily.

More formally, this book will propose that the growth of the corporate newspaper is primarily a function of increasing structural pluralism, which may be defined as growth in the number and variety of social groups in a community or social system. Two major factors explain this relationship. The first is that as a social system becomes more complex, the need for information increases, which in turn promotes the growth of large-scale media. Information is extremely crucial for coordinating and controlling

Figure 1.3
Analytical Model of Corporate Newspaper Structure

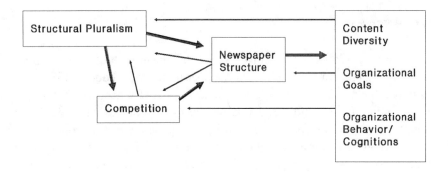

social action in systems that are highly differentiated. The second reason structural pluralism is expected to promote the growth of the corporate newspaper is increasing competition. As social systems grow and become more complex, competition between mass media for limited resources (e.g., advertising and audiences) increases, which in turn intensifies social and technological innovations and economies of scale that promote the growth of large-scale media organizations.

This theory of origins helps to explain why corporate newspapers are more profitable, have more human and financial capital, place more emphasis on quality, have more satisfied employees, and are more critical of mainstream groups, as the heavy arrows in Figure 1.3 show. The corporate newspaper is an organizational form that has survived under modern capitalism because it makes better use of human and environmental resources. These resources, in turn, have enabled the newspaper to adapt to changing conditions (feedback arrows in Figure 1.3).

From a broader perspective, the transition from the entrepreneurial to the corporate form of organization in the newspaper industry may be interpreted as supporting post-industrial theories, which claim that knowledge, rather than capital, is becoming the axial principle of modern society. Sociologist Daniel Bell argues that the coming of the post-industrial society will foster a new class structure — one based on the supremacy of professional and technical occupations, which value meritocracy — that gradually displaces the capitalists.[65] The evidence in this book suggests that corporate newspapers reflect as well as stimulate such long-term social changes.

Summary

Many scholars and journalists believe that the growth of the corporate form of organization in the U.S. newspaper industry is reducing diversity in the marketplace of ideas. Corporate newspapers are accused of placing more emphasis on profits and less on the quality of the news product, alienating employees, reducing solidarity in the community, and producing a less vigorous editorial product. Empirical research supports the notion that corporate newspapers are more profitable; however, there is relatively little evidence to suggest that they place less emphasis on product quality, alienate employees, or are less vigorous editorially.

Challenging the conventional wisdom, the alternative theory to be presented and tested in this book holds that corporate newspapers are more, not less, critical of mainstream authorities and values. The fact that corporate newspapers are more critical of the status quo does not mean they are adversaries of the system. To be sure, the content of the corporate newspaper provides broad-based support for established elites and institutions. However, as a newspaper becomes more "corporatized," news and editorial content becomes more critical, and this criticism helps to explain many of the social changes that have taken place this century. Corporate newspapers also are expected to place less emphasis on profits and more emphasis on product quality as an organizational goal, and to have more satisfied employees. Taken together, these findings suggest that diversity increases, not decreases, as a social system becomes more pluralistic.

Notes

1. A formal definition is presented subsequently.

2. Chain ownership is usually defined as two or more newspapers in different cities under common ownership. See, e.g., David Pearce Demers and Daniel B. Wackman, "Effect of Chain Ownership on Newspaper Management Goals," *Newspaper Research Journal*, 9(2):59-68 (1988).

3. For 1900 data, see Michael Emery and Edwin Emery, *The Press and America* (Englewood Cliffs, N.J.: Prentice-Hall, 1988), p. 335 and Frank Luther Mott, *American Journalism* (New York: Macmillan, 1962), p. 648. Data and estimates for 1990 are taken from *Editor & Publisher International Yearbook*; John C. Busterna, "Trends in Daily

Newspaper Ownership," *Journalism Quarterly,* 65:831-38 (1988), and U.S. Bureau of Census, *Statistical Abstract of the United States: 1990* (Washington, D.C.: U.S. Government Printing Office, 1990).

4. Cited in Doug Underwood, "When MBAs Rule the Newsroom," *Columbia Journalism Review* (March/April 1988), pp. 24-25.

5. James D. Squires, *Read All About It! The Corporate Takeover of America's Newspapers* (New York: Times Books, 1994), p. 211.

6. Cited in Jonathan Kwitney, "The High Cost of High Profits," *Washington Journalism Review* (June 1990), p. 20.

7. John H. McManus, *Market-Driven Journalism: Let the Citizen Beware?* (Thousand Oaks, Calif.: Sage, 1994), p. 197.

8. Ben H. Bagdikian, *The Media Monopoly,* 2nd ed. (Boston: Beacon Press, 1987), p. x.

9. Douglas Kellner, *Television and the Crisis of Democracy* (Boulder: Westview Press, 1990), p. 219.

10. See, e.g., C. Edwin Baker, *Ownership of Newspapers: The View from Positivist Social Science* (Cambridge, Mass.: The Joan Shorenstein Center at Harvard University, September 1994); Commission on Freedom of the Press, *A Free and Responsible Press* (Chicago: University of Chicago Press, 1947); Ted L. Glasser, Dave S. Allen and Sue Elizabeth Blanks, "The Influence of Chain Ownership on News Play: A Case Study," *Journalism Quarterly,* 66:607-14 (1989); Edward S. Herman, "Diversity of News: 'Marginalizing' the Opposition," *Journal of Communication,* 35(3):135-46 (1985); Andrew Kreig, *Spiked: How Chain Management Corrupted America's Oldest Newspaper* (Old Saybrook, Conn.: Peregrine Press, 1987); Kwitney, "The High Cost of High Profits," pp. 19-29; McManus, *Market-Driven Journalism: Let the Citizen Beware?*; Graham Murdock and Peter Golding, "For a Political Economy of Mass Communications," *The Socialist Register,* 205-34 (1973); Graham Murdock and Peter Golding, "Capitalism, Communication and Class Relations," pp. 12-43 in James Curran, Michael Gurevitch and Janet Woollacott (eds.), *Mass Communication and Society* (Beverly Hills, Calif: Sage, 1977); Doug Underwood, *When MBAs Rule the Newsroom: How the Marketers and Managers Are Reshaping Today's Media* (New York: Columbia University Press, 1993); Oswald Garrison Villard, "The Press Today: The Chain Daily," *The Nation* (May 21, 1930), pp. 597-8; and W. Powell, "The Blockbuster Decade: The Media as Big Business," *Working Papers for a New Society* (July/August 1979), pp. 26-36.

11. Gerald Stone, *Examining Newspapers: What Research Reveals About America's Newspapers* (Newbury Park, Calif.: Sage, 1987), p. 103-4.

12. Not all scholars believe the U.S. political system is "free" or "democratic." Many, including this one, argue that the U.S. political system, despite offering more freedom and democratic action than most other political systems, is nevertheless highly centralized politically and elite-driven. For more formal arguments on this point, see Martin N. Marger, *Elites and Masses* (New York: D. Van Nostrand Company, 1981) and C. Wright Mills, *The Power Elite* (New York: Oxford University Press, 1956).

13. See, e.g., H. H. Gerth and C. Wright Mills (eds.), *From Max Weber: Essays in Sociology* (New York: Oxford University Press, 1946), pp. 196-244; and Max Weber, *The Theory of Social and Economic Organization,* trans. A. M. Henderson and Talcott Parsons (New York: The Free Press, 1964 [1947]).

14. Bureaucracy is a term that historically usually referred to the state or governmental entities, but now it is widely used to refer to any large organizational structure, including businesses.

15. Weber, *The Theory of Social and Economic Organization*, pp. 145-51.

16. See Weber, *The Theory of Social and Economic Organization*, and Gerth and Mills (eds.), *From Max Weber*. It is important to point out that rationality as defined by Weber involves a means-end calculus — that is, behavior that begins with the objective of finding the most efficient way to reach a goal — not whether the behavior itself is considered "rational" by some sort of moral standard.

17. Gerth and Mills, *From Max Weber*, p. 214.

18. The list of characteristics here is distilled from Gerth and Mills, *From Max Weber*, pp. 196-8, and Weber, *The Theory of Social and Economic Organization*, pp. 329-36.

19. Contemporary research — e.g., Dean J. Champion, *The Sociology of Organizations* (New York: McGraw-Hill, 1975), pp. 36-7 — has shown that close, interpersonal relationships often flourish in bureaucratic structures. However, this does not detract from Weber's central argument that decision-making is more likely to be formal and impersonal in such organizations.

20. Gerth and Mills, *From Max Weber*, p. 215.

21. Roger Mansfield, "Bureaucracy and Centralization: An Examination of Organizational Structure," *Administrative Science Quarterly*, 18(4):477-88 (1973).

22. Weber, *The Theory of Social and Economic Organization*, pp. 346-51.

23. Mansfield, *Bureaucracy and Centralization*, p. 478.

24. Gerth and Mills, *From Max Weber*, p. 233.

25. Gerth and Mills, *From Max Weber*, p. 228. Weber also writes on p. 229: "The ruled, for their part, cannot dispense with or replace the bureaucratic apparatus of authority once it exists. For this bureaucracy rests upon expert training, a functional specialization of work, and an attitude set for habitual and virtuoso-like mastery of single yet methodically integrated functions. ... More and more the material fate of the masses depends upon steady and correct functioning of the increasingly bureaucratic organizations of private capitalism. The idea of eliminating these organizations becomes more and more utopian."

26. Gerth and Mills, *From Max Weber*, p. 224-8. Also see Robert Michels, "Oligarchy," pp. 48-67 in Frank Fischer and Carmen Sirianni, *Critical Studies in Organization and Bureaucracy* (Philadelphia: Temple University Press, 1984).

27. Robert K. Merton, *Social Theory and Social Structure* (London: The Free Press, 1957 [1949]), pp. 195-206.

28. Michael Crozier, *The Bureaucratic Phenomenon* (Chicago: The University of Chicago Press, 1964).

29. Non-rational forms of organization include the patriarchy, matriarchy, gerontocracy, patrimony, and those organizations based on collegiality or honorific criteria.

30. It is important to point out that the description here applies to the industry, not to individual newspapers, many of which never did grow but went out of business. See Chapter 2.

31. Compared to other industries, however, the newspaper industry as a whole is much closer to the entrepreneurial model. Concentration of ownership in the newspaper industry has been hindered by difficulties in centralizing production and distribution of newspapers.

32. This ontological assumption is at odds with both voluntaristic and deterministic models of social action. Like many sociologists, I argue that social actors have free will — i.e., they have the ability to make choices between alternative courses of action — but those choices are constrained (or enabled) by values, roles, laws, norms, personal tastes (etc.). For more details on the ontological assumptions of my model, see Chapter 6.

33. In the same vein, it is important to point out that the characteristics used to describe the corporate form of organization may also change over time. The first corporate groups, for example, were made up of people with similar occupations who were trying to advance or protect their own interests (much like today's professional organizations), but the division of labor in such groups was quite limited. As those groups have grown, particularly under advanced capitalism, the division of labor has also expanded greatly and traditional ways of doing things have often been challenged. See Chapter 2 for more discussion of historical development.

34. David Pearce Demers, "Corporate Structure and Emphasis on Profits and Product Quality at U.S. Daily Newspapers," *Journalism Quarterly,* 68:15-26 (1991). Chain ownership is usually defined as two or more newspapers in different cities under common ownership.

35. Only 17 percent of all businesses are legal corporations, but they account for about four-fifths of all business sales and profits. See Campbell R. McConnell, *Economics: Principles, Problems, and Policies,* 10th ed. (New York: McGraw-Hill, 1987), p. 115.

36. The correlation between circulation and number of employees, the most frequently used measure of the division of labor, is .90 or higher. See John E. Polich, "Predicting Newspaper Staff Size from Circulation: A New Look," *Journalism Quarterly,* 51:515-7 (1974); Paul J. Deutschmann, "Predicting Newspaper Staff Size from Circulation," *Journalism Quarterly,* 36:350-4 (1959); and Lori A. Bergen and David Weaver, "Job Satisfaction of Daily Newspaper Journalists and Organizational Size," *Newspaper Research Journal,* 9(2):1-13 (1988).

37. Peter M. Blau, "A Formal Theory of Differentiation in Organizations," *American Sociological Review,* 55:201-18 (April 1970) and Richard H. Hall, *Organizations: Structures, Processes & Outcomes* (Englewood Cliffs, N.J.: Prentice-Hall, 1987).

38. George A. Donohue, Clarice N. Olien and Phillip J. Tichenor, "Reporting Conflict by Pluralism, Newspaper Type and Ownership," *Journalism Quarterly,* 62:489-99, 507 (1985), p. 490.

39. James N. Rosse, "The Evolution of One Newspaper Cities," paper prepared for the Federal Trade Commission Media Symposium in Washington, D.C. (December 14-15, 1978), and James N. Rosse and James N. Dertouzos, "An Economist's Description of the 'Media Industry,'" pp. 40-192 in *Proceedings of the Symposium on Media Concentration* (Washington, D.C.: Bureau of Competition, Federal Trade Commission, December 14-15, 1978).

40. Two separate national probability surveys at the organizational level have reached the same conclusion. See Demers, "Corporate Structure and Emphasis on Profits and Product Quality at U.S. Daily Newspapers," and David Pearce Demers, "Corporate Newspaper Structure and Organizational Goals," paper presented to the Association for Education in Journalism and Mass Communication (Atlanta, August 1994). However, at the level of the social system, chain ownership (percent of newspapers owned by chains) is strongly correlated with mean circulation over time. See David Pearce Demers, "Structural Pluralism, Intermedia Competition and the Growth of the Corporate Newspaper in the United States," *Journalism Monographs,* vol. 145 (June 1994).

41. David Pearce Demers, "Effect of Corporate Structure on Autonomy of Top Editors at U.S. Dailies," *Journalism Quarterly,* 70:499-508 (1993), p. 508.

42. For more details on Munsey, see Jean Folkerts and Dwight L. Tweeter, Jr., *Voices of a Nation: A History of the Media in the United States* (New York: Macmillan, 1989), pp. 329-30.

43. William Allen White, *Emporia (Kansas) Gazette* (December 23, 1925).

44. Villard, "The Press Today: The Chain Daily."

45. George Seldes, *Lords of the Press* (New York: J. Messner, 1938). Also see his book, *Freedom of the Press* (Indianapolis: Bobbs-Merrill, 1935).

46. Commission on Freedom of the Press, *A Free and Responsible Press*, p. 51.

47. Commission on Freedom of the Press, *A Free and Responsible Press*, pp. 67-8.

48. Bagdikian, *The Media Monopoly*, pp. 3-4.

49. See, e.g., Shirley Biagi, *Media/Impact: An Introduction to Mass Media* (Belmont, Calif.: Wadsworth, 1994), various pages under index heading, "Media Ownership."

50. Bagdikian, *The Media Monopoly*, p. 3.

51. Herman, "Diversity of News: 'Marginalizing' the Opposition," p. 135.

52. William Floyd Griswold Jr., *Community Structure, Reporter Specialization and Content Diversity Among Midwest Daily Newspapers* (Ph.D. Diss., University of Minnesota, 1990), pp. 11-17.

53. Griswold, *Community Structure, Reporter Specialization and Content Diversity*, p. 14.

54. Quoted from Rufus Wilmot Griswold (ed.), *The Prose Works of John Milton*, vol. I (Philadelphia: J. W. Moore, 1856), p. 189.

55. *Abrams v. United States*, 250 U.S. 616 (1919).

56. John Locke, *The Second Treatise of Civil Government and A Letter Concerning Toleration* (Oxford: B. Blackwell, 1946 [1690]).

57. *Gitlow v. New York*, 268 U.S. 652 (1925) and *Cohen v. California*, 403 U.S. 15 (1971).

58. To support these arguments, Griswold, *Community Structure, Reporter Specialization and Content Diversity*, cites Jerome A. Barron, "Access to the Press: A New Concept of the First Amendment," pp. 9-15 in Michael C. Emery and Ted Curtis Smythe (eds.), *Readings in Mass Communications: Concepts and Issues in the Mass Media*, 2nd ed. (Dubuque: William C. Brown Co., 1974), and James S. Coleman, *Community Conflict* (New York: The Free Press, 1957), p. 21. Also see Lewis Coser, *The Functions of Social Conflict* (New York: Free Press, 1956), pp. 151-7.

59. An owner is defined here as the number of sole proprietorships, partnerships or corporations that operate a newspaper.

60. See Chapter 8 for more discussion of ownership.

61. For a review, see Keith Stamm and Doug Underwood, "The Relationship of Job Satisfaction to Newsroom Policy Changes," paper presented to the Association for Education in Journalism and Mass Communication (Washington, D.C., August 1991).

62. Adam Smith, *The Wealth of Nations* (New York: Modern Library, 1937 [1776]), p. 734, and Karl Marx, "Economic and Philosophic Manuscripts of 1844," pp. 66-125 in Robert C. Tucker (ed.), *The Marx-Engles Reader*, 2nd ed. (New York: W. W. Norton & Company, 1978), p. 74.

63. John C. Busterna, "How Managerial Ownership Affects Profit Maximization in Newspaper Firms," *Journalism Quarterly*, 66:302-7, 358 (1989), p. 307.

64. George A. Donohue, Phillip J. Tichenor and Clarice N. Olien, "Mass Media Functions, Knowledge and Social Control," *Journalism Quarterly*, 50:652-9 (1973).

65. Daniel Bell, *The Coming of the Post-Industrial Society* (New York: Basic Books, 1976 [1973]).

Part 2

BACKGROUND

Chapter 2

History of the Corporate Newspaper

The birth of the corporate newspaper in the United States is often traced to the late 1800s. This was a time, many mass communication scholars point out, that the press as well as other capitalist enterprises began to exhibit the characteristics of "big business." Mass communication historian Hazel Dicken-Garcia writes that the "emphasis shifted from news *persons* to news *selling*, and an editor-centered, personal structure gave way to corporatism, focused on advances in technology, increased competition, large circulations, diversification, and advertising as a means to profit" (emphasis in original).[1] Press historians Michael Emery and Edwin Emery argue that the transition from the entrepreneurial to the corporate form of organization began at the close of the Civil War and was reflected in the writings of Henry Watterson of the *Louisville Courier-Journal* and Harvey W. Scott of the *Portland Oregonian*.[2]

> Both enjoyed long careers that began at the close of the Civil War and continued until World War I, but both belong primarily in this transitional period of journalism history. Arthur Krock, an associate of Watterson on the *Courier-Journal* staff before becoming a *New York Times* fixture, offers one reason for setting Watterson apart from later editors: '... He was the last of those editors who wrote with the power of ownership.' The same was true of Scott. Other editors, like [Edwin Lawrence] Godkin, exercised free rein because of their relationship to the owners of their papers, and they have

continued to do so since, but admittedly with increasing difficulty as the newspaper became a corporate institution.[3]

The notion that the transition to corporate ownership occurred on such precise terms is empirically debatable.[4] More accurately, the transition was gradual and was intimately tied to the growth of cities, industries and, more specifically, retail advertising. The penny papers, in particular, might be called the first corporate newspapers because they were the first media to attract mass audiences. Yet newspapers before the Civil War were relatively small,[5] and historians are correct in pointing out that modern corporate business practices in the newspaper industry grew exponentially after the Civil War.

Although the corporate newspaper took on many of its contemporary features during this period, the origins can be traced much farther back. Understanding the historical development of the corporate form of organization is crucial for understanding the role and function of corporate media today. The central theme of this chapter is that the transition is part of an ongoing process of social differentiation, fueled by increasing urbanization and industrialization.

Pre-Press History

Although corporate groups existed during the Roman Empire, social theorists usually trace the origins of the modern corporation to the late Middle Ages and the rise of major trading centers.[6] Before then, work and other social activities revolved almost exclusively around the family and the local community. The economic and social division of labor was very limited. The vast majority of people worked the land or tended herds, and the availability of work outside of agriculture was limited in part because there was little surplus in food production. People shared a common value system and work environment. But with advances and improvements in agriculture, which increased food production, more and more people were freed from the land.

Artisan guilds, local boroughs and ecclesiastical bodies were some of the earliest corporate groups. Two key factors distinguished corporate groups from other social formations. The first was that they were consciously created instruments of self-governance designed to promote the interests of their members. Many justified their existence in part through claims that they served in the public interest and would protect the public from charlatans and quacks. They often monopolized markets, controlled prices, decided who could join their groups, and reproved members who violated organizational norms and goals. Durkheim also argues that the primary functions of these groups were to curb individual egoism, foster solidarity among workers, and act as a check on the abuses of employers, industrial organizations and the state.[7] The second factor distinguishing the corporate groups from other groups was that they survived beyond the lifetime of any single member. This permanency enhanced the power of corporate groups relative to individuals and other, more transitory social formations (i.e., kinship, friendship systems).

Contemporary professional groups, such as doctors and lawyers, and modern business corporations can trace their roots to these early corporate groups. One of the earliest forms of the business corporation was the joint-stock company, which was created in the 16th and 17th centuries to fund large public works projects, such as canal or sewer construction, or overseas trading expeditions. Through the sale of stock, such organizations could accumulate large sums of capital in a short period of time. Shares of these companies could be easily transferred from one person to another. However, unlike the modern legal corporation, the owners of joint-stock companies were personally liable for the company's debts, and many lost money because of unscrupulous promoters and risky ventures.[8]

In response to these events, England, the United States and other Western nations passed laws during the late 1700s and early 1800s limiting the liability of a stockholder to the actual amount of money invested. If the corporation went bankrupt, the personal assets of the investor were protected. The laws also were changed to give the corporation a legal personality so that it could enter into contracts, sue or be sued, and enjoy other privileges of legal citizenship. In 1837, Connecticut became the first state in the United States to pass a statute which allowed incorporation "for any lawful business."[9] These changes promoted capital investment, which, in turn, had a profound effect on the development of the business organization. In the early 1800s, most businesses were very small relative to other competitors in the market, but by the late 1800s, many had grown to powerful proportions, wielding substantial market power. At the turn of the century, for example, Standard Oil Company controlled 90 percent of the refined petroleum sold in the United States.[10]

Today, of course, the modern business corporation is the dominant form of organization. In 1980, the 100 largest corporations in the United

States held nearly 50 percent of the manufacturing assets.[11] Although the corporate organization is often praised for its efficiency and increased productive capacity, it is also strongly criticized for having too much power.[12] The major fear is that the corporate organizations will act only in their own self-interest, not in the interest of the community or their customers.

Early Press History

The first attempt to publish a newspaper in the territory that is now part of the United States took place in Boston on September 25, 1690. *Public Occurrences, Both Foreign and Domestick* contained stories about Indians who had kidnapped several children, a smallpox epidemic, a fire in Boston a week before, the possible bribery of the friendly Mohawk Indians by someone who had caused them to turn against the colonists, and a scandal involving the French king and his daughter-in-law. The last two items did not please government censors, who banned the publication after the first edition. The publisher, Benjamin Harris, originally a publisher from London, returned to running a coffee house and selling books.[13]

Kobre points out that Harris probably got the idea for the newspaper from a number of broadsides that were published in Boston in the late 1680s, some of which discussed a conflict over a new British policy that sought to gain tighter control over Massachusetts. "There were strong indications of the growing interest in printed news and the discussion of current events," Kobre writes.[14] However, Kobre argues, a complete and adequate explanation of the emergence of this newspaper as well as the *Boston News-Letter* — the first regularly published newspaper in the Colonies, which appeared April 24, 1704 — must take into account factors other than the individual actions of the publisher.

> *Public Occurrences, Both Foreign and Domestick* did not spring up by chance. The first American newspapers grew out of the peculiar conditions in the colonial environment, out of the desire for political and commercial news, foreign and domestic, and the need for an advertising medium.[15]

More specifically, Kobre contends that five "environmental" factors account for the emergence of the first newspapers in Boston. The first was population growth. By the year 1700, the population in the colonies had grown to about 250,000. Massachusetts had 45,000 settlers, and Boston was the largest city in the colonies. Although Kobre does not specifically say so, he implies that interpersonal communication alone is an inefficient or ineffective method for communicating many matters of general concern in large social systems.

The second factor affecting the development of the first newspapers, according to Kobre, was improved transportation and postal services. Until the late 1600s, news from other communities or countries was difficult to obtain, which alone would have made it difficult to publish a newspaper. Intercolonial trade and mail service was poor. Travel was chiefly by boats, which were slow and unpredictable. But by 1692, a road system was being developed and the first weekly mail service between Boston and New York had been established.

The third factor contributing to the emergence of the first newspapers was improved economic conditions. Agriculture, manufacturing, trade and commerce increased substantially during the 17th century. Dutch and English farmers, following the Hudson River Valley, raised crops that were shipped to markets in Europe. The colonies also exported cattle, tobacco, lumber, and textile products, and developed their own shipbuilding industries. By 1699, the balance of trade strongly favored the colonies, which exported goods valued at nearly twice the amount they imported.[16] All of this activity, Kobre writes,

> meant that commercial news was of value. A newspaper man could gather news about local and foreign business from these farmers, shipbuilders, shippers, ship captains. He could print this information in a newspaper and sell it. Many colonists along the seaboard wanted to know what was happening in the political and commercial life of England, the West Indies and other colonies, since they had begun to trade with these places so extensively. Commercial intelligence, or news, was needed for carrying on a profitable business. ... With services and merchandise to sell, shippers needed an advertising medium to tell prospective customers about their cargoes and to advertise their next port of call for anyone who wished to ship freight.[17]

The fourth factor influencing the development of the first newspapers was literacy. Economic development and increased productivity freed many people from long work days, giving them more leisure time which, in turn, increased interest in cultural affairs. Libraries, schools and colleges appeared in many communities. In some areas, compulsory education was instituted as early as 1647.

The fifth major factor affecting the emergence of the first newspapers was increasing tolerance of the press. During the 17th century, many religious and governmental elites opposed a free press. But the growth of democratic ideals in England, which was reflected in the English parliament's right to unlicensed publication in 1695, led to the institutionalization of the press in England and drew attention to the fact that the press could be an effective weapon for influencing public opinion in favor of the government's position.[18]

Population growth, transportation, economic development, literacy, and increased tolerance from the government were necessary conditions for the emergence of the press. But they were not sufficient. A sixth factor was financial support.[19] Many newspapers, especially before the Revolutionary War, depended on a source of income other than advertising or subscriptions for survival. For example, John Campbell, publisher of the Boston News-Letter, never had enough subscribers to turn a profit. A government subsidy saved him twice from bankruptcy. Financial problems like this were not unusual. More than half of the 2,120 newspapers founded between 1690 and 1820 folded before they were two years old; only one in four survived longer than five years.[20] One of the major problems facing newspapers at that time was limited demand for advertising. The industrial revolution, with its consumer-based economy and dependence on markets, was only in its infancy. The newspaper publisher often had to seek financial support elsewhere, including political parties, religious groups, business leaders, or the government. The publisher also was often the local postmaster.

Newspapers published before the penny press also would be considered small-scale operations by today's standards. Circulations usually were less than 1,000 and rarely exceeded 2,000. As a consequence, the owner usually wore many hats, including that of editor, reporter, printer, advertising salesperson, and circulation manager. Only the largest newspapers could afford to hire reporters, and general assignment reporting did not emerge as a significant organizational behavior until the early 1800s. Most newspapers depended heavily on other secondary sources of information to fill their pages.

Then, as now, most of the news published in newspapers originated in political and commercial centers of power.[21] Unlike today, however, the vast majority of content in early newspapers involved national or international affairs. The accounts were usually lifted from English or other colonial newspapers. Local news stories, when they appeared, were often gleaned from other colonial newspapers, private letters, correspondence and occasionally personal contacts with governmental officials. Newspapers were directed largely to elite audiences: government officials, politicians and business people. Most ordinary citizens could not read or afford a newspaper, nor was a newspaper important for them in their everyday lives.

After the Revolutionary War, newspapers entered a period of rapid expansion that coincided with the growth of urban populations. Before the war, the Colonies had 37 newspapers; in 1835, the United States had 1,258.[22] Total urban population increased nine-fold from 1790 to 1840, going from 202,000 to 1.8 million. Total population nearly quadrupled, from about 4 million to 15 million.[23] More newspapers were established in cities west of Philadelphia, including Cincinnati, St. Louis and Detroit. Yet, despite this growth, newspaper circulation remained limited, even in large urban areas. Subscription fees were high — $6 to $10 a year in advance — an amount that was more than most skilled workers earned in a week and well beyond the means of the less well-to-do.[24]

Newspapers were more lively and refined after the war,[25] but they were still highly political and commercial in content and still oriented toward national and international events. For example, in the 1820s the *Inquisitor Cincinnati Advertiser* devoted the overwhelming majority of its news hole to international, national and state political and business news. Local news, including city council minutes, typically filled less than six inches of the 144-inch news hole.[26]

Penny Press

The newspaper industry grew dramatically during the penny press era. From 1830 to 1840 alone, the number of newspapers doubled and yearly circulation tripled, going from about 68 million copies to 196 million copies.[27] On the eve of the Civil War, many metropolitan dailies were exhibiting the characteristics of large-scale organization, including a complex division of labor and a hierarchy of authority.

The first successful penny paper was the *New York Sun*, founded September 3, 1833, by Benjamin Day, a printer from Philadelphia.[28] An important part of Day's success formula was an emphasis on local and crime news. O'Brien says Day "wanted a reporter to do the police-court work, for he saw, from the first day of the paper, that was the kind of stuff that his readers devoured."[29] Day hired George Wisner, a former Bow Street reporter in London, to cover the court beat, and his reports soon took up two full columns in the newspaper.[30] Within six months the newspaper achieved a circulation of 8,000, making it twice as large as the next nearest rival in the city.

During the next decade, dozens of other penny papers were established in New York City, Albany, Boston, Philadelphia, Baltimore and New Orleans, many of which were growing rapidly.[31] But the success of the penny papers was not welcomed by all.[32] Many of the older papers criticized the coverage of crime news, arguing that it was harmful to the community.[33] Yet this criticism was short-lived. Competition from the penny papers forced many of the older papers to change their ways. As police historian Roger Lane notes:

> Both the numbers and the circulation of these (penny) papers climbed steadily, with the *Boston Times*, reportedly selling twelve thousand copies a day, leading even the established journals by 1836. All of the 'pennies' left state and national politics to their older rivals, in order to concentrate on the local news which these had ignored, especially on violent and exciting incidents. Such stories could be gathered most easily each morning in court, and the popularity of this police court reportage led the more conservative press to adopt it.[34]

Many of the established penny papers also did not welcome the arrival of the new competitors. In large urban areas, especially New York City, the papers began fighting each other for readership and advertising dollars. The battle reached a high mark in 1840, when James Gordon Bennett's rivals started a movement to boycott the *New York Herald*, which had nearly 40,000 circulation — more than one paper for every 10 residents.[35] The competitors enlisted the help of the leading clergy and accused Bennett of blasphemy. Bennett's racy style of reporting the news spilled over into the *Herald's* coverage of religious news, but Emery and Emery argue that the real cause of the "moral war" was resentment over Bennett's success.[36]

In contrast to the older papers, which were oriented toward business and governmental elites, the penny papers were directed toward the working and middle classes — two groups that were a product of an increasingly urbanized and industrialized society. From 1820 to 1860, total urban population in the United States increased tenfold, going from

693,000 to 6.2 million.[37] After the War of 1812, economic investment shifted from shipping to manufacturing and transportation. Factories were producing leather products, clothes, shoes and farm machinery. Fewer and fewer goods and services were made at home for home use. For health care, people turned from homemade remedies to patent medicines and doctors. From 1830 to 1850, the number of miles of railroad increased from less than 100 to nearly 9,000.[38]

The penny papers, unlike the older press, also placed a great deal of emphasis on local news. They covered the police, courts, churches, clubs and special interest groups, and routinized coverage of many social institutions, including Wall Street, the courts, police and government. As Schudson puts it:

> For the first time the American newspaper made it a regular practice to print political news, not just foreign but domestic, and not just national but local; for the first time it printed reports from the police, from the courts, from the streets, and from private households. One might say that, for the first time, the newspaper reflected not just commerce or politics but social life.[39]

But the key factor that distinguished the one-cent alternatives from their more expensive counterparts, according to Schiller, was that the penny papers took business success as their most fundamental goal.[40] The party press served the interests and goals of the political party. Making a profit was desired but not necessary. The penny papers, in contrast, were specifically created to make a profit. They sought to make money primarily through advertising revenues, not subscription fees, and to do this they needed to increase circulation.

Crime news played an important role in boosting circulation of the penny papers. But this was not the only factor. The penny press appealed to a broader audience because it avoided erudite political commentary and was less partisan in content. The penny papers covered church events, accidents, disasters, social news and local government. The penny papers did not eliminate political commentary and opinions, but they did de-emphasize them.[41] The party papers, in contrast, appealed to limited segments of the population — usually segments that shared the political and economic views of the newspapers. Their primary function was to promote the political and ideological interests of the parties they served.

Schiller argues that the penny press invented the concept of objectivity. Although the concept was not part of the journalism lexicon until the 20th century, Schiller writes:

Objectivity developed in tandem with the commercial newspapers' appropriation of a crucial political function — the surveillance of the public good. By means of periodic exposures of violations and infringements of public good — most notably in crime news, a blossoming genre — the newspaper at this juncture presumed to speak as "the public voice." In one jump the newspaper moved from the self-interested concerns of partisan political warfare to the apparently omniscient status of protecting the people as the whole.[42]

Increased emphasis on social news and decreased emphasis on partisan commentary boosted circulation, but it does not explain the origins of the penny press, since social news had been part of the newspaper business back to the days of John Campbell.[43] Historians argue that at least three other factors played a role in the development of the penny press.

The first of these was technology. Until the 1820s, the fastest printing presses were capable of producing only about 1,100 papers per hour. By 1830 steam power was adapted to the press which more than tripled the speed of printing.[44] These changes also were accompanied by advancements in paper-making,[45] both of which reduced per-copy costs substantially.

The second factor contributing to the rise of the penny press was literacy. Public education emerged in the early 1800s as an important social and economic issue, and the political system responded with public funding for schools and colleges. By the 1830s, a majority of adults could read,[46] and by 1870 only 20 percent of the population over 10 years of age was illiterate.[47]

Technology and literacy were necessary conditions for the rise of a mass press, but they were not sufficient. More important than either of these, according to Schudson, was the development of a "democratic market society." "A democratization of economic life was in progress," Schudson writes. "By this I mean simply that more people were entering into a cash (and credit) nexus by becoming investors and by consuming goods produced outside the household and that their attitudes and ambitions were increasingly conditioned by this fact."[48] The emergence of the penny press reflected a fundamental shift of power in the social system — a shift from the established mercantile and financial leaders to the entrepreneurial capitalists. The new class of producers needed a way of promoting their goods and services to consumers, and the penny press provided them that outlet.

Schudson also argues that the penny papers contributed to the development of a market economy in two ways. First, through advertising, the penny papers enlarged the potential market for manufactured goods. Second, the penny papers transformed the newspaper from something that was read at the club or library to a product consumed in the home. The penny papers, Schudson concludes,

> were spokesmen for egalitarianism ideals in politics, economic life, and social life through their organization of sales, their solicitation of advertising, their emphasis on news, their catering to large audiences, and their decreasing concern with the editorial.[49]

In short, the penny press became the first mass medium for delivering consumers to producers.[50]

Antebellum Press

Circulations of many newspapers continued to grow as the Civil War approached. Weeklies became dailies, and dailies began publishing on Sundays. The division of labor and role specialization expanded concomitantly. According to Emery and Emery, regularly employed reporters were rare even after the penny press had become well established in the 1840s. However, by the 1850s, chief reporters — forerunners of city editors — had emerged at larger newspapers. In 1854, for example, the *New York Tribune* had 14 reporters and 10 editors.[51]

At the large dailies, the publisher or owner played a lesser role in day-to-day operations. Editors were increasingly drawn from the ranks of the formally educated and, in many cases, knew little about printing, advertising or circulation. Their role was to fill the newspaper with news and commentary in the most efficient manner possible. The advertising and circulation tasks, in turn, were handled by other individuals who had specialized knowledge in those areas.

On the eve of the Civil War, the *New York Herald* was the world's largest daily at 77,000 circulation. Emery and Emery point out that the paper had developed the best financial section of any paper in the country,[52] which supports the notion that the penny press, as an institution, was serving the interests of the growing capitalist class. Bennett, himself once an economics teacher, wrote the "money page." The paper had a letters-to-the-editor column, a critical review column and a society news section. The paper also covered sports and church groups. It was, in other words, emerging as a highly diversified product that catered to the interests of an increasingly diverse audience.

The antebellum period also is characterized by the beginnings of concentration of ownership. In a study of Wisconsin newspapers, media historian Carolyn Dyer found that about one-fourth of the newspapers published between 1833 and 1860 were operated as parts of chains or other forms of groups.[53] She divides the group-owned newspapers into five types of ownership structures: joint-operating agreements; chains; one community, two newspaper groups; family groups; and complex family groups. About a dozen of the groups resembled modern chains in that they involved the simultaneous publication by the same people of two or more general-circulation newspapers in different communities. She notes that the distance between the two communities in "many instances" would have permitted the sharing of presses and type.[54]

Dyer argues that the depiction of "frontier journalism as the solitary pursuit of heroic individuals" is basically a myth. Very few of the newspapers she studied were capitalized solely by their operators[55] or through pre-publication subscription contributions.[56] Most depended on at least one or two other sources: chattel mortgages, in which the investment was secured by the equipment purchased, and joint-stock companies, in which ownership was sold as stock to investors. The mortgages were available from banks and printing equipment manufacturers, and the stock was usually sold to political parties and other special interest groups.

Dyer argues that the price paid for capitalization through these organizations was the loss of editorial control, particularly in the case of joint-stock companies. Dyer also contends that the joint-stock company, the precursor to today's modern corporation, was "not generally a satisfactory way to run a paper."[57] Although more likely than other types of newspapers to hire technically competent printers, the joint-stock newspaper was less able to keep them. Operator turnover was quite high because, according to Dyer, the shareholders often gave little editorial autonomy to the operator. Shareholders, she argues, usually saw the newspaper as a vehicle for promoting their political views and were often involved in day-to-day operation.

This control very well may have existed. But it is important to point out that this does not necessarily mean a loss of diversity of opinion. The present-day criticism of corporate newspapers revolves around the question of whether those newspapers place greater emphasis on profits at the expense of a robust debate of public issues. The description that Dyer gives of joint-stock newspapers suggests that, to the contrary, many were pursuing political, not just economic, goals because they were capitalized by political parties. If this is the case, one might expect that such joint-stock ownership could contribute to increased diversity.

The American Civil War brought major changes in news writing styles, including the development of fact-oriented stories, the summary lead and the inverted pyramid style of writing. To save telegraph toll costs, correspondents strived to be more concise. One way to accomplish this was to eliminate opinion and coloration from stories. Reporters from the battlefield also would relay the most important information first for fear that complete dispatches might not make it through the telegraph lines.[58] Shaw documents how objectivity in news reports increased during the war.[59]

Late 19th Century

The most explosive growth in the newspaper industry came after the Civil War. Between 1870 and 1900, the number of general-circulation daily newspapers quadrupled, going from 574 to 2,226, and the number of weekly newspapers tripled, going from 4,000 to more than 12,000.[60] Daily circulation increased five-fold, from 2.6 million copies to 15 million, and household penetration nearly tripled, from .34 to .94 copies per household (see Figure 2.1). The newspaper industry was becoming a field where fortunes could be made. In the 1890s, for example, the *New York World* was valued at $10 million and was pulling in an annual profit of $1 million a year.[61]

At the turn of the century the typical newspaper was still owned and managed by individuals or families, as opposed to joint-stock companies. But in large cities across the United States, particularly New York, such individuals increasingly had less and less say about day-to-day operations. Specialized roles had developed more fully, and functional areas such as advertising, circulation and news at large newspapers were increasingly being managed by individuals who had developed specialized skills and knowledge in those areas. Emery and Emery point out that as early as the 1870s leading metropolitan dailies had a chief editor, a managing editor or night editor, a city editor, two dozen reporters, a telegraph editor, a financial editor, a drama critic, a literary editor and editorial writers.[62] On

Figure 2.1
Household Newspaper Circulation by Year

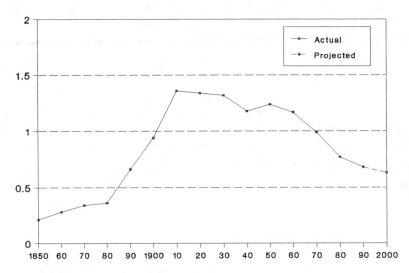

Sources: U.S. Census records and *Editor & Publisher International Yearbook.*

the production side, there were printers, pressmen, typographers, and photo-engravers, each of whom was represented by different unions.[63]

The late 19th century period also was characterized by an acceleration in the growth of the modern chain newspaper. Although chains existed before the Civil War, as Dyer points out, what distinguished the groups after the war is that they survived long beyond the death of the original owners. They had continuity, one of the factors that distinguishes complex forms of organization from more traditional forms. The Scripps family is often credited with creating the first major newspaper chain.[64] In 1880, for example, the Scripps family owned newspapers in Cleveland, Cincinnati, St. Louis, and Buffalo. Today that chain still continues to be one of the largest in the country.

One of the major consequences of this massive growth in the newspaper industry was increased competition. In 1880, about 239 of the 850 cities with an English-language daily newspaper had two more dailies. The number nearly tripled by 1910, when 689 of the 2,202 cities had competitors.[65] Competition was greater in the larger cities, especially New

York, which had 15 general circulation dailies in 1890. Newspapers also faced competition from magazines, which were taking 60 percent or more of the national advertising revenue in 1900.[66] To survive and grow, newspapers needed to increase circulation, and one way to attract more readers was through sensationalistic coverage. Hence, the latter decades of the 19th century gave birth to the period known as "yellow-journalism."

Historians have identified a number of factors to explain the dramatic growth in the newspaper industry in the closing decades of the 19th century. Two of the most important are industrialization and urbanization.[67] Total manufacturing production increased seven-fold from 1865 to 1900. From 1860 to 1900, the total number of industries tripled, going from 140,000 to 500,000. About 4 of 10 persons were engaged in nonagricultural work in 1860; 6 of 10 in 1900. The percentage of people living in urban areas also doubled, going from 20 percent to 40 percent. And between 1860 and 1900, estimated national wealth went from $20 billion to $88 billion, a four-fold increase.[68]

The growth of industry and urban populations contributed directly to the growth of newspapers. Manufacturers needed efficient ways to reach buyers. Urban residents, especially the emerging middle and upper-middle classes, needed access to information that could help them through everyday life in an increasingly interdependent, complex society. Newspapers were one mechanism for meeting both of these needs.[69]

Although the newspaper industry experienced rapid growth in the late 1800s, it is important to point out that this was a trend that characterized other industries as well. In fact, the growth of large-scale organization and concentration of ownership was even more dramatic in the railroad, oil and steel industries. The rate of growth in the daily newspaper industry probably would have been much greater had there not been major technical and transportation problems in producing and distributing a daily national publication.

Early 20th Century

During the first part of the 20th century, the trend toward concentration of ownership continued despite substantial growth in the population, the number of urban places, daily circulation and advertising revenue. Between 1910 and 1930, the population increased from 92 to 122 million. The number of cities with 8,000 or more population rose from

768 to 1,208. Circulation went from 22.5 million to 40 million. And newspaper advertising tripled between 1915 and 1929, going from $275 million to $800 million.[70] However, the number of owners declined substantially.[71]

The daily newspaper industry reached maximum diversity in about 1910, when 2,202 English-language daily newspapers were operated by 2,153 owners (see Table 2.1; column 3 + column 7). But by 1940 the number of owners had declined to 1,619, and by 1990 the number stood at 409, a 71 percent decline since 1910. Over the 90-year period, the number of dailies dropped 25 percent, going from 2,202 to 1,626.

The decline in the number of owners can be broken down into two separate trends. The first is the loss of competing newspapers through mergers or suspensions. In 1900, 559 cities with a daily, or 61 percent of the total, had two or more competing newspapers.[72] But by 1930 the number of cities with competing dailies fell to 288, or 29 percent.[73] New York City lost nearly half of its dailies during this time period. And by 1986 only 28 cities, or 2 percent, had competing papers.[74] A study by Ray in the early 1950s found that between 1910 and 1930, 1,495 dailies were founded, 1,391 newspapers suspended publication or shifted to weekly status, and 362 merged with rival papers.[75] The net result was a loss of more than 250 dailies. From 1909 to 1950, 559 dailies disappeared through consolidation or merger. According to Ray, the period 1937 to 1943 accounted for more than half of the decline.

The second trend contributing to concentration of ownership — and a more important one than the first — is the growth of the chain newspaper. Table 2.1 shows that the number of newspapers under chain or group ownership increased substantially from 1900 to 1930, going from 1.4 percent to 16 percent of the total number of dailies. The Great Depression brought the growth of chain ownership to a virtual standstill; some large national chains, including Hearst and Scripps-Howard, lost some papers.[76] But, overall, the newspaper industry held up quite well. Table 2.1 shows that between 1930 and 1940 the industry lost a net total of only 64 newspapers — fewer than it did during the previous or succeeding decade. Chains were even losing papers.[77] Yet, despite this stagnation, the number of specialists working in the newspaper organization continued to grow. In the newsroom, reporters were assigned to cover a variety of beats, including labor, science, agriculture, social work, foreign affairs and the usual political and economic beats. The political column began in the early 1920s with the writings of David Lawrence, Mark

Table 2.1
Growth of Chain Ownership in the United States

Year	No. of Dailies	No. of Groups	No. of Dailies in Groups	Percent Group- Owned	Average No. Per Group	No. of Inde- pendent Dailies
1900*	1,967	8	27	1.4%	3.4	1,940
1910	2,202	13	62	2.8%	4.8	2,140
1920	2,042	31	153	7.5%	4.9	1,889
1930	1,942	55	311	16.0%	5.7	1,631
1940	1,878	60	319	17.0%	5.3	1,559
1950*	1,772	86	427	24.1%	5.0	1,345
1960	1,763	109	552	31.3%	5.1	1,211
1970	1,748	157	879	50.3%	5.6	869
1980	1,745	154	1,139	65.3%	7.4	606
1990	1,626	129	1,217	74.8%	9.4	409

Sources: For 1900 data, Michael Emery and Edwin Emery, *The Press and America* (Englewood Cliffs, N.J.: Prentice-Hall, 1988), p. 335 and Frank Luther Mott, *American Journalism* (New York: Macmillan, 1962), p. 648; for 1910 and 1920 data, Raymond B. Nixon and Jean Ward, "Trends in Newspaper Ownership and Inter-Media Competition," *Journalism Quarterly* 38:3-24 (1961); 1930 to 1960 data, Benjamin M. Compaine, "Newspapers," pp. 27-93 in Benjamin M. Compaine, Christopher H. Sterling, Thomas Guback and J. Kendrick Noble, Jr., *Who Owns the Media: Concentration of Ownership in the Mass Communications Industry* (White Plains, N.Y.: Knowledge Industry, 1982), pp. 30, 39; and for 1990 data, *Editor and Publisher International Yearbook.*

*Number of chains and newspapers in chains estimated for these years.

Sullivan and Frank R. Kent. The political cartoon also became institutionalized.[78]

Ray attributes the decline in the number of owners in the late 1930s to the loss of advertising revenue as a result of the "recession," competition from radio, and increasing wages and newsprint prices. The loss during World War II he attributes to increased operating costs, caused by price rises, shortages and rationing of newsprint and other materials, and higher wages because of shortages of labor.[79]

> The dramatic rise of radio as an advertising medium during the 1930s and the consequent loss of advertising to radio by newspapers understandably causes publishers to seek shelter through integration. Post-war expansion of radio and television only serves to intensify the competition for advertising appropriations.[80]

But is radio responsible for concentration of ownership in the newspaper industry? Other historical data are not clear on this point.

Radio made its commercial debut in the 1920s but did not become a major medium until the depression years. As might be expected, some newspaper owners perceived the new medium as a competitive threat. Others, however, saw it as a marketing tool. The American Newspaper Publishers Association's radio committee issued a report in 1927 which showed that 48 newspapers owned radio stations, 69 sponsored programs on non-owned stations, and 97 gave news programs over the air. Many newspapers were using radio to sell themselves, and the committee concluded that it worked.[81]

Nevertheless, by the late 1920s many newspaper publishers perceived radio as a competitive threat. Chester argues that there are three major reasons for this.[82] One was the expansion of chain broadcasting by the National Broadcasting Company and the Columbia Broadcasting System. The second was the growth of radio advertising. And the third was the drop in newspaper lineage and circulation in the early years of the depression. In 1932 the American Newspaper Publishers Association formed the Publishers' National Radio Committee to develop ways to limit competition from radio. The committee drafted a "10-point agreement" in 1934 that, among other things, required CBS to withdraw from the news collection field, prohibited NBC from entering the field, and set up a Press-Radio Bureau that would control the collection and dissemination of news to radio stations.[83] The plan was implemented, but it failed to gain the support of many independent stations, especially outside of New York City, and the effort was abandoned in 1938, when the major networks withdrew their financial support and set up their own news gathering services to supplement the wire services.[84]

But was the competitive threat from radio real or imagined? A recent study by Lacy found that change in the absolute and per capita number of radio stations in 72 cities between 1929 and 1948 had no effect on whether competition between daily newspapers declined in those cities.[85] Furthermore, despite the growth of radio during the 1920s, newspaper penetration grew. Figure 2.1 shows that the number of newspapers per household peaked at 1.36 copies in 1910. Household circulation declined somewhat during the depression and began rising again in the 1940s, reaching another high point in the mid-to-late 1940s. And this growth occurred despite opinion polls by Lazarsfeld and Kendall, which showed that during World War II, 61 percent of citizens got most of their news by radio, and that during the late 1940s, 44 percent obtained most of their news by radio.[86] Whatever anxieties publishers had about radio in the early 1930s appeared to have subsided during the 1940s, as most dailies were publishing radio program listings without charge.[87]

Post World War II

The trend toward chain ownership picked up after World War II. By 1950, one-fourth of all dailies were owned by chains or groups. But newspaper penetration began to decline in the early 1950s and has continued to decline ever since (see Figure 2.1). The newspaper industry's share of total advertising dollars also has declined since the 1940s.[88] The declines coincided with the emergence of television, and, needless to say, many scholars and journalists believe the trends are no coincidence — that television has cut into newspaper circulation. However, as will be discussed in subsequent chapters, strong empirical evidence is still lacking, and some scholars argue that the two media are more complementary than competitive.[89]

The trend toward group ownership continued in the 1950s and 1960s. Bagdikian argues that this growth was fueled by high taxes and tax laws that favor investing the profits elsewhere. Newspapers, he adds, made about 12 to 15 percent profit on assets after taxes. "Tax regulations permit accumulation of undistributed earnings free of the usual tax on undistributed earnings of 38½ percent for amounts over $100,000 — if the accumulation is for buying another property of the same type," he writes. "Thus, accumulated newspaper profits tend to be used to buy other papers in other places."[90]

Bagdikian argues one of the most harmful effects of chain ownership may be that profits are not reinvested in the paper. He also contends that even though families still own a large share of the stock in many chain organizations, the idea of "a crusading proprietor" whose main interest is civic betterment, not profits, is basically a myth. Profits in the 1960s averaged 20 percent of gross before taxes. Most families had little role in the day-to-day operations. The transition from local to absentee ownership, he argues, has two major consequences for the industry. First, it means that a conventional corporate newspaper will be less concerned about local issues. "There are many cases of negligent local owners and conscientious absentee ones, but on the whole absentee owners are less sensitive to local nuances," he writes. "A locally rooted family or a personal operator whose family is part of the community is more susceptible to the social and informational needs of the paper's surroundings."[91]

Second, the transition produces a lower quality product.

> The tradition of the personally involved owner is strong and, while it produces numerous cases of entrenched morbidity, it also is the most important single factor in papers of excellence. ... Modern corporate pressures are beginning to erode the tradition of personal direction and family control of newspapers.[92]

During the 1960s, 1970s and 1980s, dailies under direct competition continued to die here and there, but, overall, the newspaper industry was relatively stable. Established papers in most communities — especially those in communities without competition from another daily — were on solid ground. And, unlike the earlier part of the century, there were few attempts to start newspapers, especially dailies. A major part of the problem was cost. Bennett founded the *New York Herald* in 1835 for $500. The capitalization of a major city daily in 1960 was about $6 million.[93] But even a small weekly would easily have run into the hundreds of thousands of dollars in start-up costs.

The diffusion of offset printing and computerized composition equipment during the 1960s and 1970s had a profound impact on staffing and role specialization at most dailies. Wright and Lavine studied a cross section of newspapers and found that from 1959 to 1980 a typical 20,000-circulation daily reduced staffing in the mechanical department (e.g., printing, typesetting) by 50 percent, but it increased the number of reporters and editors by 40 percent.[94] Not unexpectedly, this increase has been accompanied by increased role specialization. Most large newspapers now have environmental, science and technology reporters, and almost every reporter has some specialty. Some even have an information technology beat, covering such topics as e-mail.[95] For example, at the *Star Tribune* in Minneapolis, the business news section — just one of several functional areas in the news department — has 18 specialized roles, including a business editor, two general assignment reporters, Monday business editor, business forum editor, workplace reporter, retail and commercial development reporter, news assistant, technology reporter, research assistant, small-business reporter, food reporter, business-calendar correspondent, national economics correspondent, manufacturing reporter, management reporter, travel and hospitality reporter, housing reporter, consumer affairs reporter, and two columnists. Such specialization appears to correspond to increasing differentiation in business and industry in the Twin Cities metropolitan area.

Concentration and centralization of ownership also has continued. In 1900, the typical daily had a circulation of 7,500; only 27 of the 1,967 dailies, or 1.4 percent, were owned by a chain or group. But by 1990, the typical daily had a circulation of 38,000 and was owned by a chain or group headquartered in another city or state. Nearly 80 percent of the 1,626 dailies, or 1,217, were part of a chain or group.[96]

Although newspapers have become more differentiated in content since World War II, they have not been able to eliminate the decline in penetration per household, which is at its lowest point since 1890 (see Figure 2.1). DeFleur and Ball-Rokeach argue that the rise and fall of the press, as measured by penetration, follows the familiar S-shaped "curve of adoption" that is typical of growth patterns for a variety of cultural innovations.[97] They contend that limited education, transportation and printing facilities played a part in keeping the number of "early adopters" small. By 1910, many of these constraints had been overcome. However, about this time new innovations in media — including film, radio, news magazines, and television — began to appear, competing with newspapers for audience attention.

> To a greater or less extent, each of these functional alternatives to the newspaper has eaten into the circulation of the daily press. Each, in some sense, provides news, information, or entertainment in a way that once was the exclusive province of the newspaper.[98]

Kaul and McKerns argue that the evolution of the newspaper industry can be divided into four major historical periods: a prevariation stage (before 1825), in which newspapers existed as "small, formally unorganized enterprises"; a variation stage (1825-1845), when major technological and cultural changes affected the development of newspapers; a selection stage (1845-1900), in which the number of newspaper competitors grew dramatically and became crowded; and a retention stage (post 1900), in which ownership became increasingly concentrated. They now claim that newspapers are "dying in a crisis generated by the disjunction of material and knowledge technologies. In a very real sense, today's newspapers are trapped in the contradictions of their evolution."[99]

Kaul and McKerns also argue that contemporary mass communication history and theory cannot explain "the decline of the newspaper and its displacement by newly evolving communication media."[100] They propose a "dialectic ecology" model, which synthesizes the ideas of Charles Darwin and Karl Marx. Basically, the model focuses attention on contradictions and crises generated with the life history of organizations.

The historical stages articulated by Kaul and McKerns appear to provide a reasonably accurate description of the changes that the newspaper industry has undergone. The newspaper as it is currently packaged and delivered to consumers may also disappear with the advent of electronic technologies such as interactive video. But this does not necessarily mean that the organizations that publish the papers are doomed as well, because organizational forms are not simply reducible to technology. Indeed, the history of the newspaper organization has shown that it can adapt to a variety of social, economic and cultural changes, including competition from broadcast media. An alternative scenario for the future is that, while the current physical form of the newspaper may perish, newspaper organizations will make alliances with suppliers of electronic technologies (e.g., telephone companies) that will enable the former to continue to be the major producers of news and the latter to deliver the product electronically to the consumer.[101]

Summary

The corporate newspaper can trace its roots to the Middle Ages and the joint-stock company, which was created in the 16th and 17th centuries to fund large public works projects. The typical newspaper in the United States during the 17th and 18th centuries was an individually owned and managed enterprise. The organization was small, and the news focused heavily on national and international political and business events and commentary and was geared toward the needs of a small group of political and business elites. The newspaper depended heavily on subscription fees and support from political parties and other groups to finance the operation.

Today, however, the typical daily is owned by a chain or group and exhibits the characteristics of big business — a professional style of management, a highly developed division of labor and role specialization, emphasis on rules and procedures, a hierarchy of authority, and rationality in decision-making. News is aimed at a mass audience and covers a variety of economic, political and social events and issues. Financially, the newspaper now depends heavily on classified and display advertising from private businesses for survival.

A number of factors have contributed to these changes, but historically the two most important are urbanization and industrialization. As Robert Park pointed out nearly 70 years ago, the newspaper is a product of the city. "The growth of great cities has enormously increased the size of the reading public," he wrote. "Reading which was a luxury in the country has become a necessity in the city. In the urban environment literacy is almost as much a necessity as speech itself."[102] Industrialization also contributed toward the growth of the newspaper as manufacturers needed ways to reach buyers. Newspaper advertising helped deliver consumers to producers.

This review of the historical literature on changes in newspaper organization also found that household newspaper circulation generally grew throughout the 19th century, leveled off in the first half of the 20th century, and has declined ever since. The decline appears to coincide with increased competition from other media, especially television, but the historical evidence is mixed on this matter.

Notes

1. Hazel Dicken-Garcia, *Journalistic Standards in Nineteenth-Century America* (Madison, Wis.: University of Wisconsin Press, 1989), p. 60. Also see pp. 56-62.

2. Michael Emery and Edwin Emery, *The Press and America: An Interpretive History of the Mass Media*, 6th ed. (Englewood Cliffs, N.J.: Prentice-Hall), p. 182.

3. Emery and Emery, *The Press and America*, p. 182.

4. The argument that corporate newspapers give editors less autonomy than other forms of organization also is empirically questionable. See David Pearce Demers, "Effect of Corporate Structure on Autonomy of Top Editors at U.S. Dailies," *Journalism Quarterly,* 70:499-508 (1993).

5. The largest was James Gordon Bennett's *New York Herald*, with a circulation of 77,000. See Emery and Emery, *The Press and America*, pp. 120-3.

6. This early history of corporate organizations is drawn from a number of sources, including Adolf A. Berle, Jr., and Gardiner C. Means, *The Modern Corporation and Private Property* (New York: Macmillan, 1932), pp. 127-52; Emile Durkheim, *The Division of Labor in Society,* trans. W. D. Halls (New York: Free Press, 1984 [1933]), see preface to the second edition; Daniel Bell, *The End of Ideology* (Cambridge, Mass.: Harvard University Press, 1988 [1960]), pp. 39-45; Daniel Bell, *The Coming of the Post-Industrial Society* (New York: Basic Books, 1973), pp. 269-98; S. Prakash Sethi, "Corporation," in *Academic American Encyclopedia*, electronic version (Danbury, Conn.: Grolier, 1992); and William H. McNeill,

History of Western Civilization, 6th ed. (Chicago: The University of Chicago Press, 1986). There is no historical record of whether ancient Greece had corporate groups.

7. Durkheim, *The Division of Labor in Society*, see preface to the second edition.

8. McNeill, *History of Western Civilization*, p. 507.

9. Berle and Means, *The Modern Corporation and Private Property*, p. 136.

10. C. Joseph Pusateri, *Big Business in America: Attack and Defense* (Itasca, Ill.: F. E. Peacock Publishers, 1975), p. 12.

11. Campbell R. McConnell, *Economics* (New York: McGraw-Hill, 1987), p. 118.

12. See, e.g., Pusateri, *Big Business in America.*

13. Sidney Kobre, "The First American Newspaper: A Product of Environment," *Journalism Quarterly*, 17:335-45 (1940), p. 335.

14. Kobre, "The First American Newspaper," p. 344.

15. Kobre, "The First American Newspaper."

16. Kobre, "The First American Newspaper," p. 337.

17. Kobre, "The First American Newspaper," pp. 338-9.

18. Kobre, "The First American Newspaper," p. 344.

19. See, e.g., Clarence S. Brigham, *History and Bibliography of American Newspapers 1690-1820* (Worcester, Mass.: American Antiquarian Society, 1947); Willard Grosvenor Bleyer, *Main Currents in the History of Journalism* (New York: Houghton Mifflin, 1927); Emery and Emery, *The Press and America*; Frederick Hudson, *Journalism in the United States: 1690 to 1872* (New York: Harper & Brothers, Publishers, 1873); Sidney Kobre, *Development of American Journalism* (Dubuque, Iowa: Wm. C. Brown Company Publishers, 1969); and Frank Luther Mott, *American Journalism: A History 1690-1960*, 3rd ed. (New York: The Macmillan Company, 1962).

20. Brigham, *History and Bibliography of American Newspapers*, p. xii.

21. A great deal of empirical research supports the finding that news media depend heavily on elites for news and information. See, e.g., Mark Fishman, *Manufacturing the News* (Austin, Texas: University of Texas Press, 1980); Todd Gitlin, *The Whole World Is Watching: Mass Media in the Making and Unmaking of the New Left* (Berkeley, Calif.: University of California Press, 1980); Clarice N. Olien, Phillip J. Tichenor and George A. Donohue, "Media Coverage and Social Movements," pp. 139-63 in Charles T. Salmon (ed.), *Information Campaigns: Balancing Social Values and Social Change* (Newbury Park, Calif.: Sage, 1989); David L. Paletz and Robert M. Entman, *Media Power Politics* (New York: The Free Press, 1981); and Gaye Tuchman, *Making News* (New York: Free Press, 1978).

22. Hudson, *Journalism in the United States*, p. 770.

23. U.S. Bureau of the Census, *Statistical Abstract of the United States: 1989* (Washington, D.C.: U.S. Government Printing Office, 1989).

24. Emery and Emery, *The Press and America*, pp. 115-6.

25. Emery and Emery, *The Press and America.*

26. Eight months of issues (August 1819 to March 1820) for the *Inquisitor Cincinnati Advertiser* were content-analyzed, and other issues throughout the 1820s were skimmed.

27. Frank M. O'Brien, *The Story of the Sun* (New York: George H. Doran Company, 1918).

28. Emery and Emery, *The Press and America*, p. 117.

29. O'Brien, *The Story of the Sun*, p. 38.

30. Bleyer, *Main Currents*, p. 160.

31. David Pearce Demers, "Crime News and the Rise of the Modern Police Department," paper presented to the Midwest Association for Journalism and Mass Communication Historians (Evanston, Ill., April 1990).

32. Although many penny papers were successful, not all were. See Kobre, *Development of American Journalism.*.

33. Typical of that view is the following excerpt in 1828 from the *New York Statesman*, which criticized the imitators of the *London Morning Herald*'s style of reporting: "The question is asked us by a correspondent, why we do not, like a few of our contemporaries of late, keep a regular chronicle of trials before the police, for the amusement and instruction of our readers? We have to reply, that it is a fashion which does not meet with our approbation, on the score of either propriety or taste. To say nothing of the absolute indecency of some of the cases which are allowed occasionally to creep into print, we deem of little benefit to the cause of morals thus to familiarize the community, and especially the younger parts of it, to the details of misdemeanor and crime. ... Besides, it suggests to the novice in vice all the means of becoming expert in its devices. The dexterity of one knave, arrested and sent to State Prison, is adopted from newspaper instruction by others yet at large. ... There are now and then extraordinary cases, that require notice at our hands, and accordingly receive it; we also, at times, furnish from our foreign journals (for lack of other things) reports of a whimsical nature, in which there is considerable entertainment, totally unmixed with offence; but we are wholly averse to the task of dishing up the ingredients of which the majority of published trials are composed." Quote in Bleyer, *Main Currents*, p. 157. Also see Demers, "Crime News and the Rise of the Modern Police Department."

34. Roger Lane, "Policing the City: Boston 1822-1885," in Jerome Skolnick and Thomas C. Gray (eds.), *Police in America* (Boston: Little, Brown & Co., 1975).

35. Total population in New York City was about 350,000 in 1840. See Demers, "Crime News and the Rise of the Modern Police Department."

36. Emery and Emery, *The Press and America*, p. 121.

37. U.S. Bureau of Census, quoted in *The World Almanac* (New York: Pharos Books, 1988), p. 531

38. Michael Schudson, *Discovering the News* (New York: Basic Books, 1978), pp. 43-50.

39. Schudson, *Discovering the News*, p. 22.

40. Dan Schiller, "An Historical Approach to Objectivity and Professionalism in American News Reporting," *Journal of Communication*, 29(4):46-57 (1979).

41. Schudson, *Discovering the News*.

42. Schiller, "An Historical Approach," p. 47.

43. Demers, "Crime News and the Rise of the Modern Police Department."

44. Emery and Emery, *The Press and America*, pp. 112-3.

45. Schudson, *Discovering the News*, pp. 31-5

46. Emery and Emery, *The Press and America*. Also see Schudson, *Discovering the News*, pp. 35-9.

47. Mary Beth Norton, David M. Katzman, Paul D. Escott, Howard P. Chudacoff, Thomas G. Paterson and William M. Tuttle, Jr., *A People and a Nation: A History of the United States* (Boston: Houghton Mifflin, 1982), p. 543.

48. Schudson, *Discovering the News*, p. 45.

49. Schudson, *Discovering the News*, pp. 12-60.

50. George A. Donohue, Clarice N. Olien and Phillip J. Tichenor, "Reporting Conflict by Pluralism, Newspaper Type and Ownership," *Journalism Quarterly*, 62:489-99, 507 (1985), p. 491.

51. Emery and Emery, *The Press and America*, p. 212.

52. Emery and Emery, *The Press and America*, pp. 120-3.

53. Carolyn Stewart Dyer, "Economic Dependence and Concentration of Ownership Among Antebellum Wisconsin Newspapers," *Journalism History*, 7(2):42-6 (1980), p. 43.

54. Dyer, "Economic Dependence and Concentration of Ownership," p. 45.

55. Dyer uses this term to refer to the person in charge, who had various titles, including publisher, printer and editor.

56. Dyer, "Economic Dependence and Concentration of Ownership," p. 43.

57. Dyer, "Economic Dependence and Concentration of Ownership," p. 44.

58. See Emery and Emery, *The Press and America*, p. 170-1.

59. Donald L. Shaw, "News Bias and the Telegraph: A Study of Historical Change," *Journalism Quarterly*, 44:3-12, 31 (1967).

60. U.S. Department of Commerce, *Historical Statistics of the United States, 1789-1945* (Washington, D.C.: U.S. Government Printing Office, 1949).

61. Emery and Emery, *The Press and America*, p. 218.

62. Emery and Emery, *The Press and America*, p. 214.

63. Emery and Emery, *The Press and America*, p. 223.

64. Alfred McClung Lee, *The Daily Newspaper in America: The Evolution of a Social Instrument* (New York: Macmillan, 1937), p. 211.

65. Raymond B. Nixon, "Trends in Daily Newspaper Ownership Since 1945," *Journalism Quarterly*, 31:3-14 (1954). See Table 2.1. Data are for English-language dailies.

66. Emery and Emery, *The Press and America*, p. 222.

67. Education and declining illiteracy also were contributing factors. Between 1870 and 1900, the percentage of children attending public school increased from 57 to 72 percent, and illiteracy declined from 20 to 11 percent. For a sociological perspective on industrialization and urbanization, see Marvin E. Olsen, *The Process of Social Organization* (New York: Holt, Rinehart and Winston, 1968), especially Chapter 17.

68. U.S. Department of Commerce, *Historical Statistics of the United States.*

69. Newspapers are not the only way of integrating people into a community (e.g., occupation, church membership). In fact, recent research suggests that they may not be very important for newcomers (see Keith R. Stamm and Avery M. Guest, "Communication and Community Integration: An Analysis of the Communication Behavior of Newcomers," *Journalism Quarterly*, 68:644-56 [1991]). However, a large body of research evidence suggests that among established residents newspaper use is strongly correlated with community ties. See, e.g., Morris Janowitz, *Community Press in an Urban Setting,* 2nd ed. (Chicago: University of Chicago Press, 1967 [1952]).

70. Lee, *The Daily Newspaper in America*, see appendices. Advertising revenue figures are taken from the ANPA Bureau of Advertising.

71. That is, the number of individual proprietorships, partnerships and legal corporations that own newspapers declined. However, it is important to point out that the number of people who own stock or other equities in newspapers has increased with the rise of the legal corporation, mutual funds and pension funds.

72. Emery and Emery, *The Press and America*, p. 335.

73. Emery and Emery, *The Press and America*, p. 334.

74. John C. Busterna, "Trends in Daily Newspaper Ownership," *Journalism Quarterly,* 65:831-8 (1988).

75. Royal H. Ray, "Economic Forces as Factors in Daily Newspaper Concentration," *Journalism Quarterly*, 29:31-42 (1952).

76. Commission on Freedom of the Press, *A Free and Responsible Press* (Chicago: University of Chicago Press, 1947), p. 42.

77. Commission on Freedom of the Press, *A Free and Responsible Press*, p. 42.

78. Emery and Emery, *The Press and America*, p. 336.

79. Ray, "Economic Forces as Factors in Daily Newspaper Concentration," pp. 33-4.

80. Ray, "Economic Forces as Factors in Daily Newspaper Concentration," p. 41.

81. Edwin Emery, *History of the American Newspaper Publishers Association* (Minneapolis: University of Minnesota Press, 1950), Chapter 13.

82. Giraud Chester, "The Press-Radio War: 1933-1935," *Public Opinion Quarterly*, 13:252-64 (1949), see pp. 252-53.

83. Chester, "The Press-Radio War," pp. 256-7.

84. Chester, "The Press-Radio War," p. 263.

85. Stephen Lacy, "The Effect of Growth of Radio on Newspaper Competition, 1929-1948," *Journalism Quarterly*, 64:775-81 (1987).

86. Paul F. Lazarsfeld and Patricia Kendall, *Radio Listening in America* (New York: Prentice-Hall, 1948), p. 34.

87. Chester, "The Press-Radio War," p. 264.

88. Robert J. Coen, "Estimated Annual U.S. Advertising Expenditures 1935-1985," unpublished report (New York: McCann-Erickson Advertising, Inc., 1986).

89. The literature on this topic is discussed in more depth later.

90. Ben H. Bagdikian, *The Information Machines* (New York: Harper & Row, 1971), p. 131.

91. Bagdikian, *The Information Machines*, p. 117.

92. Bagdikian, *The Information Machines*, pp. 117-8.

93. Ray Eldon Hiebert, Donald F. Ungurait and Thomas W. Bohn, *Mass Media II: An Introduction to Modern Communication* (New York: Longman, 1979), p. 224.

94. B. E. Wright and John M. Lavine, *The Constant Dollar Newspaper: An Economic Analysis Covering the Last Two Decades* (Chicago: Inland Daily Press Association, 1982). Offset printing and computerized composition saved the 20,000-circulation daily about $200,000 a year. Profits did not increase substantially during the early 1980s, however, because of increased costs of newsprint.

95. The Minneapolis *Star Tribune* created the beat in February 1994. Joel Kramer, "Beats Open a Window Onto How a Paper Sees the News," *Star Tribune* (February 28, 1994), p. A29.

96. Data from Emery and Emery, *The Press and America*, p. 335, and *Editor & Publisher International Yearbook* (New York: Editor & Publisher, 1991).

97. For additional literature on the diffusion of innovations, see Everette M. Rogers, *Diffusion of Innovations*, 3rd ed. (New York: The Free Press, 1983).

98. Melvin L. DeFleur and Sandra Ball-Rokeach, *Theories of Mass Communication,* 5th ed. (New York: Longman, 1989), p. 60.

99. Arthur J. Kaul and Joseph P. McKerns, "The Dialectic Ecology of the Newspaper," *Critical Studies in Mass Communication*, 2:217-33 (1985), p. 217.

100. Kaul and McKerns, "The Dialectic Ecology of the Newspaper," p. 217.

101. John Rodden, "Ma Bell, Big Brother and the Information Services Family Feud," *Media Studies Journal*, 6(2):1-16 (1992), p. 8.

102. Robert E. Park, "The Natural History of the Newspaper," *The American Journal of Sociology*, 29:273-89 (1923), p. 274.

Chapter 3

Classical Theories of Organizational Structure

Historical research has shed a great deal of light on the growth of the corporate form of organization in the U.S. daily newspaper industry. However, such writings have been largely descriptive. They have focused heavily on what some scholars have called the "great person" theory, in which organizational changes are viewed solely or primarily as the result of decisions of individuals pursuing rational goals.[1] Moreover, even when more sophisticated explanatory schemes or models are offered, the approach taken often involves little more than presenting a list of factors intuitively considered to be important in that development — systematic empirical research rarely documents such claims.

The task of exploring the origins and consequences of the corporate form of organization has been taken up largely by sociologists, political scientists and mass communication researchers, whose theoretical and methodological approaches have been greatly influenced by the natural sciences. The key assumption underlying most social science models is that social organization, while often the product, at least in part, of intentional social action, also is shaped by historical or social factors or processes that may not be anticipated, recognized or desired by the organizations or individuals involved. Once in place, various forms of social organization also may have unintended and unrecognized consequences or functions for individuals and collectivities.

This chapter examines some of the early theories that have been offered to explain the growth and development of the corporate form of organization. The ideas of six "classical" theorists — Smith, Marx, Spencer, Durkheim, Weber and Schumpeter — are presented. None of these theorists specifically sought to explain the origins of the corporate newspaper, but their analyses contain important insights about it even to this day. This review is not a comprehensive summary of all writings on the topic, but it does cover a substantial number of the key ideas. Contemporary theories and empirical research are reviewed in the next chapter.

Adam Smith and the Division of Labor

Adam Smith was not the first scholar to write about changes in organizational structure. But his book, *An Inquiry into the Nature and Causes of the Wealth of Nations,* is widely recognized as the first major work to come to grips with the changes taking place under modern capitalism.[2]

Published in 1776, the book challenged two major schools of thought that dominated economic theory at the time.[3] In England, the Mercantilists argued that gold was the basis of wealth and that gold was to be obtained by selling goods and services to foreign nations. At the same time, the belief was that a nation should do all it can to prohibit the transfer of gold to other nations. In France, the Physiocrats praised the virtues of the farmer, not the merchant. They argued that all wealth came from the production of food. Smith rejected both positions. Wealth, he argued, was to be found in the productivity of labor. Increase the productive capacity of a nation, and an increase in the wealth will follow. And how does a nation increase its productivity? According to Smith, through the division of labor.

On the first page of the *Wealth of Nations*, Smith points out that 10 laborers working independently can scarcely produce 10 stick pins in a day. But when the tasks are broken down into a number of distinct operations and the work is coordinated, 10 men can produce as many as 48,000 pins a day.

> One man draws out the wire, another straights it, a third cuts it, a fourth points it, a fifth grinds it at the top for receiving the head; to make the head

requires two or three distinct operations ... and the important business of making a pin is, in this manner, divided into about eighteen distinct operations, which, in some manufactories, are all performed by distinct hands ... .[4]

According to Smith, three factors explain why the division of labor increases human production. First, specialization increases dexterity. When production is separated into simple tasks, a laborer becomes more proficient in performing that task. Second, the division of labor saves time that would normally be lost in passing from one job to another. "It is impossible to pass very quickly from one kind of work to another that is carried on in a different place and with quite different tools."[5] And third, when production is separated into simpler tasks, machines can be constructed that enable one person to do the work of many. "Men are much more likely to discover easier and readier methods of attaining any object when the whole attention of their minds is directed towards that single object than when it is dissipated among a great variety of things."[6]

Increased production was the major consequence of the division of labor, but it did not cause the division of labor, according to Smith. Nor was the division of labor the product of a conscious process, at least in the beginning. Smith argued that "the power of exchange" created the division of labor.[7] Humans have "a propensity" to barter and exchange one thing for another. And the motivation to make contracts for exchange, he added, comes not from benevolence but from self-interest, or the desire to increase one's own happiness. Thus, at the primitive level of production, a division of labor ensues when one individual, pursuing his or her own self-interest, finds that he or she can produce a product that can be exchanged for other desired products. Under capitalism, this productive process is moved to a higher level — it is institutionalized. Capitalists consciously seek to increase efficiency by creating a division of labor.[8]

Although Smith was not specifically concerned with developing a theory of the organization, his theory incorporates the notion that organizations grow as the division of labor increases.[9] In order to increase output, capitalists must invest more and more money to pay for the machinery and other equipment. This resulted in what Smith called accumulation, or capital investment. Although demand for labor and, concomitantly, the cost of wages would increase as businesses grew, accumulation would not fizzle out because Smith believed increasing wages also would produce an increase in the number of laborers. Increasing wages would improve living conditions.   This would reduce infant mortality, which was quite high in Smith's day, and, thus, increase the supply of workmen, which in turn would push down the costs of labor. The accumulation process could proceed in cycles of greater and lesser production, but the process would continue basically until all of the earth's resources were consumed.

Although Smith's theory incorporates the notion that businesses tend to grow in a free-market economy, Smith rejected the idea that this would lead to concentration of economic power and large-scale organization, for two reasons.   First, he believed that market forces would prevent any firm from becoming too large.   Concentration of economic power, if it did occur, was only a temporary phenomenon.   The growth of any particular firm would be checked by the emergence of other competitors.   Second, and perhaps more importantly, Smith rejected the notion that joint-stock companies, which could accumulate large sums of capital in a short period of time, were an effective form of organization for most business ventures. Joint-stock companies could function relatively well in banking and insurance industries, and they could be used to fund large public works projects (e.g., canals, water supply).   All of these required large sums of money to accomplish their tasks.   But the heart of capitalism, Smith believed, lay mainly in sole proprietorships and partnerships.   The owners in these organizations usually managed day-to-day activities and, hence, only they could be expected to look after their investments very closely. But such was not generally the case for joint-stock companies.

> The directors of such companies ... being the managers ... of other people's money than of their own ... cannot ... be expected ... (to) watch over it with the same anxious vigilance with which the partners in a private copartnery frequently watch over their own. ... Negligence and profusion, therefore, must always prevail, more or less, in the management of the affairs of such a company.[10]

Many contemporary scholars believe that history has proved Smith wrong on this point.   Indeed, today most of the large corporations that dominate many manufacturing and service industries are controlled by highly educated professionals, not the owners. The separation of ownership from control, in fact, appears to have facilitated, rather than diminished, the effectiveness of large-scale organization and its ability to adapt to changing economic, political and social conditions.[11]   But the question of whether corporate organizations are less likely than entrepreneurial forms of organization to maximize profits has not been empirically resolved.[12] Smith's beliefs were no doubt influenced by the fact that the joint-stock companies in his day were often used to fund overseas trading expeditions, which offered the potential for great rewards but often failed.[13]

Nevertheless, despite these shortcomings, Smith's analysis offers at least two major insights for the study of corporate newspaper structure: (1) Larger, more complex newspapers would be expected to be more efficient, productive and profitable because they have a more advanced division of labor; and (2) Newspapers controlled by managers would be expected to place less emphasis on profits because they typically do not benefit as directly from profits as the owners.

Karl Marx and Competition

Marx agreed with Smith that competition promotes the division of labor. He also agreed that the division of labor increases the productive capacity and wealth of a nation. But unlike Smith, Marx argued that competition would produce concentration of capital and ownership on a grand scale. One of the major problems with Smith's model, Marx's analysis suggests, is that it failed to anticipate the effects that economies of scale would have on barriers to entry in the marketplace.

Marx also disagreed with Smith in terms of who would benefit from such wealth. Smith conceded that the division of labor could have deleterious consequences for workers. Tasks that are broken down into simpler motions become more monotonous, and work becomes more mundane. But he remained generally optimistic. Wages would increase as the productive capacity of a nation increases, and this would push human happiness beyond anything dreamed of before. But by the middle of the 19th century, this sanguine assessment was of dubious merit. Laborers in many of the factories in England and other nations worked long hours, were paid little and lived in extreme poverty. The wealth generated by the division of labor went not to the laborers but, rather, as Marx observed, to the owners of the means of production.

In Volume I of *Capital*, Marx argued that competition drives capitalists to search incessantly for ways to increase productivity.[14] Capitalists innovate in one of two ways. The first is by increasing the division of labor.[15] The second is through the use of machinery.[16] In either case, the end result is that innovation allows capitalists to produce

more units at a lower per unit cost and, thus, to reap increased profits —
at least until other competitors adopt the innovation. When that happens,
the supply of the product increases, prices fall, and "surplus profits" are
eliminated. The price remains relatively stable until another innovation
comes along, and then the cycle starts over again.

Marx argued that the major consequences of innovation were
concentration and centralization of capital. "With the increasing mass of
wealth which functions as capital, accumulation increases the concentration
of that wealth in the hands of individual capitalists, and thereby widens the
basis of production on a large scale and of the specific methods of
capitalist production."[17] Marx defined concentration as growth in capital,
or an increase in the size of companies. Capitalists must continually
reinvest profits in order to remain competitive. Most of the reinvestment
goes to production and development of new machines and methods for
reducing labor costs. This increases the size and scope of mass production
and the ratio of capital to the labor process. However, Marx argued that
concentration of capital leads to an increase, not a decrease, in the number
of owners. This occurs because, over time, capital is divided among family
members, often through inheritance, and earmarked for new ventures.[18]

Although ownership tends to become decentralized as a firm grows,
this process is slow and is more than offset by centralization of capital. He
defined centralization as the combining of capitals already formed, i.e., a
reduction in the number of competitive firms in a particular sector of
industry. Centralization occurs in one of two ways. The first is when
larger, more successful companies purchase the assets of weaker, less
competitive and innovative firms. Economies of scale are primarily
responsible for this. Marx writes:

> The battle of competition is fought by cheapening of commodities. The
> cheapness of commodities depends, ceteris paribus, on the productiveness of
> labor, and this again on the scale of production. Therefore the larger capitals
> beat the smaller.[19]

The second method of centralization occurs through the formation of
joint-stock companies, which, he argued, often pool large amounts of
capital together for the purpose of gaining greater control over a particular
market. The credit and banking system plays an important role in funding
such ventures.[20]

In the broader context, Marx argued that concentration and centralization of economic power leads to increasing polarization of the classes and, eventually, revolution. Declining rates of profit will force many companies out of business. To remain competitive, others will have to lay off workers and replace them with machinery or lengthen the working day and cut wages. Over time, private enterprise as a whole becomes increasingly oligopolized and monopolized. Class consciousness will emerge as the ranks of the working and unemployed classes increase and will fuel the revolutions that overthrow the bourgeoisie.

Scholars widely agree that history generally has failed to support Marx's predictions about the declining rate of profit, polarization of the classes and revolution. There also is conflicting evidence about whether ownership of capital is becoming increasingly centralized. Some researchers claim that, despite variations across industries, the trend toward centralization has progressed monotonically since the 19th century.[21] Others contend that the degree of centralization has changed little since the 19th century — maybe even declined since World War II — and that even in highly concentrated industries there is a great deal of competition.[22] The debate continues, but few scholars dispute the general observation that concentration of capital exists in many industries, especially the manufacturing sector. For example, the four largest U.S. firms in the automobile, computer, cigarette, detergent and metal products industries account for 50 to 100 percent of total production and sales, and the 200 largest firms account for most corporate wealth and income.[23]

Marx also may have been correct in observing that innovation mediates the effects of competition on concentration of ownership. Research often finds that size of an organization and the degree of functional differentiation and specialization within organizations are positively correlated with the adoption of innovations.[24] Although larger organizations tend to adopt an innovation more quickly than smaller ones, they are not necessarily more innovative than smaller firms. New ideas and inventions often come from smaller companies.[25]

Marx's analysis offers two major implications for the study of newspaper organization. First, competition would be expected to promote the growth of large-scale newspaper organizations, since it stimulates innovation, reduces prices and runs less efficient newspapers out of business. Second, the death of entrepreneurial newspaper owners would be expected to promote dispersion of ownership as capital is divided among heirs, even though Marx pointed out that capital tends to be concentrated with centralization of ownership.

Herbert Spencer and Social Differentiation

Spencer did not share Marx's affinity for socialism or his brand of evolutionism. Spencer was an adamant supporter of capitalism and believed, like Smith, that competition primarily had benign social consequences, stimulating innovation that increased production and wealth. Spencer believed that cooperation, persuasion and altruism characterized modern industrial societies. Competition and conflict were features of more primitive societies. He wrote:

> All kinds of creatures are alike in so far as each exhibits cooperation among its components for the benefit of the whole; and this trait, common to them, is a trait common also to societies. Further, among individual organisms, the degree of co-operation measures the degree of evolution; and this general truth, too, holds among social organisms.[26]

But, unlike Smith, Spencer viewed the division of labor as one component or aspect of the evolutionary process, not just a characteristic of human societies.

Spencer's ideas are contained in *Principles of Sociology*, in which he argued that social systems, like biological systems in general, tend to specialize and differentiate as they grow.[27] Social systems can grow through internal multiplication of units (birth) or aggregation of previously unrelated units (e.g., migration).[28] In either case, as a system grows the problem of how to sustain the units within it increases, especially when there are limited resources in an environment or when the system is geographically constrained. Spencer argued that the problem of sustenance can be solved through the division of labor, which reduces competition between units and creates mutual interdependence. But for specialization to work, the system must develop mechanisms for coordinating and controlling the differentiated units, or face dissolution.[29]

Spencer argued that integrative problems could be resolved through consolidation and centralization of political power and through the development of a system of mutual interdependencies of differentiated units. Both of these organizational processes have integrating functions, but there is a dialectic between them. Too much centralization of power leads to resistance and pressures to deregulate system units; conversely, too much deregulation creates problems for sustaining linkages among diverse social units and, consequently, pressures build for the consolidation of power. Spencer asserted that social systems cycle back and forth between these tendencies, with decentralization promoting growth and differentiation and centralization resolving problems of coordination and integration.[30]

Turner argues that although Spencer did not subscribe to a unilinear view of social change, he did believe that, barring a war or other major catastrophe, over time many societies exhibited a movement toward increasing social complexity and differentiation.[31] Spencer's model contained five major types of societies, ranging from simple "headless" societies, which exhibit little complexity, to modern industrial states, which contain an extremely complex division of labor.[32] Spencer argued that modern industrial states contain regulatory, operative and distributive structures. Regulatory structures included political leaders and the government whose primary role is to govern and coordinate various parts of the system.[33] Operative structures were responsible for producing material and human resources necessary for sustenance of the system. They included kinship, religious and economic organizations and institutions.[34] And distributive structures, which include transportation, markets and channels of communication, emerge as the volume of transactions within and between the operative and regulatory structures increases. They perform the primary function of integrating the various elements.[35]

Spencer argued that complexity of structure was built up as populations experimented with different tools and methods in the effort to adapt to diverse environments. Economic production increases because of advancements in the productive process and the transmission of knowledge about these methods from one generation to the next. Like Smith, Spencer argued that the driving force behind increases in the productive process is the escalation of human needs and the happiness that increased productivity brings.[36] And although Spencer and Marx disagreed on a number of matters, they both agreed that as one set of needs is satisfied, new ones arise.

Spencer also agreed with Marx that the expansion of production under capitalism requires capital investment. One of the most effective ways to generate such capital was through the formation of joint-stock companies.[37] Spencer argued that the joint-stock company was an outgrowth of earlier trading associations and partnerships. Without such pooling, large-scale production cannot be undertaken because few individuals have sufficient wealth. Government could provide capital for such production, but Spencer contended that government would be unable to execute such projects because "conservatism and officialism would have raised immense hindrances."[38]

As production increases, Spencer argued that distribution processes must also become more elaborate. Distribution is an essential concomitant of the division of labor because a system of transference from one element (individual or group) in the system is necessary for elements to perform specialized functions.[39] Although Spencer did not directly address the role of media in this process, and newspapers were still relatively undeveloped at the time, from this theory it can be postulated that the growth and development of the mass media is the product of need for integrating and coordinating diverse elements in a social system. It is important to point out that Spencer believed that distributive structures emerged after growth in regulative and operative structures and were designed to address problems of coordination and control.

Spencer's model has been criticized for being much too mechanistic and deterministic. Indeed, Spencer drew heavily from 17th century social physics, which viewed social systems as parts of a physical universe governed by law-like properties. For example, Spencer believed that the principle of the instability of homogeneous masses accounted for a wide variety of evolutionary processes, including solar systems, cognitive complexity, skin color and values.[40] But unlike Marx, Spencer did not subscribe to a simple unilinear view of social evolution, in which society was seen as progressing from one stage to the next and headed toward some desired end-state. Rather, he argued that the societal and organizational change may be characterized as a process of growth and differentiation, equilibrium and dissolution.

Some evidence suggests that Spencer was less prone than many of his followers to organismic analogizing — an approach which sought the social analogue of the heart, brain, etc., in social systems.[41] However, Spencer nonetheless placed greater emphasis on the idea that societies were more like individuals than species. As a consequence, Buckley argues that Spencer was more likely to see differentiated societies as being characterized by cooperation than by conflict. If society is viewed as an organism, then its parts cooperate and do not compete in a struggle for survival. But if viewed as an ecological aggregate, then the Darwinian model of competitive struggle is more applicable.[42]

Yet, despite these problems, many aspects of Spencer's model can be found in contemporary theories. As Turner points out, Spencer's concept of differentiation continues to play a prominent role in the macro-sociological literature, even though Spencer himself is rarely cited.[43] But more to the point, it is interesting that Spencer's model does a fairly good job in describing in rough terms the changes that have taken place in the newspaper industry over the last 300 years. The newspaper industry grew dramatically during the 19th century, reaching its peak (as measured by household penetration) at the beginning of the 20th century and declining since the late 1940s. Newspapers continue to diversify, but nothing seems to be able to stop the decline in penetration. Still, a major shortcoming of Spencer's model is that it fails to specify the processes or forces that have contributed to the decline of the press. In this sense it is more of a descriptive than an explanatory model. The weakness here is made up in Marx's model on the effects of competition in the system.

Emile Durkheim and Social Order

Durkheim was highly critical of Smith's notion that happiness was the primary cause of the division of labor. Durkheim argued that the cause must be found in the social, not the psychological, context. Durkheim also was critical of Spencer's emphasis on physical environments as the primary cause of structural differentiation. While a diversity of external environments may accelerate the division of labor, the former was not sufficient to cause the latter. Durkheim also argued that Spencer and Smith misunderstood the function of the division of labor. Its primary function was not to advance civilization or make people happier, but to make them feel more integrated.

In *The Division of Labor in Society,* Durkheim distinguishes between two forms of social solidarity, mechanical and organic. Mechanical solidarity describes societies that are usually small and relatively undifferentiated, having achieved little control over their environment. The basis of solidarity in these societies is likeness or similarity. People cherish the same things, hold the same values, and experience things the same way. Solidarity is achieved by homogeneity in beliefs, attitudes and values.[44] Organic solidarity, in contrast, characterizes societies in which social organization is highly differentiated. The basis of solidarity in such societies is functional interdependence — people engage in different and complementary activities in which they exchange goods and services between one another.[45]

Durkheim argued that "the division of labor progresses the more individuals there are who are sufficiently in contact with one another to be able mutually to act and react upon one another."[46] He called this dynamic or moral density, which in turn was caused by two other factors: material density and social volume. The material density between individuals is reduced spatially through the growth of cities and technologically through advances in communication and technology. This effect is reinforced by the social volume, or the total number of members of the society.[47]

Borrowing from Charles Darwin, Durkheim argued that an increase in material density and social volume causes the division of labor because they increase the struggle for existence.[48] As long as resources are abundant and population size is limited, similar organisms can live side-by-side in relative peace. When organisms pursue different needs, what is beneficial to one also will be of no value to the other, and conflict will decline. But when population increases and resources become scarce, conflict and competition will increase.

Durkheim argues that humans are subject to the same law. Population growth and material density increase social conflict and competition, which advance the division of labor. The increased differentiation enables the social system to exploit limited resources more efficiently, which, in turn, moderates conflict and competition between individuals, enabling a greater number to peacefully co-exist. In Durkheim's words: "The soldier seeks military glory, the priest moral authority, the statesman power, the businessman riches, the scholar scientific renown. Each of them can attain his end without preventing the others from obtaining theirs."[49] Durkheim added that nothing in this process leads to an increase in happiness; it all takes place because of an inexorable law of social progress.[50]

However, it is important to point out that Durkheim did not believe that the division of labor would occur automatically when population and material density increased. There were other possible solutions to the struggle for existence, including emigration, colonization, or suicide. The division of labor was contingent upon a reduction in the conscience collective and heredity.[51] He defined conscience collective as the external normative order or social fact which coerced members of the group to behave and think in certain ways. As the division of labor expanded, the conscience collective declined and individualism emerged, according to Durkheim.

More specifically, the decline in the conscience collective is a function of the growth of rationality and the decline of tradition. In mechanical societies, people related to objects in the environment in the same way. The states of conscience representing this environment are parallel. The conscience collective is sharp, decisive and well-defined. But as these societies grow and their populations become more diversely situated, common objects no longer create common experiences and representations. To remain common, the conscience collective must become less concrete and well-defined, more general and abstract. For example, the animal becomes the species, the tree becomes "trees in general and in abstracto," the "Greek" and "Roman" become the concept of "man."[52] But as the conscience collective becomes less concrete and decisive, it also loses an impact on individual thought and behavior.

> The more general the common consciousness becomes, the more scope it leaves for individual variations. When God is remote from things and men, His action does not extend to every moment of time and to every thing. Only abstract rules are fixed, and these can be freely applied in very different ways. ... Because the collective consciousness becomes more rational, it therefore becomes less categorical and, for this reason again, is less irksome to the free development of individual variations.[53]

More important than the "progressive indetermination" of the conscience collective, however, is the decline of tradition. This is because the strength of the collective states of consciousness is not just that they are common to the present generation but that they are for the most part a legacy of previous generations. The authority of tradition has a familial as well as political base, but as social volume and density undermine the segmental organization individuals no longer feel bound to their kin or place of origin. Durkheim did not believe that occupational groups in modern societies could reproduce the conscience collective because the occupational "conscience" affects only occupational life and is shared by fewer people in the society, and because social volume and density undermine the conscience collective in the occupational group.[54] In short, the decline of the conscience collective and tradition were necessary for the division of labor to emerge, and Durkheim believed that both decline as material density and social volume increase. Thus, the emergence of the individual personality and freedom is a product of natural forces, not the utility of emancipation.

The second factor that had to be reduced for the division of labor to emerge is the role of heredity. Here Durkheim was responding to John Stuart Mill's argument that individuals could be classified according to their capacities given in nature.[55] Durkheim argued that the role heredity plays in the distribution of tasks declines, in the course of social evolution, for two reasons. First, heredity loses its effect over the course of evolution because new modes of activity were constituted that did not depend on its influence.[56] Second, the number and strength of those capacities that heredity can transmit, such as instincts, decline with social evolution.[57] Durkheim observed that even the degree of physiological conformity required to speak meaningfully of a "race" seems to be rapidly disappearing.

Durkheim agreed with Marx that concentration of capital is a characteristic of modern capitalism, but Durkheim disagreed with Marx on the fundamental consequences of this trend. Although concentration represents a potential threat to individual freedom and thought, Durkheim argued that a greater threat is posed by the lack of a clear-cut set of rules according to which individuals are to act. When societies undergo rapid change they initially lack the ability to impose social norms on the populace. In this state of disorganization, or anomie, individuals find that their wants exceed the means available for their realization.[58]

Left unchecked, anomie leads to anarchy. However, according to Durkheim, individual freedom can be preserved if society is able to impose a normative structure on individuals. And one of the most effective and efficient ways to accomplish this is through centralized control of economic life. Durkheim supported a strong role for the state and believed it emerged with an advancing division of labor. For Durkheim, then, differentiation of ideas and thought is a natural outcome of the division of labor, and increasing concentration of ownership and capital is the mechanism through which society is able to impose a normative structure and thereby prevent increasing differentiation from turning into social chaos or anomie.

One of the main criticisms of Durkheim's theory is that it is an illegitimate teleology. In a nutshell, Durkheim argues that moral density leads to competition, which threatens the social order which, in turn, leads to the division of labor, mutual interdependence and social solidarity. Cohen points out that the impression is left that the need for social order causes the division of labor.[59] However, Turner argues that this illegitimate teleology can be overcome by making three assumptions. First, competition must occur under conditions of scarcity of resources. Second, a law of economic utility must be evoked. And third, it must be assumed that actors are motivated to avoid competition.[60] Durkheim's theory also has been criticized for being overly deterministic and ignoring the role of individuals and elites in shaping and constructing organizations, and for placing too much emphasis on the solidarity producing aspects of the division of labor and too little on the dysfunctional aspects.

Durkheim's analysis has several important implications for the newspaper industry. First, it suggests that the cause of the division of labor in general and the corporate newspaper in particular is to be found in the social, not the psychological, environment. More specifically, the corporate newspaper may be seen as a product of population growth, a reduction of traditional ties and competition between social actors for limited resources. Second, as a social system becomes more complex, the diversity of ideas would be expected to increase. Third, the corporate newspaper may be viewed as one of the structural mechanisms that helps to prevent this diversity from destroying social order. Newspapers may be seen, in fact, as providing content that has normative as well as functional consequences, reducing social distance and integrating social actors.

Max Weber and the Bureaucracy

The factor that most distinguishes Weber from the other theorists discussed thus far is his emphasis on social action and rationality. All of the previous theorists in varying degrees gave natural forces or social structure a greater emphasis in explaining the development and evolution of social organization. But Weber argues that to understand social organization, it is also necessary to study the subjective actions or motivations of the actors involved.

Weber's description of bureaucracy was elaborated in Chapter 1. Briefly, he contends that large-scale organizations — or bureaucracies — are organizational arrangements in which behavior is goal-directed and decision-making is rational. He defines rationality as the attempt to reduce the production and distribution of goods or services into routines so as to find the most efficient and effective way to reach a goal.[61] It is important to point out that rationality as defined by Weber involves a means-end calculus — that is, behavior that begins with the objective of finding the most efficient way to reach a goal, not whether the behavior itself is considered "rational" by some sort of standard. In addition to rationality, bureaucracies are characterized by a hierarchy of authority, employment and promotion based on technical qualifications, a set of rules and procedures that define job responsibilities and show how tasks are accomplished, formalistic impersonality, and a division of labor and role specialization.[62]

Weber identified three historical conditions that favored the development of bureaucracies. The first was the development of money economies.[63] A money economy, which allows quantitative calculation of income and expenditures, gives permanence and predictability in social organization. Cash salaries, rather than other rewards, are used to compensate individuals. He argues that this creates just the right balance of dependence and independence for the faithful execution of responsibilities in the organization. In contrast, unpaid volunteers are too independent of the organization to submit unfailingly to its rules, while slaves are too dependent upon their masters to have the initiative to assume many of the responsibilities necessary for proper functioning of the organization.

The second condition that promoted the development of bureaucracies was education. In contrast to other forms of organization, bureaucracies rely heavily on written records and documents. Literacy is essential for bureaucratic work. Schools, which are themselves bureaucratically organized, also socialize individuals into bureaucratic procedures and methods. Historically, they have played an important role in breaking down traditional forms of knowledge and in ushering in the principles of rationalization of modern life.

The third condition that encouraged the development of bureaucracies was capitalism.[64] Capitalism brought with it the rational estimation of economic risks which required that the regular processes of the competitive market not be interrupted by external forces in unpredictable ways. Interference with free trade, such as banditry, piracy and social upheaval, threatens capital, and the development of a strong government is necessary to maintain social order. Capitalist enterprises, Weber argued, have as their major aim the maximization of profits, or unlimited profit accumulation, and seek to reach this goal through the rationalization of work and production. He saw the press as performing an important role in this process.

Business management throughout rests on increasing precision, steadiness, and, above all, the speed of operations. This, in turn, is determined by the peculiar nature of the modern means of communication, including, among other things, the news service of the press. The extraordinary increase in the speed by which public announcements, as well as economic and political facts, are transmitted exerts a steady and sharp pressure in the direction of speeding up the tempo of administrative reaction towards various situations. The optimum of such reaction time is normally attained only by a strictly bureaucratic organization.[65]

Weber's model goes a long way in explaining some of the characteristics of the modern newspaper organization. The development of codes of ethics in large news organizations, for example, may be interpreted as the organization's way of coordinating a large staff of reporters.[66] The hiring of more highly educated personnel and the use of objective criteria for hiring may reflect the organization's need for highly skilled, technically competent personnel.[67] Specialized news coverage is a logical consequence of the organization's expanding division of labor, which in turn depends upon increasing complexity in the larger social system. And the loss of reporter autonomy may stem from increasing role specialization in which editors spend more time managing reporters, who themselves are performing highly specialized tasks, than dealing with sources and the public.[68]

As noted in Chapter 1, one of the most significant criticisms of Weber's model is that in the real world bureaucratic organizations are not quite so efficient. As Merton pointed out, the practices that are designed to produce efficiency will, under some circumstances, produce extremely ritualistic or rigid behavior that is inefficient. "Adherence to the rules, originally conceived as a means, becomes transformed into an end-in-itself; there occurs the familiar process of *displacement of goals* whereby 'an instrumental value becomes a terminal value.'"[69]

In addition to overconformity to rules and displacement of goals, Meyer, Stevenson and Webster argue that as bureaucracies grow they become more inefficient, particularly when bureaucratic growth is disproportionate to actual tasks or outputs.[70] Large-scale organizations often have more difficulty adjusting to changes in the environment and are often said to have a low capacity for innovation. Such was the case during the 1970s in the U.S. automobile industry when sales slumped but inventories kept piling up. A number of other criticisms of Weber's model have been made,[71] but these do not detract from the overall conclusion that bureaucratic structures are still the optimum form of organization for coordinating and controlling large-scale tasks.

Weber's analysis of bureaucracies extends and reinforces the conclusions of Smith, Marx and Durkheim with respect to the division of labor and its consequences. But his analysis of the historical conditions that helped to promote the development of the bureaucracy also provides a unique contribution. A money economy, education and capitalism promoted the growth of the newspaper in modern society.

Joseph Schumpeter and the Technocrats

The economist Joseph Schumpeter agreed with Marx that innovations are an important stimulus to the development of large corporate organizations. He also agreed that competition forces prices down, which increases the pressure to find money-saving innovations. But Schumpeter disagreed with Marx in terms of who in the organization was responsible for this process. Marx argued that capitalists, the owners of the business, were behind the process. Schumpeter, on the other hand, attributed the innovative process not to the owners, but to the highly skilled managers and technical specialists in the organization. He called them "entrepreneurs."[72]

Capitalists are driven by profits. In early capitalism, the capitalist was the entrepreneur. But as organizations grew this role became more specialized and routinized, being given over to highly educated and trained specialists. Since entrepreneurs in modern corporations are not usually the direct beneficiaries of profit, according to Schumpeter, they are driven not by profits but by social status.

> First, there is the dream and the will to found a private kingdom, usually, although not necessarily, also a dynasty. ... Then there is the will to conquer: the impulse to fight, to prove oneself superior to others, to succeed for the sake, not of the fruits of success, but of success itself. ... Finally, there is the joy of creating, of getting things done, or simply of exercising one's energy and imagination.[73]

In short, the entrepreneur is not driven so much by pecuniary rewards as by prestige and status. The entrepreneur seeks to become a bourgeois. He or she is the driving force behind the system.

Schumpeter argued that the process of innovation gave rise to what he called the "creative gale of destruction." With each new technological innovation there is a scramble to adopt the innovation. As the innovation diffuses throughout the system, older technologies are displaced — they are "destroyed." Businesses that do not adopt the technology quickly enough may go out of business or be bought up by more competitive firms. Like Marx, Schumpeter argues that innovation contributes to concentration and centralization of ownership.

Schumpeter also agreed with Marx that capitalism was doomed. However, the proletariate would play little or no role in its demise, according to Schumpeter. Social change is produced not by those at the bottom of the social ladder, but, rather, by those at the top. The capitalist class itself and its rational attitude would bring the system down.

> And we have finally seen that capitalism creates a critical frame of mind which, after having destroyed the moral authority of so many other institutions, in the end turns against its own; the bourgeois finds to his amazement that the rationalist attitude does not stop at the credentials of kings and popes but goes on to attack private property and the whole scheme of bourgeois values.[74]

The new order, he argued, would consist of a planned economy driven by large-scale bureaucratic organizations in which innovation is institutionalized and routinized.

Schumpeter's ideas have had a strong impact on a number of writers, including John Kenneth Galbraith.[75] But is Schumpeter correct — is the system heading toward a kind of bureaucratic socialist system? As Heilbroner points out, in the late 1960s Schumpeter's ideas seemed profoundly prophetic.[76] But today it seems that while there is little doubt that the role of innovator has become a highly bureaucratic process, there is little evidence to suggest that capitalist values are on the demise. Emphasis on profits and faith in the system appeared to reach all-time highs during the 1980s. Furthermore, the current efforts to transform the economies of the republics that were once part of the Soviet Union and the communist Eastern block suggests that the ideology of the market model is far from decline.

Nevertheless, Schumpeter's observation that professional managers and technocrats are the force behind organizational growth and change suggests that corporate newspapers may place less emphasis on profits and more emphasis on other nonprofit goals than their entrepreneurial counterparts.

Summary

In this chapter the ideas of six early theorists on organizational development were reviewed. All agreed that the division of labor increases the productive capacity of labor which, in turn, can stimulate further organizational growth. Most also agreed that competition stimulates social and technological innovation, which promotes the division of labor and organizational complexity. But the theorists often disagreed on the causes and effects or functions of the division of labor and large-scale organization.

Smith believed the propensity of humans to bargain and exchange goods was the original cause of the division of labor, and the trend itself is encouraged by self-interest and the pursuit of happiness. Marx, in contrast, argued that competition between capitalists stimulates organizational growth — organizations that fail to innovate and reduce costs will go out of business, but those that innovate will grow and over time ownership and capital in an industry will become highly concentrated. Competition also figured prominently in Spencer, Durkheim and Schumpeter's theories; however, for them, competition was a characteristic of all forms of social organization, not just capitalism. Spencer and Durkheim both argued that as social systems grow and become more dense, the struggle for existence increases. Under certain circumstances, this promotes the division of labor, which in turn reduces competition and creates mutual interdependencies. Taking a historical approach, Weber argued that a money economy, education and capitalism promoted the growth of the division of labor and large-scale organization, or what he called bureaucracies. Schumpeter agreed with Marx that competition promotes concentration of capital and contributes to the demise of capitalism; however, it is the highly skilled and educated workers and managers, not the capitalists, who fuel innovation and organizational growth.

Smith argued that the major function or consequence of the division of labor was increased wealth for a nation, which advanced civilization and increased happiness. Marx agreed that the division of labor increased wealth, but only for the owners of the means of production, not the workers. The division of labor alienated workers and promoted class conflict that would eventually lead to a revolution. Spencer, like Smith, believed that the division of labor had primarily benign consequences, increasing the productive capacity of a social system and decreasing competition for scarce resources. In contrast, Durkheim argued that the most important function of the division of labor was not increased productivity or alienation — it was integration through increased interdependence and specialization. Weber recognized that bureaucracies were effective means for controlling and coordinating individuals and tasks, but he believed such organizations were inimical to individual freedom. Like Marx, Schumpeter believed that the growth of large-scale organizations would lead to the demise of capitalism, but this would come from a rational critique of its contradictions, not a revolution of the proletariate.

Smith's analysis of the division of labor offers at least two major insights for the study of corporate newspaper structure. Larger, more complex newspapers would be expected to be more efficient, productive and profitable. And newspapers controlled by managers would be expected to place less emphasis on profits. Marx's analysis suggests that competition would be expected to promote the growth of large-scale newspaper organizations, since it stimulates innovation, reduces prices and runs less efficient newspapers out of business. Spencer's concept of differentiation suggests that the growth and development of the mass media is the product of need for integrating and coordinating diverse elements in a social system. From Durkheim's writings, the corporate newspaper may be seen as a product of population growth, a reduction of traditional ties, and competition between social actors for limited resources. Second, as a social system becomes more complex, the diversity of ideas would be expected to increase. And third, the corporate newspaper may be viewed as one of the structural mechanisms that helps to prevent this diversity from destroying social order. Weber's analysis suggests that three historical conditions — money economy, education, and capitalism — played a major role in the growth of the corporate newspaper. Schumpeter's observation that professional managers and technocrats are the force behind organizational growth and change suggests that corporate newspapers may place less emphasis on profits and more emphasis on other nonprofit goals than their entrepreneurial counterparts.

Notes

1. Much historical research is built upon a voluntaristic conception of human nature. The incorporation of formal theoretical models is relatively new and appears to be growing in popularity. For an excellent discussion, see David Paul Nord and Harold L. Nelson, "The Logic of Historical Research," pp. 278-304 in Guido H. Stempel III and Bruce H. Westley

(eds.), *Research Methods in Mass Communication* (Englewood Cliffs, N.J.: Prentice-Hall, 1981). Three exceptions to the history-as-a-great-person-theory approach are Hazel Dicken-Garcia, *Journalistic Standards in Nineteenth-Century America* (Madison, Wis.: University of Wisconsin Press, 1989); Michael Schudson, *Discovering the News* (New York: Basic Books, 1978); and Dan Schiller, "An Historical Approach to Objectivity and Professionalism in American News Reporting," *Journal of Communication*, 29(4):46-57 (1979).

2. Adam Smith, *An Inquiry Into the Nature and Causes of the Wealth of Nations* (Chicago: William Benton, Encyclopedia Britannica, Inc., 1952 [1776]).

3. Robert L. Heilbroner, *The Making of Economic Society*, 7th ed. (Englewood Cliffs, N.J.: Prentice-Hall, 1985).

4. Smith, *Wealth of Nations*, p. 3.

5. Smith, *Wealth of Nations*, p. 5.

6. Smith, *Wealth of Nations*, p. 5.

7. Smith, *Wealth of Nations*, pp. 6-8.

8. Smith, *Wealth of Nations*, p. 37. Smith also argued that increased demand for products and services and foreign trade promote a division of labor (see, p. 327 and pp. 190-1, respectively).

9. For a more complete exposition of this model, see A. Lowe, "Adam Smith's System of Equilibrium Growth," and W. A. Eltis, "Adam Smith's Theory of Economic Growth," in Andrew S. Skinner and Thomas Wilson (eds.), *Essays on Adam Smith* (Oxford: Clarendon Press, 1975).

10. Smith, *Wealth of Nations*, p. 324.

11. Adolf A. Berle and Gardiner C. Means, *The Modern Corporation and Private Property* (New York: Commerce Clearing House, 1932) and James Burnham, *The Managerial Revolution* (New York: John Day, 1941).

12. For a review of the literature in the newspaper industry, see David Pearce Demers, "Corporate Structure and Emphasis on Profits and Product Quality at U.S. Daily Newspapers," *Journalism Quarterly*, 68:15-26 (1991) and David Pearce Demers, "Corporate Newspaper Structure and Organizational Goals," paper presented to the Association for Education in Journalism and Mass Communication (Atlanta, August 1994).

13. Smith, *Wealth of Nations*.

14. Karl Marx, *Capital: A Critique of Political Economy*, vol. 1, trans. by Samuel Moore and Edward Aveling (New York: International Publishers, 1987 [1867]).

15. Marx, *Capital*, p. 583.

16. Marx, *Capital*, p. 583.

17. Marx, *Capital*, p. 585.

18. Marx, *Capital*, pp. 582-6.

19. Marx, *Capital*, p. 586.

20. Marx, *Capital*, p. 588.

21. Sam Aaronovitch and Malcolm C. Sawyer, *Big Business: Theoretical and Empirical Aspects of Concentration and Mergers in the United Kingdom* (London: Macmillan, 1975), p. 157; J. Malcolm Blair, *Economic Concentration, Structure, Behaviour and Public Policy* (New York: Harcourt-Brace, 1972); L. Hannah, *The Rise of the Corporate Economy* (London: Methuen, 1975); Paul M. Sweezy, *The Theory of Capitalist Development* (New York: Modern Reader, 1970); and Paul M. Sweezy and H. Magdoff, *The Dynamics of U.S. Capitalism* (New York: Modern Reader, 1972).

22. Yale Brozen, *Concentration, Mergers, and Public Policy* (New York: Macmillan, 1982); William S. Comanor, "Conglomerate Mergers: Considerations for Public Policy," in R. Blair and R. F. Lanzillotti (eds.), *The Conglomerate Corporation: A Public Problem?* (Cambridge: Oelgeschlager, Gunn and Hain, 1981); and G. Warren Nutter and Henry Adler Einhorn, *Enterprise Monopoly in the United States: 1899-1958* (New York: Columbia University Press, 1969). Some of the differences between the two schools of thought may stem from differences in measurement, but no systematic treatment of this topic has been undertaken to the knowledge of this researcher.

23. Peter Asch, *Industrial Organization and Antitrust Policy* (New York: John Wiley and Sons, 1983), p. 1.

24. For reviews, see Michael K. Moch and Edward V. Morse, "Size, Centralization and Organizational Adoption of Innovations," *American Sociological Review,* 42:716-25 (1977).

25. F. M. Scherer, "Technological Change and the Modern Corporation," pp. 270-95 in B. Bock, H. J. Goldschmid, I. M. Millstein and F. M. Scherer (eds.), *The Impact of the Modern Corporation* (New York: Columbia University Press, 1984).

26. Herbert Spencer, *Principles of Sociology,* 3rd ed. (New York: D. Appleton, 1910 [1888]).

27. Spencer, *Principles of Sociology,* pp. 463-71.

28. Spencer, *Principles of Sociology,* p. 469.

29. Spencer, *Principles of Sociology,* pp. 485-518.

30. Spencer, *Principles of Sociology,* pp. 549-87.

31. Jonathan H. Turner, *Herbert Spencer: A Renewed Appreciation* (Beverly Hills, Calif.: Sage Publications, 1985), pp. 33-34.

32. See Turner, *Herbert Spencer,* pp. 85-105.

33. Spencer, *Principles of Sociology,* pp. 519-48.

34. Spencer, *Principles of Sociology,* pp. 498-504.

35. Spencer, *Principles of Sociology,* pp. 505-18.

36. Herbert Spencer, *The Principles of Sociology,* vol. III (New York: D. Appleton and Company, 1897), p. 364.

37. Spencer, *Principles of Sociology,* pp. 526-34.

38. Spencer, *Principles of Sociology,* p. 532.

39. Spencer, *Principles of Sociology,* vol. III, p. 373.

40. Herbert Spencer, *First Principles,* vol. 1 (New York: De Witt Revolving Fund, 1958 [1862]).

41. " ... [T]here exist no analogies between the body politic and a living body, save those necessitated by that mutual dependence of parts which they display in common. ... " Spencer, *First Principles,* p. 592.

42. Walter Buckley, *Sociology and Modern Systems Theory* (Englewood Cliffs, N.J.: Prentice-Hall, 1967), p. 12.

43. Turner, *Herbert Spencer.* Spencer is most remembered for coining the phrase, "survival of the fittest," and is usually interpreted as being a conservative and apologist for the status quo.

44. Emile Durkheim, *The Division of Labor in Society,* trans. W. D. Halls (New York: The Free Press, 1984 [1893]), pp. 31-67.

45. Durkheim, *The Division of Labor in Society,* pp. 68-87.

46. Durkheim, *The Division of Labor in Society,* p. 201.

47. Durkheim, *The Division of Labor in Society,* p. 205.

48. Durkheim, *The Division of Labor in Society,* pp. 208-9.

49. Durkheim, *The Division of Labor in Society*, p. 209.

50. Empirical support for Durkheim's theory of the division of labor can be found in Kenneth C. Land, "Mathematical Formalization of Durkheim's Theory of the Division of Labor," pp. 257-82 in Edgar F. Borgatta and George W. Bohrnstedt (eds.), *Sociological Methodology* (San Francisco: Jossey-Bass, 1969).

51. Durkheim, *The Division of Labor in Society*, Chapters III and IV, respectively, pp. 226-68.

52. Durkheim, *The Division of Labor in Society*, pp. 229-30.

53. Durkheim, *The Division of Labor in Society*, p. 232-3.

54. Durkheim, *The Division of Labor in Society*, pp. 242-4.

55. John Stuart Mill, *Principles of Political Economy* (New York: Appleton, 1887).

56. Durkheim, *The Division of Labor in Society*, pp. 250-61.

57. Durkheim, *The Division of Labor in Society*, pp. 261-7.

58. Durkheim, *The Division of Labor in Society*, pp. 291-309.

59. Percy S. Cohen, *Modern Social Theory* (New York: Basic Books, 1968), pp. 35-7.

60. Jonathan H. Turner, *The Structure of Sociological Theory* (Homewood, Ill.: The Dorsey Press, 1978), p. 27.

61. See Max Weber, *The Theory of Social and Economic Organization,* trans. A. M. Henderson and Talcott Parsons (New York: The Free Press, 1964 [1947]) and H. H. Gerth and C. Wright Mills (eds.), *From Max Weber* (New York: Oxford University Press, 1946).

62. The list of characteristics here is distilled from Gerth and Mills, *From Max Weber*, pp. 196-8, and Weber, *The Theory of Social and Economic Organization*, pp. 329-36.

63. Gerth and Mills, *From Max Weber*, pp. 204-9.

64. See especially, Weber, *The Theory of Social and Economic Organization*, pp. 338-9.

65. Gerth and Mills, *From Max Weber*, p. 215.

66. Douglas Anderson, "How Managing Editors View and Deal With Ethical Issues," *Journalism Quarterly*, 64:341-5 (1987).

67. David Pearce Demers and Daniel B. Wackman, "Effect of Chain Ownership on Newspaper Management Goals," *Newspaper Research Journal*, 9(2):59-68 (1988) and John W. C. Johnstone, Edward J. Slawski and William W. Bowman, *The News People* (Urbana, Ill.: University of Illinois Press, 1976).

68. David Pearce Demers, "Effect of Corporate Structure on Autonomy of Top Editors at U.S. Dailies," *Journalism Quarterly*, 70:499-508 (1993).

69. Robert K. Merton, *Social Theory and Social Structure* (London: Free Press, 1957 [1949]), p. 199.

70. Marshall W. Meyer, William Stevenson and Stephen Webster, *Limits to Bureaucratic Growth* (New York: De Gruyter, 1985).

71. For a summary, see Dean J. Champion, *The Sociology of Organizations* (New York: McGraw-Hill, 1975), pp. 36-40.

72. Joseph A. Schumpeter, *The Theory of Economic Development* (Cambridge, Mass.: Harvard University Press, 1949).

73. Schumpeter, *The Theory of Economic Development*, pp. 93-4.

74. Schumpeter, *The Theory of Economic Development*, p. 143.

75. John Kenneth Galbraith, *The New Industrial State,* 3rd ed. (New York: Mentor, 1978).

76. Robert L. Heilbroner, *The Worldly Philosophers,* 6th ed. (New York: Simon & Schuster, 1986).

Chapter 4

Social System Theory
and the Mass Media

The writings of the classical theorists reviewed in the last chapter have stimulated a great deal of interest in the growth and maintenance of societies and organizations. Many of the ideas have been synthesized into more general theories of social change. One of the most influential is social system theory, which is the general theoretical framework for this study.

A social system may be defined as two or more social actors (individuals or collectivities) in an interdependent relationship. Interdependency exists when the attempt by one actor to achieve a goal depends upon the actions of another (or others). A good example in modern society is the dependence that politicians have on the media to obtain news coverage in order to win an election and, vice-versa, the dependence that journalists have on the politicians to report the events tied to the election. Many other social actors, in turn, depend upon these two social actors to achieve their goals (e.g., voters' need for information in order to select a candidate).

The idea of society as a system can be traced to the ancient Greeks.[1] Yet, despite being one of the oldest theoretical frameworks in the social sciences, social system theory is not a highly codified system of propositions or theorems. In fact, some scholars argue that social system theory is "neither a true description of reality nor a substantive theory nor an analytical procedure. Rather, it is a conceptual device designed to facilitate the entire scientific process, from the formation of propositions to the design of research."[2]

The position taken here might be described as middle-of-the-road. Systems theory can, indeed, greatly facilitate the study of media processes and effects, but it also offers at a general level an explanation for the existence and persistence of social systems. More specifically, systems theory attempts to explain social systems in terms of institutional arrangements, values, beliefs and power. This position is contrary to some economic models, which attempt to explain social systems primarily in terms of the marketplace or contractual arrangements. While implied or formal social contracts may contribute to the maintenance of a social system, systems theorists argue that they alone cannot explain a wide range of behavior or action, including much of that exhibited by the mass media.

Since the turn of the century, a handful of mass communication researchers have used a social systems perspective to study the mass media, especially the *news* media.[3] However, the vast majority of research has been and continues to be oriented toward psychological or social-psychological explanations and the micro-level of analysis.[4] Such studies are important for understanding the consequences of mass-mediated messages, but they cannot fully account for the role of mass media in society, because media are macro-level phenomena that cannot be reduced to the sum of the cognitions or social roles of the social actors within them. The whole, in other words, is greater (or lesser) than the sum of its parts.

Although a number of factors could be cited to explain the relative lack of interest in system research on the mass media,[5] a key factor is that many contemporary media scholars continue to associate modern systems theorizing with the functionalism of Durkheim, Lazarsfeld or Parsons and, consequently, believe that it is outmoded and inherently conservative.[6] While the history of social system theory is inextricably tied to these early theorists, a systems or functional perspective does not necessarily imply a theoretical conservatism, as numerous theorists have pointed out.[7] Concepts like social action, choice, conflict, power, institution building, and the construction of social reality all play an important role in modern systems theorizing. Systems theory is opposed to logical positivism, determinism, reductionism and atomism; however, empirical analysis and quantitative research methods can inform theory and vice versa.

The purpose of this chapter is to debunk some of the myths surrounding systems theory and to show how the theory can be used to better understand the role of mass media in society. More specifically, it will be argued that systems theorizing has undergone a synthesis in which many elements of consensus, conflict and symbolic interaction theories have been incorporated into one model. This new approach still emphasizes that the mass media — like police, schools and other major institutions — are agents of social control, but concern also has increased with studying the origins and development of media institutions themselves. Media institutions are no longer taken for granted or perceived as being part of some natural order. They are a product of concrete historical conditions, social and cultural phenomena, and the goal-oriented social actors whose interests are interlocked with those of other groups in society. The history of systems theory, like the history of social systems themselves, can be viewed as part of a dialectical process in which criticism along the way has infused new ideas that have allowed the theory to adapt and change.

Intellectual History

Following Buckley,[8] the history of systems theory may be divided roughly into four major models or periods: mechanical, organic, process and general systems. The differences and boundaries between these models are not always easy to identify or define. But, heuristically, the models are useful for organizing and understanding the changes that have occurred.

Mechanical Model

The first formal social system models emerged in the 17th century and were adapted from the natural sciences, which opposed supernatural, mystical, teleological and anthropomorphic conceptions of the world. Social physics, the social counterpart to the natural science system models, regarded the human being as an elaborate machine whose actions and thoughts could be analyzed with the principles of mechanics. Society, for example, was like an astronomical system, composed of people who were bound together by mutual attraction or differentiated by repulsion. Different societies or states were seen as systems of balanced oppositions. Social organization, power and authority were believed to be the result of natural forces (i.e., social atoms and molecules), rather than being the product of human actions and will (i.e., socially constructed).[9] A number of concepts and terms emerged from this period, including the notion of moral or social space, social coordinates, equilibrium, and centrifugal and centripetal forces.

Many of the mechanical theories, according to Buckley,[10] contained elements of specious analogizing. One exception was Vilfredo Pareto, who employed only the most general principles. He was one of the first to think of society as a system in equilibrium, as a whole consisting of interdependent parts.[11] A change in one part, Pareto argued, affects other parts as well as the whole.[12] Social equilibrium is maintained by three types of factors: (1) the extra-human environment (climate, soil, etc.), (2) external conditions (society's previous states and contact with other cultures), and (3) internal elements (race, interest, knowledge, values, ideologies). Pareto believed that if a social system is subjected to pressures of external forces, inner forces will then push toward the restoration of equilibrium.

Although most contemporary systems theorists have rejected the notion of natural equilibrium, the idea of a system as a whole consisting of interdependent parts remains fundamental. In the broadest sense, a system consists of two or more units that relate to each other in a structural relationship and form an entity whose elements are functionally interdependent.[13] The opposite of a system is random variability. A social system, in particular, may be defined as a bounded set of interrelated activities that together constitute a single social entity.[14] The activities may involve those of an entire society or those of just two people or social actors (e.g., a wife and husband). Thus, societies also are conceptualized as being composed of subsystems within sub-subsystems, etc. (e.g., the society, a community within the society, a church within the community, a family within the church, a wife or husband within a family).

The mechanical model produced little in the way of systematic empirical research. Most 19th century scholars seemed content to draw upon analogies from mechanical systems (i.e., solar systems) to describe actions within social systems. Such explanations were highly deterministic and mechanistic. Furthermore, no systematic studies of the mass media using the mechanical model apparently exist. This is not too surprising, since the mechanical model was already in decline by the mid-19th century, before newspapers and social sciences had obtained major institutional status.

Organic Model

The use of the organismic metaphor is very old, but serious scientific usage of it is usually traced to Herbert Spencer.[15] Basically, this is the notion that society is like the human body: It has a number of different specialized or differentiated parts that contribute to maintenance of the overall life of the organism. Many followers of Spencer went to great lengths to find the social counterparts to the heart, brain, and other parts of the body. As noted in Chapter 3, Spencer was much more cautious.[16] Nevertheless, Spencer failed to emphasize that society is more like a species than an organism, according to Buckley.[17] When the analogy is the organism, the parts are perceived to cooperate and do not compete in a struggle for survival. In contrast to the organic analogy, the species metaphor emphasizes competition and conflict, which, of course, leads to a very different characterization of society.[18]

Historically, structural functionalists have been the major proponents of the organic model.[19] Talcott Parsons, Robert K. Merton and others analyzed relations between social systems, personalities and cultures.[20] They focused on how solidarity, trust, meaning and power are institutionalized in the construction or production of the social order. Although all of these dimensions were defined as needs that every social system must cope with in order to survive, cooperation and consensus were given a much more prominent role than power and conflict in the regulation of social activities.[21]

In their quest to explain social order, organic theorists spent a great deal of time trying to identify the functional imperatives of social systems — i.e., the needs or requisites that all social systems must solve in order to survive. Parsons, for example, developed the "four-function paradigm," which contended that all systems face four major problems — adaptation, goal attainment, integration and pattern maintenance (later renamed latent pattern maintenance-tension management). To solve these problems, he argued that social systems have developed four major subsystems or institutions: the economy to satisfy the adaptation need (i.e., the acquisition of resources from the environment); the polity to solve the goal attainment need; culture (or public associations), such as religious institutions, to meet the integration need; and the family and educational institutions to satisfy the need for pattern maintenance. Mass media were said to satisfy primarily the need for integration, albeit they as well as all other institutions were said to contribute more or less to each of the four requisite needs. A social system that resolves each of these four system needs successfully was, according to Parsons, in a state of equilibrium, or a state of balance. As Theodorson and Theodorson put it:

> [Social equilibrium is] the concept that social life has a tendency to be and to remain a functionally integrated phenomenon, so that any change in one part of the social system will bring about adjustive changes in the other parts. The initial change creates an imbalance, but a functional adjustment of the parts occurs to recreate an integrated, adjusted and relatively stable system.[22]

The equilibrium assumption led many of the functional theorists to take for granted the creation and emergence of values, norms and institutions. As a consequence, any behavior that deviated from the dominant system of values and rules was considered deviant and undesirable. The goal of social science research under such an approach was to eliminate or control such behaviors. Needless to say, the equilibrium assumption became a lightning rod for criticisms that systems theory was conservative and helped support an oppressive, inequalitarian status quo. Parsons, in particular, was frequently criticized for allegedly advancing a theory that appeared to be ideologically conservative, a label he dismissed but was never able to shake.[23]

Although the organic theorists placed a great deal of emphasis on how institutions maintain social order, they did not ignore social change, a point that is sometimes overlooked by critics. Organic theorists adopted a neo-evolutionary model of social change, in which structural differentiation and functional specialization were the primary agents. The organic theorists acknowledged that revolutionary change was possible; however, they could not account for such change because they viewed it as too complex to explain given the current state of knowledge. Parsons writes:

> ... A general theory of the processes of change of social systems is not possible in the present state of knowledge. The reason is very simply that such a theory would imply complete knowledge of the laws of process of the system and this knowledge we do not possess. The theory of change in the structure of social systems must, therefore, be a theory of particular subprocesses of change *within* such systems, not of the over-all process of change *of* the systems as systems (emphasis in original).[24]

One of the substantive areas particularly influenced by structural functionalism was comparative research on modernization in the 1950s and 1960s.[25] These studies sought to explain differences between traditional and modern societies, arguing that traditional societies were perceived as being restrictive and limited, whereas modern societies were seen as being much more adaptable to a wide range of internal and external problems, especially social and technological change. These theories assumed that the organizational dynamics of economic, political and industrial institutions provide the dynamic force of structure in any complex society. Mass media were seen as playing an important role in breaking down traditional authority and ways of life and ushering in modern values and norms.[26] Furthermore, as the world becomes more urbanized and industrialized, societies become more similar. This view was highly consistent with classical evolutionary theory, which stressed that most societies passed through relatively similar stages toward a common end-stage of modernity.[27]

Following the organic frame of reference, many mass communication researchers before and after World War II attempted to define the major functions that media perform for society. In the 1940s, Lasswell wrote about three major functions: (1) surveillance of the environment; (2) correlation of the parts of society in responding to the environment; and (3) transmission of the social heritage from one generation to the next.[28] Wright added a fourth: entertainment.[29] And Lazarsfeld and Merton added two more: status conferral and the enforcement of social norms (ethicizing).[30] Following Merton,[31] many theorists recognized that media and other institutions may have dysfunctional consequences for social systems or social actors. DeFleur argued, for example, that the function of low-taste content in mass media was "to maintain the financial equilibrium of *a deeply institutionalized social system which is tightly integrated with the whole of the American economic institution*" (emphasis in original).[32] Nevertheless, the underlying theme in such research was that media coverage, as a whole, contributed to social order.[33]

Process Model

The process model began to take shape at the turn of the century and is represented in the writings of Albion W. Small, Charles H. Cooley, Robert E. Park, George H. Mead and E. W. Burgess. However, the process model was overshadowed by the organic model (e.g., structural functionalism) until the 1960s, when symbolic interactionism emerged as a widely respected perspective. Berger and Luckmann's classic book, *The Social Construction of Reality*, also helped tremendously to legitimize this perspective.[34]

The process model views society "as a complex, multifaceted, fluid interplay of widely varying degrees and intensities of association and dissociation."[35] Structure is not something distinct from society but, rather, a temporary representation of it at any one point in time. Societies and groups continually shift their structures to adapt to changing conditions. The process model generally is opposed to the notion of equilibrium, since this idea implies that a social system could and should reach a stable or static state. Rather, society is seen as constantly changing and dynamic.

At the turn of the century, Small argued that human experience "composes an associational process," whereby social actors pursuing their own goals "enter into certain more or less persistent structural relationships with each other," also known as institutions, that carry out social functions. "These social structures and functions are, in the first instance, results of the previous associational process; but they no sooner pass out of the fluid state, into a relatively stable condition, than they become in turn causes of subsequent stages of the associational process."[36] Small predicted, somewhat presciently, that the future of sociology "is marked by the gradual shifting of effort from analogical representation of social structures to real analysis of social processes."[37]

Park and Burgess viewed society as the product of interactions between individuals who are controlled by traditions and norms that arise in a process of interaction. Social control is "the central fact and the central problem of society. ... Society is everywhere a control organization. Its function is to organize, integrate, and direct the energies resident in the individuals which compose it."[38] Park and Burgess distinguished four major social processes: competition, conflict, accommodation and assimilation. A relatively stable social order, according to Park and Burgess, is one in which the mechanisms of social control have succeeded in containing antagonistic forces in such a way that they accommodate each other. However, overall accommodation can never be permanently achieved because new social actors are likely to emerge and claim their share of scarce resources.

Writing in the 1950s, Nadel also criticized the equilibrium model, arguing that the social structure must be viewed as an "event-structure."[39] He concludes:

> ... It seems impossible to speak of social structure in the singular. Analysis in terms of structure is incapable of presenting whole societies; nor, which means the same, can any society be said to exhibit an embracing, coherent structure as we understand the term. There are always cleavages, dissociations, enclaves, so that any description alleged to present a single structure will in fact present only a fragmentary or one-sided picture.[40]

Mass media research on the process model historically has focused heavily on how the mass media construct realities and how use of those realities contributes to social integration. For example, during the early part of the 20th century, Park examined the role of the immigrant press in helping newly arrived immigrants acclimate to community life in America.[41] During the 1950s, Janowitz also analyzed the integrative role of the urban weekly, concluding that community ties contribute to reading the paper and reading contributes to integration. He concluded that urban and suburban life, in contrast to the picture created by the mass society model, entails a rich combination of community and traditional ties mixed with modern occupational roles.[42]

General Systems Theory (GST)

The general systems model can be traced to the writings of de la Mettrie, an 18th century physiologist who argued that organization was the fundamental feature of the physical, biological and social worlds.[43] However, GST did not became a potent force in the social sciences until the 1950s, when the Society for General Systems Research was formed.[44] The emergence of this organization represented the culmination of concern that specialization in the sciences was leading to the fragmentation of knowledge. GST was an attempt to integrate the various scientific disciplines by focusing on the principles of organization per se instead of what it is that is organized (i.e., physical or social phenomena).

Like organic and process models, the general systems model posits that social systems are capable of adapting to changes in their natural and social environments. However, GST places much more emphasis on the ability of social systems to transform their structure and form, rather than returning to some sort of equilibrium state, as organic models often postulate. GST also recognizes that systems may dissolve — adaption is not a necessary condition of system strain.

To adapt to changes in the environment, social systems and their actors must obtain feedback information from the environment about the consequences of various actions, social configurations and processes. According to Buckley, feedback-controlled systems are referred to as goal-directed because it is the deviations from the goal-state itself that direct the behavior of the system rather than some predetermined internal mechanism.[45] "Feedforward" describes the process when social actors in a system attempt to anticipate the probable consequences of proposed activities for the system and its environment before enacting those activities. Thus, systems are dynamic; that is, they can change in response to changes in the environment. Two basic terms are used to characterize change: morphostasis and morphogenesis. The former refers to those processes in a system that tend to preserve or maintain a system's given form, organization or state. Morphogenesis refers to those processes that tend to elaborate or change a system's form, structure or state.

Two key types of morphostasis are homeostasis and equilibrium. A social system is said to be homeostatic, or self-maintaining, if it acts to counter disruptive forces from the environment or its subsystems, as a means of maintaining some crucial system feature or features. Only certain features are protected, not the entire system. Usually these features are characteristics of the system that are important for its survival. Homeostatic actions operate to maintain the system in a "steady state." But if the actions are not successful, the key features being maintained will be changed or destroyed. Pressures also will generate for additional changes in other parts of the system, which may lead to radical alteration or dissolution of the system.

Most organic theorists postulated an inherent tendency toward equilibrium among all the parts of the system. However, general system theorists abandoned this idea and used equilibrium as a heuristic device, i.e., a starting point for analyzing changes in a system. Olsen defines equilibrium as a condition that "exists in a social system when all the parts maintain a constant relationship to each other, so that no part changes its position or relation with respect to all the other parts."[46] Dynamic processes such as homeostasis and morphogenesis may operate with the system, but basic relationships between constituent parts do not change through time. Disruptive stresses and strains may upset the equilibrium, but systems attempt to neutralize or destroy the disruptive forces. The difference between equilibrium and homeostasis is that the latter process refers to only one or a few selected features of the system that are protected, while in equilibrium every part is preserved in constant relation to the total system. In other words, a change in one part will produce changes in all other parts.

Most contemporary system theories emphasize that the equilibrium is dynamic; that is, at any particular time, one subsystem or institution may be more influential than another. At election time, for example, the mass media in a democracy are accorded unusual deference because of the importance that information is perceived to play in contributing to maintenance of the social system.[47] Contemporary theories also do not assume that a social system has a fixed equilibrium; that is, social structures do not always return to a steady state — they may disintegrate in response to environmental or internal stress and strains.

A social system is characterized as morphogenic, or developing, if the system as a whole moves toward increased order, complexity, adaptability, unity or overall effectiveness. A morphogenic system shows increased ability to deal effectively with its environment and its own subsystems. As such, it grows structurally, in terms of complexity and internal ordering, and functionally, in terms of its ability to control its activities and achieve its goals. Both homeostatic and morphogenic processes depend upon feedback, or flow of information from the environment, to operate. Neither process excludes rational thought or purposeful goal-striving, but such features are not a necessary condition for a social system to survive. System growth and change is often a process in which random occurrences that prove beneficial to the system (i.e., in terms of achieving goals) are incorporated and retained, while nonbeneficial occurrences are discarded. Social actors involved in these processes are not necessarily aware of the consequences of their activities for system maintenance or development, or the consequences that different forms of social organization may have on the system or its parts.

Several notable works in communication and sociology were produced during the 1960s and 1970s.[48] General systems theorists criticized organic theorists for placing too much emphasis on social order and not enough on social change. Such theories emphasized not only the structure-maintaining features of social systems but also the structure-elaborating and changing features of unstable systems (i.e., morphogenesis). In other words, in order for a social system to maintain a steady state (i.e., its position of power, control, influence, etc.), it may have to change its structure. General systems theory still has its protagonists in sociology[49] and organizational communication.[50] However, the effort to create a grand system theory has ultimately failed, Turner contends, because even though all systems of the universe may possess common properties, it is the unique properties and process of the systems that are more interesting to scientists.[51]

Criticisms of Social System Theory

During the 1950s and 1960s, many of the assumptions and postulates of systems models, especially structural functionalism, came under assault.

The criticisms can be summarized under six major topics or themes.

First, the approach was criticized for employing illegitimate teleologies. An explanation is said to be teleological when it attempts to explain social processes, especially social change, by reference to end states or results. An illegitimate teleology exists when causal models assume that purposes or goals cause the processes or structures without documenting the causal sequences or mechanisms that give rise to the processes or structures.[52] Durkheim's theory of the division of labor,[53] for example, is often criticized for employing an illegitimate teleology because he implied at various points that social solidarity — the end state — causes the division of labor to emerge out of competition.

Second, systems models were criticized for being tautological; that is, for having circular statements. Turner argues that this is most likely to occur with the use of terms like equilibrium and requisites.[54] Thus, a social fact is often said to contribute to maintenance of the system — to fulfill some need — and the cause of the social fact is the need it fulfills.

Third, structural functionalism was criticized for being ahistorical and Western-centric. Modern Marxists pointed out that the modernization process was not universal or present in every society. Rather, it was a unique historical situation connected with capitalism and Western expansion and the establishment of an international system of hegemonic and dependent societies. This criticism led to the development of dependency and world system theories.[55]

Fourth, many system theorists assumed that people are easily socialized. In a widely cited essay, Wrong argued that socialization provides people with a social identity, but at the same time they are creative and have the ability to evaluate social reality critically and take an autonomous stand toward concrete social roles. "When our sociological theory over-stresses the stability and integration of society we will end up imagining that man is the disembodied, conscience-driven, status-seeking phantom of current theory."[56]

Fifth, structural functionalism was criticized for being conservative — for supporting the status quo — because it placed too much emphasis on consensus in goals and values as the main integrating mechanism in social systems.[57] Social action or ideas that conflicted with dominant goals and values in a social system were perceived as deviant rather than the self-determining actions and interests of disenfranchised groups and individuals.

And sixth, the approach was criticized for failing to explain social conflict and change, particularly radical change. The possibility that integrative and regulative mechanisms will fail was recognized by structural functionalists, but social change was assumed to occur gradually.[58] Conflicts, when they occurred, were characterized as anomalies that various institutions — such as schools, police, courts and media — would address and correct to bring the system back into a state of equilibrium. As noted earlier, Parsons, in particular, has been criticized for neglecting the role of power.[59]

All of these criticisms have had some validity at one point or another. However, as Turner points out, none are insurmountable. The problem of teleology can be overcome with detailed causal analysis of how needs are actuated in the development of social structures.[60] The problem of tautology can be surmounted by focusing on how variations in social wholes are caused by variations in critical parts and vice versa, and abandoning the assumption of equilibrium. The problem of ahistoricity is not that structural functionalism is incompatible with historical analyses but, rather, so few analyses have tried to merge the two.[61] The problem of over-socialization can be addressed by focusing more on the creation of structures, not just the functions they perform. Although many functionalists have been rightly criticized for taking a conservative view, there is nothing inherent in functionalism that should lead to a conservative viewpoint, since system maintenance may be viewed as either enabling or repressive.[62] And while it is true that classical structural functionalism did not place a great deal of emphasis on explaining rapid social conflict and change, as noted earlier, criticism that it ignored the role of social change is unfounded. Parsons and others adopted a neo-evolutionary perspective which viewed change as a continual process of structural differentiation and functional specialization. Contemporary theories also have modified this slightly to place greater emphasis on the processes of de-differentiation and dissolution of structure as well.[63]

Despite these qualifications, the criticism of system models during the 1950s, 1960s and 1970s was accompanied by the growth of a number of alternative theoretical models. They included the conflict model of Ralf Dahrendorf,[64] the exchange model of George C. Homans,[65] and the symbolic structuralist model of Claude Levi-Strauss.[66] Refinements and improvements also were made to Marxist and symbolic interactionist models during this time. While there were many differences between these models, Eisenstadt points out that they all shared one major feature: an unwillingness to accept the natural givenness of any single institutional arrangement in terms of the systematic needs of the social systems to which they belonged.[67]

The conflict and symbolic-interactionist models stressed that an institutional order is developed, maintained and changed through a continuous process of interaction, negotiation and struggle among those who participate in it. Greater autonomy also was granted to groups, organizations and individuals — their goals and values may differ considerably from those of the dominant groups and institutions. In short, the argument was that the explanation of any institutional arrangement has to take into account power relations, negotiations, struggles, conflicts and coalitions.

These alternative models have altered the course of systems theory. But it is important to point out that they have not displaced many of its central tenets, particularly the idea that social control is a fundamental need in any social system. Perhaps the greatest shortcoming of early models was not that they were wrong, but that they focused too narrowly on value consensus and the natural givenness of institutional arrangements in generating social order.

Contemporary Systems Theory

Olsen argues that three major factors distinguish social system models from other types of models.[68] First, they place primary emphasis on the totality of the whole system; in other words, the whole is assumed to be greater than the sum of the parts. Emphasis on the whole does not preclude examination of the parts, but the parts can only be understood in relation to the larger whole that they constitute. Second, to define a social system, it must be bounded in some way to separate it from its environment. Such boundaries are always at least partially open to the natural and social environments in that they exchange materials, energy, individuals or information. Eisenstadt emphasizes that such boundaries are open and fragile, not closed and rigid. Social systems and the subsystems within them are in a continuous process of change (construction and deconstruction).[69] And third, the parts of a social system must be interdependent or interrelated to some degree, even though the patterns and degrees of the ordering can vary. As long as the parts of a system have some amount of functional autonomy, they can be analyzed as systems in their own rights or as subsystems of another system. These subsystems, in turn, may be composed of many sub-subsystems, etc.[70]

Unlike mechanical systems (e.g., gas-powered engines), Olsen points out that social systems are capable of adapting to changes in their natural and social environments. Social actors are assumed to be goal-oriented. Behavior is not determined or set by some outside factor or force.[71] However, the range of social action is not unlimited. Cultural, social, psychological, biological and physical elements of any system constrain or enable social action. For example, in most situations social actors have the choice of violating a social value or norm; however, the penalties or sanctions associated with such an action reduce the probability of nonconforming behavior. At the same time, rewards associated with following the norms increase the probability that people will obey. Thus, behavior in such circumstances is not determined, but the probability that action will be consistent with the dominant norm or value increases as the sanctions or rewards associated with the action increase.[72]

Currently, neofunctionalism is one of the most important intellectual movements in systems theory.[73] Alexander, one of the movement's leaders, argues that neofunctionalism: (1) models society as an intelligible system whose parts are symbiotically connected to one another and interact without *a priori* direction from a governing force; (2) concentrates on action as much as on structure, focusing on expressive activity and the ends of action as well as on practicality and means; (3) is concerned with integration as a "possibility and with deviance and processes of social control as facts" — equilibrium is a reference point for analysis; (4) posits that the distinctions between personality, culture and society are vital to social structure and the tensions between them as a continuous source of change and control; (5) implies a recognition of cultural, social and psychological differentiation as a major mode of social change and of the individuation and institutional strains that this historical process creates; and (6) implies the commitment to the independence of conceptualization and theorizing from other levels of sociological analysis.[74] Alexander adds that although each of these six theses can be identified with other lines of work in the social sciences, no other tradition can be identified with all of them.

As noted earlier, another important characteristic of modern social system theories is that they no longer take the development of institutions for granted. The process of institution building, Eisenstadt argues, is affected by three factors: (1) the level and distribution of resources among different groups (i.e., the type of division of labor); (2) the kinds of elites or institutional entrepreneurs that are available, or competing, for the mobilizing and structuring of such resources and for the major groups generated by the social division of labor; and (3) the nature of the conceptions of "visions" (or ideology) which inform the activities of these elites and which are derived from the major cultural orientations or codes prevalent in a society.[75]

According to Eisenstadt, the most important elites in any society are the political elites, because they deal most directly with the regulation of power. This group consists primarily of elites in government. They are followed by elites whose activities involve the construction of meaning and trust (e.g., churches, schools, media). Elites or, more accurately, coalitions of elites exercise control over basic resources in society through control of the major economic, political and cultural institutions. This control is achieved through a combination of organizational and coercive measures, along with the structuring of cognitive maps (or rules) of the social order (e.g., through the mass media) and the major reference orientations of social groups. The major characteristics and boundaries of social systems are shaped by the different coalitions of elites and the modes of control they exercise. These modes of control include such things as the structure of authority, the conception of justice, the structure of power and the principals of social hierarchization.[76]

Although different coalitions of elites construct the boundaries of social systems and other collectivities, no such construction is stable, according to Eisenstadt. Conflict is inherent in any setting of social interaction because of, first, the scarcity of natural and social resources; second, the plurality of actors; and third, the multiplicity of institutional principles and cultural orientations.[77] Any social setting involves a plurality of elites, movements and groups with differential control over natural and social resources who struggle continuously for control and ownership over such resources. Social conflict and competition is intensified by social differentiation, which produces groups with differing orientations and interests.

Building on the work of the early theorists (see Chapter 3) and structural functional approaches, contemporary theories of organizational growth and change have focused heavily on a neo-evolutionary perspective.[78] They vary in the extent to which structural and human agency factors shape or determine organizational structure and its outcomes. Two of the most prominent are the adaptation and selection models.

The adaptation model was a response to classical management theory, which viewed organizational performance as a product of rational decisions by managers to maximize productivity and efficiency.[79] Classical management theory fell into disfavor because it was unable to identify the principles that achieve optimal organization. Complicated tasks often exceeded the ability of any individual to find appropriate solutions. In contrast, the adaptation model proposed that organizations adapt to complexity in the environment by developing more differentiated structures. Dividing complicated tasks or decisions into subtasks or subdecisions enabled managers to make decisions within the limits of bounded rationality. In other words, organizational structures create environments that allow people to function within their abilities. This version of the adaptation model is a cognitive theory. Another version, called the resource-dependence model, contends that organizations struggle for power and resources with each other, and the outcome of this competitive process shapes organizational structure.

The adaptation model focuses on how organizations adapt to changing environmental conditions. The selection model, in contrast, attempts to explain why some organizations fail and dissolve. This model assumes that organizations are incapable of purposeful change. Several varieties of the selection model exist, but one of the most prominent is the human ecology model. Borrowing concepts and ideas from the biological sciences, this model was developed to understand better how organizations compete and coexist on limited resources in an ecological community.[80]

Basic concepts in the model include population, guild, niche and community. A population is a species. For the media ecologist, a population is a set of organizations that correspond to a medium or communication industry.[81] Thus, daily newspapers would be considered one population. A set of populations that compete for the same resources is called a guild. Hence, newspapers, radio stations, television stations and other mass media — to the extent that they compete for the same resources, such as advertising dollars or audiences — would comprise a guild. A community is a system in which the populations interact with each other and their environment. A niche is the function or role of the population within the community.

The concept of niche breadth refers to the number and amount of resources that a particular population consumes. Niche overlap is the degree to which two populations depend on the same resources. Competition refers to the indirect effect of the use of resources by one population on the availability to another. The theory assumes that resources available to the populations are finite.[82]

Overall, research suggests that many elements of organizational structure tend not to change in response to the environment.[83] This is especially true of large organizations, which have more resources to resist environmental pressures.[84] However, proponents of the selection model argue that there is prima facie evidence for its validity, since it is well known that the mortality rate among small organizations is much higher than for large ones. Pfeffer and Salancik, after reviewing the literature, also argue that there is some evidence to support the resource-dependence adaptation model in business and industry. "Mergers follow patterns of resource interdependence. Mergers made to cope with competitive interdependence are most likely when competitive uncertainty is highest — at intermediate levels of industrial concentration."[85]

In addition to external conditions, Blau and Meyer identify three internal structural factors that influence the development of organizations.[86] First, there is managerial succession. In many organizations, even bureaucratic ones, written rules may not be necessary when working relationships have been established for a long time. However, when succession occurs, the basis for these relationships disappears. The successor often has to employ bureaucratic rules and procedures — in some cases even hire additional "lieutenants" — to maintain order.

A second structural condition is the failure of simpler modes of coordination, such as through the use of contracts. Contracting was widely used in large-scale industries a century ago. Factory managers would negotiate with foremen as to the price for finished goods. The foremen would then hire workers to complete the task. But contracting had a number of problems. One was that the expertise of the foremen was limited compared to that of trained engineers. Another was that because the foremen had different ways of organizing their work and workmen, they often produced nonstandard products. Foremen also tended to be wasteful when it came to materials, tools and power, which were usually supplied by the managers. But as Weber pointed out, bureaucracy was specifically designed to overcome such problems, since expertise, precision and efficiency were its major traits.[87]

The third internal structural factor affecting the bureaucratic growth may be the quest for power in organizations. Many non-Marxist scholars contend that organizations grow and become more bureaucratized as people attempt to transform power relations, which are inherently unstable, into stable and legitimate relations of authority. Power can be legitimated through rules and regulations that substitute for the will of the boss, which often generates resentment.[88] Many Marxist scholars argue that capitalists seek growth in order to dominate a market and increase profits. Corporate managers may also seek growth in order to expand their base of power within the organization. Bureaucratic control also may have the effect of obscuring class antagonisms.[89]

Blau and Meyer also argue that the time of origin affects the bureaucratic growth of an organization. As a rule, the older the organization, the less bureaucratized. Organizations often resist change and innovation even when they would improve efficiency. However, massive reorganization efforts can stimulate the development of bureaucratic features.[90]

Mass Media and Social System Theory

Within the general theoretical framework presented above, Donohue, Tichenor and Olien point out that the mass media may be characterized as an institution, or subsystem, which, among other things, processes and disseminates information that contributes to maintenance of the social system as a whole, other subsystems, or the media subsystem itself.[91] Mass media share facets of controlling, and being controlled by, other subsystems. The researchers define a social system as "a series of interrelated subsystems with primary functions including the generation, dissemination and assimilation of information to effect further control as a means to an end or as an end in itself."[92] Social control is not the only function served by the media, but all communication processes have a control function within them, either latent or manifest.

Two key assumptions underlie the notion that the mass media are agents of social control. The first is that knowledge is a basis of social power, a proposition that is well-recognized in the literature.[93] The second, less well-known assumption is that control of knowledge is central to development and maintenance of power.[94] As collectors and disseminators of knowledge, mass media play an important role in maintenance of social power.

The maintenance function, according to Donohue, Tichenor and Olien, may be fulfilled by two sets of processes: feedback control and distribution control. Feedback control means that the media perform a feedback, or regulatory, function for other subsystems.[95] The information provided is used to make decisions or take various actions that, in turn, perform a maintenance function. The principle of feedback control is illustrated in an investigative story of a college professor who allegedly used his position and university facilities to develop a drug that made him financially wealthy. A general norm in higher education is that such behavior often creates a conflict of interest and violates basic values concerning the proper role of the university in the community. In response to the story, the university launched an investigation.[96]

Distribution control, on the other hand, can occur either independent of or jointly with feedback control and serves a maintenance function through selective dissemination and withholding of information. Censorship is the most extreme form of distribution control. A more common example is the downplaying of conflict news that occurs in small community newspapers. Numerous studies have found, in fact, that newspapers in small towns are much less likely than those in large communities to criticize local elites or institutions.[97] There are two major reasons for this. First, the amount of conflict and criticism in the small community is limited because, quite simply, the variety and number of special interest groups is limited. There are not enough individuals to create a critical mass for the development of special interest groups,[98] which in turn means less competition for limited resources and less social conflict and criticism of dominant power groups.

The second reason media in small communities tend to be less critical of local power structures is that the cultural environment does not encourage or tolerate a wide range of behaviors, opinions or values, at least openly. Social actors in such systems are expected to conform to a more narrow set of norms and values than actors in large, complex systems. As a rule of thumb, a diversity of opinion is not encouraged in a small organizational environment. Elites often share similar interests, values, goals and world views and, traditionally, decision-making relies more heavily on consensus than debate. Consensus is valued in part because social conflict usually is perceived to be disruptive of community solidarity, and small, homogeneous communities are not structurally designed to deal effectively with open conflict. Conflicts usually are handled informally, and decisions on crucial issues often are reported by local media after the fact.[99] But even when conflict or debate emerges between different groups or elites, media in small communities tend to limit reporting of such conflicts.[100]

In contrast, media in more complex, or pluralistic, communities are much more likely to publish news that is critical of elites or that is conflict-oriented.[101] Criticism and social conflict are much more common features of large, pluralistic communities because they contain a much greater variety of special interest groups competing for social, political and economic resources. Decision-making in such communities is often expected to take into account (at least to a limited extent) diverse perspectives and views, and such communities are structurally organized to deal with conflict, having mechanisms such as boards of inquiry (e.g., racial discrimination commissions, civilian police review boards), formal labor-management negotiators, formalized grievance procedures, and administrative law judges. Although stories about conflict are often viewed as threatening to the social order, such stories often play a significant role in contributing to system stability because they introduce alternative ideas or innovations that may enable organizations and institutions to change. As Donohue, Tichenor and Olien put it:

> Conflict control may include the *generation* of conflict situations as well as the direct dissipation of tension. This principle is widely recognized in the political realm; the point here is that it applies equally well to the scientific area but is expressed by different means. Media reporting of a clash between scientific opinion on supersonic transports and governmental policies regarding such technology represents a generating of conflict. From a systems perspective, such reporting is functional for maintenance of the total system in that it increases the likelihood of preserving an equilibrium state.[102]

Donohue, Olien and Tichenor argue that the notion of the mass media as a "Fourth Estate watchdog" is fundamentally a myth, in the sense of a sentinel of the general community keeping watch over central powers of government.[103] Research (see review below) strongly shows that media depend heavily on the centers of power for the news, and such dependence lends support to dominant institutions, ideologies and value systems. At the same time, the conception of the media as lapdogs of political or economic elites is inadequate. The media often attack or criticize powerful elites, who in turn are often critical of the media. Watergate and Irangate are good examples. The most appropriate canine analogy, according to Donohue, Olien and Tichenor, is the guard dog.

> The guard dog metaphor suggests that media perform as a sentry not for the community as a whole, but for those particular groups who have the power and influence to create and control their own security systems. The guard

dog media are conditioned to be suspicious of all potential intruders, and they occasionally sound the alarm for reasons that individuals in the master household, that is, the authority structure, can neither understand nor prevent. These occasions occur primarily when authority within the structure is divided.[104]

The press is most likely to "bark" at those in power when they are attacked by another powerful group or when those in power violate the rules (i.e., laws and norms) of the system. Thus, media do not protect individual elites or organizations, per se — they protect the dominant values and institutions. Any individual actor is expendable, but attacking or challenging basic elements of the system (e.g., laws, values) is much more problematic. Structural change comes slowly.

> (Elites) in the system are praised when they enjoy consensus and are subject to attack when the power structure is split. If the general welfare of the system is threatened, the welfare of the individual is at risk and there is little question that in that case the individual will be sacrificed.[105]

More formally, some of the major propositions in media system theory are summarized in Table 4.1. As with all system theories, it is assumed that social actors have needs, and among them are needs for information or entertainment (see Proposition 1). Social actors are also assumed to be goal-oriented, although the pursuit of such goals (e.g., love, money, fame) often is not formally constructed (as a business sets written objectives and goals). Some needs for information or entertainment may have a psychological or biological origin, but the majority arise in a social and cultural context that is shaped to a large extent by the interests and needs of elites, historical conditions, and dominant value and normative systems (P2 and P2a). In modern capitalist societies, large-scale business and governmental bureaucratic organizations play a disproportionate role in shaping needs for information. A white-collar worker, for example, is expected to keep up on the news that might help or hinder the competitiveness of the products his or her company sells. Such a worker also is likely to follow the stock market to keep abreast of his or her own personal investments. A general sentiment in such a society also is that each citizen should be well-informed before voting, and that each should seek out information that helps him or her make a selection.

Although needs for information and entertainment exist in all social

Table 4.1
Major Propositions of Media Systems Theory

1. Social actors have needs, among them are needs for information and entertainment.
2. Needs for information and entertainment arise primarily in a social context.
   a. Needs for information and entertainment are shaped largely by the interests and goals of those in power, historical conditions, and dominant value and normative systems.
   b. As a social system becomes more pluralistic, needs for information and entertainment increase and become more diverse.
   c. As a social system becomes more pluralistic, the number and variety of mass media and formalized means of communication increase (i.e., media systems become more complex).
      1. As the number and variety of mass media increase, competition increases.
      2. Competition promotes the growth of the corporate form of organization (i.e., large-scale, functionally complex media).
      3. Corporate organizations are more profitable and have a greater capacity to adapt to changing conditions.
3. Needs for information or entertainment can be satisfied by mass media consumption.
4. Mass media content generally promotes the interests of elite groups and dominant value systems.
   a. Elite groups seek to control the mass media to promote their interests and goals.
   b. Mass media depend heavily on elites for the news.
   c. Heavy dependence on elites helps to legitimize the news.
   d. Heavy dependence on elites for news produces a status-quo bias (i.e., media content promotes interests and goals of elites).
5. Although mass media content generally supports elite interests and dominant value systems, under some conditions it may also promote social change.
   a. As a social system becomes more pluralistic, mass media content contains more social conflict and is more critical of the status quo.
      1. The content of media in pluralistic systems is more critical of the status quo because those systems have a greater diversity of groups whose goals are unfulfilled by existing social and political arrangements.
      2. The content of media in pluralistic systems is more critical because media there have greater autonomy from established power groups.
   b. The greater the disagreement among elites on a particular issue, the greater the media coverage.
   c. The greater the power of a social group or movement, the greater its capacity to obtain media coverage.
6. The potential for social change increases as coverage of a conflict increases.
7. Social change that accommodates needs and interests of alternative or disenfranchised groups contributes to social order.
8. Mass media content that satisfies social actors' needs for information or entertainment contributes to social order.

systems, as a system grows and becomes more pluralistic, needs increase and become more diverse (P2b), and the number and variety of mass media also increase (P2c). As noted in Chapter 2, the emergence of the modern newspaper and other media is directly related to the growing demands for information brought on by urbanization and industrialization. Manufacturers need access to markets, and advertising was one efficient method for reaching such markets. The penny press emerged in the 1830s as the first mass media to offer access to mass markets, and the dramatic growth of the newspaper in the 19th century is directly related to the growth of advertising. As urban populations grew, so did needs for information, and newspapers were one mechanism for meeting both of these needs.

More formally, Ball-Rokeach and DeFleur have argued that dependence on mass media, at the individual as well as organizational and subsystem levels, increases as a social system becomes more complex.[106] Several factors explain this. First, as a social system grows and becomes more complex, the amount of personal contact people and organizations have with each other decreases, which in turn means greater dependence on formalized communication to accomplish tasks. Second, increasing complexity gives rise to problems of coordination and control. Mass media are one type of formalized method of communication for reducing such problems and integrating social actors.[107]

One consequence of the growth in the number and variety of media in a social system is increasing competition (P2c1). Competition promotes the growth of the corporate form of organization (i.e., large-scale, functionally complex media), primarily because, as Marx pointed out, it stimulates the innovative process which in turn generates economies of scale (P2c2). Media systems may expand as long as demand exceeds supply. This was the case in the United States until the early 1920s, when the number of newspapers began to decline. The more a newspaper exhibited the characteristics of the corporate form of organization, the more profitable it was and the greater was its capacity to adapt to changing conditions (P2c3).

The system model also assumes that needs for information or entertainment can be satisfied (P3). In capitalistic systems, the satisfaction of such needs is usually determined by the marketplace. Mass media programming or publications that attract enough advertising, viewership and/or readership survive, while those that do not perish. In noncapitalist economies, the satisfaction of needs is determined by elite groups who control the media. These groups may or may not obtain feedback from other segments of the population. If viewers or readers are satisfied with the media content they consume, then it is also posited that such content has the effect of integrating them into the system, reducing the potential for social action that challenges dominant power groups (P8). This integrating effect may be viewed as coercive or benign, depending upon whose interests are being served.

Mass media content generally promotes the interests of elite groups and dominant value systems (P4). The legitimacy of the media, in fact, depends heavily on serving such interests. Elite and challenging groups seek to control the media to promote their own interests (P4a), but elites are much more successful partly because they confer greater status, legitimacy and rewards to media. Challenging groups also seek to use media to reach their goals, but they are often marginalized by established powers and, thus, are perceived by the media to be less credible and newsworthy.[108] As a general rule, then, the greater the power of a group or organization, the greater its ability to command the attention of the media. Dominant values and norms in a system also shape media content, which in turn reinforces them.[109]

Media also depend heavily on elites and dominant institutions (police, courts, legislature, president) for the news because they offer a predictable, daily supply of news (P4b). Media have limited capacity to independently determine the social and political agenda — that power is reserved to the elites and the institutions they run. One consequence of this dependence is increased legitimacy for the role of the mass media in society (P4c). Another, however, is a status-quo bias. Social problems and conflicts are usually framed from the perspective of the elite groups and dominant value systems. News and entertainment programming provides strong support for such values as capitalism, social order, the family, Western religion, representative democracy, and moderatism in politics.[110]

Although mass media content generally supports the status quo, under some conditions it may also promote social change (P5). Social change may be defined as the difference between current and antecedent conditions in social organization or social structure. As a system becomes more pluralistic, media content contains more social conflict and is more critical of the status quo (P5a). Such content does not guarantee change, but it is an antecedent condition. One reason content becomes more critical as a system becomes more pluralistic is that those systems have a greater diversity of groups whose goals are unfulfilled by existing social and political arrangements (P5a1). Another reason is that media in pluralistic systems have more autonomy from established power groups (P5a2). A major factor contributing to this autonomy is the decline of the owner-manager and the rise of the professional manager and technocrats. Increasing complexity associated with news production has forced owners to rely more heavily on specialists. These technocrats, in turn, have developed their own codes of ethics and professional standards which seek to legitimate their roles and give them more autonomy. The movement toward autonomy also has been enhanced by the dispersion of ownership; that is, the proportion of stock or equity that any single individual or entity owns in newspapers has declined since the turn of the century. Dispersion of ownership occurs when a media owner's holdings are divided among heirs, when the media company goes public, or when capital requirements increase substantially beyond the means of any single stockholder.

The probability that mass media may promote social change also increases when elite groups themselves disagree over basic policy issues (P5b). Although elite groups share a number of concerns and have many similar goals and values (e.g., inflation is bad, family is good), they disagree often on the best policy or approach for reaching those goals or enhancing those values.[111] This disagreement is responsible for a large proportion of the news that appears in media situated in representative democratic systems and, in turn, increases the probability of change (P6). The probability of change also is proportional to the power of the group (P5c), which explains in part why media defer to established authorities and elites (P4a-d). As a rule of thumb, the more radical the group or idea, the less media coverage it will receive. One exception is when violence breaks out, in which case media focus on restoring social order and usually cast the challenging groups as lawbreakers. Alternative groups or social movements are most successful when their needs can be accommodated without disrupting in any major way the existing distribution of power. Finally, to the extent that media content satisfies needs for information, such content can be expected to contribute to social order (P7 and P8).

It is important to point out that the theoretical perspective taken here does not mean that the content of the media is always functional for maintenance of the system as a whole, subsystems, organizations or individuals. News coverage is sometimes dysfunctional for many elite groups, particularly when those groups fight over fundamental questions of resource allocation. Empirical evidence presented below also will demonstrate that news reports sometimes are favorable toward alternative or challenging groups. Some studies also indicate that exposure to media reports may produce beliefs that run counter to the dominant values.

Nevertheless, the fact that mass media rely much more heavily on established power groups for news means that news content generally legitimizes those groups and the dominant values in the system. Under a systems model, the argument is that media content, when taken as a whole, contributes to social order — it serves the needs of various elite groups and helps them to achieve their goals, often to the disadvantage of less powerful groups. Social change can occur and the ideas of challenging groups can make their way into the general value system (e.g., the changing role of women in society). But mainstream media do not normally challenge the basic institutions and values of the system, nor do they produce major shifts of power. Instead, they play an important role in regulating and controlling change.

Research and Media System Theory

Empirical research provides a great deal of support for the general media system model outlined above. Studies show that mass media are highly responsive to political and economic centers of power and promote values generally consistent with capitalist ideals and elite interests.[112] Journalists rely heavily on bureaucratic, especially governmental, institutions for the news, and they eschew alternative, unorthodox points of view.[113] One consequence of this is that social problems are usually framed from the position of those in power.[114] Agenda-setting studies show that media play an important role in transmitting the political and economic priorities of elites to the masses.[115] Challenging groups also seek to use media to reach their goals, but they are often marginalized by established powers and, thus, are perceived by the media to be less credible and newsworthy.[116] For example, the Glasgow University Media Group has documented how media blame labor unions, not management, for industrial disputes.[117] During the 1960s, police and the media often portrayed student activists as unkempt brats who needed old-fashioned discipline.[118] Political groups that are perceived as deviant by newspaper editors are generally given less favorable coverage.[119] And media coverage of protests by anarchist groups focused most heavily on their violations of social norms, rather than the substantive nature of their protests.[120] As a general rule of thumb, then, the greater the power of a group or organization, the greater its ability to command the attention of the media.

The system-maintenance function of the media also is served by the finding that journalists tend to support the dominant values and social norms in a social system, such as "responsible capitalism."[121] Evidence of bias in coverage of Latin America and other foreign countries is well-documented.[122] Reporters often identify or sympathize with their sources, expressing strong support, for example, in the goals of city hall.[123] Studies of television programs suggest that institutionalized power groups, such as the police, are usually portrayed humanely and sympathetically, while other characters, including victims, are portrayed as stereotypes, often with negative overtones.[124] As a rule of thumb, media fail to report class conflict, ignore common working-class interests and take for granted a national consensus.[125] A well-documented finding in both England and the United States is that ownership of newspapers is relatively concentrated in the hands of a few powerful corporations or individuals,[126] which is often interpreted to mean that content is becoming less diverse or more homogeneous. Competition in the U.S. daily newspaper field also has declined over the last 80 years.[127] And prominent elite media companies, such as the publishers of the *New York Times* and *Washington Post,* are strongly interconnected with other power centers via memberships on boards of directors.[128]

Although journalists tend to support the dominant system of values, other research shows that they generally are more liberal than elites, as well as the general public, on a wide variety of social and political issues.[129] These findings and those from other studies suggest that, contrary to some critical theories of ideology,[130] media have the capacity at times to produce content that is critical of dominant groups and beneficial to disadvantaged groups. Polls and historical research show that conservatives are more critical than liberals of investigative reporting and that journalists often are sensitive to the concerns of minorities and consumers groups, are critical of business, and believe that private business is profiting at the expense of Third World countries.[131] One analysis of U.S. network television news coverage of Latin America also failed to produce evidence of a conservative, status-quo bias.[132] Media reports also helped to legitimize rural protest groups in Minnesota, whose goal was to block construction of a power line that would serve a large, Midwestern metropolitan area.[133] Studies often find that media coverage influences governmental policy at the national level[134] as well as the local.[135] And a recent study found that, contrary to the expectations of the researcher, media coverage of separate protest marches in Washington sponsored by gay and lesbian organizations and pro-choice groups were much more favorable than unfavorable to each of those challenging groups.[136]

Although media need a consistent, inexpensive supply of news and depend heavily on political and economic elites for the news,[137] it is also important to point out that elites depend heavily on the media to achieve their goals. It is widely agreed, for example, that a state or national politician cannot be elected today without effective media coverage. Candidates rely less and less on the political party machine and more and more on direct coverage in media to get elected. This dependence, in turn, has lessened to some extent the power of the traditional political parties.

Although ownership of newspapers is becoming more centralized (i.e., reduction in number of owners), to date there is little evidence showing that this has led to a reduction in message diversity[138] or that other media sectors, like magazines and broadcast television stations, are experiencing the same trends.[139] In fact, some studies have found that media in larger, more pluralistic communities cover a broader range of topics and contain more news.[140] A systems perspective is that current declines in newspaper circulation and national network television penetration reflect increasing differentiation of the social structure and that such differentiation nevertheless can, under some circumstances, promote increased criticism of established institutions and greater diversity in media content.[141] For example, even though research shows that small, community newspapers often omit news that is critical of established institutions and elites, media in more pluralistic communities are much more likely to publish news that is critical of elites or conflict-oriented.[142] Another study showed that veteran reporters at mainstream newspapers can write stories that challenge components of the dominant ideology.[143] Studying Canadian press coverage of disarmament, peace and security issues, another reported that commentaries, columns and op-ed pieces often challenged the dominant view of bureaucrats.[144] And a study of the press in India suggests that the news media have the potential to challenge the status quo.[145] The researcher found that such challenges may not be direct or comprehensive, but some kinds of news stories may represent a challenge indirectly by contributing, for example, to public awareness of problems with the status quo, which in turn can promote discontent and support for social change.

Research also shows that alternative media often challenge dominant ideologies and contribute to mobilizing and promoting social movements or causes. Challenging the arguments of the "routines theorists,"[146] one participant observation study found that reporters at an alternative radio station could create oppositional news using conventional routines and reportorial techniques.[147]   A historical review reported that alternative media have helped to promote the American Revolution, abolitionism, and equality for women, minorities, and gay rights groups.[148] And even though one study discussed earlier found that the mainstream mass media marginalize anarchist groups, the study also found that the alternative press idolized them.[149]

Although social control is one of the major functions of media, it does not explain the origins and nature of media themselves.[150] As noted earlier, a basic proposition in media system theory is that the structure of a social system sets parameters or constraints on the number and type of media in that system, as well as media content.[151] Specifically, Tichenor, Donohue and Olien point out that homogeneous, traditional societies or communities have a limited number of mass media sources, and those sources tend to represent the interests and concerns of a homogeneous, undifferentiated audience. But, as the level of structural pluralism increases, demand for specialized sources of information and news increases, and social actors respond by increasing the number and diversity of print and electronic media. The rapid proliferation of newsletters, cable systems, highly specialized academic journals and fax machines are examples of how social actors have responded to increasing pluralism. Pluralism also is a strong predictor of the amount and percentage of news space allocated to public affairs issues[152] and to the number and variety of media in a community.[153]

Research on the ideological effects of the media indicates that the media may have dysfunctional consequences for some groups, but this is not always the case and, furthermore, media consumers are not easily manipulated. Hartmann and Husband found that English children's use of mass media leads to distorted perceptions of immigrants. More specifically, the researchers found that: (1) Children living in areas of low immigration rely more heavily on the media for their information about "coloured people" than others; (2) Media reports about immigrants contain the inference of conflict more often than other sources; and (3) Children who rely on media are more prone to think about race relations in terms of conflict, even though they are more likely to live in areas where racial conflict is absent.[154] In contrast, two other studies conducted in the United States have reached opposite conclusions. One, which was conducted during the 1960s, reported that the greater the number of mass media messages white Southerners attended to, the less likely they were to have strict segregationist attitudes.[155] Although this relationship was not particularly strong, it did hold up when controlling for education. Mass media, the researchers argued, often subvert traditional, patrimonial ways and usher in modern attitudes that promote social change. Researchers behind the *Great American Values Test* concluded that a specially designed 30-minute television program broadcast in 1979 also was able to increase anti-racist beliefs and the importance of equality itself as a basic social value.[156] The researchers also found that people who have a high dependency on television changed their values more and contributed more money to groups that promote anti-racism and equality than people with low dependence on television.

Cultivation analysis also has been interpreted as supporting the systems model.[157] This research shows that television exaggerates the amount of crime and violence in society and that such content is cognitively translated into increased support for authoritarian measures by police and the state.[158] Gerbner and his colleagues argue that television "is the central cultural arm of American society" whose primary function is "to spread and stabilize social patterns, to cultivate not change but resistance to change."[159] Some re-analysis of the original cultivation data, however, fails to support the theory,[160] and cross-cultural research suggests that cultivation effects may depend on a variety of factors.[161] In contrast to some critical theories of media, a large body of research also indicates that media often impact public policy. Researchers at Northwestern University, for instance, found that investigative stories on police brutality "produced swift and fundamental revisions of regulations regarding police misconduct."[162] Another study found that media coverage of murder cases influences the way prosecutors handle cases.[163] And Viswanath and his colleagues reported that a mass media campaign to reduce diet-related cancer risks was effective in transmitting knowledge about the dangers of high-fat and low-fiber diets.[164]

Another study suggests that television may actually promote beliefs that oppose economic inequalities.[165] The data, obtained from personal interviews with a probability sample of U.S. adults in 1986, show that people who benefit most from the system — men, whites, conservatives, and those who have high incomes, education and occupational prestige — are most likely to favor economic inequalities. However, the study found that television viewing reduces support for beliefs that promote economic inequality, even when controlling for all of the other factors. Gamson's peer group study also suggests that people often use media to challenge and criticize established authorities. He challenges both the radical view that working people are incorporated by the dominant ideology and the mainstream social science view that working people are uninterested in politics and unable to engage in well-reasoned discussions. Using data collected in peer group sessions with 188 "working people," he concludes that "(a) people are not so passive, (b) people are not so dumb, and (c) people negotiate with media messages in complicated ways that vary from issue to issue."[166]

In short, the empirical research suggests that media content provides broad-based support for the status quo, but it can, in many instances, promote conflict, criticism and social change. As Herbert Gans puts it:

> News is not so much conservative or liberal as it is reformist; indeed, the enduring values are very much like the values of the Progressive movement of the early twentieth century. The resemblance is often uncanny, as in the common advocacy of honest, meritocratic, and anti-bureaucratic government, and in the shared antipathy to political machines and demagogues, particularly of populist bent.[167]

And, comparing the mass media to legal systems, Jeffrey Alexander observes:

> In distinguishing the news media from the law, the significant point is the media's flexibility. By daily exposing and reformulating itself vis-à-vis changing values, group formations, and objective economic and political conditions, the media allows "public opinion" to be organized responsively on a mass basis. By performing this function of information-conduit and normative-organizer, the news media provides the normative dimension of society with the greatest flexibility in dealing with social strains.[168]

Summary

Modern social system theory was built upon the ideas of Spencer, Marx, Durkheim and others. This theory is distinguished from other perspectives by its emphasis on the totality of the whole, its notion of boundary maintenance, and its idea of interdependence of the parts. The general model of social change in system theory can be described as neo-evolutionary — as social systems grow, they become, under certain conditions, more differentiated, functionally specialized and interdependent. The mass media, like other major institutions, are a product of increasing differentiation and play an important maintenance function. The media, in turn, are controlled by other subsystems. Mass media are not a necessary condition for social organization, but they are for complex social organization.

A review of the empirical literature clearly shows that media play an important role in explaining the persistence and stability of modern capitalism. Media depend heavily on political and economic centers of power for the news. One consequence of this is that the construction of social problems usually is framed from the position of those in power, and news content generally promotes values consistent with capitalist ideals and elite interests. Mainstream media rarely, if ever, facilitate or cause radical social change. The watchdog function of the press is largely a myth. Like police and schools, media are an important agent of social control.

At the same time, however, this review shows that it would be inaccurate to argue that social actors are slaves to a dominant ideology or that media are lapdogs of the powerful. Depending in part on what they read and see in the media, ordinary citizens also can develop highly critical views of those in power and the social system in general. As a group, journalists are more liberal than elites and the public, and media content, especially in pluralistic systems, is much more critical of those elites and dominant values than content in small, homogeneous systems. Investigative reporting and news about social movements often promotes change and reform, often to the displeasure of conservatives and sometimes to the benefit of underprivileged groups. More accurately, the news media may be characterized as a guard dog, which provides broad-based support for dominant institutions and values in a social system but can criticize those in power, especially when they violate laws or norms.

The notion that mass media can criticize those in power or promote social reform has not gone unnoticed in studies of ideology. As noted earlier, nearly all contemporary theories of ideology acknowledge that news may be critical of those in power. However, virtually none of these theories has specified the conditions in which alternative or challenging ideas and groups may emerge and gain access to media. Such access or the structural changes that sometimes result from criticisms of the dominant ideology are usually viewed either as anomalies that have little impact on the system or as accommodations that contribute to greater hegemonic control. As a consequence, such theories are at a loss to explain many of the contributions that mass media have made to social and political reforms during the 19th and early 20th centuries (e.g., the emergence of minimum wage laws, social security, labor laws, anti-trust laws, welfare, progressive income tax system), as well as more recent challenges to some dominant values regarding health care reform, parenthood (e.g., the Murphy Brown television show and the single motherhood issue) and homosexuality (e.g., coverage of the social protests in Washington regarding military policies; TV movies about fired military personnel). These reforms (or reforms in progress) should not be summarily dismissed as meaningless or as mere accommodations. They should be seen as changes that have from time to time worked to the benefit of disadvantaged or challenging groups and the working classes.

Notes

1. M. Francis Abraham, *Modern Sociological Theory* (Delhi, India: Oxford University Press, 1982).

2. Marvin E. Olsen, *The Process of Social Organization* (New York: Holt, Rinehart & Winston, 1968), p. 227.

3. Warren Breed, "Mass Communication and Sociocultural Integration," *Social Forces,* 37:109-16 (1958); Warren Breed, "Social Control in the Newsroom: A Functional Analysis," *Social Forces,* 33:326-55 (1955); Melvin L. DeFleur and Sandra Ball-Rokeach, *Theories of Mass Communication,* 5th ed. (New York: Longman, 1989); Morris Janowitz, *The Community Press in an Urban Setting* (New York: Free Press, 1952); Robert E. Park, *The Immigrant Press and Its Control* (New York: Harper, 1922); Eric W. Rothenbuhler, "Neofunctionalism for Mass Communication Theory," *Mass Communication Yearbook,* vol. 6 (Newbury Park, Calif.: Sage, 1987); Kim A. Smith, "Newspaper Coverage and Public Concern About Community Issues: A Time-Series Analysis," *Journalism Monographs,* vol. 101 (February 1987); Phillip J. Tichenor, George A. Donohue and Clarice N. Olien, *Community Conflict and the Press* (Beverly Hills, Calif.: Sage, 1980); and Charles R. Wright, *Mass Communication: A Sociological Perspective,* 3rd ed. (New York: Random House, 1986).

4. Joseph T. Klapper, *The Effects of Mass Communication* (New York: The Free Press, 1960); Sidney Kraus and Dennis Davis, *The Effect of Mass Communication on Political Behavior* (University Park, Penn.: Pennsylvania State University Press, 1976); Werner J. Severin and James W. Tankard, Jr., *Communication Theories: Origins, Methods, Uses* (New York: Hastings House, 1979); Gaye Tuchman, "Mass Media Institutions," pp. 601-26 in Neil J. Smelser (ed.), *Handbook of Sociology* (Beverly Hills, Calif.: Sage, 1988).

5. Historically, research questions on the media were framed in individualistic, rather than systemic, terms. For example, the Payne Fund Studies examined the psychological and physiological effects of movies on children. See Shearon T. Lowery and Melvin L. DeFleur, *Milestones in Mass Communication* (New York: Longman, 1989). The research agenda also was heavily influenced by the advertising industry's need to understand and control the effects of advertising. See Todd Gitlin, "Media Sociology: The Dominant Paradigm," *Theory and Society,* 6:205-53 (1978).

6. Carl P. Burrowes, "The Functionalist Tradition and Communication Theory," paper presented to the Association for Education in Journalism and Mass Communication (Kansas City, Mo., August 1993); Gitlin, "Media Sociology: The Dominant Paradigm"; Denis

McQuail, *Mass Communication Theory: An Introduction,* 3rd ed. (London: Sage, 1994), p. 78; and Tuchman, "Mass Media Institutions."

7. Abraham, *Modern Sociological Theory;* Jeffrey C. Alexander (ed.), *Neofunctionalism* (Beverly Hills, Calif.: Sage, 1985); Lewis Coser, *The Functions of Social Conflict* (New York: The Free Press, 1956); William J. Goode, "A Theory of Role Strain," *American Sociological Review,* 25:483-96 (1960); Alvin W. Gouldner, "The Norm of Reciprocity," *American Sociological Review,* 25:161-78 (1960); Olsen, *The Process of Social Organization;* Rothenbuhler, "Neofunctionalism for Mass Communication Theory"; Arthur L. Stinchcombe, *Constructing Social Theories* (Chicago: University of Chicago Press, 1968); and Jonathan H. Turner, *The Structure of Sociological Theory* (Homewood, Ill.: The Dorsey Press, 1978).

8. Walter Buckley, *Sociology and Modern Systems Theory* (Englewood Cliffs, N.J.: Prentice-Hall, 1967), Chapter 1.

9. Peter L. Berger and Thomas Luckmann, *The Social Construction of Reality* (New York: Anchor Books, 1966).

10. Buckley, *Sociology and Modern Systems Theory,* p. 9.

11. See, e.g., Abraham, *Modern Sociological Theory,* pp. 42-3.

12. Vilfredo Pareto, *The Mind and Society: A Treatise on General Sociology* (New York: Dover, 1973).

13. Abraham, *Modern Sociological Theory,* p. 39.

14. A. D. Hall and R. E. Fagen, "Definition of Systems," *General Systems,* 1:18-28 (1956).

15. Herbert Spencer, *First Principles,* vol. 1 (New York: De Witt Revolving Fund, 1958 [1862]). Also see Herbert Spencer, *Principles of Sociology,* vol. III (New York: D. Appleton, 1897) and Emile Durkheim, *The Division of Labor in Society,* trans. by W. D. Halls (New York: The Free Press, 1984 [1893]).

16. Spencer, *First Principles,* p. 592.

17. Buckley, *Sociology and Modern Systems Theory,* p. 12.

18. Some scholars have made a distinction between the organismic metaphor, which uses the human body as the basis for comparison, and the organic metaphor, which uses the species metaphor. No distinction is made here because the similarity of the terms invites misinterpretation.

19. Olsen points out that a social system model can be used by exchange, symbolic interactionist, ecological, and power theorists as well. However, he says the perspective appears to be most compatible with a functionalist perspective.

20. Robert K. Merton, *Social Theory and Social Structure,* 3rd ed. (New York: The Free Press, 1968 [1949]) and Talcott Parsons, *The Social System* (New York: The Free Press, 1951).

21. See, e.g., Parsons, *The Social System,* and Ralf Dahrendorf, *Class and Class Conflict in Industrial Society* (Stanford, Calif.: Stanford University Press, 1959 [1957 German version]).

22. G. A. Theodorson and A. G. Theodorson, *A Modern Dictionary of Sociology* (New York: Crowell, 1969), p. 133.

23. Parsons dismissed such criticisms, but many researchers who were attracted to functionalism took the existing power structure for granted. Neofunctionalism is not subject to the same shortcomings. See Ruth A. Wallace and Alison Wolf, *Contemporary Sociological Theory* (Englewood Cliffs, N.J.: Prentice-Hall, 1986), pp. 35-6 and 59-60.

24. Parsons, *The Social System,* p. 46. Parsons' observations appear to be as true today as they were in his time. See, e.g., James B. Rule, *Theories of Civil Violence* (Berkeley, Calif.: University of California Press, 1988).

25. Chin-Chuan Lee, *Media Imperialism Reconsidered* (Beverly Hills, Calif.: Sage, 1980) and Alvin Y. So, *Social Change and Development: Modernization, Dependency and World-System Theories* (Newbury Park, Calif.: Sage, 1990).

26. Daniel Lerner, *The Passing of Traditional Society* (New York: Macmillan, 1958).

27. August Comte, "The Progress of Civilization Through Three States," in A. Etzioni and E. Etzioni-Halevy (eds.), *Social Change* (New York: Basic Books, 1973) and Herbert Spencer, "The Evolution of Societies," in A. Etzioni and E. Etzioni-Halevy (eds.), *Social Change* (New York: Basic Books, 1973).

28. Harold D. Lasswell, "The Structure and Function of Communication in Society," pp. 84-99 in Wilbur Schramm and Donald F. Roberts (eds.), *The Process and Effects of Mass Communication* (Urbana, Ill.: University of Illinois Press, 1971).

29. Charles R. Wright, *Mass Communication: A Sociological Perspective* (New York: Random House, 1959).

30. Paul Lazarsfeld and Robert Merton, "Mass Communication, Popular Taste and Organized Social Action," pp. 95-118 in L. Bryson (ed.), *The Communication of Ideas* (New York: Harper and Brothers, 1948).

31. Merton, *Social Theory and Social Structure.*

32. Melvin L. DeFleur, "Mass Media as Social Systems," pp. 63-83 in Wilbur Schramm and Donald F. Roberts, *The Process of Effects of Mass Communication* (Urbana, Ill.: University of Illinois Press, 1971), p. 83. Italics in original.

33. Breed, "Mass Communication and Sociocultural Integration"; Janowitz, *The Community Press in an Urban Setting*; and Charles R. Wright, "Functional Analysis and Mass Communication," *Public Opinion Quarterly,* 24:605-20 (1960).

34. Berger and Luckmann, *The Social Construction of Reality.*

35. Buckley, *Sociology and Modern Systems Theory,* p. 18.

36. Albion W. Small, *General Sociology* (Chicago: University of Chicago Press, 1905), pp. 619-20.

37. Small, *General Sociology,* p. ix.

38. Robert E. Park and E. W. Burgess, *Introduction to the Science of Sociology* (Chicago: The University of Chicago Press, 1921), p. 42.

39. S. F. Nadel, *The Theory of Social Structure* (New York: The Free Press, 1957), p. 128).

40. Nadel, *The Theory of Social Structure,* p. 153.

41. Park, *The Immigrant Press and Its Control.*

42. Janowitz, *The Community Press in an Urban Setting.*

43. To escape the philosophical dilemma between mechanistic and vitalist conceptualizations of life, de la Mettrie argued that "matter was in itself neither organic nor inorganic, neither living nor dead, neither sensible nor insensible. The difference between these states or properties of material things sprang, not from the intrinsic natures of their raw materials, but from the different ways in which these materials were organized." Quoted in S. Toulmin and J. Goodfield, *The Architecture of Matter* (New York: Harper & Row, 1962), p. 318.

44. Ludwig von Bertalanffy, "General System Theory," pp. 6-21 in Brent D. Rubin and John Y. Kim (eds.), *General Systems Theory and Human Communication* (Rochelle Park, N.J.: Hayden Book Company, 1975).

45. Buckley, *Sociology and Modern Systems Theory,* pp. 58-62.

46. Olsen, *The Process of Social Organization,* pp. 234-5.

47. See Marion J. Levy, Jr., *The Structure of Society* (Princeton, N.J.: Princeton University Press, 1952), pp. 76-83.

48. Buckley, *Sociology and Modern Systems Theory,* and Rubin and Kim (eds.), *General Systems Theory and Human Communication.*

49. Kenneth D. Bailey, *Sociology and the New Systems Theory* (Albany, N.Y.: State University of New York Press, 1992).

50. For review, see Stephen W. Littlejohn, *Theories of Human Communication* (Belmont, Calif.: Wadsworth, 1983). Also see Peter Monge, "The Systems Perspective as a Theoretical Basis for the Study of Human Communication," *Communication Quarterly,* 25:19-29 (1977).

51. Jonathan H. Turner, *Herbert Spencer: A Renewed Appreciation* (Beverly Hills, Calif.: Sage, 1985), p. 31.

52. Turner, *The Structure of Sociological Theory,* p. 105.

53. Durkheim, *The Division of Labor in Society.*

54. Turner, *The Structure of Sociological Theory,* pp. 110-11.

55. See, e.g., Lee, *Media Imperialism Reconsidered*; So, *Social Change and Development: Modernization, Dependency and World-System Theories*; and Immanuel Wallerstein, *The Modern World-System I: Capitalist Agriculture and the Origins of the European World-Economy in the Sixteenth Century* (New York: Academic Press, 1974) and *The Modern World-System II: Mercantilism and the Consolidation of the European World-Economy, 1600-1750* (New York: Academic Press, 1980).

56. Dennis H. Wrong, "The Oversocialized Conception of Man in Modern Sociology," *American Sociological Review,* 26:183-93 (April 1961).

57. See, e.g., Robert Cooley Angell, *The Integration of American Society* (New York: Russell & Russell, 1975 [1941]).

58. As van den Berghe put it: "Dysfunctions, tension and 'deviance' do exist and can persist for a long time, but they tend to resolve themselves or to be 'institutionalized' in the long run. In other words, while perfect equilibrium or integration is never reached, it is the limit towards which social systems tend. ... Change generally occurs in a gradual, adjustive fashion, and not in a sudden, revolutionary way. Changes which appear to be drastic, in fact affect mostly the social superstructure while leaving the core elements of the social and cultural structure largely unchanged." Pierre L. van den Berghe, "Dialectic and Functionalism," in R. Serge Denisoff et al. (eds.), *Theories and Paradigms in Contemporary Sociology* (Itasca, N.Y.: F. E. Peacock Publishers, 1974), p. 281.

59. Dahrendorf, *Class and Class Conflict in Industrial Society.*

60. He also suggests abandoning the concept of function — which may be defined as contribution that the part makes to the whole — because it takes for granted what should be part of the empirical investigation. See Turner, *The Structure of Sociological Theory,* p. 110.

61. Jeffrey C. Alexander, "The Mass News Media in Systemic, Historical and Comparative Perspective," pp. 17-51 in Elihu Katz and T. Szecskö (eds.), *Mass Media and Social Change* (Beverly Hills, Calif.: Sage, 1981), does a superb job of integrating the two in his comparative, historical and systemic analysis of the development of newspapers in the United States and Europe.

62. Dick Atkinson, *Orthodox Consensus and Radical Alternation* (New York: Basic Books, 1972).

63. As noted in Chapter 3, the idea that structures may dissolve was addressed by Spencer, although Parsons and other structural functionalists gave little attention to de-differentiation and dissolution. See Edward A. Tiryakian, "On the Significance of De-

Differentiation," pp. 118-34 in S. N. Eisenstadt and H. J. Helle (eds.), *Macro-Sociological Theory* (Beverly Hills, Calif.: Sage Publications, 1985).

64. Dahrendorf, *Class and Class Conflict in Industrial Society.*

65. George C. Homans, *Social Behavior: Its Elementary Forms* (New York: Harcourt Brace Jovanovich, Inc., 1974).

66. Claude Levi-Strauss, *Totemism* (Boston: Beacon Press, 1963).

67. S. N. Eisenstadt, "Macro-Societal Analysis — Background, Development and Indications," pp. 7-24 in S. N. Eisenstadt and H. J. Helle, *Macro-Sociological Theory: Perspectives on Sociological Theory* (Newbury Park, Calif.: Sage Publications, 1985), p. 19.

68. Olsen, *The Process of Social Organization.*

69. Eisenstadt, "Macro-Societal Analysis."

70. Olsen, *The Process of Social Organization*, pp. 229-31.

71. The growth of functionalism during the early part of the 20th century was a reaction in part to the failure of deterministic, mechanical and positivist theories to explain human behavior.

72. See Chapter 6 for a brief discussion of social action, determinism and quantitative research methods.

73. Alexander (ed.), *Neofunctionalism*; Kenneth E. Boulding, *The World as a Total System* (Beverly Hills, Calif.: Sage, 1985); Niklas Luhmann, *The Differentiation of Society* (New York: Columbia University Press, 1982); Richard Münch, "Parsonian Theory Today: In Search of a New Synthesis," pp. 116-55 in Anthony Giddens and Jonathan H. Turner (eds.), *Social Theory Today* (Stanford, Calif.: Stanford University Press, 1987).

74. Alexander (ed.), *Neofunctionalism,* pp. 9-10.

75. Eisenstadt, "Macro-Societal Analysis."

76. Eisenstadt, "Macro-Societal Analysis," pp. 20-1.

77. The first item in this list was added by this author.

78. See, e.g., Richard P. Applebaum, *Theories of Social Change* (Chicago: Markham, 1970); Peter M. Blau and Marshall W. Meyer, *Bureaucracy in Modern Society*, 3rd ed. (New York: Random House, 1987), Chapter 6; and Howard E. Aldrich and Peter V. Marsden, "Environments and Organizations," pp. 361-92 in Neil J. Smelser (ed.), *Handbook of Sociology* (Newbury Park, Calif.: Sage, 1988).

79. Frederick Taylor, *Scientific Management* (New York: Harper & Row, 1964 [1947]).

80. A. H. Hawley, *Human Ecology: A Theory of Community Structure* (New York: Ronald Press, 1950) and Michael T. Hannan and John H. Freeman, "The Population Ecology of Organizations," *American Journal of Sociology*, 82:929-64 (1977).

81. See, e.g., John Dimmick and Eric Rothenbuhler, "The Theory of the Niche: Quantifying Competition Among Media Industries," *Journal of Communication*, 34(1):103-19 (1984).

82. Dimmick and Rothenberger, "The Theory of the Niche," p. 107.

83. Blau and Meyer, *Bureaucracy in Modern Society.*

84. Aldrich and Marsden, "Environments and Organizations," p. 365.

85. Jeffrey Pfeffer and Gerald R. Salancik, *The External Control of Organizations* (New York: Harper & Row, 1978), pp. 139-40.

86. Blau and Meyer, *Bureaucracy in Modern Society,* pp. 33-8.

87. H. H. Gerth and C. Wright Mills, *From Max Weber: Essays in Sociology* (New York: Oxford University Press, 1946), p. 214.

88. For this view, Blau and Meyer cite Jeffrey Pfeffer, *Power in Organizations* (Marshfield, Mass.: Pitman, 1981).

89. Richard Edwards, *Contested Terrain* (New York: Basic Books, 1979), p. 145.

90. Blau and Meyer, *Bureaucracy in Modern Society*, p. 38-41.

91. George A. Donohue, Phillip J. Tichenor and Clarice N. Olien, "Mass Media Functions, Knowledge and Social Control," *Journalism Quarterly*, 50:652-9 (1973). Also see Breed, "Mass Communication and Sociocultural Integration"; Janowitz, *The Community Press in an Urban Setting*; and Clarice N. Olien, Phillip J. Tichenor and George A. Donohue, "Media Coverage and Social Movements," pp. 139-63 in Charles T. Salmon (ed.), *Information Campaigns: Balancing Social Values and Social Change* (Newbury Park, Calif.: Sage, 1989).

92. Donohue, Tichenor and Olien, "Mass Media Functions, Knowledge and Social Control," p. 652.

93. See, e.g., Ben H. Bagdikian, *The Information Machines: Their Impact on Men and the Media* (New York: Harper and Row, 1971); Coser, *The Functions of Social Conflict*; John K. Galbraith, *The New Industrial State*, 3rd ed. (Boston: Houghton Mifflin, 1978); and Robert E. Park, "News as a Form of Knowledge," *American Journal of Sociology*, 45:669-86 (1940).

94. Donohue, Tichenor and Olien, "Mass Media Functions, Knowledge and Social Control."

95. Donohue, Tichenor and Olien, "Mass Media Functions, Knowledge and Social Control," p. 653.

96. The first story appeared in the (Minneapolis) *Star Tribune*, May 30, 1992. The university professor was later forced to resign and was prosecuted by federal authorities.

97. Breed, "Mass Communication and Sociocultural Integration"; Janowitz, *Community Press in an Urban Setting*, and Arthur J. Vidich and Joseph Bensman, *Small Town in Mass Society* (Princeton, N.J.: Princeton University Press, 1968), p. 31.

98. Thomas C. Wilson, "Community Population Size and Social Heterogeneity: An Empirical Test," *American Journal of Sociology*, 91:1154-69 (1986).

99. Clarice N. Olien, George A. Donohue and Phillip J. Tichenor, "The Community Editor's Power and the Reporting of Conflict," *Journalism Quarterly*, 45:243-52 (1968).

100. One exception is when conflict erupts between the local community and an outside source of power (e.g., state or federal government), in which case local media coverage tends to support local norms and interprets the conflict through the perspective of local elites.

101. George A. Donohue, Clarice N. Olien and Phillip J. Tichenor, "Reporting Conflict by Pluralism, Newspaper Type and Ownership," *Journalism Quarterly,* 62:489-99, 507 (1985) and Tichenor, Donohue and Olien, *Community Conflict and the Press.*

102. Donohue, Tichenor and Olien, "Mass Media Functions, Knowledge and Social Control," pp. 653-4. Also see Coser, *The Functions of Social Conflict,* for a discussion of how conflict may contribute to social stability.

103. George A. Donohue, Phillip J. Tichenor, and Clarice N. Olien, "A Guard Dog Perspective on the Role of Media," *Journal of Communication,* 45(2):115-32 (1995).

104. Donohue, Tichenor and Olien, "A Guard Dog Perspective on the Role of Media," p. 116.

105. Donohue, Tichenor and Olien, "A Guard Dog Perspective on the Role of Media," p. 126.

106. Sandra J. Ball-Rokeach, "The Origins of Individual Media System Dependency: A Sociological Framework," *Communication Research,* 12:485-510 (1985); Sandra J. Ball-Rokeach and Melvin L. DeFleur, "A Dependency Model of Mass Media Effects," *Communication Research,* 3:3-21 (1976); and DeFleur and Ball-Rokeach, *Theories of Mass Communication.*

107. David Pearce Demers, "Structural Pluralism, Intermedia Competition and Growth of the Corporate Newspaper in the United States," *Journalism Monographs,* vol. 145 (June 1994).

108. Mark Fishman, *Manufacturing the News* (Austin, Texas: University of Texas Press, 1980); Edward S. Herman, "Diversity of News: Marginalizing the Opposition," *Journal of Communication,* 35(3):135-46 (1985); Todd Gitlin, *The Whole World Is Watching: Mass Media and the New Left* (Berkeley, Calif.: University of California Press, 1980); C. N. Olien, G. A. Donohue and P. J. Tichenor, "Media and Stages of Social Conflict," *Journalism Monographs,* vol. 90 (November 1984); and David L. Paletz and Robert M. Entman, *Media Power Politics* (New York: Free Press, 1981).

109. Herbert J. Gans, *Deciding What's News* (New York: Vintage, 1979) and Jack Newfield, "Journalism: Old, New and Corporate," in Ronald Weber (ed.), *The Reporter as Artist: A Look at the New Journalism* (New York: Hastings House, 1974).

110. Gans, *Deciding What's News.*

111. Jonathan H. Turner and David Musick, *American Dilemmas: A Sociological Interpretation of Enduring Social Issues* (New York: Columbia University Press, 1985).

112. Karen E. Altman, "Consuming Ideology: The Better Homes in America Campaign," *Critical Studies in Mass Communication,* 7:286-307 (1990); W. Lance Bennett, *News: The Politics of Illusion,* 2nd ed. (New York: Longman, 1988); Stuart Ewin, *Captains of Consciousness: Advertising and the Social Roots of the Consumer Culture* (New York: McGraw Hill, 1976); Fishman, *Manufacturing the News;* Doris A. Graber, *Mass Media and American Politics,* 3rd ed. (Washington, D.C.: Congressional Quarterly Press, 1989); Gans, *Deciding What's News;* Gitlin, *The Whole World Is Watching;* Harvey Molotch and Marilyn Lester, "Accidental News: The Great Oil Spill as Local Occurrence and National Event," *American Journal of Sociology,* 81:235-60 (1975); Paletz and Entman, *Media Power Politics;* Fred Powledge, *The Engineering of Restraint* (Washington, D.C.: Public Affairs Press, 1971); Tichenor, Donohue and Olien, *Community Conflict and the Press;* and Gaye Tuchman, *Making News: A Study in the Construction of Reality* (New York: The Free Press, 1978).

113. J. Herbert Altschull, *Agents of Power* (New York: Longman, 1984); Robert Cirino, *Power to Persuade* (New York: Bantam Books, 1974); Stanley Cohen and Jock Young (eds.), *The Manufacture of News* (London: Constable, 1981); Edward Jay Epstein, *News From Nowhere* (New York: Random House, 1973); Gitlin, *The Whole World Is Watching;* Molotch and Lester, "Accidental News," Powledge, *The Engineering of Restraint;* Michael Schudson, "The Politics of Narrative Form: The Emergence of News Conventions in Print and Television," *Daedalus,* 11:97-112 (1982); Lawrence C. Soley, "Pundits in Print: 'Experts' and Their Use in Newspaper Stories," *Newspaper Research Journal,* 15(2):65-75 (1994); Tichenor, Donohue and Olien, *Community Conflict and the Press;* Tuchman, *Making News;* and Jeremy Tunstall, *Journalists at Work* (London: The Anchor Press, 1971).

114. Mayer N. McCarthy and John D. Zald, "Resource Mobilization and Social Movements: A Partial Theory," *American Journal of Sociology,* 82:1212-41 (1977) and Mayer N. McCarthy and John D. Zald (eds.), *The Dynamics of Social Movements: Resource Mobilization, Social Control and Tactics* (Cambridge, Mass.: Winthrop Publishers, 1979).

115. David Pearce Demers, Dennis Craff, Yang-Ho Choi, and Beth M. Pessin, "Issue Obtrusiveness and the Agenda-Setting Effects of National Network News," *Communication Research,* 16:793-812 (1989); Graber, *Media Power in Politics,* pp. 75-150; Gerald M. Kosicki, "Problems and Opportunities in Agenda-Setting Research," *Journal of Communication,* 43(2):100-28 (1993); Maxwell McCombs, "News Influence on Our Pictures of the World," pp. 1-16 in Jennings Bryant and Dolf Zillmann (eds.), *Media Effects: Advances in Theory and Research* (Hillsdale, N.J.: Lawrence Erlbaum Associates, 1994); and

Maxwell E. McCombs and Donald L. Shaw, "The Agenda-Setting Function of the Mass Media," *Public Opinion Quarterly,* 36:176-87 (1972).

116. Fishman, *Manufacturing the News*; Herman, "Diversity of News"; Gitlin, *The Whole World Is Watching*; Olien, Donohue and Tichenor, "Media and Stages of Social Conflict"; and Paletz and Entman, *Media Power Politics*.

117. Glasgow University Media Group, *Bad News* (London: Routledge & Kegan Paul, 1976).

118. Gitlin, *The Whole World Is Watching*.

119. Pamela Shoemaker, "Media Treatment of Deviant Political Groups," *Journalism Quarterly,* 61:66-75, 82 (1984).

120. Douglas M. McLeod and James K. Hertog, "The Manufacture of 'Public Opinion' by Reporters: Informal Cues for Public Perceptions of Protest Groups," *Discourse and Society,* 3(3):259-75 (1992).

121. Gans, *Deciding What's News*; Newfield, "Journalism: Old, New and Corporate"; Robert A. Peterson, Gerald Albaum, George Kozmetsky and Isabella C. M. Cunningham, "Attitudes of Newspaper Business Editors and General Public Toward Capitalism," *Journalism Quarterly,* 61:56-65 (1984).

122. Edward S. Herman and Noam Chomsky, *Manufacturing Consent: The Political Economy of the Mass Media* (New York: Pantheon, 1988).

123. Walter Gieber and Walter Johnson, "The City Hall Beat: A Study of Reporter and Source Roles," *Journalism Quarterly,* 38:289-97 (1961); Paletz and Entman, *Media Power Politics*; and David L. Paletz, P. Reichert and B. McIntyre, "How the Media Support Local Government Authority, *Public Opinion Quarterly,* 35:808-92 (1971).

124. G. Hurd, "The Television Presentation of the Police," in T. Bennett et al. (eds.), *Popular Television and Film* (London: BFI/Open University Press, 1981).

125. Stuart Hall, "Culture, the Media and the Ideological Effect," pp. 315-48 in James Curran, Michael Gurevitch and Janet Woollacott (eds.), *Mass Communication and Society* (London: Edward Arnold, 1977) and John Hartley, *Understanding News* (London: Methuen, 1982).

126. Bagdikian, *Media Monopoly*; Compaine, Sterling, Guback and Noble, *Who Owns the Media*; Peter Dreier and Steven Weinberg, "Interlocking Directorates," *Columbia Journalism Review* (November/December 1979), pp. 51-68; and Graham Murdock and Peter Golding, "Capitalism, Communication and Class Relations," pp. 12-43 in James Curran, Michael Gurevitch and Janet Woollacott (eds.), *Mass Communication and Society* (Beverly Hills, Calif.: Sage, 1977).

127. Demers, "Structural Pluralism, Intermedia Competition and the Growth of the Corporate Newspaper in the United States."

128. Dreier and Weinberg, "Interlocking Directorates."

129. John W. C. Johnstone, Edward J. Slawski, and William W. Bowman, *The News People: A Sociological Portrait of American Journalists and Their Work* (Urbana, Ill.: University of Illinois Press, 1976); David Shaw, "Public and Press — Two Viewpoints," *Los Angeles Times* (August 11, 1985); and David H. Weaver and G. Cleveland Wilhoit, *The American Journalist: A Portrait of U.S. News People and Their Work* (Bloomington, Ind.: Indiana University Press, 1986).

130. The Frankfurt school has played an important role in shaping theories of ideology. Space prohibits a detailed examination of all of the theorists of this school, but it is important to point out that a wide range of views emerged from the school. Adorno and Horkheimer, for example, were pessimistic about the potential for emancipation — the culture of neocapitalism is a mass culture, imposed from above, not by any indigenous culture; it

promotes obedience, impedes critical judgment, and displaces dissent. Benjamin, on the other hand, was more optimistic, believing that the media had the power to raise consciousness and critical ideas. One of the best-known critiques comes from Marcuse, who argued that technology has played a major role in the survival of modern capitalism. A highly technologized culture, he asserted, generates affluence, which removes dissent; promotes development of a bureaucratic welfare state that dominates people's lives; increases leisure time that creates the illusion of freedom; stimulates automation which shifts the labor force into white-collar positions and reduces the sense of work-place repression; and blurs the distinction between consumption patterns. More than Gramsci, Marcuse emphasizes the structural controls that contribute to maintenance of capitalism and represses the development of class consciousness. See Theodore Adorno and Max Horkheimer, *Dialectic of the Enlightenment* (London: Verso, 1979) and Herbert Marcuse, *One-Dimensional Man* (Boston: Beacon Press, 1964).

131. S. Robert Lichter and Stanley Rothman, "Media and Business Elites, " *Public Opinion Quarterly,* 4:42-6 (1981).

132. W. Q. Morales, "Revolutions, Earthquakes, and Latin America: The Networks Look at Allende's Chile and Somoza's Nicaragua," pp. 79-116 in W. C. Adams (ed.), *Television Coverage of International Affairs* (Norwood, N.J.: Ablex, 1982).

133. The state supreme court eventually allowed construction of the power line, after which the media coverage of the protest groups took on a more negative tone. See Olien, Donohue and Tichenor, "Media and Stages of Social Conflict."

134. For review, see David L. Altheide, *Media Power* (Beverly Hills, Calif.: Sage, 1985). Also see Wayne Wanta, Mary Ann Stephenson, Judy VanSlyke Turk and Maxwell E. McCombs, "How President's State of Union Talk Influenced News Media Agendas," *Journalism Quarterly,* 66:537-41 (1989).

135. David Pritchard, "Homicide and Bargained Justice: The Agenda-Setting Effect of Crime News on Prosecutors," *Public Opinion Quarterly,* 50:143-59 (1986).

136. Jane R. Ballinger, "Media Coverage of Social Protest: An Examination of Media Hegemony," paper presented to the Association for Education in Journalism and Mass Communication, Kansas City, Mo. (August 1993).

137. See, e.g., Fishman, *Manufacturing the News,* and Tuchman, *Making News.*

138. See, e.g., Benjamin Compaine, "The Expanding Base of Media Competition, *Journal of Communication,* 35(3):81-96 (1985) and Maxwell McCombs, "Effect of Monopoly in Cleveland on Diversity of Newspaper Content, *Journalism Quarterly,* 64:740-4, 792 (1987).

139. Compaine, Sterling, Guback and Noble, *Who Owns the Media.* See chapter on magazine industry, which actually grew during the 1970s. David Waterman, "A New Look at Media Chains and Groups: 1977-1989," *Journal of Broadcasting & Electronic Media,* 35:167-78 (1991).

140. W. R. Davie and J. Lee, "Television News Technology: Do More Sources Mean Less Diversity?" *Journal of Broadcasting & Electronic Media,* 37:453-64 (1993), and Donohue, Olien, and Tichenor, "Reporting Conflict by Pluralism, Newspaper Type and Ownership."

141. David Pearce Demers, "Corporate Newspaper Structure and Editorial Page Vigor," paper presented to the International Communication Association (Albuquerque, N.M., May 1995) and David Pearce Demers, "Effects of Competition and Structural Pluralism on Centralization of Ownership in the U.S. Newspaper Industry," paper presented to the Association for Education in Journalism (Minneapolis, August 1990).

142. Donohue, Olien and Tichenor, "Reporting Conflict by Pluralism, Newspaper Type and Ownership," and Tichenor, Donohue and Olien, *Community Conflict and the Press.*

143. Marion Meyers, "Reporters and Beats: The Making of Oppositional News," *Critical Studies in Mass Communication,* 9:75-90 (1992).

144. Peter Bruck, "Strategies for Peace, Strategies for News Research," *Journal of Communication,* 39(1):108-29 (1989).

145. Hemant Shah, "News and the Self-Production of Society," *Journalism Monographs,* vol. 144 (April 1994).

146. See e.g., Epstein, *News From Nowhere*; Gitlin, *The Whole World Is Watching*; Schudson, "The Politics of Narrative Form."

147. N. Eliasoph, "Routines and the Making of Oppositional News," *Critical Studies in Mass Communication,* 5:313-34 (1988).

148. John Downing, "Alternative Media and the Boston Tea Party, " pp. 180-91 in John Downing, Ali Mohammadi and Annabelle Sreberny-Mohammadi (eds.), *Questioning the Media* (Newbury Park: Sage, 1990).

149. McLeod and Hertog, "The Manufacture of 'Public Opinion' by Reporters."

150. Following Durkheim, a distinction is made here between the functions and causes.

151. See, e.g., Tichenor, Donohue, and Olien, *Community Conflict and the Press.*

152. G. A. Donohue, C. N. Olien, P. J. Tichenor and D. P. Demers, "Community Structure, News Judgments and Newspaper Content," paper presented at the annual meeting of the Association for Education in Journalism and Mass Communication (Minneapolis, August 1990).

153. Demers, "Structural Pluralism, Intermedia Competition, and the Growth of the Corporate Newspaper in the United States."

154. Paul Hartmann and Charles Husband, "The Mass Media and Racial Conflict," pp. 288-302 in Stanley Cohen and Jock Young (eds.), *The Manufacture of News* (London: Constable, 1981).

155. Donald R. Matthews and James W. Protho, *Negroes and the New Southern Politics* (New York: Harcourt, Brace & World, 1966), p. 344.

156. Sandra J. Ball-Rokeach, Melvin Rokeach and Joel W. Grube, *The Great American Values Test: Influencing Behavior and Belief Through Television* (New York: Free Press, 1984) and Sandra J. Ball-Rokeach, Melvin Rokeach and Joel W. Grube, "Changing and Stabilizing Political Behavior and Beliefs," pp. 280-90 in Sandra J. Ball-Rokeach and Muriel G. Cantor (eds.), *Media Audience and Social Structure* (Newbury Park, Calif.: Sage, 1986).

157. George Gerbner and Larry Gross, "Living With Television: The Violence Profile," *Journal of Communication,* 26(2):173-99 (1976) and George Gerbner, Larry Gross, Michael Morgan and Nancy Signorielli, "Growing Up With Television: The Cultivation Perspective," pp. 17-41 in Jennings Bryant and Dolf Zillman (eds.), *Media Effects: Advances in Theory and Research* (Hillsdale, N.J.: Lawrence Erlbaum Associates, 1994).

158. From the perspective of the individual, the distorted image of crime conveyed on television is generally dysfunctional, leading to the development of the irrational beliefs, or a "mean world syndrome." However, from the perspective of the social system as whole, such "mean world" beliefs may be very functional for supporting authoritarian actions.

159. Gerbner and Gross, "Living With Television," p. 175.

160. Paul M. Hirsch, "The 'Scary World' of the Nonviewer and Other Anomalies: A Reanalysis of Gerbner et al.'s Findings on Cultivation Analysis, Part I," *Communication Research,* 7:403-56 (1980); Paul M. Hirsch, "On Not Learning From One's Own Mistakes: A Reanalysis of Gerbner et al.'s Findings on Cultivation Analysis, Part II," *Communication Research,* 8:3-37 (1981); and M. Hughes, "The Fruits of Cultivation Analysis: A Re-

Examination of Some Effects of Television Watching," *Public Opinion Quarterly,* 44:287-302 (1980).

161. Gerbner, Gross, Morgan and Signorielli, "Growing Up With Television."

162. David L. Protess, Fay Lomax Cook, Jack C. Doppelt, James S. Ettema, Margaret T. Gordon, Donna R. Leff, and Peter Miller, *The Journalism of Outrage: Investigative Reporting and Agenda-Building in America* (New York: Guilford Press, 1991).

163. Pritchard, "Homicide and Bargained Justice."

164. K. Viswanath, Emily Kahn, John R. Finnegan, Jr., James Hertog and John D. Potter, "Motivation and the Knowledge Gap: Effects of a Campaign to Reduce Diet-Related Cancer Risk," *Communication Research,* 20:546-63 (1993). The researchers also found that knowledge gaps did not narrow when controlling for motivation.

165. David Pearce Demers, "Media Use and Beliefs About Economic Equality: An Empirical Test of the Dominant Ideology Thesis," presented to the Midwest Association for Public Opinion Research (Chicago, November 1993).

166. William A. Gamson, *Talking Politics* (Cambridge, Mass.: Cambridge University Press, 1992), p. 4.

167. Gans, *Deciding What's News,* pp. 68-9.

168. Alexander, "The Mass News Media in Systemic, Historical and Comparative Perspective," p. 21.

Part 3

ORIGINS

Chapter 5

Empirical Research on Corporate Newspaper Origins

Thus far the literature review has focused on the historical development of the corporate newspaper, early theories of organizational structure and change, contemporary social system theory, and mass media system theory. Two major variables have been offered to explain the growth of the corporate form of organization in the newspaper industry: (1) competition and (2) structural pluralism, or the amount complexity in a social system (i.e., urbanization and industrialization).

As noted in Chapter 3, the notion that competition promotes the growth of corporate newspapers can be traced to the writings of Karl Marx. Competition stimulates innovation and material and social technology, which increases economies of scale and reduces per unit costs. As prices fall, weaker competitors are eliminated, and the survivors grow even larger and become more structurally complex. Marx saw competition as a specific structural feature of capitalism, not a characteristic of all social organization. Under communism, competition would give way to cooperation and harmony.[1] Marx identified three types of competition under capitalism: (1) between capitalists to control the market, (2) between workers to secure employment, and (3) between capital and labor. This book focuses on the first of these.

Structural pluralism also is said to contribute directly to the growth of newspapers. As markets and industries grow, manufacturers and retailers need efficient ways to reach buyers. Urban residents, especially the emerging middle and upper-middle classes, also need access to information that can help them through everyday life in an increasingly interdependent, complex society. Newspapers purportedly help to satisfy both needs.[2]

But does the empirical evidence support the argument that competition and structural pluralism promote the growth of corporate newspapers? The purpose of this chapter is to answer this question. This review is divided into three parts. The first examines the effects of competition on corporate newspaper structure. The second examines the effects of structural pluralism. The third briefly examines other explanations and incorporates them into a larger, more comprehensive theoretical model.

Competition and the Corporate Newspaper

Competition may be defined as a normatively regulated social process wherein two or more organizations or individuals make a common attempt to achieve a goal that precludes full goal achievement by others. Competition may or may not be recognized or intended by the participants and may be distinguished from social conflict in that the latter is less rule-bound and may involve the use of force or violence. Competition also may be unregulated (i.e., natural selection and the competition for survival of a species), but the focus here is on competition in a market economy, a particular form of social organization with its own values and rules.

In media research, competition is usually defined as a condition that exists when: (1) increases in usage of one medium (e.g., TV viewing) produces decreases in usage of another (e.g., newspaper circulation); (2) increases in advertising or subscription prices for one medium increases the quantity of advertising or subscriptions for another;[3] (3) increases in the number or quantity of one medium produces declines in another; or (4) increases in the number or quantity of one medium produces increases in the amount and proportion of news in another. Research on the effects of competition has primarily involved testing two major propositions: (1) *the intramedia hypothesis*, or competition between daily newspapers in the same market or geographical territory; and (2) *the intermedia hypothesis*, or competition between newspapers and other media forms.

Intramedia Competition

The notion that two or more daily newspapers in the same city compete with each other for readers and advertisers is well-documented empirically.[4] This form of competition is usually cited as the most important factor contributing to the growth of corporate newspapers through mergers and consolidations.[5] The primary explanation given for this is economies of scale. According to Rosse, Dertouzos, Robinson and Wildman:

> Economies of scale have played a pivotal role in the dominance of one-newspaper towns. It is a fact of newspaper technology that, all things equal, a larger firm is able to produce output (in terms of circulation and/or space) at lower per unit costs than a smaller establishment.[6]

Rosse and his colleagues argue that there are three sources of economies of scale — those incurred in creating and composing content, reproduction, and distribution.[7] More specifically, Blau points out that as an organization grows the supervisory span of control widens, reducing management costs per employee.[8] Larger organizations also reduce costs through sharing of news stories, through bulk purchases of newsprint and other raw materials and through centralized printing facilities.[9]

Some researchers have questioned the argument that economies of scale are solely responsible for the decline of daily newspaper competition and the growth of large-scale newspapers.[10] Litman criticizes Rosse's analysis because it considers short-term rather than long-term costs.[11] Dertouzos and Thorpe examined the impact of new technology on newspaper costs and found that economies of scale are not distributed equally across all sizes of newspapers.[12] Blankenburg also found that economies of scale are related to number of pages but not to circulation for medium-sized newspapers.[13] Nevertheless, despite these qualifications, few researchers have questioned the argument that economies of scale have played a substantial role in the decline of intracity newspaper competition. Moreover, few would argue that economies of scale are the sole determinant of intracity competition.

Rosse, for example, argues that the decline in competitive newspaper markets also stems from a lack of effective market segmentation — that is, a failure by newspapers to target specific audience segments with different informational needs.[14] He attributes this to a downward shift in advertising demand, a weakening of advertising preference for differentiated audiences, a downward shift in reader demand, growth of alternative media, increasing costs, and new technologies that have reduced the cost of differentiated newspaper products. Many daily newspapers in the United States could have survived, Rosse argues, if they had appealed to various segments of the population. Under this model, it may be argued that the *New York Daily News* and the *New York Times* survive because the former primarily targets a mass or blue-collar market and the latter, an elite or white-collar one.

Rosse also argues that despite the decline in the number of cities with two or more dailies, competition between newspapers is still alive and well in most large, metropolitan areas. He argues that metropolitan dailies are in direct competition with satellite city and suburban newspapers. The "umbrella hypothesis," as this has come to be called, posits that newspapers serving different but overlapping geographical areas often compete with each other. More specifically, Rosse identifies four layers of competition — metropolitan dailies, satellite city newspapers, suburban dailies, and weekly newspapers and shoppers — and contends that the competition is between layers, not within.[15]

According to Rosse, the competition is sharpest in the affluent suburbs, where metropolitan dailies compete with satellite city newspapers and suburban newspapers for audience attention. The development of zoned editions by the metropolitan dailies reflects this type of competition. In contrast, Rosse says there is little or no competition between two weekly suburban newspapers that serve different communities, since the coverage areas do not overlap. Although newspapers from different levels compete for readers and advertising, the level of competition, as well as the penetration of the metropolitan daily, declines as the distance between the metropolitan center and the community served by the smaller newspaper increases, according to Rosse. The local newspaper has an advantage over the large metropolitan daily because it can cover local news more effectively. In fact, Rosse believes that suburban newspapers and other media would eventually erode the penetration of the metropolitan dailies.

There is some evidence to support the umbrella hypothesis, but there is little evidence to suggest that smaller papers are running the metropolitan papers out of town. Olien, Donohue and Tichenor show that suburban communities with a heavy dependence on metropolitan centers for jobs also rely heavily on metropolitan dailies, even if a local paper is available.[16] In a later study, those researchers found that the circulation of regional dailies in Minnesota increases when the state's major metropolitan daily reduces circulation in nonmetropolitan areas.[17] Although the increase in circulation for the regional dailies does not fully compensate for the metro daily pullback in circulation from rural areas, these data strongly support the notion that newspapers from different layers may be functional substitutes.[18]

The pullback hypothesis is fully compatible with the idea that newspapers adapt to changing conditions. The withdrawal of circulation from some areas may be seen as a way to reduce costs and improve the efficiency of the newspaper. However, the pullback hypothesis does not explain why household circulation of metropolitan newspapers also is declining rapidly in the suburbs,[19] areas that generally represent the most attractive target markets for newspaper advertisers. One possible explanation is increased competition in those areas from television, especially cable television — a topic that is explored in more depth in the next section.

Several studies by Lacy also provide some support for the umbrella hypothesis. In a survey of newspaper executives in the 13 Standard Metropolitan Statistical Areas in southwest states, he found that umbrella competition decreased as the distance of the smaller dailies from the metropolitan centers increased.[20] In a separate study, Lacy later found that metropolitan dailies in monopoly markets are more likely than those in competitive markets to compete with outlying small daily and weekly newspapers for circulation.[21] However, just the opposite was true for advertising revenue competition, and in a more recent study he and his colleagues conclude that daily competition or absence of it has minimal impact on circulation or existence of suburban newspapers.[22] Lacy and Dalmia also studied the newspaper industry in non-metropolitan areas of Michigan from 1980 to 1989 and found that as daily and Sunday metropolitan daily newspaper penetration increased, penetration of satellite dailies decreased, and vice versa. Daily penetration of satellite dailies also was negatively related to penetration of weeklies, but a positive relationship was found for Sunday penetration. A positive but weak relationship for Sunday penetration also was found between metropolitan dailies and weeklies.[23]

Devey found no support for the umbrella hypothesis when she compared aggregate circulation figures of metro dailies and the combined figures of newspapers in the satellite and suburban layers between 1945 and 1985.[24] However, Lacy and Dalmia criticized this study because "the fact that population growth in suburban and satellite areas equaled the circulation growth of newspapers in these layers does not necessarily show a lack of interlayer competition."[25] In contrast, Tillinghast, in a study of the Los Angeles-Orange County newspaper market, concluded that the *Los*

Angeles Times competes with both suburban newspapers and satellite city papers for advertising and circulation.[26] And at least one study of news content also supports the umbrella hypothesis: Lacy found that as the level of competition increased, the amount of news hole space in metro, suburban and satellite dailies also increased, and the amount of local coverage increased in the suburban papers.[27]

Intermedia Competition

Many researchers believe that competition from non-newspaper media, especially television, also has contributed to a decline in readership of the daily newspaper and, consequently, to the growth of the corporate newspaper.[28] As noted in Chapter 2, newspaper circulation per household has declined steadily since the late 1940s (see Figure 2.1), when television first emerged as a powerful medium. Yet, despite the intuitive appeal of the intermedia-competition hypothesis, much of the contemporary research fails to support this hypothesis, or the research that does support it is methodologically flawed. A fundamental question to be resolved is the extent to which broadcast media are functional alternatives for newspapers.[29]

Scott conducted one of the earliest studies, concluding in 1954 that declines in circulation among metropolitan daily newspapers in Los Angeles during that year and the three previous years were due in part to "the rapid rise of television" there. However, the study did not empirically correlate the rise of the television penetration with the decline in circulation — it merely assumed the decline in circulation stemmed from the growth of the number of homes with television.[30]

Two other studies in the 1950s failed to support the intermedia competition hypothesis. The first, an international survey covering the period 1954 to 1958, concluded that although television was capturing a larger share of the total advertising dollars in the United States, the United Kingdom and Japan, "in absolute figures the advertising revenues for daily newspapers nevertheless continued to increase in all three countries: fastest in Japan with a rise of over 60 per cent, in England with roughly 50 per cent and in the U.S.A. 20 per cent."[31] The study found declines in circulation and advertising in 1958 but attributed them to subscription rate increases and a recession. The second study, conducted in Britain in the late 1950s, also concluded that the effects of television on the reading and buying of newspapers and magazines "are small and do not parallel recent circulation changes. The direct implication of this is that we must go beyond television for any adequate explanation of the recent decline in press circulation figures."[32] In addition, the study found that television appears to stimulate reading of the popular press, including news items in general and items dealing with TV programs, and "in the long term, television increases slightly the reading of daily and Sunday papers at the expense of weekly and monthly magazines."[33]

During the 1970s, at least one study found support for the intermedia-competition hypothesis. McCombs proposed that the proportion of money people and advertisers spend on the mass media remains relatively constant over time, despite changes in the types and availability of media in the marketplace. When the relative amount of advertising in or usage of one media increases, there must be parallel decreases in other media. He refers to this as the "relative constancy hypothesis." McCombs examined trends in the newspaper industry since the early 1900s and concluded that "the combination of rising costs, limited consumer and advertising spending on media, and competition from new communication media have resulted in fewer newspapers."[34]

Competition from new media may very well explain the growth of the corporate model and the decline of newspaper competition. However, the theoretical and empirical soundness of the constancy hypothesis may be challenged.[35] Historically, the amount of time social actors have spent with media has risen dramatically during the 20th century, partly because of the increasing division of labor. In this capacity, media may be seen as playing an important role in providing information that helps to integrate individuals and organizations into a larger social system.[36] Consequently, one would expect an increase, not a constant, in the amount of time people spend with formalized means of communication as a social system becomes more pluralistic.[37] Thus, assuming costs for media remain constant, actual expenditures on media should increase over time. However, empirically this has not been the case because the costs of new forms of media change dramatically as they become more diffused. Media expenditures throughout the 20th century have risen and fallen a number of times.[38]

A number of other empirical studies that have specifically tested the constancy hypothesis also fail to support it. Blankenburg reasoned that if demand for newspapers is relatively constant, then the total circulation in a market should be unrelated to the number of dailies published in that market when the number of households is controlled. But he found that circulation was higher in areas with more dailies and concluded that "the proposition of no effect on total circulation by number of dailies is only marginally tenable at this time."[39] Studying the development of new video technology, Wood and O'Hare found a dramatic upturn in consumer spending on the mass media. "The data show that consumers' willingness to spend an increased share of income on the mass media in 1979-1988 prevented major losses by print and conventional audiovisual media."[40] Robinson and Jeffres reported that the proportion of GNP spent on mass media rose from 2.7 percent in 1965 to 3.2 percent in 1975.[41] And Demers, using time-series analysis, found that relative spending on advertising increased significantly from 1850 to 1920, and that spending increased and decreased significantly four times during the 20th century. He found, however, that structural pluralism was directly or indirectly related to increases in absolute levels of spending.[42] In short, the findings from these studies support the argument that demand for formalized sources of information and news increases in absolute as well as relative terms as social systems become more structurally diverse.

   Although the McCombs' study supports the intermedia hypothesis, two more empirical studies conducted in the 1970s fail to support it. Bogart reported that viewing of evening television news is not significantly greater in areas where newspapers lost circulation than in areas in which they gained.[43] The second study, conducted by Robinson and Jeffres, found that even though time devoted to newspapers declined from 1965 to 1975 as time devoted to national television news increased, cross-sectional data indicated that time spent with the two media is positively, not negatively, correlated.[44]

   During the 1980s most of the empirical research also failed to support the intermedia hypothesis. Blankenburg found that the physical distance between a weekly newspaper and the next-nearest daily or weekly newspaper, or radio station and shopper that was not co-owned had no significant effect on advertising prices charged by the weeklies.[45] Lacy reported that change in the absolute and per capita number of radio stations in 72 cities between 1929 and 1948 had no effect on whether newspaper competition declined in those cities.[46] Furthermore, despite the growth of radio during that time, newspaper circulation per capita generally continued to increase.[47] Busterna found that the relative price of national advertising for other media, including television, over a 15-year period had no significant impact on the quantity of national newspaper advertising.[48] And Ferguson found that the number of radio and television stations in a city decreases daily newspaper advertising rates but increases daily newspaper circulation. "The circulation result is surprising," he writes. "One would expect the increase in the number of alternative news and entertainment sources to cause people to spend less time reading newspapers, thereby reducing circulation."[49] He did not have an explanation for the finding.

One exception to the rule of no support for the intermedia hypothesis during the 1980s was a study by Dimmick and Rothenbuhler.[50] Using an ecological model, they examined changes in the proportion of advertising dollars spent on newspapers, television, radio and outdoor advertising in three major categories — spot, local and national advertising. They found that since 1957 the newspaper's strongest competitor has been radio because both rely heavily on local advertising. Newspapers compete less strongly with television and outdoor advertising, but the level of competition with television has increased since 1970 and with outdoor advertising it has declined. In the late 1940s and early 1950s, the amount of competition between radio, television and outdoor advertising was extremely strong, because all three relied heavily on national advertising revenues.[51] Dimmick and Rothenbuhler argue that radio survived heavy competition from television by decreasing its dependence on national advertising and increasing its share of local advertising. Their data suggest that television is now increasing its dependence on local advertising, while no significant changes have occurred in the newspaper industry.

The data in the Dimmick and Rothenbuhler study help to keep the door open on the question of intermedia competition. However, one shortcoming in the study is that the data account only for relative market share, not absolute. Thus, if the total amount of advertising dollars in a market increases, theoretically, these absolute increases could support additional media even with increased competition. During the time period studied, absolute advertising revenues for newspapers increased even while its relative market share declined.

On balance, the empirical evidence to date suggests that broadcast media and newspapers are more complementary than competitive. Each seems to have carved out its own niche. But even if the intermedia competition hypothesis is valid, it is important to point out that there is little reason to expect that a competition model can provide a full explanation of the changes that have taken place in the newspaper industry. As Smelser points out, the view that behavior in business organizations is guided solely by economic factors is too simplistic.[52] Research shows, in fact, that trade unions, government, tax laws and many other forces play a significant role in the behavior of the firm.[53]

Structural Pluralism
and the Corporate Newspaper

One alternative explanation for the growth of the corporate newspaper employs structural pluralism — a term whose intellectual heritage can be traced to Spencer and his concept of structural differentiation — as the key independent variable. Tichenor, Donohue and Olien define structural pluralism as "the degree of differentiation in the social system along institutional and specialized interest group lines, in a way that determines the potential sources of organized social power."[54] They have operationalized structural pluralism as an index consisting of one or more of the following measures: the proportion of labor force outside agriculture; per capita income; population; distance from a major metropolitan area; and number of businesses, voluntary groups, schools and churches in a community.[55]

The concept of structural pluralism has been used in a variety of different analyses of the media and usually is employed as an independent variable.[56] The analysis here focuses on Tichenor, Donohue and Olien's argument that as communities become more pluralistic, the tradition of family ownership gives way to corporate ownership.[57]

> Corporate ownership of multiple newspapers has occurred primarily in larger, more pluralistic communities and among the larger operations deemed to be better investments, i.e., more profitable in the world of journalism. Such ownership involves a pattern of organization, division of responsibility and discreteness of work which differs markedly from the individually owned enterprise, but without necessarily having negative effects on the news gathering process.[58]

Corporate ownership, the researchers argue, should be viewed as an outgrowth of the same forces driving a consumption-based economy. Modern marketing requires access to large, heterogeneous markets which must be reached through secondary rather than primary contacts, and newspapers become principal outlets for delivering consumers to producers. The trend toward media conglomeration, in which a media organization becomes just one part of a large corporate organization that produces a variety of different goods and services, may also be interpreted as supporting the idea that the principal motivation in corporate organizations today is optimum return.[59] As Tichenor, Donohue and Olien put it:

Media today operate to an increasing degree on whether the "bottom line" is increased or decreased by changes in the organization. ... The guiding theme in the past was that media were necessary to an informed public, and constituted a profession at which one labored with the expectation of a reasonable return for one's investment. Now it appears that the journalism profession is an enterprise which should be gauged more by how one maximizes profit. One might say that the familiar slogan "all the news fit to print" has evolved to "all the news that maximizes a profit."[60]

Tichenor, Donohue and Olien's research provides support for this model. During the 1960s, about 90 percent of the weeklies and 82 percent of the nonmetropolitan dailies in Minnesota were locally owned. By 1979, after those communities had become much more pluralistic, about a fourth of the weeklies and semi-weeklies and nearly two-thirds of the nonmetropolitan dailies were owned outside the local communities. The dailies, which are located in more pluralistic communities, also were more likely than the weeklies to be owned by an out-of-state corporation.

Several other studies may be interpreted as supporting the hypothesis that corporate newspaper structure is a function of structural pluralism. Tillinghast found that newspaper circulation increases as urbanization, one indicator of structural pluralism, increases.[61] Using national data from 1910 to 1980 and time-series analysis, Demers found that the percentage of newspapers owned by chains increases as structural pluralism increases.[62]

Two recent empirical studies also support the notion that larger newspaper organizations are more profitable. Blankenburg found that the profit rate on revenues for a typical newspaper with a circulation of 100,000 was 20.8 percent compared to 18.5 percent for a newspaper with a circulation of 50,000.[63] Tharp and Stanley found that the average profit increased as the size of a newspaper increased: 6.4 percent for those under 10,000; 11.5 percent for those 10,000 to 15,000; 17.3 percent for those 15,000 to 25,000; and about 19 percent for those 25,000 or more.[64]

Most of the empirical literature has viewed competition as an exogenous variable; that is, few researchers have sought to explain competition itself. But competition itself may be seen as a product of increasing pluralism. As noted in Chapter 3, the notion that competition between individuals and groups increases as a social system grows and becomes more complex is widely recognized in the sociological literature and can be traced to the writings of Spencer and Durkheim. They essentially argued that as population in an area increases, competition between individuals and groups over scarce resources increases. Left unchecked, competition can threaten the existence of the society or community, but integration is possible and the efficiency of the society or community can be improved through a division of labor and role specialization. These social configurations raise problems of coordination and control, which in turn can be resolved through more formalized methods of communication. Written rules and regulations, media and in-house correspondence and publications play an important role in integrating various elements of an organization or social system.[65]

More recently, Tichenor, Donohue and Olien have argued that the number and variety of media increase as structural pluralism increases.[66] Undifferentiated, homogeneous communities, they contend, generally have a limited number of mass media sources, and those sources tend to represent the interests and concerns of an undifferentiated, homogeneous audience. But as the division of labor expands and interdependence increases, demand for information and news increases and social actors respond to this need by increasing the number and diversity of media.

There is strong empirical support for this hypothesis in the newspaper industry, both in terms of cross-sectional and longitudinal research. Using circulation as a measure of community size, data collected by Sobel and Emery show that competition between dailies increases substantially as circulation increases. Fewer than 4 percent of the newspapers under 50,000 circulation had competition, compared to 12 percent of those between 50,000 to 99,999 circulation, 27 percent of those between 100,000 and 249,999 circulation, 61 percent of those between 250,000 and 499,999 circulation, and all of the newspapers with 500,000 or more circulation.[67] Rosse also found that the probability of a newspaper having direct competition increases as size of the community increases, but over time daily newspaper competition in all communities has declined.[68] In 1948, 96 percent of the U.S. cities with a population of one million or more had competition, compared with 74 percent in 1973. And Hagner reported that population was a good predictor of the level of newspaper competition in a Standard Metropolitan Statistical Area. However, the number of cities was the best predictor, and proximity to a larger SMSA (closer to one) and land area also were predictors of competition.[69]

Intermedia competition also appears to increase as a social system becomes more pluralistic. Olien, Tichenor and Donohue point out that pluralistic communities have multiple sources of news and information, including several locally based television stations, cable systems with more channels, and a plethora of AM and FM radio stations.[70] The variety and number of broadcast media also has grown dramatically in recent decades. From 1965 to 1986, the number of radio stations more than tripled, and the number of television stations doubled.[71] Compaine also points out that although direct competition between daily newspapers has declined, the number of book publishers and magazines has grown dramatically. He writes: "The empirical evidence indicates that the media structure in the United States is by far more open, diverse, and responsive to public needs and wants than at any time in history, notwithstanding the contrary sense that is suggested by the headlines created when media companies merge."[72]

Other Explanations for Corporate Newspaper Growth

Competition and structural pluralism are two key factors that have been offered to explain the growth of corporate newspapers. Others include growth of the suburbs, decline of partisanship, poor management, changes in tax laws, increasing greed, the decline of the rural economy, increased wages, labor union resistance to technological change, and the lack of investment capital in family-owned newspapers for new technology. Many of these factors, it will be argued, can be incorporated under the concept of structural pluralism.

Growth of the Suburbs
Nixon and Ward argue that the growth of the suburbs has contributed to concentration of ownership. Suburbanites are less likely than city dwellers to subscribe to and read two or more metropolitan dailies because they "prefer one downtown and one suburban paper."[73] Rosse also argues that the growth of the suburbs resulted in a "downward shift of subscriber demand for the center city newspapers" and an increased demand for suburban newspapers.[74] National data collected by Olien, Tichenor, and Donohue show that metropolitan daily newspaper penetration declined faster from 1965 to 1987 in suburban (34% to 20%, a 43 percent drop) than in center city counties (93% to 57%, a 37 percent drop). It is unclear, however, whether penetration of suburban daily newspapers has increased in suburban areas.[75]

Janowitz, in his study of urban community newspapers, provides a theoretical rationale for the decline in metro newspaper circulation in suburban areas. He argues that the urban residential community is a community of "limited liability," meaning that people in pluralistic systems have multiple identities and roles and have less attachment to any single local institution or group.[76]   He found that the greater the degree of attachment to a community, the higher the newspaper readership. People who were highly integrated in the community — i.e., those who had children, owned homes, worked in the local community, and lived in the community a long time — spent more time reading the local paper. The paper provided information and news that was useful in their everyday lives.   Thus, it would be expected that the penetration of metropolitan newspapers will decline as social roles and identities become more diversified and specialized.[77]

A structural explanation for the decline in readership of metropolitan dailies in suburban communities also would emphasize the fact that those communities have a greater number of media, or more competition. The media mix in the suburbs includes daily newspapers, shoppers, weekly community newspapers, network television stations, radio stations, and cable television. This multiplicity of sources might be expected to lead to greater diversity in media use patterns — a hypothesis supported in another study conducted by Tichenor, Donohue and Olien.[78]

Decline of Partisanship

In addition to the growth of the suburbs, Nixon and Ward argue that the decline of partisanship and the growth in objectivity in reporting has contributed to concentration of ownership. "Few newspapers are started or kept alive today for political reasons," they write; "the modern political party or pressure group hires a public relations director and makes use of all the available mass media."[79]   The growth of objectivity means newspapers have become more similar in their coverage and, hence, "there has come to be little more reason for two competing newspapers than there would be for two competing telephone companies."[80]   This explanation parallels Rosse's argument that dailies have failed to differentiate and target specific audience segments.

Poor Management

Another factor contributing to the growth of the corporate newspaper, according to Compaine, Sterling, Guback and Noble, is poor management.[81] As Marx noted, ownership of a family business tends to become increasingly diffused as the business is handed down from generation to generation.   Of course, from a structural perspective, the chances for disputes among owners increase as the number of owners increases. But perhaps more importantly, as the social system becomes more pluralistic and the newspaper grows, family ownership, as an organizational form, may be unable to coordinate and control the organization as effectively as a corporate organization. Many of the owners of family-owned newspapers have little or no specialized knowledge in modern business practices or in the newspaper business. In contrast, publicly owned newspapers are structurally organized to employ modern management practices as well as the specialized talent and people to get the job done.

Changes in Tax Laws

Bagdikian argues that tax laws are the "chief force" in the growth of corporate newspapers because they "favor investing the profits elsewhere."[82] Under the tax laws, profits distributed to owners or shareholders are taxed at a much higher rate than profits that are reinvested in other newspapers. Bagdikian also points out that inheritance taxes have contributed to the demise of the family-owned newspaper. Tax laws permit the first owner to leave the property to his or her heirs without taxes, but the taxes are "very large" when it passes to the third generation. To avoid such taxes but retain family control, the owners may sell public stock and retain a block large enough to control policy but not large enough to pay death duties. Another option is to form a tax-free foundation to own most of the stock and to retain enough voting shares in the foundation to exercise control.[83]

While changes in the tax laws may certainly have contributed to the growth of large-scale organization, this is not really an explanation. The question not answered is: Why did the tax laws change?

Increasing Greed

Another popular explanation for the growth of chain ownership is that "greed" is the driving force.[84] Owners of chains or large media corporations are believed to be more susceptible to such tendencies because tax laws and economies of scale give their companies significant competitive advantages in the marketplace.[85] This perspective is based on the classical economic assumptions that self-interest is the driving force behind human behavior and that competition is necessary to prevent profit-hungry individuals from holding the community hostage.[86] Although there is some evidence to support the notion that chains are more profit-oriented and that chains and large-scale organizations are more profitable,[87] there is little evidence to suggest that people are more greedy now than they were in the past. The emphasis on profits appears to be more a consequence than a cause of changes in organizational style.[88]

Additional Factors

Other factors cited as contributing to the growth of the corporate newspaper include: (1) the decline of the rural economy,[89] (2) increased wages,[90] (3) labor union resistance to technological change,[91] and (4) the lack of investment capital in family-owned newspapers for new technology.[92]

Many of these causes, as well as the ones above, may be subsumed under the explanatory umbrella of structural pluralism. The decline of partisanship and growth in objectivity, for example, may be seen as the structural response to increasing pluralism, i.e., increasing rationalization of the news production process that enables news organizations to reach and retain large, heterogeneous audiences. Tax laws that favor large-scale organization also reflect a shift of power in the system from small-scale, family-owned businesses to large, corporate organizations, which have dominated the economy since the late 19th century. And the decline of the rural economy and increased wages are often employed as indicators of pluralism.[93]

Summary

Competition is widely believed to be an important factor promoting the growth of the corporate newspaper. Research provides some support for the intramedia hypothesis (competition between dailies) and the umbrella hypothesis but generally fails to support the intermedia competition hypothesis (competition between dailies and nondaily media). In particular, there is little empirical evidence to suggest that television has contributed to the rise of the corporate newspaper, despite the intuitive appeal of that hypothesis.

Although structural pluralism is not widely recognized in mass communication research as a factor that promotes the development of the modern corporation, empirical research supports the argument that pluralistic communities are more likely to have newspapers with the characteristics of a modern corporation. Media in pluralistic communities are larger, have a greater division of labor and role specialization, and historically were more likely to be part of a chain organization. Empirical research suggests that competition between media increases as structural pluralism increases. Larger, heterogeneous communities have a greater number and variety of mass media.

In addition to competition, the growth of the suburbs, the decline in partisanship and the growth of objectivity, poor management, changes in the tax laws that favor large-scale organization, decline of the rural economy and increased wages all have been cited as factors explaining the growth of the corporate newspaper. Theoretically, these may be seen as components of a larger, more comprehensive concept — structural pluralism.

Notes

1. Because of this, some scholars argue that Marx was not really the conflict theorist that he is often described to be. Weber, in contrast, argued that conflict was inherent in all forms of social organization.

2. Later in this chapter, it will be argued that competition mediates part of the effects of structural pluralism on corporate newspaper structure.

3. The concept of cross-elasticity of demand is also used to refer to this proposition.

4. See, e.g., James M. Ferguson, "Daily Newspaper Advertising Rates, Local Media Cross-Ownership, Newspaper Chains, and Media Competition," *The Journal of Law & Economics*, 26:635-54 (1983).

5. Raymond B. Nixon and Jean Ward, "Trends in Newspaper Ownership and Inter-Media Competition," *Journalism Quarterly*, 38:3-14 (1961), p. 9.

6. James N. Rosse, James N. Dertouzos, Michael Robinson and Steven Wildman, "Economic Issues in Mass Communication Industries," paper prepared for the Federal Trade Commission Media Symposium (Washington, D.C., December 14-15, 1978), p. 63. Also see James N. Rosse, "The Evolution of One Newspaper Cities," paper prepared for the Federal Trade Commission Media Symposium (Washington, D.C., December 14-15, 1978).

7. Rosse, Dertouzos, Robinson and Wildman, "Economic Issues in Mass Communication Industries."

8. Peter M. Blau, "A Formal Theory of Differentiation in Organizations," *American Sociological Review*, 55:201-18 (1970).

9. David Pearce Demers, "Structural Pluralism and the Growth of Chain Ownership in the U.S. Daily Newspaper Industry," paper presented to the Association for Education in Journalism and Mass Communication (Minneapolis, August 1990).

10. For a general discussion, see Stephen Lacy and Robert G. Picard, "Interactive Monopoly Power in the Daily Newspaper Industry," *The Journal of Media Economics*, 3(2):27-38 (1990).

11. Barry R. Litman, "Microeconomic Foundations," pp. 3-34 in Robert G. Picard, James P. Winter, Maxwell E. McCombs and Stephen Lacy (eds.), *Press Concentration and Monopoly* (Norwood, N.J.: Ablex, 1988).

12. James N. Dertouzos and K. E. Thorpe, *Newspaper Groups: Economies of Scale, Tax Laws, and Merger Incentives* (Santa Monica, Calif.: Rand, 1985).

13. William B. Blankenburg, "Newspaper Scale and Newspaper Expenditures," *Newspaper Research Journal*, 10(2):97-103 (1989).

14. Benjamin M. Compaine, Christopher H. Sterling, Thomas Guback and J. Kendrick Noble, Jr., *Who Owns the Media? Concentration of Ownership in the Mass Communications Industry* (White Plains, N.Y.: Knowledge Industry, 1982) and James N. Rosse and J. N. Dertouzos, "An Economist's Description of the 'Media Industry,'" pp. 40-192 of *Proceedings of the Symposium on Media Concentration, December 14 and 15, 1978*, vol. 1 (Washington, D.C.: Federal Trade Commission, 1979).

15. Rosse and Dertouzos, "An Economist's Description of the 'Media Industry.'"

16. C. N. Olien, G. A. Donohue and P. J. Tichenor, "Metropolitan Dominance and Media Use," *American Newspaper Publishers Association News Research Report*, no. 36 (1986).

17. G. A. Donohue, P. J. Tichenor and C. N. Olien, "Metro Daily Pullback and Knowledge Gaps Within and Between Communities," *Communication Research*, 13:453-71 (1986).

18. Metro daily newspapers are pulling out of rural areas, according to the researchers, because rural areas are not attractive target markets. Incomes in such areas are generally lower than those in metropolitan areas and, geographically, the rural markets are too far removed from the metropolitan area to be attractive markets for metropolitan advertisers. Bagdikian also argues that newspapers are pulling circulation out of inner city areas because they are not attractive markets to advertisers. See Ben H. Bagdikian, *The Media Monopoly* (Boston: Beacon Press, 1987), pp. 105-17.

19. Clarice N. Olien, Phillip J. Tichenor and George A. Donohue, "Media Redistribution in the U.S.: A Growing Information Gap Between Metro and Nonmetro Areas?" paper presented to the American Association for Public Opinion Research (Phoenix, May 1991).

20. Stephen Lacy, "Competition Among Metropolitan Daily, Small Daily and Weekly Newspapers," *Journalism Quarterly*, 61:640-44, 742 (1984).

21. Stephen Lacy, "Monopoly Metropolitan Dailies and Inter-City Competition," *Journalism Quarterly*, 62:640-4 (1985).

22. Walter E. Niebauer, Jr., Stephen Lacy, James M. Bernstein and Tuen-yu Lau, "Central City Market Structure's Impact on Suburban Newspaper Circulation," *Journalism Quarterly*, 65:726-32 (1988).

23. Stephen Lacy and Shikha Dalmia, "The Relationship Between Daily and Weekly Newspaper Penetration in Non-Metropolitan Areas," paper presented to the Association for Education in Journalism and Mass Communication (Montreal, August 1992).

24. Susan M. Devey, "Umbrella Competition for Circulation in the Boston Metro Area," *Journal of Media Economics*, 2(1):31-40 (1989).

25. Lacy and Dalmia, "The Relationship Between Daily and Weekly Newspaper Penetration in Non-Metropolitan Areas," p. 4.

26. Diana Stover Tillinghast, "Limits of Competition," pp. 71-87 in Robert G. Picard, James P. Winter, Maxwell E. McCombs and Stephen Lacy (eds.), *Press Concentration and Monopoly* (Norwood, N.J.: Ablex, 1988).

27. Stephen Lacy, "The Impact of Intercity Competition on Daily Newspaper Competition," *Journalism Quarterly*, 65:399-406 (1988).

28. See, e.g., Robert M. Entman, *Democracy Without Citizens: Media and the Decay of American Politics* (New York: Oxford University Press, 1989), p. 91.

29. For a discussion of functional alternatives as used in social system theory, see Robert K. Merton, *Social Theory and Social Structure* (New York: The Free Press, 1957 [1949]).

30. Paul T. Scott, "The Mass Media in Los Angeles Since the Rise of Television," *Journalism Quarterly*, 31:161-6, 192 (1954).

31. L. F. Tijmstra, "The Challenge of TV to the Press," *Journal of Broadcasting*, 4(1):3-13 (1959-60), p. 4. Tijmstra, who was the Deputy Director of the International Press Institute, presented the results of this study to the Eighth General Assembly of the IPI, held in Berlin in 1959.

32. William A. Belson, "The Effects of Television on the Reading and the Buying of Newspapers and Magazines," *The Public Opinion Quarterly*, 25:366-81 (1961), p. 378.

33. Belson, "The Effects of Television."

34. Maxwell McCombs, "Mass Media in the Marketplace," *Journalism Monographs*, vol. 24 (August 1972), pp. 55-6.

35. David Pearce Demers, "The Relative Constancy Hypothesis, Structural Pluralism and National Advertising Expenditures," *Journal of Media Economics*, 7(4):31-48 (1994).

36. This does not mean that media messages always perform an integrating function for every individual or group, only that the sum total of such messages produces an outcome which contributes to system stability.

37. Demers, "The Relative Constancy Hypothesis." Also see Olien, Tichenor and Donohue, "Media Redistribution in the U.S." One of the problems with McCombs methodology is that he measures the amount of money spent on the media rather than amount of time. The amount of money spent may fluctuate considerably because the price of new media technologies frequently declines as the innovation is diffused throughout the system.

38. See Demers, "The Relative Constancy Hypothesis."

39. William B. Blankenburg, "Structural Determination of Circulation," *Journalism Quarterly*, 58:543-51 (1981), p. 548.

40. William C. Wood and Sharon L. O'Hare, "Paying for the Video Revolution: Consumer Spending on the Mass Media," *Journal of Communication*, 41(1):24-30 (1991), p. 28.

41. John P. Robinson and Leo W. Jeffres, "The Changing Role of Newspapers in the Age of Television," *Journalism Monographs*, vol. 63 (September 1979).

42. Demers, "The Relative Constancy Hypothesis."

43. Leo Bogart, "How the Challenge of Television News Affects the Prosperity of Daily Newspapers," *Journalism Quarterly*, 52:403-10 (1975).

44. Robinson and Jeffres, "The Changing Role of Newspapers."

45. William B. Blankenburg, "Determinants of Pricing of Advertising in Weeklies," *Journalism Quarterly*, 57:663-6 (1980).

46. Stephen Lacy, "The Effect of Growth of Radio on Newspaper Competition, 1929-1948," *Journalism Quarterly*, 64:775-81 (1987).

47. Rosse and Dertouzos, "An Economist's Description," p. 73.

48. John C. Busterna, "The Cross-Elasticity of Demand for National Newspaper Advertising," *Journalism Quarterly*, 64:346-51 (1987).

49. Ferguson, "Daily Newspaper Advertising Rates," p. 636.

50. John Dimmick and Eric Rothenbuhler, "The Theory of the Niche: Quantifying Competition Among Media Industries," *Journal of Communication*, 34(1):103-19 (1984).

51. No data for newspapers is available for these years because of problems in the data. See Dimmick and Rothenbuhler, "The Theory of the Niche," pp. 108-9.

52. Neil J. Smelser, *The Sociology of Economic Life* (Englewood Cliffs, N.J.: Prentice-Hall, 1963), pp. 79-80.

53. Andreas G. Papendreou, "Some Basic Problems in the Theory of the Firm," pp. 183-219 in Bernard F. Haley (ed.), *A Survey of Contemporary Economics,* vol. II (Homewood, Ill.: Irwin, 1952).

54. Phillip J. Tichenor, George A. Donohue and Clarice N. Olien, *Community Conflict and the Press* (Beverly Hills, Calif.: Sage, 1980), p. 16.

55. Tichenor, Donohue and Olien, *Community Conflict and the Press,* and G. A. Donohue, C. N. Olien and P. J. Tichenor, "Structure and Constraints on Community Newspaper Gatekeepers," *Journalism Quarterly* 66:807-12, 845 (1989).

56. See, e.g., Tichenor, Donohue and Olien, *Community Conflict and the Press.*

57. George A. Donohue, Clarice N. Olien and Phillip J. Tichenor, "Reporting Conflict by Pluralism, Newspaper Type and Ownership," *Journalism Quarterly,* 62:489-99, 507 (1985).

58. C. N. Olien, P. J. Tichenor and G. A. Donohue, "Relation Between Corporate Ownership and Editor Attitudes Toward Business," *Journalism Quarterly,* 65:259-66 (1988), p. 261.

59. Olien, Tichenor and Donohue, "Reporting Conflict by Pluralism," p. 491.

60. Donohue, Olien and Tichenor, "Reporting Conflict by Pluralism," pp. 490-1.

61. William A. Tillinghast, "Declining Newspaper Readership: Impact of Region and Urbanization," *Journalism Quarterly,* 58:14-23, 50 (1981).

62. Demers, "Structural Pluralism and the Growth of Chain Ownership."

63. Blankenburg, "Newspaper Scale and Newspaper Expenditures," p. 100.

64. Marty Tharp and Linda R. Stanley, "A Time Series Analysis of Newspaper Profitability by Circulation Size," *The Journal of Media Economics,* 5(1):3-12 (1992). Also see Marty Tharp and Linda R. Stanley, "Trends in Profitability of Daily U.S. Newspapers by Circulation Size, 1978-1988," paper presented to the Association for Education in Journalism and Mass Communication (Minneapolis, August 1990).

65. Herbert Spencer, *Principles of Sociology,* vol. III (New York: D. Appleton, 1897) and Emile Durkheim, *The Division of Labor in Society,* trans. W. D. Wells (New York: The Free Press, 1984 [1893]). As noted in Chapter 3, it is important to point out that even though Spencer believed increasing population would generally increase the level of competition between individuals, he argued that cooperation between individuals was greater in advanced, complex societies than in primitive societies. The division of labor controlled competition and increased cooperation between individuals and groups.

66. Tichenor, Donohue and Olien, *Community Conflict and the Press,* and George A. Donohue, Phillip J. Tichenor and Clarice N. Olien, "Mass Media Functions, Knowledge and Social Control," *Journalism Quarterly* 50:652-9 (1973).

67. Judith Sobel and Edwin Emery, "U.S. Dailies' Competition in Relation to Circulation Size: A Newspaper Data Update," *Journalism Quarterly,* 55:145-9 (1978).

68. Rosse, "The Evolution of One Newspaper Cities."

69. Paul R. Hagner, "Newspaper Competition: Isolating Related Market Characteristics," *Journalism Quarterly,* 60:281-7 (1983).

70. G. A. Donohue, C. N. Olien and P. J. Tichenor, "A Changing Media Environment in the U.S.," paper presented to the Association for Education in Journalism and Mass Communication (Boston, August 1991), and C. N. Olien, G. A. Donohue and P. J. Tichenor, "Media Mix and the Metro-Nonmetro Knowledge Gap: Information Deprivation in an Information Age?" paper presented to the Midwest Association for Public Opinion Research (Chicago, November 1990).

71. Olien, Tichenor and Donohue, "A Changing Media Environment in the U.S."

72. Benjamin M. Compaine, "The Expanding Base of Media Competition," *Journal of Communication*, 35(3):81-96 (1985), p. 95.

73. Nixon and Ward, "Trends in Newspaper Ownership," p. 9.

74. Rosse, "The Evolution of One Newspaper Cities," pp. 55-6.

75. No studies examining this issue could be located.

76. Morris Janowitz, *The Community Press in an Urban Setting*, 2nd ed. (Chicago: University of Chicago Press, 1967 [1952]). For a more recent review of the literature, see David Pearce Demers, "Does Personal Experience in a Community Increase or Decrease Newspaper Reading?" *Journalism Quarterly* (in press) and John R. Finnegan, Jr. and Kasisomayajula Viswanath, "Community Ties and Use of Cable TV and Newspapers in a Midwest Suburb," *Journalism Quarterly*, 65:456-63 (1988).

77. It might also be argued that advertisers, too, should be less attracted to those newspapers, since their products and services — in response to an increasingly diversified market — have become increasingly differentiated. In a highly pluralistic system, advertisers need more efficient and effective means of reaching specific target markets. But this should be treated as an empirical question, since many department stores and discount stores still need market saturation.

78. C. N. Olien, G. A. Donohue and P. J. Tichenor, "Media Competition and Community Structure," report to the American Newspaper Publishers Association (March 1981).

79. Nixon and Ward, "Trends in Newspaper Ownership," p. 9.

80. Nixon and Ward, "Trends in Newspaper Ownership," p. 9.

81. Compaine, Sterling, Guback and Noble, *Who Owns the Media?*

82. Ben H. Bagdikian, *The Information Machines* (New York: Harper & Row, 1971), p. 131.

83. Bagdikian, *The Information Machines*, pp. 120-21.

84. Gerald Stone, "A Mellow Appraisal of Media Monopoly Mania," pp. 44-60 in Michael C. Emery and Ted Curtis Smythe, *Mass Communication: Concepts and Issues in the Mass Media* (Dubuque, Iowa: Wm. C. Brown Company, 1980), p. 50.

85. Bagdikian, *The Media Monopoly*, pp. 12-16, and Compaine, Sterling, Guback and Noble, *Who Owns the Media?* pp. 46-57.

86. Adam Smith, *An Inquiry Into the Nature and Causes of the Wealth of Nations* (Chicago: William Benton, Encyclopedia Britannica, Inc., 1952 [1776]).

87. For a review of literature, see David Pearce Demers, "Corporate Structure and Emphasis on Profits and Product Quality at U.S. Daily Newspapers," *Journalism Quarterly*, 68:15-26 (1991).

88. Tharp and Stanley, "Trends in Profitability of Daily U.S. Newspapers."

89. Nixon and Ward, "Trends in Newspaper Ownership."

90. Yale Brozen, *Concentration, Mergers and Public Policy* (New York: Macmillan, 1982).

91. Rosse, "The Evolution of One Newspaper Cities," p. 56.

92. Compaine, "The Expanding Base of Media Competition."

93. Tichenor, Donohue and Olien, *Community Conflict and the Press.* Also see George A. Donohue, "Adaptation Isn't Enough: Rural Communities Need Mutation," *Sociology of Rural Life*, 11(1):1-2, 7 (1990).

Chapter 6

A Theory of
Corporate Newspaper Origins

The previous chapter showed that as a social system becomes more complex, the number and variety of mass media increase. Despite widespread awareness of this phenomena, few researchers have sought to explain this process.[1] Many are content to believe that complex social systems have more media simply because they have more social actors. While the sheer number of social actors does, indeed, set parameters on the development of media systems, numbers alone do not explain the growth of the mass media in general or the rise of the corporate form of organization in particular.

Drawing on social system theory, this chapter will develop and test a theory which holds that the growth of the corporate newspaper is largely a function of structural pluralism. There are two major reasons for this. The first is that the need for information increases as a social system becomes more complex, which in turn promotes growth of large-scale media.[2] Information and formalized communication processes are extremely crucial for coordinating and controlling social action in systems that are highly differentiated. The second reason structural pluralism promotes the growth of the corporate newspaper is competition. As social systems grow and become more complex, competition between mass media for limited resources (e.g., advertising and audiences) increases, which intensifies social and technological innovations that eliminate inefficient competitors and promote the growth of complex media organizations.

Many of the basic ideas comprising this theory of origins are not new, as the literature reviews in the previous chapters have shown. However, the theoretical model presented here is unique in that it represents the first attempt to integrate many of these ideas into one comprehensive model. The purpose of this chapter is to formally present this theory of origins and to empirically test it. But before doing that, some background assumptions are presented, and some key concepts are defined.

Science, Assumptions and Concepts

All theories, explanations or interpretations of the world or human action contain assumptions about the nature of reality (ontology) and how people come to know it (epistemology). Many social scientists do not explicitly identify these assumptions in their research because other colleagues in their field of study are familiar with them. The familiarity factor is less applicable to the field of mass communication research, however, for at least two reasons. First, the field is extremely diverse. It is populated with scholars trained in a number of social science disciplines (communication, sociology, political science, psychology, journalism) who employ a variety of research methods and theories, some of which are not widely known or understood.[3]   And second, the field of mass communication also contains a large number of researchers with professional backgrounds (e.g., journalism, public relations, advertising), many of whom have had little or no formal training in philosophy of science issues.

Space prohibits a detailed examination of all of the ontological and epistemological assumptions underlying this study. However, some of the key ones are briefly outlined below.

Assumptions

One of the most important assumptions underlying this study is that scientific explanation should involve both formal theory and empirical observation. As Tichenor puts it:

> Science is neither theory alone nor pure gathering of evidence in the absence of higher-order reasoning. Science requires both, pursued in an atmosphere of rigor in logic and measures that allows others to determine whether they,

using that combination of reasoning and procedure, would come to similar conclusions.[4]

The notion that science should involve both formal theory and empirical observation might seem obvious or trite to many social scientists. But a great deal of research on mass media actually lacks formal theory. In fact, Potter, Cooper and Dupagne surveyed major mass communication journals and found that only 13 percent of the "social scientific" studies published are theory-driven — most are data-driven (inductive and quantitative).[5] Much of the research on newspapers, if not most, also could be classified as data-heavy and theory-light.

The idea that explanation should focus exclusively or more heavily on empirical observation rather than on formal theory is a major tenet of logical positivism, which posits that the only valid knowledge is that derived by sensory experience.[6] Logical positivists reject formal deductive theoretical systems, preferring instead an inductive approach that seeks to understand or explain phenomena primarily through experience and the senses. The assumption logical positivists make is that reality and truth can be directly and accurately perceived by the senses, independent of any formal, deductive theoretical framework.

The inductive model of logical positivism has been largely discredited.[7] Scholars have demonstrated that theory-neutral observation is impossible. No explanation of phenomena can be built solely through inductive logic or tested solely on the basis of phenomenal evidence. Data are not self-explanatory. They need a logical system to be interpreted. Alexander argues, in fact, that theorizing at a general level, without reference to particular empirical problems, is a significant and crucial endeavor for the social sciences. He also argues that the social sciences will always be overdetermined by theory and underdetermined by fact.

> There is no clear indisputable reference for the elements that compose social science — definitions, concepts, models, or "facts." Because of this, there is not neat translatability between different levels of generality. Formulations at one level do not ramify in clear-cut ways for the other levels of scientific concern. For example, while precise empirical measurements of two variable correlations can sometimes be established, it is rarely possible for such a correlation to prove or disprove a proposition about this interrelationship that is stated in more general terms. The reason is that the existence of empirical and ideological dissensus allows social scientists to operationalize propositions in a variety of different ways.[8]

This dissensus, Alexander argues, means that facts are never directly interpretable. Truth claims involve reference to nonempirical phenomena, including reason and logic. As a consequence, scientific analysis involves not just explanation but also discourse. "Discourse seeks persuasion through argument rather than prediction. Its persuasiveness is based on such qualities as logical coherence, expansiveness of scope, interpretive insight, value relevance, rhetorical force, beauty, and texture of argument."[9]

While some scholars are critical of formal theoretical frameworks, others, especially in the humanities, take the opposite view, rejecting empiricism as a valid form of inquiry. They seek truth and knowledge not in sensory experience but in pure logic and reason, a moral system, an inspirational moment, or a spiritual essence. They believe that empiricists, especially quantitative ones, oversimplify the complexity of the social world and overestimate their ability to measure it. In fact, some critical and cultural scholars believe quantitative research methods are deterministic and contribute to hegemonic order. Human action does not conform to the kind of universal laws that one finds in the physical sciences, they argue. Humans are not robots. They have the ability to choose between alternative courses of action. They are not chained to any deterministic, mechanical forces of nature.

Few researchers, quantitative or otherwise, would dispute the argument that human behavior is very complex. But the anti-empiricist perspective, it is argued here, is often based on faulty assumptions about the nature of human behavior and social action. Quantitative research need not be grounded in a deterministic model of human action, nor is it opposed to free-will or human agency perspectives. The alternative is a probabilistic model, which holds that social actors have the power to make choices, but those choices are constrained or enabled by the physical, organic, psychological, social and cultural phenomena. At the social and cultural levels, for example, the probability of engaging in any particular behavior or action increases as the social sanctions increase. In other words, social actors are more likely to engage in certain kinds of behaviors if they are rewarded for it, while they avoid certain kinds of behaviors if they are punished. Thus, the goal of quantitative research is to develop probabilistic generalizations about populations based upon these constraints or enablements.

A probabilistic model also means that quantitative methods are not necessarily incompatible with qualitative and interpretive research methods. Qualitative methods focus more on idiosyncratic actions or mental processes of individual actors and, thus, can provide great depth and insight into a particular case. However, findings from such studies usually cannot be generalized to larger populations. Quantitative methods, on the other hand, enable researchers to make generalizations to populations of actors, at the price of an in-depth analysis or understanding. Thus, the two methods often complement each other.[10]

Although the goal of this book is to explain the origins and consequences of the corporate form of organization in the U.S. daily newspaper industry, it is important to point out that no theory or model can provide a full explanation of a phenomenon (i.e., explain all of the variance). The growth of any specific corporate newspaper is the product of a multitude of factors, including the idiosyncratic actions of many individual actors pursuing various goals, such as profits or social power. The theory to be developed in this chapter focuses on how the structure of a social system sets parameters or constraints on individual-level decisions and actions. This approach does not mean individuals are powerless. Rather, individual decisions and actions are viewed as being broadly shaped by the structure of a social system, and it is these processes which this study attempts to identify.

The perspective taken in this study, then, is post-positivist. It places a great deal of importance on formal theoretical frameworks in developing explanations of the world — in fact, theory generally takes precedence over data. But even though all theories will be composed of many more propositions than can be operationalized or tested, empirical observation is considered to be important for testing key elements of those theories. Alternative nonempirical approaches to understanding and knowing the world are not necessarily wrong or false, as logical positivists would contend. But they are not classified as nonscientific explanations. Thus, religious accounts of the creation of the world very well may be correct. However, the question of whether God created the world cannot be empirically tested — it must be taken as a matter of faith. As an explanation for the existence of the world, creationism is a philosophical doctrine, not a scientific theory. Evolutionism, in contrast, is classified as a scientific doctrine, since it contains a logical, abstract system of propositions (a theory) and has been supported by empirical observation in the field.

In this study the corporate form of organization also is assumed to be a social construction; that is, it has been created by social actors seeking to solve certain problems — it is not given in nature. The actors themselves may not always be aware of the consequences of their actions, but such actions do have consequences for social organization and its effects. The sources or origins of social constructions are shaped to a large extent by the social structure. Although the boundaries of newspaper organizations (corporate or noncorporate) are open and are in a continual process of construction, for analytical purposes the boundaries are temporarily closed.

Finally, it should be noted that nothing in the theory to be presented here is intended to imply that the corporate form of organization is desirable from a social policy perspective. The goal of this chapter is to explain the origins and growth of the corporate newspaper, not to pass judgment on its role and function in society. This does not mean the findings from this study are not useful from a public policy-making perspective. They are, but the author presents his views in Chapter 11.

Concepts

Definitions for some of the key concepts that encompass the theory to be developed here follow:

• A *social actor* is an individual or organization (e.g., newspaper) engaged in purposeful, goal-oriented action. Social actors are presumed to have needs and to pursue goals, and goal-oriented action is directed toward satisfying those needs. However, the causes and consequences of such action may not be recognized or intended by the actors themselves. Those needs and goals may have their origins in personality, biological or physical systems, but they are shaped to a large extent by the structure and culture of the social system. Needs for information and entertainment, in fact, emerge primarily from a social context.

• *Social structure* is defined as the enduring, patterned and orderly relationships between elements of a society, which includes the values, norms or laws that shape social action. Many social scientists exclude values, norms or laws from social structure, preferring instead to classify them as cultural phenomena. No distinction is made here, since social relationships themselves cannot exist in the absence of such phenomena.

• A *social system* is "a series of interrelated subsystems with primary functions including the generation, dissemination and assimilation of information to effect further control as a means to an end or as an end in itself."[11] A social system may be as small as two social actors (e.g., marriage) or as large as a nation-state. The unit of analysis here is primarily at the community and national level. Daily newspapers and other mass media are assumed to be institutions or subsystems that generate and disseminate information that contributes to maintenance of the national or local community, other subsystems within those units (e.g., legal, education, political), or the media subsystem itself. The theory presented in this chapter, however, is primarily concerned with explaining the evolution of the corporate newspaper, rather than its integrative or social control functions, which are addressed in Chapters 9 and 10.

 • *Structural pluralism* is the degree of differentiation along institutional and specialized interest group lines. In plain language, pluralism is the number and variety of groups in a society. As social systems become more industrialized and urbanized, pluralism increases. Furthermore, in communities that are more pluralistic, power generally is more diffused, and decision-making generally is more likely to involve open debate and compromise.

 • *Competition* is defined as a normatively regulated social process wherein two or more social actors (e.g., media) make a common attempt to achieve a goal that precludes full goal achievement by others. Competition may or may not be recognized or intended by the participants. Media that compete with each other also are functional substitutes for each other, but they need not be perfect substitutes. This book considers two types of competition: intramedia, or competition between units of the same medium (i.e., newspapers), and intermedia, competition between units of different mediums (e.g., newspapers versus television and radio).

 • A *corporate newspaper* is an organization that exhibits the characteristics of a complex bureaucracy — i.e., a complex hierarchy of authority, a highly developed division of labor and role specialization, formalized rules and procedures, employment and promotion based on technical qualifications, formalistic impersonality, and greater rationality in decision-making. A newspaper need not be legally incorporated to fit the definition espoused here, but newspapers that are incorporated typically are more complex than those that are organized as sole proprietorships or partnerships. Legal incorporation enables organizations to sell stock to raise capital, to limit the liability of the owners to the amount invested, and to continue to function as an entity even when individual managers or owners leave the organization or die — factors that contribute to the complexity of the organization. Chain ownership is one measure of organizational complexity and is defined as two or more newspapers located in separate communities under common ownership.

 • *Social change* is defined as the difference between current and antecedent conditions in the social structure.

A Theory of Corporate Newspaper Origins

To explain the growth of the corporate newspaper in the United States, it is necessary to view that phenomenon, first, as the product of a growing need for information that develops as a social system grows and becomes more structurally pluralistic, and, second, as the product of increasing competition in the marketplace.

Structural Pluralism and the Corporate Newspaper

All social systems need information and knowledge to survive and adapt to their environment. However, as social systems grow and become more complex, needs for information and communication also generally grow.

Social systems may grow through one of two processes: aggregation of previously unaggregated units (migration, conquest, unification) or internal growth (procreation). In either case, if a social system grows, competition for material and social resources normally increases. Two exceptions are when social actors pursue different goals and resources or when resources are in unlimited supply. In these cases the social system may continue to grow with minimal conflict between social units. But in most situations such resources are not unlimited, and the resulting competition between social actors for those resources often threatens the stability of the system.[12]

The division of labor is one possible solution to the increased competition and conflict, because it enables a social system or organization to exploit resources more efficiently. The division of labor increases human production through three major means. First, specialization increases dexterity, which reduces the time required to perform a task. Second, the division of labor saves time that normally would be lost in passing from one job to another. And third, when production is separated into simpler tasks, machines or robots can be constructed that enable a small number of people to do the work of many. The division of labor also can create interdependencies that contribute to social solidarity. But the route to the division of labor is not automatic or necessary. If elites or those in power fail to perceive these changes, the system may disintegrate as resources are exhausted. Other possible outcomes or solutions to increased competition are emigration, colonization, civil war or genocide. The emergence of the division of labor is not a necessary condition of increased competition but is itself contingent upon several other structural factors.

The first, and most important, is the strength of traditional rules and values that prohibit the emergence of social and technological innovations. Where traditional ways hold strong sway over the actions of individuals, alternative methods of achieving goals will not be easy to institute. For example, where law or custom determines and limits the occupation of people, the division of labor cannot develop. Relaxation of traditional rules and values is most likely in systems where elites stand to benefit from the changes or where their power is least likely to be threatened.

A second major factor influencing the growth and development of the division of labor is a money economy. This gives permanence and predictability in social organization and enables the creation of a wage system. A third factor is mass education. Education trains social actors for highly specialized roles and socializes people into dominant value systems, such as the pursuit of profits. A fourth factor is capitalism, which brings rational estimation of economic risks and, more importantly, institutionalizes innovation. Capitalism is not a necessary condition for the development of the corporate form of organization, as developments in Marxist countries have shown. But competition under capitalism intensifies the development of the corporate form of organization because capitalism stimulates social and technological innovation.

The division of labor enables social systems to exploit their resources more effectively and efficiently, but it also creates other problems that threaten system stability and integration. Specifically, the actions of the now differentiated parts must be coordinated and controlled in order for the parts and the system as a whole to achieve their goals as well as to maintain the system itself. To coordinate and control the parts, decision-making often must be centralized and formalized, and more efficient means of communication must be developed. Why? Because interpersonal communication alone is inadequate for maintaining complex relationships.

Nearly all of the activities crucial for maintaining a small, homogeneous system can be accomplished through interpersonal communication.[13] Most social and economic activities take place within a few basic types of organization, particularly the extended family and the community. Such organizations are multipurpose — they serve a number of different functions for the social system. The social division of labor is limited. Group solidarity and homogeneity in shared sentiments and values are high.

Competition between social actors for scarce resources (economic, social and political) and social conflict are limited.

However, as a social system grows and becomes more differentiated, interpersonal communication as the sole basis for social organization becomes inadequate. The primary reason is that it is inefficient. In large organizations, it is impossible for even one individual to communicate personally with all others on a regular basis. More generally, as the number of social actors in a system or organization increases, the amount of interpersonal contact between any single social actor and all of the others declines. But even if interpersonal communication on a grand scale were possible, it could not, by itself, deal with the problems of coordination and control that accompany increases in the division of labor and role specialization. For the division of labor to expand, various tasks, functions and jobs often must be routinized, formalized and standardized, and to accomplish these tasks efficiently, organizations and social systems develop formal, secondary sources of information and communication.

The types of secondary sources and media employed depend in part on the level of analysis. Within organizations, such sources include, but are not limited to, the development of formalized goals and policy statements, written rules and procedures, job descriptions, interdepartment memos and letters, bulletin boards, newsletters and e-mail.[14] Within industry segments, specialized media, such as magazines and newsletters, emerge to help organizations cope with management problems and changes in the industry. And within communities or social systems as a whole, mass media, including newspapers, television and radio, provide information about system-wide problems and issues that cut across organizational boundaries and subsystems. Such media are also important vehicles for connecting consumers to producers via advertising. Although the types of media and content may vary considerably within and between levels, in all cases they perform at least one similar function: They link social actors to one another, reducing social distance and enabling them to accomplish their goals more effectively and efficiently.

A hypothetical example of a small marketing-research company will help to illustrate this process. One of the major goals of this organization — though certainly not the only one — is to produce a product (market research) for clients in a way that earns the company a profit. To accomplish this goal, a number of needs must be met.

First, the organization will need to recruit interviewers. The recruiting could be done by sending an employee to a street corner to ask people walking by if they would like a job. But this approach is not very efficient. Only a small fraction of the passersby would qualify for or be interested in an interviewing job. The research company could not continue to function efficiently if it had to depend solely on interpersonal communication for recruiting. So, instead, the organization depends heavily on classified advertising in the local newspaper, which is an extremely cost-effective method of recruiting.[15]

A second major need the organization has is to keep up with changing technology. More efficient and less expensive methods of conducting surveys, such as computer-assisted interviewing, are constantly being devised and marketed. An organization that fails to keep up with such innovations may find itself at a competitive disadvantage. One way to fulfill this need is to establish personal contacts with universities and private business organizations on a regular basis to learn about the latest in new technology. However, this approach would be extremely inefficient — few organizations could afford to monitor their environment this thoroughly. So, instead, the organization typically subscribes to a number of magazines and newsletters (e.g., *Marketing News, Advertising Age*) that specialize in providing information that meets the research firm's needs.

A third need the market research company has is to keep up with changes in the government regulations, tax laws and the economy. Increased government regulations, higher taxes, or a failing economy may have serious ramifications for the bottom line. If the organization is going to lessen the impact of any change and adapt, it must monitor general political and economic news. To get this news, the organization could contact city hall, the chamber of commerce and other organizations directly. Again, though, this would not be very efficient, not to mention the fact that the organizations called likely would be unable to employ enough people to assist all of the calls they would get from businesses. Instead, the market research company's executives turn to newspapers (e.g., *Wall Street Journal*), magazines (e.g., *Business Week*) and television programs (e.g., CNN, CNBC), which provide news and information that help to meet such needs.

This example touches on only a fraction of the needs for information that a modern organization has. But it illustrates how many organizations in pluralistic systems depend upon the mass media to accomplish their goals.

Historically, the emergence of the modern newspaper and the growth of the corporate form of organization are directly related to the growing demands for information brought on by urbanization and industrialization. The pioneer farm typically produced most of the goods and services (e.g., food, clothing) it needed for everyday life — it was a relatively autonomous social unit. Urban residents, in contrast, depend heavily upon other individuals and organizations for food, clothing, shelter, and for public services, such as water and police protection. To monitor their environment, urban residents rely more heavily on newspapers and other mass media.

Urbanization and industrialization also mean that large numbers of people must cooperate to achieve common goals. Urbanization, for example, requires collective cooperation to deal with a broad number of social problems, including crime, poverty, waste disposal, public health, pollution and land control. Political elites — who have most of the power for dealing with such problems — depend heavily upon the mass media for information to help them make policy decisions. They also depend upon news reports to help generate support from other elites and the public for the decisions they make. Media coverage helps to legitimize such actions, while at the same time conveying the notion that the citizenry in general plays a major role in the decision-making process.

Industrialization also requires that people work together, but now the purpose is to produce products and services for sale in a market that ultimately earns a profit for the business firms. Manufacturers need access to large, heterogeneous markets, and one efficient method for reaching such markets is through advertising. The dramatic growth of the newspaper in the 19th century is directly related to the growth of advertising in the private sector, with the penny press emerging in the 1830s as the first mass media to offer access to mass markets. News about markets, politics and natural disasters also is crucial for running a profitable business. Business managers must constantly monitor their economic and political environments to adapt to changing conditions and to lobby for change when necessary.

The increasing need for information is one of the most important factors which explains why increasing pluralism promotes the growth of the corporate newspaper. But there are others, including:

• *Concentration of ownership in the system as a whole.* The growth of retail chain stores has meant increased demand for advertising in large-scale media that penetrates across communities and geo-political boundaries. In other words, a corporate organization with a number of chain stores in a large metropolitan area prefers to advertise in one, large-circulation newspaper, rather than in many small, community based newspapers, since it is normally more cost efficient, and this preference promotes the development of large-scale, complex newspaper organizations.

• *Changes in tax laws.* Concentration of economic power in the 19th century contributed to a shift in political power from the individual entrepreneur to the industrial capitalist, who then used that power to promote changes in the tax laws which benefit large-scale organizations. The U.S. tax law that allowed newspapers to reinvest undistributed earnings of more than $100,000 tax free is one example of this.

• *Development of the "objective" news reporting model.* This change, which broadened the base of readership for newspapers, occurred most quickly in large, pluralistic systems, where a large diversity of interests exists. As a professional ideology, objective reporting helps maintain the attention of large, heterogenous audiences and, as such, contributes to organizational growth.[16]

• *Historical factors.* The development of roads, postal services, literacy, technology (i.e., the invention of the printing press) and increased tolerance from government also contributed to the establishment and growth of the newspaper. However, urbanization and industrialization are the two most important factors that have contributed to the growth of the corporate newspaper, because they increased needs for information.

• *Competition from other media.* This factor is addressed in more depth below.

In sum, the following hypothesis may be derived from the preceding:

H1: *The greater the structural pluralism, the greater the likelihood a newspaper will exhibit the characteristics of the corporate form of organization.*

Structural Pluralism and Media Competition

The discussion above implies that as the need for information in a social system increases, the number and variety of mass media also increase. This proposition gets a great deal of support when looking at media systems as a whole. The total number and variety of media have grown dramatically in the United States since the 19th century.[17]

Daily newspapers have faced increased competition not only from other dailies but from the introduction of other media forms as well. This includes, in rough order of appearance, national magazines, motion pictures, radio, over the air television, suburban newspapers and cable television. The appearance of these media and the increased competition they bring to the marketplace did not occur by happenstance. They, too, are a product of increasing pluralism, and for the same reason that newspapers grew during the 19th century — the increasing need for information.

The rise of suburban daily and weekly newspapers, for example, is directly related to the growth of suburban communities around major metropolitan areas. Such communities, although highly dependent on the core city for jobs and services, have unique social and political problems and have their own governmental units for dealing with such problems. This, along with the development of retail businesses to service such areas, contributed to the emergence and growth of the community newspaper.

Although pluralism has contributed to the growth of the suburban daily and weekly newspapers, this does not mean that such newspapers will displace the large metropolitan daily, as some economists have argued. This will depend in part on the extent to which political power is centralized in a social system. Suburban newspapers depend on local autonomy and community identity for survival. However, increasing centralization of decision-making in the political system can undermine local community identity. Since the degree to which individuals are integrated into a community is a strong predictor of newspaper readership, a loss of community identity should be translated into lower readership of the local paper. Thus, if concentration of ownership in the retail industry and centralization of power in the political system continues, as would be expected as a system becomes more pluralistic, metropolitan dailies will gain a competitive edge.

Like suburban newspapers, radio and television first emerged in pluralistic communities and grew in numbers as those areas expanded. The relatively low cost of setting up and operating a radio station also later led to its expansion in small communities and rural areas. However, the number and variety of media continues to be much greater in larger communities. Although initially cable television was extended to some remote areas difficult to reach by over-the-air signals, the diffusion of cable television throughout the 1970s and 1980s occurred much more rapidly in the pluralistic metropolitan communities because it was much more cost efficient and profitable there. In short:

H2: *The greater the structural pluralism, the greater the media competition.*

Media Competition and the Corporate Newspaper

Although the total number of formalized media in a system increases as the level of pluralism increases, not all forms of media grow or will continue to grow and expand as a social system becomes more differentiated. The telegraph, for example, is no longer a competitive medium, having been replaced by more sophisticated electronic media. The future of the video stores also is in doubt, with expectations that movie watchers will be able to select movies electronically through their televisions or telephone lines. More germane to the topic of this book, the total number of daily newspapers and household newspaper penetration has declined during the 20th century. These changes in the newspaper industry, at first glance, seem paradoxical. If the need for information is supposed to increase as a system becomes more pluralistic, why has the daily newspaper — an important source of information — been in decline?

The answer, as Marx pointed out (see Chapter 4), is competition and innovation. Competition from other newspapers and broadcast media stimulates innovation in material and social technology, which has had a profound impact upon the growth and development of the newspaper. More generally, in a market economy, competition drives capitalists to innovate, which in turn increases productivity. Social and technological innovation lowers the per unit cost of production and increases profits — at least until other competitors adopt the innovation. When that happens, the supply of the product increases, prices fall, and profits decline. The price remains relatively stable until another innovation comes along, and then the cycle starts over again.

The major consequences of innovation are concentration of capital and organizational growth. Capitalists must continually reinvest profits in order to remain competitive and, as a consequence, their organizations increase in size. As long as resources crucial for sustaining organizations remain abundant, a number of new organizations may enter the market, and all can grow. However, if resources decline or are limited, over time the number of media outlets will decline as a consequence of the innovative process. This occurs primarily because larger, more successful companies purchase the assets of weaker, less competitive and less innovative firms. Economies of scale help to drive this process; that is, larger organizations are able to reduce costs and produce higher profit margins.

The newspaper industry is particularly responsive to economies of scale in production. The cost of printing each copy normally declines as circulation increases. This explains why the number of cities with two or more dailies decreased so dramatically during the 20th century. During the 19th century, the number of dailies continued to increase in many cities because resources — i.e., number of readers and advertising dollars — were abundant. But the increased competition helped to promote further innovations in technology that enabled larger newspapers to lower advertising rates and win the battle for advertisers.

Historically, intracity daily newspaper competition explains the decline of daily competition within cities. Economies of scale have driven inefficient competitors out of business. However, intracity daily competition fails to explain the decline in newspaper penetration since the late 1940s, since most dailies have faced no competition from another daily newspaper. Instead, the argument put forth here is that *inter*media competition — that is, competition from radio, television, suburban newspapers and other media forms — is responsible in part for the decline in daily newspaper penetration.

To be sure, broadcast media are not perfect substitutes or functional alternatives for daily newspapers. Each has carved out a niche. The newspaper is primarily a source of news and information; the television is primarily a theatrical entertainment medium; and radio is primarily a music entertainment medium. Historically, the introduction of a new medium initially is often perceived as a threat by the existing media. But the threat posed by radio to newspapers dissipated rather quickly when both media came to the realization that they could coexist and survive. Part of the reason for this is that advertising revenues in the late 1930s were growing for both media. When television came on the scene in the late 1940s, radio advertising leveled off and then declined until 1959, when revenues began increasing again. During this time radio made a number of format changes (e.g., from comedy/drama to music format) that enabled the medium to carve out a new niche, or unique market position. And during the 1960s, 1970s and 1980s, all three media generally experienced increases in total advertising dollars. Resources in the system were expanding, enabling each to coexist comfortably.[18]

Yet, despite the distinctive market positions of newspaper, radio and television, all these media can, at various times, be substituted for each other. All three carry news reports about politics and the economy. All three offer entertainment programming or content. And all three can reach large, heterogeneous audiences, which is attractive to many advertisers.[19] In short, although the level of competition between newspapers and broadcast media is limited, this nonetheless explains in part why household penetration of metropolitan dailies has declined and why the newspaper, to survive in an increasingly competitive environment, continues to become more complex.

A key assumption under this argument is that the marketplace must be free of outside, especially governmental, interference. To the extent that anti-trust legislation is enforced or the government puts a cap on the number of media that any one company or individual can legally own, trends toward concentration of ownership will be contained. For example, despite widespread beliefs to the contrary, increasing chain ownership is a characteristic largely limited to the newspaper industry. The levels of centralization in radio, television and cable television have not changed significantly during the last 30 years, primarily because of government regulations on ownership. On the other hand, it is very interesting to note that between 1947 and 1977 the magazine publishing industry actually became less centralized, apparently because of increasing product differentiation and target marketing.[20] In sum:

H3: The greater the competition from non-newspaper media, the greater the likelihood a newspaper will exhibit the characteristics of a corporate organization.

Effects of Corporate Organization

The need for information and competition are two of the major factors that explain why, as a system becomes more pluralistic, newspapers increasingly develop the characteristics of the corporate form of organization. But it is important to mention that the relationship also is reciprocal: As newspapers grow and become more complex, they can generate or increase needs for information and they become more competitive. The corporate organization is especially suited to meet the needs of social actors in a highly complex system, and it is structurally designed to maximize profits, which enables it to adapt more readily to changing conditions. In short, the relationship between organizational structure and organizational outcomes should be seen as a process, not a static. The focus in this chapter, however, is on the origins of corporate structure. Effects or consequences are addressed in depth in Chapters 8 through 10.

Implications of the Model

As noted earlier, it is important to point out that nothing in the theory presented in this chapter is intended to imply that the corporate form of organization is desirable from a social policy perspective. The fact that formal sources of communication, such as newspapers, help social actors achieve their goals does not mean those goals are appropriate. In a capitalistic economic system, a major goal is to make profits, which may or may not have negative consequences for various groups and individuals. The normative question of whether the corporate newspaper has negative consequences for society will be examined in Chapter 11.

Summary

A theory that attempts to explain the origins and growth of the corporate newspaper was presented in this chapter. The theory posits that the rise of the corporate form of organization in the U.S. daily newspaper industry is primarily an outgrowth of structural pluralism. Two major reasons were given for this relationship. The first was that the need for information increases as a social system becomes more complex, which in turn promotes the growth of large-scale media. Information is extremely crucial for coordinating and controlling social action in systems that are highly diversified. The second reason structural pluralism promotes the growth of the corporate newspaper revolves around the effect of competition. As social systems grow and become more complex, competition between mass media for limited resources (e.g., advertising and audiences) increases, which intensifies social and technological innovations that eliminate competitors and promote the growth of large-scale media organizations.

Notes

1. One exception has been the research program of Phillip J. Tichenor, George A. Donohue and Clarice N. Olien at the University of Minnesota. See, e.g., *Community Conflict and the Press* (Beverly Hills, Calif.: Sage, 1980).

2. This relationship should be seen as a reciprocal or nonrecursive process, in which organizational complexity generates needs for information, which in turn increases the probability that social actors will create formalized media to satisfy those needs, which in turn enables the organization to increase its complexity, etc.

3. Everett M. Rogers and Steven H. Chaffee, "Communication and Journalism from 'Daddy' Bleyer to Wilbur Schramm," *Journalism Monographs*, vol. 148 (December 1994).

4. Phillip J. Tichenor, "The Logic of Social and Behavioral Science," pp. 10-28 in Guido H. Stempel III and Bruce H. Westley (eds.), *Research Methods in Mass Communication* (Englewood Cliffs, N.J.: Prentice-Hall, 1981).

5. W. James Potter, Roger Cooper and Michel Dupagne,"The Three Paradigms of Mass Media Research in Mainstream Communication Journals," *Communication Theory*, 3:317-35 (1993).

6. For an excellent introductory discussion of positivism and science, see Loïc J. D. Wacquant, "Positivism," pp. 495-8 in William Outhwaite and Tom Bottomore (eds.), *The Blackwell Dictionary of Twentieth-Century Social Thought* (Oxford, England: Blackwell, 1994).

7. See, e.g., Thomas Kuhn, *The Structure of Scientific Revolutions* (Chicago: University of Chicago Press, 1962) and Imre Lakatos, "Falsification and the Methodology of Research Programmes," pp. 91-196 in Imre Lakatos and A. Musgrave (eds.), *Criticism and the Growth of Knowledge* (Cambridge, England: Cambridge University Press, 1970).

8. Jeffrey C. Alexander, "The New Theoretical Movement," pp. 77-101 in Neil J. Smelser (ed.), *Handbook of Sociology* (Newbury Park, Calif.: Sage, 1988), p. 81.

9. Alexander, "The New Theoretical Movement," p. 80.

10. A more general distinction that social scientists often draw is that between ideographic and nomothetic methods of research. The former involves investigation of individual or unique experiences, while the latter is concerned with generalities. Although qualitative research often fits the ideographic model and quantitative fits the nomothetic, this is not necessarily the case. For example, a researcher could use quantitative methods (e.g., aggregated responses in a public opinion poll over time) to describe the ideosyncratic actions of a nation without drawing generalizations to other nations.

11. G. A. Donohue, P. J. Tichenor and C. N. Olien, "Mass Media Functions, Knowledge and Social Control," *Journalism Quarterly*, 50:652-59 (Winter 1973), p. 652.

12. Competition between social actors may also increase when resources decline, but growth of the social system is a necessary condition for continued expansion in the division of labor.

13. This principle may also be extended to small groups or organizations, such as the family or a local club, in complex systems. But in complex systems, many small groups (e.g., academic departments) also publish a newsletter to keep their members informed.

14. This does not mean that secondary sources of communication always accomplish the goals, only that for the system or organization to be maintained, the net balance must be such that they resolve the problems.

15. As a rule of thumb, the amount of interpersonal communication also increases as a system or organization becomes more pluralistic. The "meeting" has become an institutionalized method of decision-making in large organizations.

16. The "objective" reporting model also appears to be functional for system maintenance, in that news about social issues is distributed to large, heterogeneous audiences, rather than highly segmented, specialized groups, as is the case with media pursuing specific political goals.

17. For more detailed information, see Chapter 2.

18. These trends are documented in Robert J. Coen, "Estimated Annual U.S. Advertising Expenditures, 1935-1987," unpublished report (New York: McCann-Erickson, Inc., 1987).

19. Newspapers and television are more effective than radio at reaching large, heterogeneous markets. In metropolitan areas, radio often targets specialized audiences with different music and news formats.

20. See Benjamin M. Compaine, Christopher H. Sterling, Thomas Guback and J. Kendrick Noble, Jr., *Who Owns the Media? Concentration of Ownership in the Mass Communications Industry* (White Plains, N.Y.: Knowledge Industry, 1982).

Chapter 7

Testing a Theory of
Corporate Newspaper Origins

The theory presented in the previous chapter is a theory of social change — newspapers are said to acquire the characteristics of the corporate form of organization as a social system (e.g., community or nation) becomes more structurally complex. The ideal dataset for testing such a theory would consist of multiple indicators of corporate newspaper structure, competition and structural pluralism, measured yearly over the last 150 years or so. Unfortunately, such data do not exist. Even measures of role specialization in news organizations do not exist at the national level.[1] The amount of advertising dollars spent on alternative media, one possible measure of competition, also was not systematically generated or collected until the 1930s.

Nevertheless, using governmental and private sources, including U.S. Bureau of Census reports and *Editor & Publisher International Yearbook*, it is possible to develop datasets with reasonably good measures. More specifically, this analysis employs one cross-sectional dataset and two longitudinal datasets covering time periods between 1900 and 1993. Traditional correlation and regression analyses will be used to test the hypotheses in the cross-sectional dataset. Time-series regression analysis will be used to test the data in the longitudinal datasets. Because this technique is somewhat complex and not widely used in mass communication research, this chapter also will include a brief discussion of it.

Datasets

Two of the three datasets used in this study were created using secondary data sources. One is called the Decennial Dataset because the observations were collected at 10-year intervals. The other is referred to as the Yearly Dataset. In both of these datasets, the United States is the population to which generalizations are being made. The third dataset contains primary data collected through a national probability survey of newspapers in the United States during 1993. The population consists of daily newspapers.

Dataset #1 — Decennial Dataset, 1900-1990

This dataset contains 10 observations, one for each decennial year from 1900 to 1990. Over this time period, data for only two of the three major key concepts — structural pluralism and corporate structure — are available. As noted above, before the 1930s, data on the amount of advertising spent on media or the number of alternative media (magazines, movies, radio) — two possible measures of competition — were not collected or are not readily available through standard governmental sources. Thus, only the first hypothesis, which posited a relationship between structural pluralism and corporate newspaper structure, will be tested with this dataset.

Two measures of corporate newspaper structure are employed. The first is the percentage of newspapers owned by chains or groups in each decennial year. A chain or group is defined as two or more daily newspapers in different cities under the same principal ownership or control.[2] This measure is frequently used in studies of newspaper organization.[3] The data values and sources used to generate this data are presented in Table 2.1 in Chapter 2. Descriptive statistics are shown in Table 7.1.

The second measure of corporate newspaper structure is mean daily newspaper circulation. Previous studies show that circulation is a powerful indicator of organizational size, which in turn is a strong indicator of organizational complexity (i.e., division of labor). For example, using log transformed variables, Polich found a zero-order correlation of .97 between circulation and number of editorial employees.[4] Bergen and Weaver found a correlation of .90.[5] For the Decennial Dataset, newspaper circulation was calculated by dividing the total circulation by the total number of daily

Table 7.1
Descriptive Statistics
- Decennial Dataset (1910-1990) -

Corporate Structure Variables	Mean	Std Dev	Minimum	Maximum	N
1. Overall Corporate Index (a+b)†	.00	1.00	-1.45	1.50	10
a. Proportion owned by chains	.29	.26	.01	.75	10
b. Mean circulation	44,750	17,753	15,102	62,649	10
Structural Pluralism Measures					
1. Pluralism Index (a+b+c+d)†	.00	1.00	-1.40	1.71	10
a. Total resident population (000)	154,229	58,743	76,094	248,709	10
b. Number of urban areas with					
100,000+ population	109	51	38	189	10
c. Number of people employed (000)	62,334	28,570	29,073	117,914	10
d. Number of businesses (000)	2,273	646	1,174	3,366	10

†Items composing index were standardized before creating index.

newspapers. This information was obtained from U.S. Bureau of Census reports.[6]

The zero-order correlation between percent of newspapers and mean newspaper circulation in this longitudinal dataset was .83 (p<.01).[7] The two items were standardized and summed to create a single corporate newspaper measure (see Table 7.1).

Four measures of structural pluralism are employed: (1) total resident population, (2) number of urban areas with 100,000 or more people, (3) number of people employed, and (4) number of businesses. Previous research shows that population size is a strong predictor of social heterogeneity.[8] Data for the first three measures were obtained from Bureau of Census records.[9] Data for the last measure was derived from the *Dun & Bradstreet Reference Book*.[10] Zero-order correlations between the pluralism measures ranged from .78 to .94.[11] The four items were standardized and summed to create a single structural pluralism measure (see Table 7.1).

Dataset #2 — Yearly Dataset, 1955-1986

Unlike the Decennial Dataset, the Yearly Dataset includes a measure of competition and covers the period 1955 to 1986, which yields a total 32 observations. The data were restricted to the years 1955 and after because information on the number of newspapers owned by chains as reported in

Editor & Publisher International Yearbook may be less reliable for some previous years.[12] All three hypotheses are tested with the Yearly Dataset.

Like the Decennial Dataset, two measures of corporate newspaper structure are employed. The first is the percentage of newspapers owned by chains or groups as reported in *Editor & Publisher International Yearbook*. The second measure of corporate newspaper structure is mean daily newspaper circulation, calculated by dividing the total circulation by the total number of daily newspapers. Again, this information was obtained from U.S. Bureau of Census reports and *Editor & Publisher*. The zero-order correlation between percent of newspapers and mean newspaper circulation is .55 ($p<.01$).[13] The two items were standardized and summed to create a single corporate newspaper measure (see Table 7.2).

Three indicators of structural pluralism are used: (1) total resident population, (2) number of workers employed in non-agricultural jobs, and (3) number of women employed in the workforce. Yearly data on urbanization is not collected by the U.S. government. But the number of women employed in the workforce is a good indicator of pluralism because as women enter the workforce, they take on new roles and new social affiliations (i.e., union membership, professional affiliations) that increase the complexity of a social system. Where women are restricted to traditional roles, such as mother and housewife, pluralism is typically very low. Data for all three measures were obtained from Bureau of Census records. Zero-order correlations between the pluralism measures ranged from .92 to .99, even after removing the effects of autocorrelation.[14] The three items were standardized and summed to create a single structural pluralism measure (see Table 7.2).

Six measures of competition were employed: (1) total number of television stations; (2) total number of AM and FM radio stations; (3) percent of total estimated national advertising revenues spent on television; (4) percent of total estimated local advertising revenues spent on television; (5) percent of total estimated national advertising revenues spent on radio; and (6) percent of total estimated local advertising revenues spent on radio. The first two indicators were obtained from *The Broadcasting Yearbook*.[15] The third through sixth measures were compiled by McCann-Erickson Advertising[16] and included both network and cable television revenues combined. Similar measures of competition have been used in other studies.[17]

An overall broadcast media competition index also was created from the six individual measures. Factor analysis showed that all six loaded on

Table 7.2
Descriptive Statistics
- Yearly Dataset (1955-1986) -

Corporate Structure Variables	Mean	Std Dev	Minimum	Maximum	N
1. Overall Corporate Index (a+b)†	.00	1.00	-1.40	1.71	32
a. Proportion owned by chains	.50	.14	.27	.71	32
b. Mean circulation	34,816	1,340	31,901	37,809	32
Structural Pluralism Measures					
1. Pluralism Index (a+b+c)†	.00	1.00	-1.49	1.75	32
a. Total resident population (000)	205,399	22,201	166,000	242,000	32
b. Number of workers employed in non-agricultural jobs (000)	77,888	15,813	55,722	106,434	32
c. Number of women employed (000)	31,492	9,200	19,550	48,706	32
Broadcast Competition Measures					
1. Broadcast Competition Index† (a+b+c+d+e+f)	.00	1.00	-1.66	1.42	32
a. Number of TV stations	802	238	439	1,236	32
b. Number of AM/FM radio stations	6,622	2,140	3,221	9,973	32
c. Proportion of total local advertising revenues spent on TV	.09	.03	.06	.15	32
d. Proportion of total national advertising revenues spent on TV	.24	.04	.15	.29	32
e. Proportion of total local advertising revenues spent on radio	.10	.01	.09	.12	32
f. Proportion of total national advertising revenues spent on radio[a]	.04	.003	.03	.04	32

†Items composing index were standardized before creating index.
[a]This item was reversed before creating competition index.

one factor, which explained 91 percent of the variance. One item — national radio advertising — loaded negatively. An examination of the scatterplot revealed, in fact, that national radio advertising declined from 1955 to 1986, going from 4.05 percent to 3.05 percent. This finding supports Dimmick and Rothenbuhler's study, which found that since the 1950s radio has reduced its dependence on national advertising and increased its dependence on local advertising. They attributed this change to competition from television.[18] Before creating the broadcast competition index for this study, the scale on the national radio advertising measure was reversed (see Table 7.2).[19]

Dataset #3 — Cross-Sectional Dataset, 1993

A two-page, 66-item questionnaire was mailed in September 1993 to the highest-ranking manager (e.g., publisher, general manager), the highest-ranking editor and a police reporter at 250 daily newspapers randomly selected from the *1993 Editor & Publisher International Yearbook*. The mailings to the highest ranking manager and top editor were personally addressed; the mailing to the reporters was simply addressed "police reporter" because no list of names exists. Police reporters were included in the sample to obtain a sampling of positions in the lower levels of the organization's hierarchy. They, rather than another reporting position, were selected because virtually every daily general circulation newspaper has a police reporter or someone who performs that function.[20]

Two follow-up mailings were conducted.[21] Of the 750 questionnaires mailed, responses were obtained from 409 journalists, for a total response rate of 55 percent. No significant differences in response rates emerged for the three groups (top manager, 52%; top editor, 56%, and police reporter, 55%).[22] There also was no significant correlation between the type of respondent (top manager, top editor, reporter) and newspaper circulation (r=.01).[23]

Although individuals responded to the questionnaire, it is important to point out that the newspaper — not the journalist — is the unit of analysis for this part of the study. To conduct such an analysis, the findings were aggregated for each newspaper that had more than one respondent. This meant that 223 of the 250 newspapers sampled, or 89 percent, were included in the analysis. For continuous measures (i.e., ordinal, interval and ratio level measures) and dichotomous nominal measures,[24] the final value used in the analysis represented the mean of the ratings given. In cases where the values for one of the respondents were missing (e.g., failure to answer a question), the values of the other respondent(s) were substituted. No nominal variables containing more than three values were included in this analysis.

Max Weber's conceptual framework was used as a guide to create measures of corporate structure. Respondents were asked to provide information on 14 individual measures. The first set of measures was designed to measure the division of labor, or organizational complexity. The most frequently used measure here is the number of workers or employees.[25] Three measures were employed:[26] number of full-time employees (mean=205); number of full-time reporters and editors (mean=40);[27] and number of beats or departments (mean=5.3).[28] Hierarchy of authority was operationalized as the number of promotions needed for a reporter to become top editor (mean=3.1).[29] Three indicators of the presence of rules and procedures were used: whether the newspaper has "its own formal, written code of ethics" (33%); whether the newspaper has "its own employee handbook of rules and procedures" (66%); and whether the newspaper has its own "style book (in addition to AP or UPI)" (51%). Staff expertise was measured by a question which asked whether "reporters normally need a bachelor's degree to be considered for employment at your newspaper" (73%). Rationality was operationalized as the amount of importance top management places on "finding the most efficient way to solve problems" (mean=4.78 on 7-point scale).[30] Five measures of ownership structure were included: whether the newspaper was owned by chain or group (67%);[31] whether public ownership was possible (31%);[32] whether their newspaper was a legally incorporated business (81%);[33] whether the newspaper was *not* controlled by one family or individual (28%);[34] and the number of daily newspapers in chain (mean=25).[35]

The 14 items were factor-analyzed using principal components, oblique rotation.[36] Oblique rotation was used because it was expected that corporate structure is a multidimensional concept whose dimensions are not orthogonal. In other words, it was not expected that the items for division of labor would load on the same factor as the items for rules and procedures; however, these two factors should be positively correlated to some extent. Many researchers also prefer oblique rotation to varimax, especially in exploratory analysis, because if all of the factors identified are orthogonal, the results of the oblique rotation will be very similar to a varimax rotation.[37] A factor loading of .60 was used as a rule of thumb for determining whether a measure should be included with a particular factor, and measures that had two or more loadings greater than .30 and less than .60 were considered problematic.

Using an eigenvalue of 1.00 as a minimum for defining a factor, the analysis initially produced a four-factor solution. However, this solution produced multiple factor loadings for several variables. A five-factor solution was then extracted, and this stabilized most of the loadings. The results are presented in Table 7.3. As expected, the division of labor items loaded heavily together, on the first factor, but the hierarchy of authority measure also loaded strongly there. Conceptually one may be able to distinguish between division of labor and hierarchy of authority, but operationally they could not be separated in this study.

Table 7.3
Corporate Newspaper Measures Factor-Analyzed[a]
- Cross-Sectional Dataset (1993) -

Corporate Measures	Factor Loadings					CE[b]
	F1	F2	F3	F4	F5	
1. Structural Complexity						
Number full-time reporters/editors	.98	.02	-.04	-.13	.02	.91
Number full-time employees	.93	-.01	-.08	-.11	.00	.81
Number beats or departments	.91	-.05	.03	.09	.01	.88
Number promotions needed for						
reporter to become top editor	.68	-.00	.15	.23	.04	.65
2. Ownership Structure						
Owned by chain or group	-.16	.78	.11	-.05	-.01	.63
Public ownership possible	.18	.78	-.01	.07	-.02	.67
Legally incorporated business	.00	.73	.15	-.27	-.02	.57
Not owned/controlled by one						
individual/family	.01	.65	-.07	.17	.39	.65
Number of newspapers in chain[c]	-.05	.56	-.39	.49	-.18	.75
3. Rules & Regulations						
Has employee handbook of rules	-.04	-.03	.88	.06	.05	.78
Has formal, written code of ethics	.06	.22	.73	.10	.00	.66
4. Hire College Graduates						
Reporters need bachelor's degree	-.03	-.16	.12	.78	.14	.66
Has own style book[c]	.21	.09	.24	.45	-.16	.43
5. Rational Decision-Making						
Importance placed on finding most						
efficient way to solve problems	.05	.04	.05	.02	.92	.87
EIGENVALUES	3.73	2.64	1.53	1.08	.95	9.93
PERCENT OF VARIANCE	26%	19%	11%	8%	7%	71%

[a]Principal components, oblique rotation (N=199).
[b]Communality Estimates (i.e., total variance explained)
[c]Measures excluded from indices because of low or mixed loadings.

For purposes here, the first factor was defined as "structural complexity." Newspapers that score higher are more complex. The ownership items loaded heavily on the second factor, with one exception — number of newspapers in chain — which also loaded moderately high on the third and fourth factors (rules and regulations and staff expertise, respectively). Because of these mixed loadings, this item was excluded from the ownership index. The third factor included two of the three rules and regulations measures: whether the newspaper has an employee handbook of rules and a formal, written code of ethics. The other measure, whether the newspaper has its own style book, loaded most highly on the fourth factor (staff expertise) and posted the lowest final communality estimate (i.e., had the lowest explained variance). As such, it also was excluded from subsequent analysis. The fifth factor consisted solely of the rationality measure.

In sum, the factor analysis produced five empirically distinct factors composed of 12 of the 14 original measures, which altogether explained 71 percent of the total variance in those variables. An overall corporate index variable was created after the values for the individual measures were standardized and summed (missing values reduced the total sample size for the index measure to 199; see Table 7.4).

Zero-order correlations among the five factors or dimensions are shown in Table 7.5. Structural complexity is correlated with every dimension except ownership structure. In fact, none of the four individual ownership indicators was even moderately correlated with the structural complexity index (data not shown). These findings are consistent with recent research which has found little or no correlation between circulation (a proxy measure for complexity) and chain ownership in cross-sectional studies.[38] This has not always been the case. Previous research has shown that chain ownership and circulation have been moderately correlated; that is, larger papers are more likely than smaller ones to be part of a chain.[39] However, chain ownership has become so diffused in the newspaper industry (about 80 percent are now owned by chains) that it no longer appears to be a sensitive measure of corporate complexity in cross-sectional studies.[40] This analysis will retain the ownership index because it is still correlated with the rules and rationality dimensions.

Table 7.5 shows that the dimension exhibiting the strongest intercorrelations is rules and procedures. All of the correlations between it and the other indices are greater than .20. This finding supports Mansfield's argument that rules may be at the heart of the bureaucratic structure — it is the one element in this data that links all of the other dimensions together.[41] Rationality is correlated with all of the dimensions except hiring college graduates for reporting positions, which in turn is correlated with structural complexity and rules but not ownership. Overall, then, ownership structure and hiring college graduates are the two weakest indicators of corporate structure.

Table 7.4
Descriptive Statistics
- Cross-Sectional Dataset (1993) -

Corporate Structure Variables	Mean	Std Dev	Minimum	Maximum	N
1. Overall Corporate Index (2+3+4+5+6)†	.00	1.00	-2.56	2.80	199
2. Structural Complexity Index†	.00	1.00	-1.20	4.58	218
a. Number of promotions reporter needs to become top editor	3.12	1.14	1	6.50	221
b. Number of beats employing full-time reporters	5.26	4.19	0	18	223
c. Number of full-time reporters/editors	39.73	66.64	3	500	221
d. Number of full-time employees	205.20	562.58	5	7,000	219
3. Ownership Structure Index†	.00	1.00	-1.65	1.56	207
a. Proportion that are incorporated businesses	.81	.34	.00	1.00	221
b. Proportion publicly owned	.31	.44	.00	1.00	219
c. Proportion in which one family/ individual does not own 50 percent interest in newspaper	.28	.42	.00	1.00	213
d. Proportion owned by chain/group	.67	.45	.00	1.00	223
4. Rules and Procedures Index†	.00	1.00	-1.34	1.38	221
a. Proportion that have their own formal, written code of ethics	.33	.41	.00	1.00	221
b. Proportion having own employee handbook of rules and procedures	.66	.44	.00	1.00	222
5. Rational Decision-Making (mean)	4.78	1.38	1	7	222
6. Proportion Requiring a College Degree for Reporters	.73	.40	.00	1.00	216

Structural Pluralism Measures	Mean	Std Dev	Minimum	Maximum	N
1. Index (2+3+4) (before rank-ordering)†	0	1.00	-.75	7.20	217
Index (2+3+4) (after rank-ordering)†	0	1.00	-1.72	1.72	217
2. County Measures†	.00	1.00	-.89	5.00	223
a. County population (000)	527	1483	8	9054	223
b. Proportion with bachelor's degree	.18	.07	.07	.50	223
c. Number of businesses	10607	31201	235	192689	223
3. City Measures†	.00	1.00	-.44	10.70	223
a. City population (000)	137	586	3	7312	223
b. Proportion with bachelor's degree	.09	.12	.08	.68	223
c. Number of businesses	2688	11263	666	132489	223
4. Self-Reported Community Size (000)	272	678	5	5500	217

Competition Measures	Mean	Std Dev	Minimum	Maximum	N
1. Number of TV and Radio Stations	4.90	7.11	0	41	223
2. Open Ad Rate per 1,000 Circulation ($)	96.73	59.88	27.79	510.49	216

†Items composing index were standardized before creating index.

Table 7.5
Zero-Order Correlations Between Corporate Measures
- Cross-Sectional Dataset (1993) -

Corporate Indices/Measures	1	2	3	4	5
1. Structural Complexity	1.00	.06	.26**	.11*	.18**
2. Ownership Structure	.06	1.00	.23**	.10*	.07
3. Rules & Procedures	.26**	.23**	1.00	.26**	.22**
4. Rational Decision Making	.11*	.10*	.26**	1.00	.05
5. Hire College Graduates	.18**	.07	.22**	.05	1.00

*p<.05; **p<.01

In the Cross-Sectional Dataset (see Table 7.4), structural pluralism was measured as an index composed of three dimensions: (1) county pluralism, (2) city pluralism, and (3) self-reported size of community the newspaper serves. The first two dimensions (county and city pluralism) were themselves composed of three measures: population of the county/city in which the newspaper is located, percent of population in the county/city with a four-year college degree, and number of businesses in the county/city.[42] These data were obtained from the *1994 County and City Data Book*.[43] Data on education and number of businesses were not available for cities under 25,000 population, so in these cases population was used as the sole indicator of city pluralism.[44]

For most newspapers in this study, county and city pluralism are relatively good measures of the complexity of the community the newspaper serves. However, in cases where the community the newspaper serves is not identical to the boundaries of the county or city, some measurement error is introduced. In particular, the error is likely to be greatest when a newspaper that serves a small city is located in a large, metropolitan county, or when a newspaper that serves a large metropolitan area is located in a relatively small city. In the former case, the county pluralism measure may overestimate the complexity of the community the newspaper serves, and in the latter case the city pluralism (and perhaps the county measure as well) may underestimate the complexity of the community. To help correct for these measurement problems, respondents in the survey were asked to estimate the "population of the community your newspaper serves," the third indicator in the structural pluralism index.

The zero-order correlation between the county and city pluralism measures is .56 (p<.001). City pluralism is somewhat more strongly correlated with the self-reported community size measure (.58, p<.001 compared with .43, p<.001, for the county pluralism measure). This suggests that city pluralism is a slightly better measure of complexity of the market a newspaper serves. The three pluralism indicators were standardized and summed to create a structural pluralism index, which was positively skewed (see Table 7.4). The skewness reflects a non-normal distribution in the population: The number of newspapers located in smaller communities is much larger than the number in large communities. Because skewness can affect the values of inferential statistics (i.e., increase the chances of making a Type I error), it was necessary to transform the variable. Log-transformations did not normalize the distribution, so the newspapers were rank-ordered (no two newspapers had the same rank), and the values were standardized (mean=0, SD=1).[45]

Two measures of intermedia competition were employed in the Cross-Sectional Dataset (see Table 7.4). The first is the number of radio and television stations located in the city in which the newspaper is located. The data were recorded from the 1993 edition of *The Working Press of the Nation: TV and Radio Directory* (Volume 3).[46] One possible shortcoming of this indicator is that it does not account for stations that broadcast into the newspaper market if they are not physically located in the newspaper's city — such data are available only for ADI markets, not smaller markets. On the other hand, the fact that a station broadcasts into a newspaper market does not necessarily mean it is competing for the same advertising dollars or audience. The assumption behind the measure used here is that the intensity of competition is much higher when a broadcast station is located in the same city as a newspaper. The mean number of broadcast stations was 4.9, with some markets having no stations and one (New York) having 41 (see Table 7.4).

The second measure of competition is the open advertising rate per 1,000 circulation. The expectation is that the advertising rate will decline as the number of broadcast stations increases (controlling for total newspaper circulation).[47] More specifically, the advertising rate variable should mediate the impact of the first competition measure (number of broadcast stations) on corporate structure (i.e., number of broadcast stations → open advertising rate per 1,000 circulation → corporate newspaper index). The open advertising rate and circulation data were obtained from the *1993 Editor & Publisher International Yearbook*. The advertising rate variable was calculated by dividing the open advertising rate by daily circulation and multiplying that figure by 1,000. The mean of the sample was about $97, with a range of $28 to $510 (see Table 7.4).

Analytical Approach

Regression and correlation analysis are used to test the hypotheses in the Cross-Sectional Dataset. Time-series regression analysis is used for the longitudinal datasets. This is a powerful tool for assessing relationships between variables. A brief discussion follows. For more detailed information, readers should consult the sources cited.

Time-Series Models. A simple time-series regression equation may be written as follows:

$$Y_t = a + bX_t + e_t$$

where Y_t is the endogenous variable, X_t is the exogenous variable, e_t is the random disturbance term, a and b are the unknown parameters, and the subscript t indicates that X_t and Y_t are a series of equally spaced observations through time. Six key assumptions underlie the use of a time-series regression model:

1. *Linearity:* the relationship between Y and X is linear,
2. *Nonstochastic X:* $E[e_t X_t]=0$, or X is uncorrelated with error term,
3. *Zero Mean:* $E[e_t]=0$, or the expected value of the error term is equal to 0,
4. *Homoskedasticity:* $E[e_t^2]=\sigma^2$, the variance of the error term is constant for all values of X_t,
5. *Normality:* the error term, e_t is normally distributed,
6. *Non-autocorrelation:* $E[e_t e_{t-m}]=0$ ($m \neq 0$), or the error terms are uncorrelated.

The first five assumptions are widely recognized and discussed in the literature on regression analysis.[48] The attention here will focus on the sixth assumption, since it often creates substantial problems in time-series analysis and is not normally a significant problem in cross-sectional analysis.

Autocorrelation is a condition that exists when the disturbance or error term in a regression equation is not independently distributed over time. Markus points out that autocorrelation is caused primarily by (a) the omission of relevant predictor variables and (b) measurement error.[49] Leaving out relevant predictor variables is particularly problematic when the lag between sets of observations is relatively short and when lagged values of the dependent variable are used.[50] Autocorrelation is analogous to spuriousness, in which the correlation between two variables, X and Y, is partly due to the effects of a third variable, Z. To estimate the effect of X on Y, Z must be controlled.

When there is no autocorrelation in a regression model, the error terms are randomly distributed around the mean with no discernable pattern. Negative autocorrelation produces a series that tends to alternate rapidly above and below the average, and positive autocorrelation produces a series that tends to drift above and below the mean for longer periods of time. Positive autocorrelation is typical in most time-series analyses that involve political and economic data, since changes over time tend to occur in trends (either up or down for two or more successive points in time). An example of a positive autocorrelation would be changes over time in public opinion toward capital punishment, which tends to go up or down gradually over time. An example of a negative autocorrelation would be government spending on road construction, which may be high one year and low the next.

Positive autocorrelation results in an underestimate of the variance of the disturbance term, which means that statistics based on the error variance, including R^2, F, and the t ratios for coefficients, become inflated. This increases the risk of Type I errors — that is, concluding that there is a relationship between two or more variables when in reality there is none. The opposite is true for negative autocorrelation, which increases the risk of Type II errors. Autocorrelation will yield unbiased estimates of the unstandardized regression coefficients (i.e., the slope), which means the expected value of the estimates is the true population parameter value; however, they will be inefficient, which means that they have a larger variance (i.e., standard error).[51]

In ordinary least squares regression, the presence of autocorrelation is indicated by the Durbin-Watson D statistic.[52] The value of this statistic ranges from 0 to 4, with 2 indicating no autocorrelation. Values less than 2 indicate the presence of positive autocorrelation, while those greater than 2 indicate the presence of negative autocorrelation. The value necessary to reject the hypothesis that autocorrelation is significantly different from zero varies depending upon the number of cases and number of independent variables. A Durbin-Watson table is available in most econometric textbooks.

In statistical analysis, there are a number of ways to control for autocorrelation. If no lagged values of the dependent variables are used as predictor variables,[53] Ostrom points out that generalized least squares regression is the preferred approach.[54] The simplest GLS approach is called first differences; that is, an observation at time 1 is subtracted from the observation at time 2, etc., creating new values for each of the dependent and independent variables. Regression analysis is then performed on the "differenced" variables. One serious shortcoming with first differences, however, is that this procedure works well only when the autocorrelation is positive and near perfect (i.e., a Durbin-Watson value of zero). In other cases, it can seriously underestimate the effects of an independent variable.[55] Since the amount of autocorrelation in most time-series rarely approaches zero, researchers usually use more-complex statistical procedures. The default procedure in SPSS/PC+™ is Prais-Winsten.[56]

Findings

The findings are organized by each hypothesis.

H1: Pluralism and Corporate Newspaper Structure

Data from all three datasets support the first hypothesis — that the greater the structural pluralism, the greater the likelihood a newspaper will exhibit the characteristics of the corporate form of organization.

Decennial Dataset. Figure 7.1 shows that the relationship between structural pluralism and the corporate newspaper index is highly linear. The scatterplot suggests that there is a slight "s"-shaped curve over the 90-year time period, but additional analysis (not shown) indicates that the curve is not substantial enough to develop a nonlinear model. The values for pluralism and corporate newspaper index increase substantially from each decennial year to the next except from 1930 to 1940, when both measures remained relatively flat. Only one of the pluralism measures — total population — increased during the period of the Great Depression. The other three — number of urban areas with 100,000 or more people, number of people employed, and number of businesses — declined slightly. Newspaper circulation and the percentage of newspapers owned by chains increased only slightly.

An ordinary least squares regression for the relationship shown in Figure 7.1 detected no significant autocorrelation. Table 7.6 indicates that with 10 cases and one variable, the null hypothesis of no positive autocorrelation can be rejected at the 95 percent level (p<.05) if the

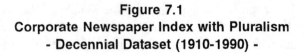

Figure 7.1
Corporate Newspaper Index with Pluralism
- Decennial Dataset (1910-1990) -

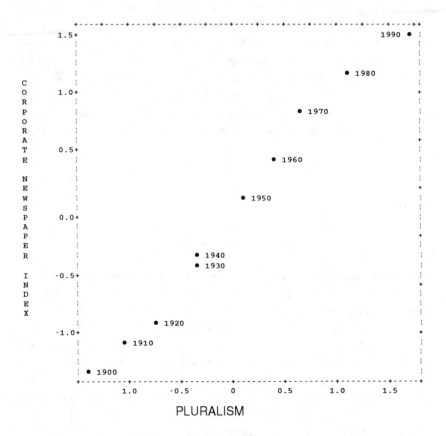

PLURALISM

*Values are standardized, with a mean of zero and a standard deviation of one.

Durbin-Watson value is less than 1.32. The actual value from the regression is 1.37, indicating no autocorrelation. The autocorrelation and partial autocorrelation plots (not shown) also support the conclusion of no autocorrelation: The correlations at each lag are not statistically significant. The absence of autocorrelation probably stems from the large time periods between observations (10 years).

The slope or unstandardized regression coefficient indicates that the corporate newspaper index increases by nearly one standard deviation

Table 7.6
Corporate Index Regressed on Pluralism
- Decennial Dataset (1910-1990) -

Model[a]	Slope	SE of Slope	p=	Adjusted R^2	SE of Regression	Durbin-Watson[b]
1. Ordinary Least Squares	.988	.048	.000	.98	.14	1.37
2. Prais-Winsten Regression	.949	.064	.000	.96	.15	1.41

[a]Sample size for each model is 10.
[b]Durbin-Watson values less than 1.32 indicate the possible presence of positive autocorrelation; those greater than 2.68 indicate a negative autocorrelation.

(.988) when pluralism increases by one standard deviation. The standard error is small (.048) and highly significant (p<.001). R^2 is very high (.98), suggesting the relationship is strong, but this statistic is probably inflated because the value of R^2 is highly sensitive to the number of degrees of freedom — i.e., it increases as the degrees of freedom declines, all other things being equal. In this case there are only 8 degrees of freedom. R^2 also is sensitive to changes in variances across populations, which makes comparisons across regressions difficult. Because of these problems, most statisticians prefer the unstandardized statistics in time-series analysis.[57] For example, the standard error of the regression, a measure of goodness-of-fit, indicates that for any observed value of the corporate newspaper index there is a 68 percent chance that the true population value lies within ±0.14 standard deviations.

For illustrative purposes, the results from a Prais-Winsten general least squares regression, which controls for first-order autocorrelation, also are shown in Table 7.6. The values are nearly identical to the ordinary least squares results, supporting the earlier conclusion that autocorrelation poses few problems in the model. In sum, the data from the Decennial Dataset strongly supports the first hypothesis that changes in pluralism are positively related to changes in the corporate newspaper index.

Yearly Dataset. The Yearly Dataset also supports the hypothesis that changes in pluralism are related to changes in the corporate newspaper index. Consistent with the findings in the Decennial Dataset, Figure 7.2

Figure 7.2
Corporate Newspaper Index With Pluralism
- Yearly Dataset (1955-1986) -

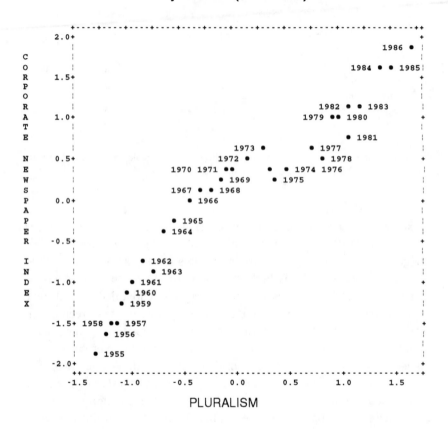

PLURALISM

*Values are standardized, with a mean of zero and a standard deviation of one.

shows that the relationship between pluralism and the corporate newspaper index in the Yearly Dataset is linear, with the exception of a slight dip that occurs when the values for pluralism are between 0.25 and 0.50. Additional analysis (not shown) revealed that the dip occurred in 1974, when national newspaper circulation dropped sharply, after reaching an all-time high in 1973. Circulation began another slow climb in 1976. Hiebert, Ungurait and Bohn suggest that the decline occurred because of inflation and recession in the mid-1970s, and because of the combining of morning

Table 7.7
Corporate Index Regressed on Pluralism
- Yearly Dataset (1955-1986) -

Model[a]	Slope	SE of Slope	p=	R^2	SE of Regression	Durbin-Watson[b]
1. Ordinary Least Squares	.940	.049	.000	.92	.27	.36
2. Prais-Winsten Regression	1.046	.116	.000	.72	.16	2.39

[a]Sample size for each model is 32.
[b]Durbin-Watson values less than 1.50 indicate the possible presence of positive autocorrelation; those greater than 2.50 indicate a negative autocorrelation.

and evening newspapers.[58] Another factor, though, could have been the oil embargo, which might have led some newspapers to reduce circulation to remote areas because of the increased cost of delivery. At any rate, logarithmic transformations did not straighten the slight curve or alter the strength of the relationship between pluralism and the corporate newspaper index, so the original values were used in the analysis.

In contrast to the Decennial Dataset, autocorrelation is a problem for interpreting the findings from an ordinary least squares regression in the Yearly Dataset. Model #1 in Table 7.7 shows that the Durbin-Watson statistic is .36, which is substantially lower than 1.50, the minimum value needed to reject the null hypothesis of no positive autocorrelation with 32 cases and one independent variable. An examination of the autocorrelation and partial autocorrelation plots (not shown) also indicates the presence of first-order autocorrelation.

When the effects of the autocorrelation are removed using Prais-Winsten regression (Durbin-Watson=2.39), model #2 in Table 7.7 shows that R^2 drops (from .92 to .72), and the standard error of the slope more than doubles (from .049 to .116). However, pluralism remains a powerful and significant predictor of the corporate newspaper index (p<.001). The findings are nearly identical to those in the Decennial Dataset: A one standard deviation change in pluralism produces about a one standard deviation change in the corporate newspaper index (1.046).[59] The standard error of the regression is .16.

Cross-Sectional Dataset. Consistent with the findings in the Decennial and Yearly datasets, the cross-sectional data also support the hypothesis that changes in pluralism are related to changes in the corporate newspaper index. Figure 7.3 shows that the relationship between pluralism and the corporate newspaper index is linear and moderately strong. Regression analysis shows that a one standard deviation change in the pluralism index produces a .44 standard deviation change in the corporate structure index (slope=.436, standard error=.066, R^2=.18, p<.0001, n=194). Table 7.8 shows that the zero-order correlation is moderately strong (r=.43, p<.01). Of the three individual pluralism indicators, city pluralism is the best predictor (r=.47, p<.01), but self-reported community size and county pluralism are both significantly related to the pluralism index (r=.34 and r=.23, respectively). For comparative purposes, the correlation between the log of the pluralism index and the corporate index also is shown in the table, and it is nearly identical to the rank-ordered index (r=.42 vs. r=.43).

The pluralism measures are most strongly correlated with the structural complexity dimension of the corporate index (see Table 7.8). Most of the pluralism measures also are significantly related to the rules and hiring college graduates dimensions. However, the pluralism measures are not significantly related to the ownership structure and rationality dimensions.

H2: Pluralism and Media Competition

Data in the Yearly and the Cross-Sectional datasets generally support the second hypothesis: the greater the structural pluralism, the greater the media competition.

Yearly Dataset. Table 7.9 shows that all of the broadcast competition measures except one are positively and significantly related to pluralism. For example, a one standard deviation increase in pluralism produces a 3.9 percent share increase in national television advertising and an increase of about 234 television stations (models #2 and #4, respectively). (Note: A one standard deviation increase in pluralism is a very large change, approximating that which would take place over a 10- to 15-year period.)

The exception to the rule involves national advertising revenues for radio: As pluralism increases, the percentage of national advertising revenues that went to radio decreases (model #5). This finding supports Dimmick and Rothenbuhler's study, which found that since the 1950s radio increasingly has relied on local, rather than national, advertising. They attributed this change to increasing competition from television,[60] but it is important to point out that with the advent of national programming via

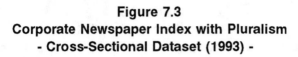

Figure 7.3
Corporate Newspaper Index with Pluralism
- Cross-Sectional Dataset (1993) -

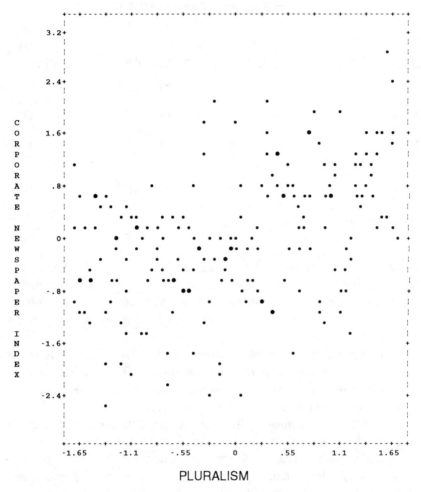

PLURALISM

*Values are standardized, with a mean of zero and a standard deviation of one.

•=1 case; •=2 cases.

satellite transmission, the shift to local advertising is not necessarily permanent. Moreover, although radio is capturing a smaller share of national advertising revenues, Table 7.9 shows that its competitive position relative to newspapers actually may have improved because the total

Table 7.8
Zero-Order Correlations Between
Corporate Newspaper and Pluralism Measures
- Cross-Sectional Dataset (1993) -

Pluralism Measures	Corp. Index	Structural Complexity	Ownership Structure	Rules	Rationality	Hire College Grads
1. Rank-Order Index (3+4+5)	.43**	.67**	.04	.25**	.05	.23**
2. Log of Pluralism Index (3+4+5)	.42**	.74**	.08	.23**	-.01	.13*
3. County Pluralism	.23**	.44**	.01	.10*	-.04	.12*
4. City Pluralism	.47**	.63**	.07	.21**	.03	.18**
5. Self-Reported Community Size	.34**	.70**	.08	.18**	.03	.01

*p<.05; **p<.01

number of radio stations and radio's share of local advertising revenues have increased as pluralism has increased. A one standard deviation increase in the pluralism produces nearly a 0.878 percent increase in local advertising revenues and an increase of about 2,100 radio stations (models #6 and #7, respectively).

The upshot of all these findings is that the overall broadcast competition index is strongly related to pluralism — for each one standard deviation increase in pluralism, the broadcast competition index increases by nearly one standard deviation (.944; p<.001).[61]

Cross-Sectional Dataset. The cross-sectional data also show that as the level of pluralism increases, competition from broadcast media increases (data not shown). The zero-order correlation between pluralism and number of broadcast stations is .53 (p<.001). The correlation between pluralism and number of radio stations is identical to the correlation between pluralism and number of television stations (r=.52, p<.001).

H3: Media Competition and Corporate Structure
The yearly data do not support the third hypothesis, which posits that the greater the competition from other media, the greater the likelihood a daily newspaper will exhibit the characteristics of the corporate form of

Table 7.9
Broadcast Competition Measures
Regressed on Pluralism
- Yearly Dataset (1955-1986) -

Model[a] Dependent Variable	Slope	SE of Slope	p=	R^2	SE of Reg.	Durbin-Watson[b]
1. Broadcast Index[c]	.944	.042	.000	.94	.10	1.82
2. National TV Advertising	3.901	.520	.000	.64	.79	1.58
3. Local TV Advertising	2.782	.235	.000	.82	.29	1.99
4. TV Stations	233.6	20.480	.000	.81	37.30	1.55
5. National Radio Advertising	-.262	.047	.000	.49	.13	1.95
6. Local Radio Advertising	.878	.134	.000	.57	.26	1.62
7. Radio Stations	2100.2	77.5	.000	.96	170.70	1.71

[a]Sample size for each model is 32. Estimates obtained from Prais-Winsten regression procedure.
[b]Durbin-Watson values less than 1.50 indicate the possible presence of positive autocorrelation; those greater than 2.50 indicate a negative autocorrelation.
[c]Values for national radio advertising are reversed before creating the index.

organization. However, the cross-sectional data generally support the hypothesis.

Yearly Dataset. Bivariate analysis shows that the media competition measures are related to the corporate newspaper index (data not shown), but these relationships generally disappear when controlling for pluralism (see Table 7.10). In other words, competition does not appear to mediate the effects of pluralism on corporate newspaper structure — the bivariate relationships appear to be spurious, a product of their joint correlation with pluralism.

All of the bivariate correlations between the media competition measures are significantly related to the corporate newspaper index (data not shown). Adding a television station to a market, for example, has more effect than adding a radio station — for each television station added, the corporate newspaper index increases by .003, compared with .001 for each radio station. The overall broadcast competition index also is significantly

Table 7.10
Corporate Newspaper Index Regressed on
Pluralism and Competition Measures
- Yearly Dataset (1955-1986) -

Model/[a] Independent Variable	Slope	SE of Slope	p=	R^2	SE of Reg.	Durbin- Watson[b]
1. Pluralism	.891	.304	.007	.69	.16	2.33
Broadcast Index[c]	.175	.302	.566			
2. Pluralism	.832	.117	.000	.76	.16	2.23
National TV Advertising	.052	.037	.176			
3. Pluralism	1.954	.211	.000	.94	.15	2.09
Local TV Advertising	-.339	.071	.000			
4. Pluralism	.966	.000	.000	.70	.16	2.42
TV Stations	.001	.001	.654			
5. Pluralism	1.004	.139	.000	.69	.16	2.34
National Radio Advrtsng	-.170	.220	.447			
6. Pluralism	1.147	.148	.000	.72	.16	2.44
Local Radio Advertising	-.125	.115	.284			
7. Pluralism	.580	.371	.130	.71	.16	2.29
Radio Stations	.001	.001	.189			

[a]Sample size for each model is 32. Estimates obtained from Prais-Winsten regression procedure.
[b]Durbin-Watson values less than 1.50 indicate the possible presence of positive autocorrelation; those greater than 2.50 indicate a negative autocorrelation.
[c]Values for national radio advertising are inverted before creating the index.

related to the corporate newspaper index. The data show that a one standard deviation change in the competition index produces a .996 standard deviation increase in the corporate newspaper index (data not shown).

These findings support the hypothesis that media competition is related to corporate newspaper structure — however, when pluralism is controlled, the partial unstandardized regression coefficients for the media competition measures become nonsignificant. Table 7.10 shows that the value of the slope for pluralism drops slightly when controlling for the overall broadcast competition index, from 1.046 (see Table 7.7) to .891 (p<.007). However, the unstandardized coefficient for the media competition index (b=.175) is not statistically significant (p=.566). Furthermore, only one of the individual competition measures — local television advertising — is

Table 7.11
Corporate Newspaper Index and Advertising Measure
Regressed on Competition and Pluralism Measures
- Cross-Sectional Dataset (1993) -

Model/Variables	Slope	SE of Slope	p=	Beta	R^2
1. Corporate Index regressed on:					
Pluralism	.436	.066	.001	.43	.18
2. Corporate Index regressed on:					
Broadcast Index	.456	.073	.001	.40	.16
3. Corporate Index regressed on:					
Pluralism	.364	.079	.001	.36	.30
Broadcast Index	.287	.082	.001	.27	
4. Advertising Rate regressed on:					
Pluralism	.093	.084	.275	.09	.08
Broadcast Index	-.236	.093	.012	-.25	
Circulation	-.141	.091	.120	-.15	
5. Corporate Index regressed on:					
Pluralism	.308	.084	.001	.30	.29
Broadcast Index	.222	.095	.010	.21	
Circulation	.208	.111	.032	.17	
Advertising Rate	.073	.094	.220	.06	

statistically significant when controlling for pluralism, but the coefficient is inverse, i.e., opposite of expectations (b= -.339, p<.001) and does reduce the size of the pluralism coefficient. One competition measure — number of radio stations — produces a significant decline in the slope coefficient for pluralism (from 1.046 to .580); but the coefficient for the media measure is not statistically significant (p=.189).

In sum, pluralism is a significant and strong predictor of the corporate newspaper index in the Yearly Dataset. However, the data do not support the argument that competition from broadcast media mediates part of this relationship.

Cross-Sectional Dataset. The cross-sectional data support the hypothesis that broadcast competition mediates the effect of pluralism on corporate newspaper structure, but advertising rates did not mediate the effect of competition. Models #1 and #2 in Table 7.11 show the bivariate relationships between the corporate newspaper index and pluralism and the broadcast competition index. In both cases the relationships are moderately strong and significant: As the level of pluralism increases and the number of broadcast media increases, the corporate newspaper index increases. Model #3 also shows that the broadcast index mediates some of the effect of pluralism. The slope coefficient for pluralism drops from .436 in the bivariate model to .364, and beta also declines from .43 to .36. The effect of the broadcast index also declines but remains significant. In short, pluralism has direct effects on the corporate newspaper index and indirect effects via broadcast competition.

A further question was whether the impact of the broadcast index could be mediated by open advertising rates per 1,000 circulation. The answer appears to be no. The broadcast index is significantly related to the advertising rate measure; that is, as the number of broadcast media in a community increases, advertising rates decline (see Model #4). This relationship holds even while controlling for circulation. However, the advertising rate measure is not significantly related to the corporate newspaper index when controlling for the broadcasting index, pluralism and circulation.[62]

Summary

A theory that attempts to explain the growth of the corporate newspaper was tested in this chapter using data from two longitudinal studies and one cross-sectional study. The data provide strong support for the first hypothesis: Pluralism is a significant and strong predictor of all of the corporate newspaper indices in the three datasets. The more complex the community, the more likely its newspapers will acquire the characteristics of the corporate form of organization. The cross-sectional data indicate that pluralism is a strong predictor of the structural complexity of the newspaper (division of labor and hierarchy of authority), the number of rules and regulations, and whether the newspaper only hires reporters with a college degree (staff expertise). Ownership structure (including chain ownership), as well as rationality in decision-making, had little relation to pluralism.

The data also support the second hypothesis, which posited that competition from broadcast media would increase as structural pluralism increases. Large, complex communities have a greater number of radio and television stations.

The data provide only partial support for the third hypothesis, which expected that intermedia broadcast competition would mediate the effect of structural pluralism on corporate newspaper structure. The yearly dataset failed to support that hypothesis. The cross-sectional study found that competition from broadcast stations did mediate some of the effects of pluralism. Additional analysis showed that newspaper advertising rates also declined as the number of broadcast stations increased, indicating that competition is stiffer in pluralistic communities. However, advertising rates failed to explain the correlation between number of broadcast stations and the corporate newspaper index.

At least two explanations may be offered for the failure to find strong support for the notion that competition mediates some of the effects of pluralism. The first is that the measures of competition in this study — i.e., number of competitive media, proportion of advertising obtained by alternative media and newspaper advertising rates — are not sensitive enough to measure the effects of competition. Indeed, one problem with these measures is that they do not take into account the intensity of competition in a market; that is, it is conceivable that one market with two major media may have more intense competition than another market with three or more media. The second explanation for the lack of strong support for the competition hypotheses is that the empirical model may be too simplistic. The model assumes that intermedia competition promotes organizational growth because it enhances the innovation process which, in turn, leads to economies of scale. No empirical measures of innovation or economies of scale were included in this study, but such measures may be necessary to demonstrate an empirical relationship between competition and corporate newspaper structure.

Neither of these two explanations can be rejected outright. But it is also important to point out that the finding that intermedia competition has little or no direct effect on the growth of the corporate newspaper certainly is not inconsistent with a large portion of the empirical literature. Taken together, these studies suggest that even though television, radio, and newspapers offer information and news that is redundant in some ways, in most other respects they cannot be considered functional substitutes. In other words, each has a unique element — i.e., radio has immediacy, television has the power of images, and newspapers have depth of analysis — that has enabled it to develop its own niche and to survive.

Additional research is necessary to sort out which explanation is most appropriate. Such research should explore more closely the effect of intermedia competition on the innovation process, economies of scale, product quality, and profitability. Research that examines the effect of organizational size on these variables also is encouraged. Most likely this will mean studies conducted at the organizational level, as opposed to the national or market level.

But even if additional research shows that intermedia competition plays little or no role in the growth of the corporate newspaper, it is important to point out that this does not mean competition plays no role. This study focused on intermedia competition — competition from broadcast media. Intracity daily newspaper competition, most scholars agree, has played a major role in promoting the growth of large-scale dailies through mergers via economies of scale in production and intracity mergers. Nevertheless, intracity newspaper competition cannot explain the continued trend toward the corporate form of organization in the newspaper industry, since few cities have two or more competing newspapers. To explain this continued growth, the findings in this study strongly suggest that increasing complexity in the social structure, or structural pluralism, is a key factor.

Notes

1. William Floyd Griswold, Jr., *Community Structure, Reporter Specialization and Content Diversity Among Midwest Daily Newspapers* (Ph.D. Diss., University of Minnesota, 1990), p. 98.

2. *Editor & Publisher International Yearbook* (New York: Editor & Publisher Company, 1988), p. I-374

3. See, e.g., Robert G. Picard, James P. Winter, Maxwell E. McCombs and Stephen Lacy (eds.), *Press Concentration and Monopoly* (Norwood, N.J.: Ablex, 1988).

4. John E. Polich, "Predicting Newspaper Staff Size from Circulation: A New Look," *Journalism Quarterly*, 51:515-7 (1974) and Paul J. Deutschmann, "Predicting Newspaper Staff Size from Circulation," *Journalism Quarterly*, 36:350-4 (1959).

5. Lori A. Bergen and David Weaver, "Job Satisfaction of Daily Newspaper Journalists and Organizational Size," *Newspaper Research Journal*, 9(2):1-13 (1988), p. 4.

6. U.S. Bureau of Census, *Historical Statistics of the United States, Colonial Times to 1970* (Washington, D.C.: U.S. Government Printing Office, 1975) and U.S. Bureau of Census, *Statistical Abstract of the United States, 1991* (Washington, D.C.: U.S. Government Printing Office, 1991).

7. This was the correlation after removing the effects of a first-order autocorrelation. For more information on autocorrelation in time-series analysis, see discussion that follows in this chapter.

8. Thomas C. Wilson, "Community Population Size and Social Heterogeneity: An Empirical Test," *American Journal of Sociology*, 91:1154-69 (1986).

9. U.S. Bureau of Census, *Historical Statistics of the United States, Colonial Times to 1970*, and U.S. Bureau of Census, *Statistical Abstract of the United States.*

10. Dun & Bradstreet, *Dun & Bradstreet Reference Book of Corporate Managements* (New York: Dun & Bradstreet, 1968-1980).

11. Correlations after the effects of a first-order autocorrelation are removed.

12. The source of this claim is a personal conversation in the summer of 1989 with Raymond B. Nixon, professor emeritus of journalism at the University of Minnesota. Nixon, who began tracking ownership trends for *Editor & Publisher* in 1955, said prior to that year *E&P* editors did not always update the section on chain ownership on a yearly basis.

13. This was the correlation after removing the effects of a first-order autocorrelation.

14. Correlations after effects of a first-order autocorrelation removed.

15. Broadcasting Publications, *The Broadcasting Yearbook* (Washington, D.C.: Broadcasting Publications, 1991), p. H-55.

16. Robert J. Coen, "Estimated Annual U.S. Advertising Expenditures 1935-1985," unpublished report (New York: McCann-Erickson Advertising, Inc., 1986).

17. See, e.g., John C. Busterna, "The Cross-Elasticity of Demand for National Newspaper Advertising," *Journalism Quarterly*, 64:346-51 (1987).

18. John Dimmick and Eric Rothenbuhler, "The Theory of the Niche: Quantifying Competition Among Media Industries," *Journal of Communication*, 34(1):103-19 (1984).

19. Although this measure indicates that radio is less of a competitive threat to newspapers or other media, this does not mean that radio is no longer a competitive threat, since its share of local advertising has increased.

20. Police reporters typically occupy the lowest-status position in reporting. At only two newspapers did one person hold both the highest ranking manager and editor role. In these two cases, the editor survey was mailed to the next highest ranking editor.

21. One was a post card reminder, mailed about a week later. After about a month, a second follow-up that included a questionnaire was mailed to those who did not respond.

22. The author of this paper thought the response rate for the police reporter group would have been the lowest because the mailings were not personally addressed. This was not the case.

23. A respondent's position in the organizational hierarchy may have a substantial effect on perceptions of organizational goals, etc. Had there been a correlation between role and circulation, it would have been necessary to control for role when examining the effects of corporate structure (see Chapter 10).

24. For dichotomous measures, the proportion is just a special case of the mean when the values are zero and one.

25. See, e.g., Peter M. Blau and Marshall W. Meyer, *Bureaucracy in Modern Society*, 3rd ed. (New York: Random House, 1987).

26. Circulation also is a good indicator of the division of labor and organizational complexity, but it was not used in the index here because it also measures consumer demand.

27. The first two measures were worded as follows: "How many full-time reporters and editors and how many full-time employees are employed at your newspaper? (Please estimate if exact number not known)."

28. "In which of the following beats or areas does your newspaper employ at least one full-time reporter? (Please check all that apply): business, sports, book reviews, arts, real estate, health, national, state, food, home, science, technology, metro, international, lifestyles, travel, fashion and education."

29. "For a general assignment reporter to become the top editor of the newspaper, how many promotions typically would he or she have to receive? (For example, if a newspaper employs assistant city editors, a city editor and an editor-in-chief, the total number of promotions needed to become the top editor is three.)"

30. Respondents were asked to rate 22 items in terms of the amount of importance top management places on them. Responses were recorded on a 7-point scale ranging from "not very important" to "extremely important."

31. "Is your newspaper owned by a chain or group, or is it independently owned?" Chain ownership was coded "1"; independent ownership, "0." The value for this measure (67%) was slightly lower than the estimate in *Editor & Publisher International Yearbook* (about 80%). The discrepancy probably stems from an under-reporting of chain ownership; that is, some publishers and journalists who work for small chains that are family owned do not appear to see their newspapers as chains because that term connotes a large, impersonal organization. In terms of measurement error, this would not appear to pose a major problem, however, since many small chains come closer to matching the characteristics of the entrepreneurial than the corporate model.

32. "Is your newspaper owned privately or can the public through the purchase of stock or other means own part or all of your newspaper?" Public ownership coded "1"; all others "0."

33. "Is your newspaper a sole proprietorship, a partnership or a corporation?" Corporation coded "1"; all others a "0."

34. "Does one *individual or family* own or control more than a 50 percent interest in your newspaper?" A "no" response was coded "1"; a "yes" was "0."

35. This item was coded from *Editor & Publisher International Yearbook.*

36. Some of the ownership measures are dichotomous. Although factor analysis technically requires continuous measures, like regression analysis it is a very robust technique and there is no evidence to suggest that the analysis distorted the data.

37. For a discussion of factor analysis, see Jae-On Kim and Charles W. Mueller, *Introduction to Factor Analysis* (Beverly Hills, Calif.: Sage, 1978) and *Factor Analysis: Statistical Methods and Practical Issues* (Beverly Hills, Calif.: Sage, 1978).

38. David Pearce Demers, "Corporate Structure and Emphasis on Profits and Product Quality at U.S. Daily Newspapers," *Journalism Quarterly,* 68:15-26 (1991).

39. Polich, "Predicting Newspaper Staff Size from Circulation." It will be argued later, however, that chain ownership is no longer a good measure of organizational complexity in cross-sectional studies because it is so widely diffused.

40. David Pearce Demers, "Corporate Newspaper Structure and Editorial-Page Vigor," paper presented to the International Communication Association (Albuquerque, May 1995). Chain ownership is still a useful measure in longitudinal studies, however, since the variance is being measured over time.

41. Roger Mansfield, "Bureaucracy and Centralization: An Examination of Organizational Structure," *Administrative Science Quarterly,* 18:477-88 (1973).

42. The business measure was itself created by adding together the number of manufacturing plants, wholesale establishments, retail establishments and service-based businesses.

43. U.S. Bureau of the Census, *County and City Data Book: 1994* (Washington, D.C.: U.S. Government Printing Office, 1994).

44. One-hundred-twenty-seven of the 223 newspapers were located in cities with fewer than 25,000 residents.

45. The substantive hypotheses were tested using untransformed and log-transformed variables. The results, which will not be presented, were nearly identical to the rank-ordered transformation.

46. National Research Bureau, *The Working Press of the Nation: TV & Radio Directory*, vol. 3 (Chicago: National Research Bureau, 1993).

47. It is important to control for circulation in order to rule out possible confounding effects from economies of scale (i.e., larger newspapers have lower advertising rates per 1,000 circulation because of economies of scale).

48. See, e.g., Michael S. Lewis-Beck, *Applied Regression: An Introduction* (Beverly Hills, Calif.: Sage, 1980).

49. Gregory B. Markus, *Analyzing Panel Data* (Beverly Hills, Calif.: Sage Publications, 1979), p. 50.

50. Lagged value means the value in the previous point in time.

51. Markus, *Analyzing Panel Data*, p. 50, and Charles W. Ostrom, Jr., *Time Series Analysis: Regression Techniques*, 2nd ed. (Beverly Hills, Calif.: Sage, 1990), p. 15.

52. The discussion here focuses only on first-order autocorrelation, since this is by far the most common type of autocorrelation.

53. Another assumption is that the autocorrelation is first-order, which is almost always the case.

54. Ostrom, *Time Series Analysis*, pp. 32-5.

55. See, e.g., J. Kmenta, *Elements of Econometrics* (New York: Macmillan, 1986), pp. 321-2.

56. SPSS Inc., *SPSS/PC+ Trends* (Chicago: SPSS, Inc., 1990), pp. B65-B78. See Ostrom, *Time Series Analysis*, pp. 32-5 for a comparison of Prais-Winsten to other GLS procedures.

57. Herbert M. Blalock, "Causal Inferences, Closed Populations, and Measures of Association," *American Political Science Review*, 61:130-6 (1967), and G. W. Bohrnstedt, "Observations on the Measurement of Change," in E. F. Borgotta (ed.), *Sociological Methodology* (San Francisco: Jossey-Bass, 1969).

58. Ray Eldon Hiebert, Donald F. Ungurait and Thomas W. Bohn, *Mass Media II: An Introduction to Modern Communication* (Longman: New York, 1979), p. 226.

59. Note that the slopes in the OLS and P-W regressions are nearly identical. As noted earlier, positive autocorrelation inflates inferential statistical values but has little effect on slope estimates, which are unbiased though inefficient with the presence of autocorrelation.

60. Dimmick and Rothenbuhler, "The Theory of the Niche."

61. Note that values for the national radio advertising were inverted before creating the broadcast competition index.

62. Hierarchical regressions were also conducted, and they yielded the same results.

Part 4

EFFECTS

Chapter 8

Empirical Research on Corporate Newspaper Effects

Most of the research on the corporate newspaper has examined the effects rather than the origins of that organizational form. This is not too surprising. From a public policy perspective, the key concern is whether changes in ownership or organizational structure promote or hinder the development of a social system's political and social goals (e.g., democracy, diversity of ideas, freedom of information).

As outlined in Chapter 1, the corporate newspaper is widely perceived to be a menace to democracy and good journalism. Among other charges, critics claim that the corporate newspaper places more emphasis on profit-making than on product quality or meeting the informational needs of the community, and that it restricts journalists' autonomy, fosters worker alienation and job dissatisfaction, is less vigorous editorially, and destroys community solidarity. Are the critics right? Does the empirical evidence support these charges?

The goal of this chapter is to begin answering these questions with a review of the empirical literature on the consequences or effects of the corporate form of organization. Some of the major theories or models that have been devised to explain the effects of the corporate newspaper are outlined in the first section below. This is followed by a review of the empirical literature. The question of effects will be taken up again in Chapters 9 and 10, when this author's theories are presented and empirically tested.

Theories of Effects

As noted in Chapter 5, few mass communication researchers have constructed formal theories of corporate newspaper effects. However, at least four major explanatory frameworks or models can be gleaned from the literature: critical, economic, managerial revolution and competition contingency.

1. Critical Model

This is by far the most popular model of corporate newspaper effects. The large number of scholars and professionals believe corporate newspapers are more interested in profits than in product quality, are exerting greater control over journalists' behavior, are producing more highly dissatisfied employees, are ruining community solidarity, and are less vigorous editorially.[1] According to Herman:

> The dominant media companies are large profit-seeking corporations, owned and controlled by very wealthy boards and individuals. Many are run completely as money-making concerns, and for the others as well there are powerful pressures from stockholders, directors, and bankers to focus on the bottom line. These pressures intensified over the 1980s as media stocks became stock market favorites and actual or prospective owners of media properties were able to generate great wealth from increased audience size and advertising revenues (e.g., Rupert Murdoch, Time-Warner, and many others). This encouraged the entry of speculators and takeovers, and increased the pressure and temptation to focus more intensively on profitability.[2]

Three arguments are often put forth to support the notion that corporate media are more profit-oriented. The first is that they have more market power, i.e., they are less constrained by competition. The assumption here is that newspaper owners are profit maximizers and that competition is necessary to keep them from holding the community hostage. Corporate newspapers derive their market power in part from economies of scale, lack of competition at the local level, greater knowledge of the marketplace, tax laws that favor corporate enterprises, more efficient operations, and greater rationality in decision-making.[3] In particular, chains and large-scale media organizations are perceived to be more profit-oriented because they have more market power than independently owned and small newspapers, respectively.

The second argument supporting the notion that the corporate newspaper is more profit-oriented revolves around ownership structure. Because corporate newspapers are more likely to be publicly owned, it is believed that they must be constantly oriented to the bottom line to keep stockholders happy and investment dollars flowing in. Competition under these conditions is not just a matter of producing a better and less expensive product than a competitor — it means generating a profit that is higher than at companies in other industries as well. According to Hirsch and Thompson:

> In this demanding environment, performance is continually assessed by analysts and investors using the quarterly report on earnings. Analysts use information about a firm's operations to generate forecasts about the company's long-term productivity and performance, which are reflected in the stock price. "Working for the numbers" has several important consequences for how newspapers operate. Strategies and activities geared toward creating value in the long run that require heavy investment in the short run become less attractive to executives because they decrease earnings in the current period.[4]

The third argument supporting the idea that corporate newspapers are more profit-oriented stems from the belief that locally owned newspapers are more responsive to the social and moral concerns of the local community. Chain newspapers are perceived to be less responsive because their owners rarely live in the communities their newspapers serve and because their managers are less involved in local community organizations, are oriented more toward the organization,[5] and change jobs more frequently.[6] Without strong ties to the local community, the chain organization is believed to be more interested in pursuing profits than the goals or interests of readers or the community (e.g., moral development).[7] The notion that corporate newspapers are less oriented to the local community also is expected to diminish community identity and solidarity. One expectation here is that the chain newspaper will publish less local news.

Because corporate newspapers are assumed to be profit-maximizers, they also are assumed to place less emphasis on product quality. The assumption most critics make follows a zero-sum formula: If a newspaper maximizes profits, then it has less money to spend on newsgathering, improving the product, or serving the public. In particular, critics charge that chain newspapers often sacrifice good journalism for profits. Chains and publicly owned newspapers often have been accused of hiring fewer reporters and spending less money on local news production. As Hirsch and Thompson argue:

> The move to public ownership led to the emergence of not only a new set of stakeholders in newspapers but a new logic for managing newspapers. Performance that is measured more in terms of economic than editorial accomplishments undermines newspaper executives' autonomy to pursue nonfinancial goals.[8]

In addition to more emphasis on profits and less on product quality, the critical model holds that the corporate newspaper is robbing journalists of their professional autonomy and destroying job satisfaction.[9] Autonomy may be defined as the freedom to conduct work in accordance with one's own discretion.[10] In many occupations, autonomy is considered to be more of a luxury than a necessity. But in journalism, autonomy is considered a prerequisite for a diversity of ideas.[11]

Johnstone, Slawski and Bowman have identified two major reasons to support the loss-of-autonomy argument. First, control of editorial operations at larger organizations is more hierarchical, which means proportionately fewer journalists are participating in key decisions. And second, work at larger organizations is more specialized, which means journalists are removed from the final products of their labor. "Just as in other spheres of the industrial order, growth in news operations is accompanied by increasing bureaucratization and by increasing specialization; ... these conditions in turn should make it more difficult for a journalist to maintain professional autonomy over his work."[12]

The notion that journalists at corporate newspapers are less satisfied with their jobs than journalists at entrepreneurial newspapers can be traced to the writings of Adam Smith and Karl Marx. Both argued that the division of labor created work that was dissatisfying and alienating. The division of labor involves breaking down complex tasks into a number of simpler, more discrete steps or tasks that can often be performed by machines and unskilled labor. Under such conditions, work becomes more mundane and monotonous. Smith and Marx disagreed, however, about the long-term consequences of increasing specialization.

Smith was an optimist. He conceded that a worker who repeats a task over and over again "generally becomes as stupid and ignorant as it is possible for a human creature to become."[13] And he was concerned that over-specialization would hinder the development of a sense of community among people. But the division of labor, he pointed out, substantially increases the productive capacity of a nation,[14] and as production increases, wages would increase, pushing human happiness to levels never dreamed of before.[15]

Marx disagreed. He pointed out that most of the wealth generated by the division of labor went not to the laborers but, rather, to the owners of the means of production. For workers, the primary consequence of the division of labor was not profits but alienation — from the objects they produce, from themselves, from the process of production and from the community.

> The fact that labour is external to the worker, i.e., it does not belong to his essential being; that in his work, therefore, he does not affirm himself but denies himself, does not feel content but unhappy, does not develop freely his physical and mental energy but mortifies his body and ruins his mind. The worker therefore only feels himself outside his work, and in his work feels outside himself.[16]

In the larger scheme of things, Marx's theory of alienation played an important role in explaining the emergence and growth of class consciousness, which he believed was a necessary condition for mobilization of the proletariat in the revolution against the capitalist class.[17]

Finally, another major complaint is that corporate newspapers publish fewer editorials about local issues, publish fewer editorials that are critical of mainstream groups and ideas, and exercise greater control over their editorial editors and the editorials they write. Corporate newspapers are less vigorous editorially, the critics contend, because they are afraid of offending advertisers, readers or sources, who may pull their advertising, buy fewer newspapers, or refuse to cooperate with reporters. The effect of this alleged editorial timidity is a reduction in the diversity of ideas.

2. Classical and Neoclassical Economics Models

Economic models basically hold that there should be no difference between corporate and entrepreneurial newspapers in terms of the bottom line, product quality or any of the other factors identified above. The theory of the firm assumes that businesses have but one primary goal: to make as much money as possible.[18] This is true regardless of who owns or manages the company. Business people may not even consciously maximize their profits, but competition will drive them to act as if they did.

Historically, mainstream economists have taken a sanguine view of the structural changes (e.g., growth of chains) that have occurred in the newspaper industry. They believe that marketplace forces are producing the most efficient organization possible — and one that produces the most socially desirable outcomes as well.

3. Managerial Revolution Model

In contrast to the previous models, the managerial revolution model implies that corporate newspapers are less profit-oriented, are more quality-driven, give journalists more autonomy and job satisfaction, are more vigorous editorially, and are more likely to serve the needs of the community. This model has a rich and extensive intellectual history in economics and sociology, albeit its exact origins are not known. Ironically, some of the seeds appear to have been planted by Smith and Marx, neither of whom likely would have received it with much favor.

Smith popularized the idea that joint-stock companies (precursor to the modern corporation, see Chapter 2), which are more likely to be controlled by managers, place less emphasis on maximizing profits than owner-controlled firms. He believed the heart of capitalism lay mainly in sole proprietorships and partnerships, i.e., businesses that typically are owned and managed by the same people. Owner-managers could be expected to keep an eye on the bottom line because their pocketbooks were directly affected. But such was not generally the case for joint-stock companies.[19]

Marx is partly responsible for the idea that as businesses grow and capital becomes more concentrated, ownership becomes more, not less, dispersed. As noted in Chapter 3, he defined concentration of ownership as growth in capital, or an increase in the size of companies. Capitalists must continually reinvest profits in order to remain competitive, which in turn increases the size and scope of mass production. However, concentration of capital leads to an increase, not decrease, in the number of owners, because, over time, capital is divided among family members because of inheritance and the need to fund new ventures.[20] Although ownership tends to become diffused and decentralized as a firm grows, Marx countered that this process is slow and is more than offset by centralization of capital, which he defined as the combining of capitals already formed (i.e., a reduction in the number of competitive firms in a particular sector of industry through merger, bankruptcy or acquisition).[21]

Despite these observations, the idea that power could shift from capitalists to professional managers apparently did not emerge until the turn of the century. An early proponent was Social Democratic theoretician Eduard Bernstein, who argued that the corporate form of organization led to the splitting up of property into "armies of shareholders" who represented a new "power." The shareholder, he argued, expropriates the capitalist class,[22] transforming it "from a proprietor to a simple administrator." Max Weber's writings at the turn of the century also may be interpreted as anticipating more formal arguments of later writers, even though he personally disagreed with the idea that managers were gaining power over capitalists.[23] The appropriation of managerial functions from the owners, he argued, does not mean the separation of control from ownership; rather, it means the separation of the managerial function from ownership.[24] Nevertheless, Weber's writings are ambiguous. Elsewhere, he observed that bureaucrats, or the technical experts of government, often control the flow of information to both policy makers and the public.

> The question is always who controls the existing bureaucratic machinery. And such control is possible only in a very limited degree to persons who are not technical specialists. Generally speaking, the trained permanent official is more likely to get his way in the long run than his nominal superior, the Cabinet minister, who is not a specialist.[25]

But the first comprehensive analysis of the notion that the owners of the means of production may be losing control over their organizations did not come until the early 1930s. In *The Modern Corporation and Private Property,* Berle and Means argued that "ownership of wealth without appreciable control and control of wealth without appreciable ownership appear to be the logical outcome of corporate development."[26] They defined control as the "actual power to select the board of directors (or its majority)."[27] The trend toward separation of ownership from management, they argued, occurs because the capital required to operate and own large corporations is often beyond the resources of any single individual or company. As companies grow, they need to draw upon more and more sources of capital, which over time diminishes the percentage of shares owned by any single individual or entity. Berle and Means viewed this change as largely having positive outcomes for society: Managers, unlike the owners, would be guided by a broader social conscience and professional values, rather than a selfish profit motive.

In the early 1940s, sociologist James Burnham took Berle and Means' argument one step further.[28] He argued that the trend toward separation of management from ownership was leading to the rise of a new class that would replace the capitalists. Growth of business means more than just increasing scale; it also means increasing technical complexity, and this in turn means that the owners must depend more and more on experts and highly skilled managers to run the new means of production. Organizational skills and technical knowledge are the foundation of managerial power. Burnham predicted that the "revolution" would be completed by about 1970.[29] However, in contrast to Berle and Means, Burnham was not as optimistic about the consequences of the transition of power. He believed managers would act in their own self-interest, not necessarily in the public interest.

During the 1940s, Schumpeter made similar arguments.[30] As noted in Chapter 3, he attributed the innovative process in modern capitalism not to the owners, but to the highly skilled managers and technical specialists in the organization.[31] In early capitalism, the capitalist, who is driven by profits, was the entrepreneur. But as organizations grew this role became more specialized and routinized, being given over to highly educated and trained specialists. Since entrepreneurs in modern corporations are not usually the direct beneficiaries of profit, according to Schumpeter, they are driven not by profits but by social status.

By the 1950s many social theorists treated the managerial revolution as an empirical fact rather than as a hypothesis or theory, according to Zeitlin.[32] Parsons and Dahrendorf both believed that class relations were being replaced by an occupational system based on individual achievement, in which status was determined by functional importance. "The basic phenomenon seems to have been the shift in control of enterprise from property interests of founding families to managerial and technical personnel who as such have not had a comparable vested interest in ownership," Parsons wrote.[33] According to Dahrendorf, the basic source of social conflict in a modern capitalist nation is no longer between capital and labor, because "in post-capitalist society the ruling and the subjected classes of industry and of the political society are no longer identical; ... there are, in other words ... two independent conflict fronts. ... This holds increasingly as within industry the separation of ownership and control increases and as the more universal capitalists are replaced by managers."[34]

During the 1960s and 1970s, John Kenneth Galbraith and Daniel Bell continued this line of thinking, incorporating the managerial revolution hypothesis into larger, more comprehensive theories of social change. Galbraith argues that the "decisive power in modern industrial society is exercised not by capital but by organization, not by the capitalist but by the industrial bureaucrat."[35] One consequence of the shift in power, he says, is less emphasis on profit maximization as an organizational goal. Profit maximizing becomes less important because professional managers receive most of their income through a fixed salary, not from the profits; hence, it would be irrational to argue that those in control (i.e., managers) will maximize profits for others (i.e., stockholders).[36] More important to managers than maximizing profits is prevention of loss, since low earnings or losses make a company vulnerable to outside influence or control. Galbraith believes all businesses must earn a minimum level of profit, but professional managers place greater emphasis on organizational growth, planning, knowledge, autonomy and expertise, because these factors are recognized as the basis of power in the organization and are essential for long-term survival of the organization.

These ideas are reinforced and extended in Bell's famous book, *The Coming of the Post-Industrial Society*,[37] which contends that theoretical knowledge, rather than capital or practical knowledge, is the primary source of innovation and social organization in a post-industrial society. In the economy, this change is reflected in the decline of manufacturing and goods and the rise of service industries, especially health, education, social welfare services and professional/technical services (research, evaluation, computers, systems analysis). Universities play a central role in the production of knowledge and technology. A post-modern society is an information society. Education, rather than social position, is the key means of advancement, and rewards are based less on inheritance or property than on education and skill (i.e., a meritocracy). Bell contends that these structural changes foster a new class structure — one based on the supremacy of professional, managerial, scientific and technical occupations (the knowledge or intellectual class) — that gradually replaces the bourgeoisie as the ruling class. Many European sociologists also have made similar arguments about other Western countries.[38]

Since the late 1960s, much of the scholarship has focused on empirically testing the managerial revolution thesis. This research is reviewed later.

4. Competition Contingency Model

This model represents a synthesis of the economic model with the critical or managerial revolution models. If there is competition, then the expectation is that there will be no difference between corporate and entrepreneurial newspapers in terms of emphasis on profits. If there is no competition, then making predictions boils down to whether a researcher believes corporate newspapers are located in markets that have more or less competition than entrepreneurial newspapers.[39]

Although economic theory assumes that the profit motive is no stronger in large corporations than it is in individually owned enterprises, many economists believe the structure of an industry can alter the behavior and performance of firms in the marketplace. Under conditions of perfect or near-perfect competition, profits are held in check — no firm is sufficiently large enough to control prices, and competition produces the lowest price. Thus, under conditions of competition, the expectation is for no difference between corporate and entrepreneurial newspapers because, even though the former are more likely to be managed by professionals rather than the owners, competition forces all newspapers to keep an eye on the bottom line.

However, because many scholars believe corporate newspapers are located in markets that have less competition, the critical competition contingency model is that corporate newspapers will place more emphasis on profits. Corporate newspapers are expected to maximize profits by restricting output and setting price above marginal cost. In addition, product quality is expected to suffer. Under monopoly conditions, there is little incentive to produce a better widget. Many scholars contend that monopolies tolerate waste and inefficiency.[40]

In contrast, a managerial revolution competition contingency perspective would hold that corporate newspapers will place less emphasis on profits under monopoly-like conditions because they are assured profits and are managed by professionals, not the owners, who place less emphasis on profits. As Busterna puts it, "Without much pressure from competitors, the manager-controlled firm is more likely to have sufficient profitability secured even if management pursues some other goals. ... Since newspapers operate in such highly concentrated markets, we might expect ... significant differences in profit maximizing behavior between owner and manager-controlled firms ... ."[41] At the same time, this contingency model expects that corporate newspapers will place greater emphasis on product quality, since product quality has direct benefits for professionals (prestige and other material rewards) and can help the organization maintain its competitive position and help it grow. The assumption is that consumers prefer products of high quality, and firms that produce inferior products will experience a loss of sales to competitors.

Empirical Research on Effects

Empirical research on newspaper and non-newspaper organizations fails to provide unqualified support for any of the models presented above. However, when viewed as a whole, the weight of the evidence does provide more support for the managerial revolution model than the others.

This conclusion is supported by several key findings from the research literature: (1) As an organization grows in size, capitalists (or the owners) play less and less of a role in the day-to-day operations and decision-making — professional managers, specialists and technocrats play a bigger role, which increases the potential for nonowner control; and (2) As a newspaper grows and becomes more structurally complex, it: (a) places less emphasis on profits as an organizational goal, (b) places more emphasis on product quality, (c) produces a product that is deemed to be of higher quality on a number of dimensions, and (d) becomes more vigorous editorially.

To be sure, some findings do not support the managerial revolution model. One of the most important is that large organizations and chains appear to be more profitable, and chains also appear to place more emphasis on profits. The evidence on autonomy and job satisfaction also produces mixed results.

Research on the Managerial Revolution Hypothesis

A number of criticisms have been directed at the managerial revolution hypothesis through the years,[42] but one of the most prominent is that there is no empirical evidence to support it. In 1974, Zeitlin argued that predictions of the demise of the capitalist class were grossly premature and that there was relatively little empirical evidence to support such claims. "... I believe that the 'separation of ownership and control' may well be one of those rather critical, widely accepted, pseudofacts with which all sciences occasionally have found themselves burdened and bedeviled."[43] More recently, Jary and Jary write that "Bell's concept (post-industrial society) has also been widely criticized as failing to demonstrate that the undoubted increase in the importance of knowledge in modern societies actually does lead to a shift of economic power to a new class, especially to a new noncapitalist class."[44] Other reviewers have made similar arguments.[45]

While it is true that the empirical research fails to provide uncontested support for the managerial revolution thesis, charges that the weight of the evidence is against it are not supported. Research on the question of whether ownership is becoming more diversified strongly supports the conclusion that owners or capitalists play less and less role in the day-to-day operations and decision-making as an organization grows and becomes more complex. Many key decisions must be delegated to managers and lower-level technocrats, which suggests they have more potential for control. Research on the question of whether managers serve the interests of the owners before their own is more mixed. But many of the studies that fail to support the managerial revolution hypothesis are based on samples of only the largest organizations, not all organizations, which truncates variance and increases the risk of Type II errors.

• *Is Ownership Becoming More Diversified?* The research on this question is primarily descriptive and focuses on how much stock is controlled by families or individuals and the extent to which they are involved in top management. These studies usually use 4-10 percent stock ownership, membership on the board of directors or in top management, or a combination of both to determine whether organizations are owner-controlled. But regardless of the different definitions used, most support the notion that ownership becomes more diversified as an organization grows. This finding should not be taken to mean that managers are displacing capitalists as the key decision-makers, since managers may be incorporated or co-opted into the ideology of the capitalist class or be coerced to follow its orders. But it does imply that owners are less involved in decision-making at lower levels, and thus do not have the same level of involvement as owner-managers.

Berle and Means appear to have conducted the first quantitative empirical analysis of ownership.[46] Using data compiled from Standard's *Corporation Records, Moody's* manuals, *The New York Times* and *The Wall Street Journal,* they concluded that families or groups of business associates owned more than half of the outstanding voting stock in only 11 percent of the top 200 largest nonfinancial corporations. Using 10 percent stock ownership as the minimum criterion for family control, they classified 44 percent of the top 200 largest nonfinancial corporations as management controlled.

In 1937, the Securities and Exchange Commission, using more reliable and comprehensive data, reported that minority ownership control existed in the vast majority of the nation's largest corporations.[47] However, R. A. Gordon challenged the government study, pointing to a number of shortcomings and concluding that probably fewer than a third of the companies were controlled by families or a small group of individuals.[48] A study by *Fortune* magazine in the 1960s also concluded that 71 percent of the 500 largest industrial corporations were controlled by management,[49] but the methods and data have been criticized by some scholars.[50]

Using a methodology similar to Berle and Means, Larner concluded that only 3 percent of the largest 200 nonfinancial corporations were controlled by families in 1963.[51] At the same time, 84 percent of the companies were controlled by managers, nearly double what Berle and Means had found. The remaining 13 percent were partially controlled. Larner argued that the managerial revolution was nearly complete, fulfilling

Burnham's prediction (ahead of time). "A corporation may reach a size so great that, with a few exceptions, its control is beyond the financial means of any individual or interest."[52]

However, a year later Burch challenged Larner's and Berle and Mean's findings, arguing that they had used a definition of control that was too restrictive.[53] Burch argues that control should include not only some measure of stock ownership but also membership in top management or on the board of directors. Using this broader definition, he found that about 36 percent of the top 300 public and private industrial corporations were probably family controlled in 1965. However, Burch also found that the proportion of family-controlled firms had declined about 3 to 5 percent a year since 1938, when they controlled about 50 percent of all large companies. These data support Larner's and Berle and Mean's argument that family or individual control declines as a company grows.

In sum, these studies strongly suggest that owners play less and less of a role in the day-to-day operations as organizations grow, that the proportion of manager-controlled firms has increased, and that most large businesses are manager- rather than owner-controlled.

• *Do Managers Serve Themselves or the Owners?* The second line of research has focused to a large extent on Smith's 200-year-old hypothesis of whether managers are less likely to serve the interests of the owners than themselves. Often this has involved examining whether managerial-controlled firms or large corporations are less profitable or place less emphasis on profits. Noneconomic researchers have also examined the impact on organizational goals and practices, with the expectation that managers will place greater value on organizational growth, product quality, and innovation. Findings are mixed.

Several studies are interpreted as supporting the managerial revolution thesis. Monsen, Chiu and Cooley examined the impact of ownership structure on the level of profitability for the 500 largest industrial firms.[54] A firm was considered to be owner-controlled if one party (individual, family, family holding company, etc.) is represented on the board of directors and owns 10 percent or more of the voting stock, or if one party owns more than 20 percent of the voting stock. Manager-controlled firms were defined as those in which no single owner held more than 5 percent of the voting stock and where there is no evidence of recent owner control. Using these definitions and government data, the researchers were able to track 36 firms of each type over a 12-year period. The result: the net income to net worth ratio (return on owner's equity) for owner-controlled firms was 12.8 percent, compared with 7.3 percent for manager-controlled firms.

Palmer's study also provides support for the economic-managerial revolution competition contingency model.   He found that manager-controlled firms operating in markets with a high degree of monopoly power report significantly lower profit rates than owner-controlled firms, but no major differences emerged between firms in moderate or low monopoly markets.[55] The logic here is that managers can pursue goals other than maximum profits only in the absence of competition, which acts as a constraint on all types of organizational structure. Larner also reported that manager-controlled firms have slightly lower profit rates.[56]

In contrast, other studies have found no differences between manager- and owner-controlled firms, or that manager-controlled firms are more profitable.   Fligstein and Brantley, for example, found that manager-controlled firms actually outperformed family- or bank-controlled firms in terms of profits.[57] However, they argue that ownership overall has little effect on the economic actions undertaken by large firms; rather, the key determinants are existing power relations within the firm, the concept of control that dominates the firm's actions, and the action of competitors (or what they collectively call a "sociology of markets" model). Several other studies also have found that managerial control exerts no important influence on profit rates.[58]   James and Soref studied the relationship between dismissal of corporate chiefs and five measures of managerial/owner control, with the expectation under the managerial revolution thesis that corporate chiefs at managerial-controlled organizations would have more job security.[59] However, they concluded that corporate heads are retained or fired on the basis of profit performance, not ownership structure.

These studies have contributed a great deal toward understanding organizational effects, but they should be interpreted cautiously.   The findings in most of them are based on samples of the 100 to 500 largest corporations in the United States — smaller firms are excluded — and, thus, the findings cannot be generalized to the entire population of businesses. These studies truncate variance on both the dependent (e.g., profit maximization) and independent (ownership structure) variables, increasing the risk of Type II errors.

• *Front-Page Attributions and the Managerial Revolution Hypothesis.*
Demers has suggested an alternative method of testing the managerial revolution thesis, one that does not suffer from the shortcoming noted above.[60] It involves examining changes in source attributions in news stories over time.   The logic is straightforward. Since media content reflects in a crude way the power structure of a society (see Chapter 4), changes in the power structure theoretically should be reflected in the

sources that journalists use to report on the news. More specifically, under the managerial revolution thesis, it would be expected that *during the 20th century attributions of capitalists and their representatives will have declined, while attributions of scientists, technicians, researchers and others whose roles involve the production of theoretical knowledge will have increased.*

To test this hypothesis, Demers content-analyzed source attributions on the front page of the *New York Times* at four points in time over a 90-year period during the 20th century (1903, 1933, 1963 and 1993). The *Times* was selected because it is widely recognized as the most powerful and respected newspaper in the country. Two constructed weeks of front pages in each time period were analyzed.[61] The titles or positions of the sources cited in those stories were recorded, yielding a total of 553 different sources over the 90-year period. From this list, three coders were then instructed to categorize the sources into two groups: (1) technocrats, which includes "educators, economists, academics, scientists, engineers and researchers"; and (2) capitalists, which includes "business owners, company executives, employers, corporations, companies, businesses and banks, excluding any financial company associated with government." Although company executives may not have significant holdings in their companies and, thus, technically could not be classified as a member of the ownership class, they were included in that group under the assumption that they are agents of or are controlled by the owners. This classification actually produces a more rigorous test of the hypothesis (i.e., reducing the risk of making a Type I error).[62]

Demers found support for the managerial revolution hypothesis. Figure 8.1 shows that change is quite dramatic, declining more than 50 percent for capitalists and increasing more than four-fold for technocrats. In 1903, 8.8 percent of the sources cited on the front page of the *New York Times* during the two weeks sampled were capitalists or their representatives. The attributions dropped to 6.3 percent in 1933; 5.2 percent in 1963; and 4 percent in 1993. The decline is linear and statistically significant ($r=-.26$, $p<.05$). Conversely, attributions for technocrats increased. In 1903, 2.7 percent were technocrats. This increased to 3.7 percent in 1933; 5.2 percent in 1963; and 10.5 percent in 1993. Visually the relationship for technocrats appears to be slightly exponential, but the trend was not statistically significant ($p>.05$). The zero-order correlation between time and proportion of citations for technocrats is .40 ($p<.001$).

Figure 8.1
Percent of Front Page Sources in The NYT
Who Are Capitalists or Technocrats

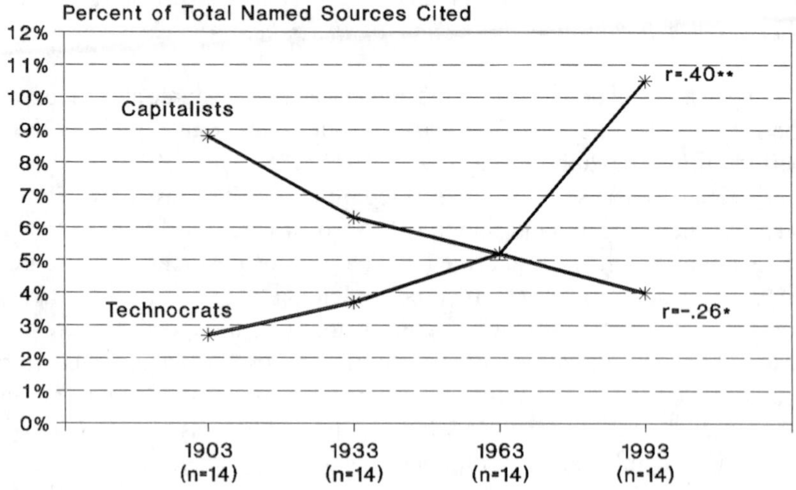

Percent of Total Named Sources Cited

12%			
11%			r=.40**
10% Capitalists			
9%			
8%			
7%			
6%			
5%			
4%			
Technocrats			r=-.26*
3%			
2%			
1%			
0%			

1903	1933	1963	1993
(n=14)	(n=14)	(n=14)	(n=14)

*p<.05; **p<.001

Source: David Pearce Demers, "Front-Page Story Attribution and the Managerial Revolution," unpublished paper (University of Wisconsin—River Falls, Wis., October 1994).

Corporate Structure and Profits

Research on the relationship between profits and newspaper structure suggests that large newspapers and chain newspapers are more profitable, but large newspapers appear to place less emphasis on profits, while chains appear to place more.

• *Size and Profits.*   Several studies support the argument that larger newspapers are more profitable.   Blankenburg, using self-reported costs and revenue data from newspapers in the Inland Press Association, found that the profit rate on revenues for a typical newspaper with a circulation of 100,000 was 20.8 percent, compared with 18.5 percent for a newspaper with a circulation of 50,000.[63]   Tharp and Stanley also found that the average profit increased as the size of a newspaper increased: 6.4 percent for those under 10,000; 11.5 percent for those 10,000 to 15,000; 17.3 percent for those 15,000 to 25,000; and about 19 percent for those 25,000 or more.[64]   The data in these studies also are supported by research which shows that large organizations benefit from tax laws and economies of scale.[65]

Although larger papers are more profitable, they appear to place less emphasis on profits as an organizational goal. Demers found that top editors at larger daily newspapers in the United States were less likely than top editors of smaller dailies to say profit was one of the top three goals driving their organization.[66] Drawing on the research of Olien, Tichenor and Donohue (see below), he argues that increasing role specialization, which is a characteristic of larger organizations, removes the editor from concern over the bottom line and increases concern with the news production process.

• *Ownership and Profits.* Research generally suggests that chain newspapers place more emphasis on profits, but the evidence is mixed on the effects of owner versus manager-control.

Case studies by Soloski and by McGrath and Gaziano concluded that chain ownership increases the pressure for greater profits and reduced costs.[67] Blankenburg and Busterna, in separate studies, also found that Gannett newspapers, one of the largest chains in the United States, charge higher advertising prices than other papers.[68] Blankenburg argues that while all organizations act rationally in the pursuit of profits, chains "have more information with which to be rational."[69] Demers and Wackman surveyed top managers at daily newspapers and found that chain editors are much more likely than editors at independent newspapers to say profit is a purpose, goal or objective that drives their organization.[70] Demers also replicated this finding in a national study of daily newspapers.[71]

Contrary to the managerial revolution model, Busterna hypothesized that owner-controlled newspapers would place less emphasis on profits because they "place more value on 'externalities,' factors external to the pure economic efficient considerations of the profit maximizer."[72] He surveyed top-level managers, mostly publishers, at small weeklies and dailies in Minnesota and found that those who owned 50 percent or more of their newspapers did, indeed, place less emphasis than other publishers on profits. Blankenburg and Ozanich also found that among newspaper companies with more than $100 million in revenues, those with less insider control (i.e., more public ownership) generally were more profitable.[73] They, too, concluded that the data failed to support the managerial revolution model.

However, Olien, Tichenor and Donohue found that editors of independently owned or locally headquartered weekly and semi-weekly newspapers in Minnesota are more, not less, likely to mention profits when asked to list reasons for being satisfied or dissatisfied with their jobs.[74]

They argue that role specialization removes the editor from concern about the bottom-line. A second study by the researchers found that ownership structure had no effect on the importance of advertising as a concern for decisions that editors make, but editors in pluralistic communities were less likely to rank advertising and more likely to rank news and editorial as important concerns.[75] These findings may be seen as contradicting the notion that chains are more profit-oriented, but this need not be the case. It is possible that even as editorial employees become less concerned about profits as a result of increased role specialization, emphasis on profits as an organizational goal may increase.

Corporate Structure and Product Quality

Research generally supports the argument that larger newspapers produce a higher quality product and place more emphasis on product quality as an organizational goal. The evidence suggests that ownership structure has no significant impact on quality.

• *Size and Quality.* Blankenburg found that even though large newspapers are more profitable than smaller ones, larger papers also proportionately spent more money on news-editorial costs. "So if news-editorial quality can be equated with expenditures, then it's better to have a single large daily than two half its size," he concluded.[76] Demers also found that editors at large daily newspapers were much more likely to mention product quality when asked to name the three most important goals in their organizations.[77] Beam surveyed daily newspaper managers and found that the larger the newspaper, the higher its score on seven of eight professional indices. For example, larger newspapers devote more resources for professional development and to news gathering, are editorially more aggressive, are more likely to fight an order to divulge confidence source or fight to get access to a public meeting, and are less partial to advertisers and friends of the publisher.[78]

In a national survey, Gladney reported that editors at large newspapers place more value on staff enterprise, professionalism and comprehensive news coverage than editors at small dailies and weeklies.[79] As noted in Chapter 4, a large body of research also shows that small newspapers, which tend to be located in small, homogeneous communities, are much less likely than larger newspapers to report on social conflict and news critical of local elites.[80] Weeklies, especially, often play the role of community booster, which limits the diversity of ideas in those communities.

Larger newspapers also appear to be more insulated from advertising pressures. In a national probability survey, Soley and Craig found that almost all newspapers are pressured to write stories that appease advertisers. However, "small newspapers reported in-house pressure to write or tailor news stories to please advertisers significantly more often than large newspapers."[81] They concluded that "media with narrow advertising bases seem to be more susceptible to advertising pressures because advertising withdrawals by individual advertisers hurt the bottom line more."[82] Other studies show that larger newspapers make fewer spelling and editing errors,[83] devote more space to news and features, are more likely to have codes of ethics,[84] hire more highly educated journalists,[85] conduct more opinion polls,[86] launch more investigative reporting projects,[87] have more ombudsmen,[88] and win more Pulitzer Prizes.[89]

• *Ownership and Quality.* Research on differences between chain and independently owned newspapers in terms of quality is more mixed. Becker, Beam and Russial found that chain ownership correlates positively with an index of press performance.[90] Lacy reported that chain papers had larger news staffs.[91] Parsons, Finnegan and Benham found that chains were more likely to have written codes of behavior that discouraged membership in organizations not connected with the professions.[92] A case study by Flatt concluded that a chain's managerial incentives encourage quality journalism.[93] And the weight of the evidence from a number of studies suggests that chain newspapers are more vigorous editorially — i.e., they publish more local editorials and are more critical of local elites. These studies are reviewed in depth below under the heading, "Corporate Structure and Editorial-Page Vigor."

In contrast, some of the research has found that chains place less importance on product quality or produce a less diverse product. Litman and Bridges, for example, reported that chains have smaller news staffs.[94] Glasser, Allen and Blanks content-analyzed newspapers that subscribe and do not subscribe to the Knight-Ridder chain's wire service and found that newspapers which subscribed to the news wire gave more and better play to a major story which was first reported by a Knight-Ridder paper — a finding which supports the criticism that chain wire services promote homogeneity, rather than diversity, in news coverage.[95]

But most studies have produced mixed results or found no differences between chain and independent newspapers. For example, although Litman and Bridges found that chains have smaller news staffs, they and Drew and Wilhoit found few differences in terms of newshole size.[96] Using regression analysis, Grotta found no differences in terms of size of editorial staff, size of newshole, percentage of local news, size of the editorial-page newshole, and the percentage of editorials as content.[97] A book edited by Ghiglione that presented the findings of 10 different case studies of newspapers purchased by chains concluded that in three cases the newspapers had improved, in three cases there were no significant changes, and in four cases they deteriorated.[98] Examining the editorial content of 36 chain and 32 independent daily newspapers, Daugherty reported that independent newspapers published more stories on the front page, but there were no differences in terms of the amount of content devoted to local news, state news, international news, features and local photos.[99] He did find, however, that chains published more local editorials and letters to the editor (see review below under "Corporate Structure and Editorial-Page Vigor").

In a national content analysis of group-owned and independent newspapers, Lacy and Fico found virtually no differences between chain and independent newspapers using an eight-item indicator of newspaper quality.[100] Coulson found that journalists at independent papers gave their papers higher ratings in terms of commitment to quality local coverage; nevertheless, on most other measures there were no differences between chain and independent newspapers — journalists at both "generally held positive opinions about their publications' local news coverage."[101] Similarly, Beam found that total circulation of a chain organization was positively correlated with four of eight professional indices, but there were virtually no differences between chain and independent newspapers on these measures, and larger chains (in terms of numbers of newspapers) were less professional.[102] In a national probability survey of daily newspapers, Demers found no relationship between chain ownership and emphasis on product quality as an organizational goal.[103] Research examining the impact of ownership on radio and television broadcasting also has reached similar mixed conclusions.[104]

Corporate Structure and Autonomy

Research that examines the effects of circulation and ownership (i.e., chain vs. independent) on decision-making and editorial content provides some support for the loss-of-autonomy model.[105] However, some recent studies suggest that, consistent with the managerial revolution hypothesis, editors at larger newspapers have more, not less, autonomy. Research on nonmedia organizations also has reached similar conclusions; in fact, some sociologists now argue that decision-making generally is more, not less, decentralized in large, differentiated organizations.[106]

• *Autonomy and Nonmedia Organizations.* Much of the nonmedia research on the relationship between organizational structure and autonomy stems from the writings of Max Weber.[107] Most theorists have interpreted Weber as arguing that professional autonomy declines with increasing complexity of organization, because large-scale organizations need a hierarchy of authority and many rules and procedures to coordinate social action.

During the 1950s and 1960s, organizational theorists generally assumed that bureaucratization and professional autonomy were antithetical.[108] For example, Scott points out that a professional carries out a complete task on the basis of specialized knowledge acquired through training. The professional is loyal to other professionals and has arrived at a terminal status and seeks no higher position. In contrast, a bureaucrat carries out a limited set of tasks which must be coordinated with others. The bureaucrat is supervised by a hierarchical superior and sanctioned for not following the rules. Loyalty is to the organization and the rules.[109]

Empirical research sometimes supported this model. For example, Hall found that autonomy was negatively related to a division of labor, a hierarchy of authority, the number of rules and procedures, and the amount of impersonality. "This suggests that increased bureaucratization threatens professional autonomy," he writes.[110] But by the early 1970s this conclusion was being challenged. In fact, Benson reviewed the literature and found that bureaucratization and professionalism are often complementary.[111]

Mansfield also argues that Weber never suggested that centralization of decision-making was a characteristic of bureaucracy.[112] In fact, Mansfield contends that Weber proposed just the opposite: "When the principle of jurisdictional 'competency' is fully carried through, hierarchical subordination — at least in public office — does not mean that the 'higher' authority is simply authorized to take over the business of the 'lower.' Indeed, the opposite is the rule."[113] Mansfield posits that increasing size forces top-level managers to create more rules to govern behavior and to reduce the range of potential problems. Increased use of rules and paperwork allows these managers to delegate decisions to lower-level managers without losing overall control.[114]

Mansfield criticizes studies like Hall's because they operationalize autonomy using individual perceptions rather than objective measures. "Studies based on (perceptions) may tell a great deal about the subjective experience of those working in organizations, but must at best be regarded as weak indicators of the objective structure of organizations."[115] To support his argument, Mansfield cites three large-scale empirical studies, all of which had found a negative relationship between "objective" measures of centralization in decision-making and bureaucracy.[116]

Although some studies of perceptions have supported the loss-of-autonomy thesis, it is important to point out that not all have. Engel found that physicians working for a moderate-sized, privately owned medical organization generally reported having more autonomy than those in solo practice or those who worked for a highly bureaucratic government agency. She reasoned that some bureaucracies, especially professional bureaucracies, can serve the needs of professionals by supplying them with funds, equipment, technical personnel and other resources in a stimulating intellectual climate for interchanging information and controlling quality of performance. "The nonbureaucratically employed may have experienced a lack of essential physical facilities, while those who worked in the highly bureaucratic organization might have felt limited by its rigid administrative structure."[117]

Since the early 1970s, a number of other studies have supported the proposition that "the larger an organization, the greater the likelihood that authority over decisions is delegated by top management to lower levels."[118] Blau and Meyer point out that this does not mean that the top managers of large organizations command fewer resources or have less power than heads of small organizations. Rather, because of their greater responsibilities, heads of large organizations must delegate more decisions to subordinates and reserve only the most important ones for themselves.[119]

Blau and Meyer also argue that several other factors can affect centralization of decision-making. First, vertical differentiation promotes decentralization of decision-making because it removes top executives from operations, whereas horizontal differentiation promotes centralization. Second, decentralization of decision-making is positively correlated with the complexity of the job and formalization of procedures. Specialized jobs and expertise reduce the extent to which authority is centralized. Qualified people need less supervision. And third, contrary to popular belief, formal rules and procedures that make work more routine and predictable also promote decentralization because there is less need for directives from supervisors.[120]

• *Autonomy and Media Organizations.* Most of the research in mass communication has been conducted on the assumption that bureaucracy (or corporate structure) and autonomy are incompatible. In a national survey of journalists in 1971, Johnstone, Slawski and Bowman found support for this assumption. Reporters at news organizations with 26 or more editorial employees had less freedom than reporters at organizations with fewer than 26 employees when it came to controlling their story assignments, to deciding which stories to report and to determining what to emphasize in a story. They also found that stories written by reporters at large news organizations are more likely to be edited by someone other than the reporter. Twelve years later Weaver and Wilhoit replicated these findings and also reported that freedom to decide news story emphasis had declined.[121] A national survey of journalists by Coulson also found that more than four of 10 group journalists agreed that group ownership restricts diversity of news and editorial opinion.[122]

In contrast, other studies employing subjective evaluations of autonomy have reached the opposite conclusion. A 1979 survey by the American Society of Newspaper Editors found that editors at chain-owned newspapers were more, not less, likely than those at independently owned newspapers to: (1) take stands that would be opposed by their publishers, (2) choose who their newspaper would endorse in a national election, and (3) say they never had to check with a newspaper's headquarters or owner before taking a stand on controversial issues.[123] These findings support a number of anecdotal stories as well.[124]

Results from studies employing "objective" measures of autonomy also are mixed. Wackman, Gillmor, Gaziano and Dennis examined newspapers' editorial endorsements of presidential candidates from 1960 to 1972 and concluded that chain newspapers exhibit a high degree of homogeneity.[125] "Clearly these data run counter to the insistence of chain spokesmen that their endorsement policies are independent from chain direction. At an overt level, in terms of formal structural controls, this may be true, but at an informal level questions should be raised about the degree to which hiring practices, management procedures and peer pressure push chain newspapers toward uniformity of editorial posture."[126]

In 1989 Gaziano expanded this dataset to include the 1976, 1980, 1984 and 1988 elections. She concluded that chains still tend to be homogeneous in their presidential choices; however, as chains increase in size, the degree of homogeneity declines. "Being bigger often has been equated with being more restrictive of editorial freedoms," she writes. "This study suggests, on the other hand, being bigger inhibits such restrictive control, at least on decisions about support for presidential candidates."[127] Busterna and Hansen, on the other hand, contend that the statistical methods used in the Wackman et al. and Gaziano studies are faulty and that there is little evidence to substantiate the chain homogeneity argument.[128] And another study of newspapers in Canada found no relationship between editorial slant and ownership structure.[129]

Although most mass communication researchers assume that autonomy and corporate structure are incompatible, there is at least one exception. Olien, Tichenor and Donohue posit that autonomy is a product of increasing interdependence. They argue that role specialization — a characteristic of large organizations — relieves editors of concerns about profits, circulation and advertising, and increases their concern with news production. Consequently, editors who work for corporate organizations should have more, not less, autonomy then editors at entrepreneurial newspapers when it comes to producing news and information. Their research supports this model. Editors of daily newspapers rate news-editorial matters as more important concerns for decisions that they make than do editors of weekly newspapers.[130]

Three other studies can be interpreted as supporting the role specialization hypothesis. Wilhoit and Drew reported that editorial editors at group-owned newspapers were far more likely than those at family or independently owned newspapers to say publishers have no influence or very little influence when it comes to "determining the priority given to editorial topics."[131] Demers hypothesized that, because of role specialization, editors at chain-owned newspapers and large newspapers would have more freedom when it came to making decisions about what they do and how to improve the quality of the editorial content. The hypothesis for ownership was not supported, but the hypothesis for organizational size was — the larger the organization, the greater the autonomy.[132] Gladney found that editors on large dailies placed greater emphasis on editorial independence than editors at small dailies and weeklies.[133]

Corporate Structure and Community Involvement

Relatively little research has examined the relationship between corporate newspaper structure and community involvement or support. But there is some evidence to suggest that (1) chain or corporate newspapers publish less information about the local community, and that (2) journalists at chain newspapers are oriented less to the local community and more oriented to their careers and the organization. The number and proportion of local stories and loyalty to the community are not direct measures of community solidarity, but the implication is that these factors will foster a decline in community solidarity.

Donohue, Olien and Tichenor studied the impact of organizational structure on the amount of local conflict news in Minnesota newspapers.[134] They divided the sample into papers owned by Minnesotans or a Minnesota company and those owned by out-of-staters. From 1965 to 1979, the amount of conflict news in "locally" owned newspapers increased by about a third, while the out-of-state papers decreased their coverage by nearly one-half. This finding has been widely interpreted as evidence that chain newspapers are systematically excluding stories that could possibly offend local groups. However, another interpretation is that the emphasis on nonlocal news represents the chain newspaper's orientation to the larger social system. In an increasingly interdependent society, such an orientation may help local communities adapt to changing social and economic conditions.[135] In fact, Gladney reported that small newspapers placed more emphasis on "strong local coverage" and on "news coverage that focuses on common community values and helps give readers a sense of individual existence and worth," while large papers placed more emphasis on comprehensive coverage (i.e., "coverage of news from beyond the newspaper's immediate distribution area").[136]

Parsons, Finnegan and Benham, using role-theory, hypothesized that journalists at chain newspapers would express a greater desire than journalists at independently owned newspapers to move out of the community and to leave the local paper in order to advance within the broader organization.[137] They also expected that chain editors would be more mobile. They found support for their hypotheses. Chain editors were much less likely to say they expect to remain in their current jobs until retirement, had been at their newspapers a shorter period of time, were more likely to say they had worked for another paper, and had lived in the community their newspaper served for a shorter period of time. They add, however, that these findings should not be taken to mean chain editors did not have the same desire to serve their communities. In fact, the data showed that they spent similar amounts of time meeting with and talking to members of the local community. Parsons, Finnegan and Benham point out that increased commitment to the organization and the presence of codes of conduct might serve to insulate the newspaper from the community and reinforce professional norms. However, the codes also could "increase organizational commitment at the cost of community and professional commitment."[138]

> The model of communicator behavior derived from this role-theory approach suggests that chain editors will be socialized into organizational role expectations that transcend the local community and therefore reduce the salience of community role expectations. In situations of role conflict, this may result in greater organizational commitment and resolution of the conflict in favor of the organization.[139]

Research on nonmedia organizations also supports the finding that managers of absentee-owned businesses are less involved in local community organizations and are oriented more toward the organization than the local community.[140]

Corporate Structure and Job Satisfaction

Empirical research provides a great deal of support for the notion that workers who have more autonomy and freedom in the workplace are more satisfied with their jobs. However, research on the relationship between the size of organization and satisfaction has produced mixed results — some studies even have found that workers in larger organizations are more satisfied.

• *Satisfaction and Nonmedia Organizations.* In one of the earliest nonmedia studies, Worthy reported that employees in the Sears, Roebuck and Company organization who work in smaller units and in smaller communities had higher morale than employees working in larger units and larger communities. They have higher morale because, in part, they "can see its (work's) relation and importance to other functions and to the organization as a whole." However, Worthy also reported that units with many supervisory levels and narrow spans of control had lower levels of satisfaction than those with few supervisory levels and wide spans of control. He argued that supervisors with narrow spans of control supervised their subordinates more closely, whereas those with a larger span were forced to spend more time coordinating work activity than concentrating attention on any single employee.[141]

Similarly, Kohn interviewed 3,101 men representative of all men employed in civilian occupations in the United States in 1964 and found, as expected under Marx's theory, that closeness of supervision, routinization of work, and work that is less complex are related to several measures of alienation, including powerlessness, self-estrangement and normlessness. However, the size of the firm was negatively related to these measures: Employees of highly bureaucratized firms and organizations were less likely to feel powerless, estranged and normless than those of non-bureaucratized firms and organizations.[142] He concluded that the data

> consistently imply that neither capitalism nor bureaucracy is the primary source of alienation in this industrial society. ... My findings point instead to occupational conditions that impinge more directly and immediately on the worker, in particular, to his opportunities to exercise self-direction in his work.[143]

Other research on nonmedia organizations provides strong support for the idea that decentralization of decision-making, the elimination of formalization in organization and other measures of autonomy contribute to high job satisfaction.[144] Studies of media organizations also support this finding. However, research on the relationship between size of the media organization and satisfaction is mixed. The early studies tended to support the argument that journalists in large organizations were less satisfied.

• *Satisfaction and Media Organizations.* In the early 1960s, Samuelson surveyed journalists at daily newspapers in the United States and found that those working at newspapers with circulations of more than 50,000 were significantly less satisfied with their management and personal duties than journalists at smaller newspapers.[145] Also less satisfied on one or more of the six different satisfaction measures used in the study were journalists who worked under Guild contracts, made less than $130 a week, had less than four years of newspaper experience, worked on two or more newspapers, and were under age 35.

Samuelson did not provide an explanation for the findings relating size to satisfaction. But during the early 1970s, Donohue, Tichenor and Olien suggested that reporters at smaller newspapers may be more satisfied because, even though they are paid less than reporters at larger newspapers, they have fewer highly paid colleagues for comparison and perform a greater variety of tasks.[146] This explanation was based in part on reference group theory and the concept of relative deprivation, which emerged from studies of soldiers during World War II.[147] The basic notion is that people do not evaluate their positions in life on the basis of absolute, objective standards, but, rather, on the basis of comparisons with others in their reference group. For example, one of the studies found that even though soldiers serving in the Military Police were less likely to be promoted than soldiers serving in the Army Air Corp, the MPs were more satisfied with their jobs. Why? Because they were less likely to know of a lesser qualified buddy who had been promoted.[148]

Consistent with Samuelson's data, a national survey of more than 1,300 journalists conducted in 1971 by Johnstone, Slawski and Bowman found that those working for large news organizations were less satisfied with their jobs than those at small organizations. However, these researchers did not attribute this finding to relative deprivation; rather, they argued that it stemmed from the loss of autonomy associated with work in large bureaucratic institutions.[149] Johnstone argued that smaller organizations "afford them (journalists) a greater voice in organizational decision-making, less fragmentation of reportorial tasks, and more face-to-face contact with superiors."[150] He added:

> The principal sources of alienation are the fragmentation and routinization of work tasks brought about through excessive specialization, and the impersonality of the contemporary bureaucracy. We would conclude that the strain which emanates from the conflict between the needs of individual professionals for autonomy and a voice in organizational decision-making is

becoming especially acute in American journalism because of increasing centralization in the news industry.[151]

In the late 1970s, Becker, Sobowale and Cobbey reanalyzed the Johnstone data and also found an inverse relationship between size of controlling company and job satisfaction.[152] They questioned the importance the original researchers placed on the link between organizational size and autonomy, arguing that media type (i.e., weekly vs. daily newspaper) was a more important predictor of autonomy. But these findings are not contradictory, since media type and newspaper size conceptually are measuring the same underlying concept — degree of organizational complexity.[153]

Although these early media studies generally supported the argument that journalists in larger organizations are less satisfied with their jobs, studies conducted during the 1980s and 1990s generally failed to support this finding. For example, Weaver and Wilhoit replicated the Johnstone study in a 1982-83 national survey of 1,001 journalists and found that, even though journalists were less satisfied 12 years later, those at larger organizations were no less satisfied than those at smaller ones. The best predictors of satisfaction were esteem for the organization's performance, frequent communication with supervisors and perceived job autonomy.[154] Another follow-up by Weaver and Wilhoit in the early 1990s produced evidence that job satisfaction had declined even more.[155]

Reanalyzing the same data several years later, Bergen and Weaver also found no significant relationship between organizational size and job satisfaction. The single best predictor was respondents' perception of how good a job informing the public they thought their news organization was doing. Older respondents also were more satisfied, along with those who sought out reactions or comments on their work from other people, those who believed that editorial policies are important when rating a job in their field, and those who were most likely to work in the media in the next five years.[156]

In a recent study, Stamm and Underwood interviewed 429 journalists at 12 daily newspapers in California, Idaho and Washington. Using measures they obtained from Samuelson, they found that newspaper size was not a major factor in job satisfaction. However, ownership structure was: Journalists who work for chain newspapers were less satisfied than those who worked for family owned newspapers. They argue that newsroom policies are responsible for these differences.

Job satisfaction at family papers was enhanced by a greater emphasis on reporter initiative, and by a greater tendency for recent changes to improve the balance between business and journalism (or at least not make it worse). The lower job satisfaction at chain papers was in part due to the perception that they discourage unions and the perception that journalism is beginning to take a back seat to business and marketing.[157]

In another recent study, Cook, Banks and Turner administered the Maslach Burnout Inventory to 120 reporters and copy editors from 10 daily newspapers of dissimilar size across the country.[158] The Inventory is a psychological test designed to measure "job burnout" and is composed of three subscales: emotional exhaustion, depersonalization and personal accomplishment.[159] They found that the size of a newspaper was not significantly related to the emotional exhaustion or depersonalization scales, but journalists at larger newspapers were less likely to feel a sense of personal accomplishment. Later, using data from a similar study, Cook and Banks found that reporters at larger newspapers exhibited lower levels of emotional exhaustion.[160] And a study commissioned by the Associated Press Managing Editors Association found that journalists at medium-sized newspapers (50,000 to 150,000 circulation) were less satisfied with their jobs than those at smaller and larger newspapers.[161]

Drawing on reference group theory and the concept of relative deprivation, Demers hypothesized that top editors at large newspapers would be more satisfied with their jobs than top editors at small newspapers because increased role specialization gives them greater autonomy and because they make more money and their jobs are more prestigious. Income did not mediate the effect of size on satisfaction, but autonomy did — editors at larger newspapers were more satisfied. Demers speculated, however, that this finding may not hold for lower-level positions.

> Reporting positions at larger organizations ... also are accorded higher social status and prestige than positions at smaller organizations, and relative comparisons here would be expected to produce higher levels of satisfaction. However, when reporters at larger newspapers compare themselves to other reporters in their organization, the probability for dissatisfaction increases because, structurally, the probability also is greater that the reporter will know of a lesser qualified reporter who has been promoted or rewarded differentially.[162]

In sum, the empirical research is mixed about whether satisfaction among journalists is higher or lower in larger news organizations.

However, the data strongly suggest that autonomy is a consistent and powerful predictor of satisfaction.

Corporate Structure and Editorial-Page Vigor

Despite the popularity of the notion that corporate newspapers are "soft" editorially, only three empirical studies that have examined the effects of ownership structure on editorial-page content support it. The weight of the evidence suggests that large newspapers and chain newspapers are more, not less, vigorous editorially.[163]

A review of the literature produced 18 studies that have examined the effect of organizational structure on editorial-page content or practices. Most employed chain ownership (chain vs. independent newspapers) or some variant of it (e.g., number of newspapers in chain) as the independent variable.[164] Of the 16 studies examined, three generally support the critical model, eight show no relationship or have mixed findings, and seven suggest that chain organizations are more vigorous or create conditions conducive for more diversity.

The earliest study located was published in 1956 by Borstel, who wanted to know whether "home-owned, non-chain papers show a greater interest in local affairs of public interest than chain papers where the owners live hundreds or thousands of miles away," or whether "chain papers, because of their greater financial strength, show greater forthrightness, greater tendencies to speak frankly, regardless of consequence, on local questions."[165] He content-analyzed editorials, columns, letters to the editor and cartoons over a six-week period in 20 small dailies located in northern cities with under 25,000 population. He found "no consistent differences" by ownership structure. In 1971, Grotta published the findings from a study which found no significant differences between independent and chain newspapers in terms of size of the editorial-page newshole and the percentage of editorials as content.[166] Four years later another study reached similar conclusions. Wagenberg and Soderlund studied Canadian newspapers and found no correlation between ownership structure and slant in the treatment of competing political parties or the number of articles written about a variety of editorial themes, including welfare, federalism, and tax reform.[167]

In contrast to those studies, Wackman, Gillmor, Gaziano and Dennis examined newspapers' editorial endorsements of presidential candidates from 1960 to 1972 and concluded that chain newspapers exhibit a high degree of homogeneity.[168] In 1989, Gaziano expanded this dataset to include later elections and concluded that chains still tend to be homogeneous in their presidential choices; however, as chains increase in size, the degree of homogeneity declines.[169] Busterna and Hansen, on the other hand, contend that there is little evidence to substantiate the chain homogeneity argument.[170]

Thrift compared editorials in 24 West Coast chain and independent newspapers before and after the chain-owned newspapers were purchased by a chain.[171] He found that after the purchase, newspapers that became part of a chain were less likely to write editorials that dealt with topics of controversy, local or otherwise, and were less likely to write "argumentative" (as opposed to explanatory) editorials. In contrast, independently owned newspapers posted significant increases on these measures. He concluded that "independently owned daily newspapers' editorials do become less vigorous after the newspapers have been purchased by chains."[172]

In contrast, the 1979 survey by the American Society of Newspaper Editors mentioned earlier found that editorial-page editors at chain-owned newspapers had more freedom to take stands that would be opposed by their publishers and to write on controversial issues.[173] A study by Goodman also produced results that generally supported the ASNE study.[174] He read three months of editorials in 45 chain-owned and 25 independent Illinois weeklies and found that, although independent newspapers published a slightly higher proportion of editorials about local and state subjects, independent papers published fewer editorials overall. The chain weeklies actually published more editorials, more column inches of editorials and made more political endorsements than independent weeklies. And Daugherty's Ph.D. dissertation also supported these studies.[175] Examining the editorial content of 36 chain and 32 independent daily newspapers, he reported that chain papers published more letters to the editor and more editorials, and had more editorials about local issues. No differences were found in the number of presidential endorsements.

St. Dizier reported the findings from a survey of editorial-page editors, which found that chain newspapers were more likely to endorse the Republican candidate for U.S. president in the 1980 election (i.e., Reagan).[176] He also found that chains were more likely to have Republican publishers. About the same time, however, a study of 51 California newspapers by Rystrom found that chains were more likely to endorse Democratic candidates and that the gap had widened from 1970 to 1980.[177]

Hale studied the editorial-page content of 28 daily newspapers when they were independently owned and after they had been purchased by a large chain (groups that own six or more dailies).[178] He concluded that for most of the papers the change in ownership resulted in "only modest change and slight improvement or deterioration."[179] The papers published about the same number of editorial pages, editorials, and letters to the editor after the conversion. For only one of 16 measures was there a significant change: Chain newspapers published slightly fewer miscellaneous articles. Romanow and Soderlund also reported that the purchase of *The* (Toronto) *Globe and Mail* — which is considered to be Canada's "national newspaper" — by the often-criticized Thomson Newspaper chain resulted in few editorial changes. The chain actually doubled the number of local reporters after acquisition, and it was somewhat more vigorous editorially on international issues that involved Britain or the United States.[180]

Akhavan-Majid, Rife and Gopinath found a high level of agreement among editorial positions taken by Gannett newspapers compared with a matched sample of independently owned newspapers; however, the Gannett newspapers were far more likely to editorialize on the three national issues studied and to oppose the positions taken by dominant elites (e.g., President, Supreme Court).[181] A more recent study by Akhavan-Majid and Boudreau found that editors at chain newspapers are more likely than their counterparts at independently owned newspapers to say that the role of their newspaper is to provide critical evaluation of local government performance and to function as a watchdog of business on behalf of consumers.[182] Large newspapers also were more likely to say the role of their newspaper is to function as a watchdog of business. Beam's recent survey of daily newspaper managers supports this finding: Large newspapers are more aggressive editorially and are less partial to advertisers and friends of the publisher.[183] And, finally, Wilhoit and Drew found that editorial editors at group-owned newspapers are far more likely than those at family or independently owned newspapers to say publishers have no influence or very little influence when it comes to "determining the priority given to editorial topics."[184]

In sum, the weight of the empirical evidence fails to support the critical model; rather, the findings suggest just the opposite — that chain newspapers are slightly more vigorous editorially or have the capacity to be more vigorous than independent newspapers.

Summary

Critics charge that the corporate newspaper places more emphasis on profit-making than on news-making, and that it restricts journalists' autonomy, creates a work environment that fosters alienation and dissatisfaction, is less vigorous editorially, and is destroying community solidarity.

Three arguments are put forth to support the first charge: Corporate newspapers are said to have more market power, to be more oriented to the bottom line because they are more likely to be publicly owned, and to be less concerned about the local community than about their own careers and the news organization. The assumption is that greater emphasis on profits means less concern for product quality. Charges that corporate newspapers restrict journalists' autonomy and produce less satisfied employees are based primarily on the argument that decision-making becomes more centralized as an organization grows and becomes more bureaucratized. Corporate newspapers are said to be less vigorous editorially because they cannot afford to alienate advertisers, readers or sources if they expect to maximize profits. And corporate newspapers are destroying community solidarity because their workers are oriented to their own careers and the corporation, not the local community.

This review of the literature provides some support for these arguments. Chain newspapers appear to place greater emphasis on profits, and larger newspapers and chains appear to be more profitable. Some evidence also suggests that chain newspapers devote less space to local news coverage and that their editors are less-oriented to the local community.

However, when taken as a whole, the evidence fails to provide strong support for the critical model. Although corporate newspapers appear to be more profitable, there is little evidence to suggest that this has had an adverse impact on the editorial product or on journalistic freedom and autonomy. Overall, in fact, the evidence suggests that chain newspapers are more vigorous editorially and that large newspapers place much more emphasis on product quality and produce a paper that is deemed to be of higher quality on a number of dimensions. Other research indicates that as an organization grows in size, capitalists (or the owners) play less and less of a role in the day-to-day operations and decision-making — managers play a bigger role. And a content analysis of the *New York Times* indicates that attributions of capitalists have declined while attributions of technocrats have increased. Overall, then, these findings provide more support for the managerial revolution model than the critical model.

Two major contemporary proponents of the managerial revolution thesis are Galbraith and Bell. Galbraith argues that large, corporate organizations should place less value on profit maximization because they are controlled not by the owners (i.e., stockholders), who benefit directly from the profits, but by professional managers, who obtain most of their income through a fixed salary. Galbraith believes that, aside from earning a minimum level of profit, managers place greater emphasis on autonomy, organizational growth, planning, knowledge and expertise. These factors are recognized as the basis of power in the organization and are essential for long-term survival of the organization.

Bell also argues that control of corporate organizations in modern societies is gradually being transferred from the owners to knowledge-based professional and scientific groups (or intellectuals). This shift is part of what he calls the "coming of the post-industrial society." A post-industrial society is one in which knowledge is the primary source of innovation and social organization. In the economy, this is reflected in the decline of manufacturing and goods and the rise of service industries, especially health, education, social welfare services and professional/technical services (research, evaluation, computers, systems analysis). This fosters a new class structure — one based on the supremacy of professional and technical occupations — that gradually replaces the bourgeoisie. Rewards in a post-industrial society are based less on inheritance or property than on education and skill (i.e., the meritocracy).

Notes

1. Ben H. Bagdikian, *The Media Monopoly*, 2nd ed. (Boston: Beacon Press, 1987); Ben H. Bagdikian, "The U.S. Media: Supermarket or Assembly Line?" *Journal of Communication* 35(3):97-109 (1985); C. Edwin Baker, *Ownership of Newspapers: The View from Positivist Social Science*, (Cambridge, Mass.: The Joan Shorenstein Center at Harvard University, September 1994); Commission on Freedom of the Press, *A Free and Responsible Press* (Chicago: University of Chicago Press, 1947); Edward S. Herman, "Diversity of News: 'Marginalizing' the Opposition," *Journal of Communication* 35(3):135-46 (1985); Andrew Kreig, *Spiked: How Chain Management Corrupted America's Oldest Newspaper* (Old Saybrook, Conn.: Peregrine Press, 1987); Jonathan Kwitney, "The High Cost of High Profits," *Washington Journalism Review* (June 1990), pp. 19-29; Graham Murdock and Peter Golding, "Capitalism, Communication and Class Relations," pp. 12-43 in J. Curran, M. Gurevitch and J. Woollacott (eds.), *Mass Communication and Society* (Beverly Hills, Calif.: Sage, 1977); James D. Squires, *Read All About It: The Corporate Takeover of America's Newspapers* (New York: Times Books, 1993); John Soloski, "Economics and Management: The Real Influence of Newspaper Groups," *Newspaper Research Journal*, 1:19-28 (1979); and Doug Underwood, *When MBAs Rule the Newsroom: How the Marketers and Managers Are Reshaping Today's Media* (New York: Columbia University Press, 1993).

2. Edward Herman, "Media in the U.S. Political Economy," pp. 75-87 in John Downing, Ali Mohammadi, and Annabelle Sreberny-Mohammadi (eds.), *Questioning the Media: A Critical Introduction* (Newbury Park, Calif.: Sage, 1990), p. 79.

3. Bagdikian, *The Media Monopoly*, pp. 12-6; William B. Blankenburg, "A Newspaper Chain's Pricing Behavior," *Journalism Quarterly*, 60:275-80 (1983); Leo Bogart, *Press and Public*, 2nd ed. (Hillsdale, N.J.: Lawrence Erlbaum Associates, 1989); Benjamin M.

Compaine, Christopher H. Sterling, Thomas Guback and J. Kendrick Noble, *Who Owns the Media? Concentration of Ownership in the Mass Communications Industry* (White Plains, N.Y.: Knowledge Industry, 1982); Don R. Pember, *Mass Media in America* (Chicago: Science Research, 1974); and Gerald Stone, "A Mellow Appraisal of Media Monopoly Mania," in Michael Emery and T. C. Smythe (eds.), *Mass Communication: Concepts and Issues in the Mass Media* (Dubuque, Iowa: William C. Brown Company, 1980), p. 50.

4. Paul M. Hirsch and Tracy A. Thompson, "The Stock Market as Audience: The Impact of Public Ownership on Newspapers," pp. 142-58 in James S. Ettema and D. Charles Whitney (eds.), *Audiencemaking: How the Media Create the Audience* (Thousand Oaks, Calif.: Sage, 1994), pp. 149-50. Also see Ben H. Bagdikian, "Conglomeration, Concentration, and the Media," *Journal of Communication*, 30(2):59-64 (1980). The newspaper field is very profitable relative to other industries (see, e.g., Bogart, *Press and Public*, Chapter 2).

5. Roland J. Pellegrin and Charles H. Coates, "Absentee-Owned Corporations and Community Power Structure," *American Journal of Sociology*, 61:413-9 (1956).

6. Patrick Parsons, John Finnegan, Jr. and William Benham, "Editors and Their Roles," pp. 91-104 in Robert G. Picard, James P. Winter, Maxwell E. McCombs and Stephen Lacy (eds.), *Press Concentration and Monopoly* (Norwood, N.J.: Ablex, 1988).

7. Large newspapers also are believed to be less responsive to the local community because of increased emphasis on formalized rules and procedures that often result in impersonal relationships within the organization as well as with external publics. In response to these charges, some economists would argue that a bottom-line orientation means that the newspaper is responsive to the community's needs.

8. Hirsch and Thompson, "The Stock Market as Audience," p. 150.

9. See, for example, Bagdikian, *The Media Monopoly*, pp. 212-8, and Doug Underwood, "When MBAs Rule the Newsroom," *Columbia Journalism Review* (March/April 1988), pp. 23-40.

10. This definition is adopted from Gloria V. Engel, "Professional Autonomy and Bureaucratic Organization," *Administrative Science Quarterly*, 15:12-21 (1970), p. 12. Engel defines autonomy as having individual and group dimensions. She further refines the individual dimension into personal autonomy, or freedom to conduct tangential work activities in a normative manner in accordance with one's own discretion, and work-related autonomy, freedom to practice in accordance with one's professional training. This study does not distinguish between the two but does assume that either contributes to greater diversity of ideas in the marketplace.

11. For a more thorough discussion of the concept of diversity, see William Floyd Griswold, Jr., *Community Structure, Reporter Specialization and Content Diversity Among Midwest Daily Newspapers* (Ph.D. Diss., University of Minnesota, 1990), pp. 11-7.

12. John W. C. Johnstone, Edward J. Slawski, and William W. Bowman, *The News People* (Urbana, IL: University of Illinois Press, 1976), p. 85.

13. Adam Smith, *The Wealth of Nations* (New York: Modern Library, 1937 [1776]), p. 734.

14. Smith gave three reasons why the division of labor increases production: (1) Workers become more dexterous and proficient when they perform a limited number of tasks over and over again; (2) Time is saved when passing from one task to another; and (3) Machines can be used to perform simple tasks.

15. Smith also argued that a number of other factors affected job satisfaction, including high wages, power, prestige, autonomy and creativity. For a review, see Margaret H. DeFleur, "Foundations of Job Satisfaction in the Media Industries," *Journalism Educator*,

47(1):3-15 (1992).

16. Quoted in Robert C. Tucker (ed.), *The Marx-Engles Reader*, 2nd ed. (New York: W. W. Norton & Company, 1978), p. 74, from the "Economic and Philosophic Manuscripts of 1844."

17. Many other writers have built on the ideas of Smith and Marx. Most notably, C. Wright Mills has argued that large bureaucracies also alienate professional workers and managers. He wrote: "The objective alienation of man from the product and process of work is entailed by the legal framework of modern capitalism and the modern division of labour. The worker does not own the product or the tools of his production. In the labour contract he sells his time, energy, and skill into the power of others ... a person instrumentalizes and externalizes intimate features of his person and disposition. In certain white-collar areas, the rise of personality markets has carried self and social alienation to explicit extremes." Source: C. Wright Mills, *White Collar* (New York: Oxford University Press, 1953), pp. 225-7.

18. A good summary of economic theory of the firm can be found in Ernest Gellhorn, *Antitrust Law and Economics* (St. Paul, Minn.: West, 1986), pp. 51-4.

19. Smith, *Wealth of Nations*, p. 324. Also, see page 62 in Chapter 3 of this book.

20. Karl Marx, *Capital: A Critique of Political Economy,* vol. 1, Samuel Moore and Edward Aveling, trans. (New York: International Publishers, 1987 [1867]), pp. 582-6.

21. For more detailed information, see Chapter 3.

22. Eduard Bernstein, *Evolutionary Socialism* (New York: Schocken, 1961 [1899]), p. 54.

23. Max Weber, *The Theory of Social and Economic Organization*, trans. A. M. Henderson and Talcott Parsons (New York: Free Press, 1947).

24. Weber, *The Theory of Social and Economic Organization*, pp. 248-9.

25. Weber, *The Theory of Social and Economic Organization*, p. 338.

26. Adolph A. Berle and Gardiner C. Means, *The Modern Corporation and Private Property (*New York: Commerce Clearing House, 1932), p. 69.

27. Berle and Means, *The Modern Corporation and Private Property*, p. 69.

28. James Burnham, *The Managerial Revolution* (New York: John Day, 1941).

29. Burnham, *The Managerial Revolution*, p. 71.

30. Joseph A. Schumpeter, *The Theory of Economic Development* (Cambridge, Mass.: Harvard University Press, 1949).

31. Schumpeter, *The Theory of Economic Development.*

32. Maurice Zeitlin, "Corporate Ownership and Control: The Large Corporation and the Capitalist Class," *American Journal of Sociology,* 79:1073-119 (1974).

33. Talcott Parsons, "A Revised Analytical Approach to the Theory of Social Stratification," in Richard Bendix and Seymour Martin Lipset (eds.), *Class, Status, and Power* (Glencoe, Ill.: Free Press, 1953), pp. 122-3.

34. Ralph Dahrendorf, *Class and Class Conflict in Industrial Society* (Stanford, Calif.: Stanford University Press, 1959 [1957 German Edition]), pp. 275-6.

35. John Kenneth Galbraith, *The New Industrial State,* 2nd ed. (New York: Houghton Mifflin, 1971), p. xix.

36. Galbraith calls the belief that professional managers are more profit-maximizing the "approved contradiction."

37. Daniel Bell, *The Coming of the Post-Industrial Society* (New York: Basic Books, 1976 [1973]).

38. See, e.g., Alaine Touraine, *The Post-Industrial Society* (New York: Random House, 1971).

39. The evidence on whether daily newspapers face significant competition from broadcast media or weekly newspapers is mixed. For a review, see David Pearce Demers, "Structural Pluralism, Intermedia Competition and the Growth of the Corporate Newspaper in the United States," *Journalism Monographs,* vol. 145 (June 1994).

40. Gellhorn, *Anti-Trust Law and Economics*, p. 63.

41. John C. Busterna, "How Managerial Ownership Affects Profit Maximization in Newspaper Firms," *Journalism Quarterly,* 66:302-7, 358 (1989), p. 303. Busterna actually hypothesizes the opposite — that owner-controlled newspapers would place less emphasis on profits.

42. Scholars have argued that even if managers run the day-to-day operations, this does not mean they control the organization, since top management is accountable to the board of directors. Moreover, others have argued that even though there is no direct evidence that owners exert direct control of corporate organizations, they retain potential for control. Zeitlin and others also have argued that corporate leadership, even if it does not have sole ownership of a company, nevertheless makes its decisions on the basis of continued acquisition of power and wealth.

43. Zeitlin, *Corporate Ownership and Control,* p. 1107.

44. David Jary and Julia Jary, *The HarperCollins Dictionary of Sociology* (New York: HarperCollins, 1991), p. 375.

45. Nicholas Abercrombie, Stephen Hill and Bryan S. Turner, *Dictionary of Sociology,* 2nd ed. (London: Penguin Books, 1988), p. 191, and John Scott, "Managerial Revolution," pp. 353-5 in William Outhwaite and Tom Bottomore (eds.), *The Blackwell Dictionary of Twentieth-Century Social Thought* (Oxford, England: Blackwell, 1994).

46. Berle and Means, *The Modern Corporation and Private Property.*

47. U.S. Temporary National Economic Committee, *The Distribution of Ownership in the 200 Largest Nonfinancial Corporations,* Monograph 29 (Washington, D.C.: U.S. Government Printing Office, 1940), p. 104.

48. Robert Aaron Gordon, *Business Leadership in the Large Corporation* (Berkeley, Calif.: University of California Press, 1961 [1945]).

49. Robert Sheehan, "There's Plenty of Privacy Left in Private Enterprise," *Fortune* (July 15, 1966), pp. 224-5, 327-8, 334, 343, 348.

50. Philip H. Burch, *The Managerial Revolution Reassessed* (Lexington, Mass.: D.C. Heath and Company, 1972).

51. Robert J. Larner, *Management Control in the Large Corporation* (Cambridge, Mass.: Dunellen, 1970).

52. Larner, *Management Control in the Large Corporation,* p. 20.

53. Burch, *The Managerial Revolution Reassessed.*

54. Joseph R. Monsen, Jr., John S. Chiu and David E. Cooley, "The Effect of Separation of Ownership and Control on the Performance of the Large Firm," *Quarterly Journal of Economics,* 82:435-51 (1968).

55. John Palmer, "The Profit-Performance Effect of the Separation of Ownership from Control in Large U.S. Industrial Corporations," *Bell Journal of Economics and Management Science,* 4:299-303 (1973).

56. Larner, *Management Control in the Large Corporation.*

57. Neil Fligstein and Peter Brantley, "Bank Control, Owner Control, or Organizational Dynamics: Who Controls the Large Modern Corporation," *American Journal of Sociology,* 98:280-307 (1992).

58. Brian V. Hindley, "Separation of Ownership and Control in the Modern Corporation," *The Journal of Law and Economics,* 13:185-221 (1970), and David R. Kamerschen, "The Influence of Ownership and Control on Profit Rates," *American Economic Review,* 58:432-47 (1968).

59. David R. James and Michael Soref, "Profit Constraints on Managerial Autonomy: Managerial Theory and the Unmaking of the Corporate President," *American Sociological Review,* 46:1-18 (1981).

60. David Pearce Demers, "Front-Page News Story Attribution and the Managerial Revolution," unpublished paper (University of Wisconsin—River Falls, Wis., October 1994).

61. The sampling dates in each year were as follows: 4th Monday in January; 4th Tuesday in February; 2nd Wednesday in March; 2nd Thursday in April; 1st Friday and 4th Sunday in May; 1st Saturday in June; 1st Sunday in July; 4th Monday in August; 3rd Tuesday in September; 3rd Wednesday in October; 1st Saturday and 4th Thursday in November; and 1st Friday in December. Research shows that two weeks is optimal for obtaining stable reliability estimates. See Daniel Riffe, Charles F. Aust, and Stephen R. Lacy, "The Effectiveness of Random, Consecutive Day and Constructed Week Sampling in Newspaper Content Analysis," *Journalism Quarterly,* 70:133-9 (1993).

62. The intercoder reliability coefficients for the three pairs of coders ranged between 73 percent and 92 percent for the technocrats and between 79 percent and 85 percent for the capitalists. The overall means were 79 percent and 81 percent, respectively. The final listing of sources for each group was created if two or more of the coders were in agreement. A total of 42 sources fell into the technocrats group, including scientists, campaign experts, director of Harvard Observatory, government economists, professor of economics and finance at Princeton, United Federation of Teachers, professor of New York university, legal scholars, budget director, U.S. advisors, and wide range of experts. A total of 48 sources fell into the capitalists group, including bank president, secretary of the stock exchange, stockholders, Hearst corporation, prominent oil men, a banker, president of Associated General Contractors of America, spokesman for Ford, vice president of AT&T, many business leaders, Paramount Pictures, chairman of Ford, and president of railroad.

One shortcoming of this methodology is that only front-page attributions were coded. Ideally, the entire newspaper should be content-analyzed, but this was not practical because of limited resources. As a consequence, one assumption underlying this classification scheme is that changes reflected on the front page are indicative of changes in power in the entire social system. A critic might counter that front-page attributions are not a good indicator of changes in the power structure because of the growth of specialized business sections. However, it is important to point out that this study focuses on relative, not absolute, changes in power, and the growth of specialized business sections also has been accompanied by growth in other specialized sections that depend heavily on technocrats.

63. William B. Blankenburg, "Newspaper Scale and Newspaper Expenditures," *Newspaper Research Journal,* 10(2):97-103 (1989).

64. Marty Tharp and Linda R. Stanley, "A Time Series Analysis of Newspaper Profitability by Circulation Size," *The Journal of Media Economics* 5(1):3-12 (1992). Also see Marty Tharp and Linda R. Stanley, "Trends in Profitability of Daily U.S. Newspapers by Circulation Size, 1978-1988," paper delivered at Association for Education in Journalism and Mass Communication (Minneapolis, August 1990).

65. Bagdikian, *The Media Monopoly*; Compaine, Sterling, Guback and Noble, *Who Owns the Media?*; James N. Rosse and J. N. Dertouzos, "An Economist's Description of the 'Media Industry,'" pp. 40-192 in *Proceedings of the Symposium on Media Concentration, December 14 and 15, 1978,* vol. 1 (Washington, D.C.: U.S. Government Printing Office,

1979).

66. David Pearce Demers, "Corporate Structure and Emphasis on Profits and Product Quality at U.S. Daily Newspapers," *Journalism Quarterly,* 68:15-26 (1991). No relationship was found for a closed-ended measure of profit-orientation.

67. Soloski, "Economics and Management: The Real Influence of Newspaper Groups," and Kristine McGrath and Cecilie Gaziano, "Dimensions of Media Credibility: Highlights of the 1985 ASNE Survey," *Newspaper Research Journal,* 7(2):55-67 (1986).

68. William B. Blankenburg, "A Newspaper Chain's Pricing Behavior," and John C. Busterna, "National Advertising Pricing: Chain vs. Independent Newspapers," *Journalism Quarterly,* 65:307-12 (1988).

69. Blankenburg, "A Newspaper Chain's Pricing Behavior," p. 276.

70. David Pearce Demers and Daniel B. Wackman, "Effect of Chain Ownership on Newspaper Management Goals," *Newspaper Research Journal,* 9:59-68 (1988).

71. Demers, "Corporate Structure and Emphasis on Profits and Product Quality at U.S. Daily Newspapers."

72. Busterna, "How Managerial Ownership Affects Profit Maximization in Newspaper Firms." This argument is consistent with the first model (critical model) presented in the previous section in this paper.

73. William B. Blankenburg and Gary W. Ozanich, "The Effect of Public Ownership on the Financial Performance of Newspaper Corporations," *Journalism Quarterly,* 70:68-75 (1993). Also see William B. Blankenburg and Gary W. Ozanich, "Public Ownership of Newspaper Corporations: A Cause in Search of Effects," paper delivered at Midwest Association for Public Opinion Research annual meeting (Chicago, November 1990).

74. C. N. Olien, P. J. Tichenor and G. A. Donohue, "Relation Between Corporate Ownership and Editor Attitudes About Business," *Journalism Quarterly,* 65:259-66 (1988).

75. G. A. Donohue, C. N. Olien and P. J. Tichenor, "Structure and Constraints on Community Newspaper Gatekeepers," *Journalism Quarterly,* 66:807-12, 845 (1989).

76. Blankenburg, "Newspaper Scale and Newspaper Expenditures," p. 101.

77. Demers, "Corporate Structure and Emphasis on Profits and Product Quality at U.S. Daily Newspapers."

78. Randal A. Beam, "The Impact of Group Ownership Variables on Organizational Professionalism at Daily Newspapers," *Journalism Quarterly,* 70:907-18 (1993).

79. George A. Gladney, "Newspaper Excellence: How Editors of Small and Large Papers Judge Quality," *Newspaper Research Journal,* 11(2):58-72 (1990).

80. Warren Breed, "Mass Communication and Sociocultural Integration," *Social Forces,* 37:109-16 (1958); Morris Janowitz, *The Community Press in an Urban Setting* (New York: Free Press, 1952); Clarice N. Olien, George A. Donohue and Phillip J. Tichenor, "The Community Editor's Power and the Reporting of Conflict," *Journalism Quarterly,* 45:243-52 (1968); and Arthur J. Vidich and Joseph Bensman, *Small Town in Mass Society* (Princeton, N.J.: Princeton University Press, 1968).

81. Lawrence C. Soley and Robert L. Craig, "Advertising Pressures on Newspapers: A Survey," *Journal of Advertising,* 21(4):1-9 (1992), p. 7.

82. Soley and Craig, "Advertising Pressures on Newspapers," p. 7.

83. Philip Meyer and David Arant, "A Test of the Neuharth Conjecture: Searching an Electronic Database to Evaluate Newspaper Quality," paper delivered at Association for Education in Journalism and Mass Communication (Kansas City, Mo., August 1993).

84. Douglas Anderson, "How Managing Editors View and Deal With Ethical Issues," *Journalism Quarterly,* 64:341-5 (1987).

85. Johnstone, Slawski, and Bowman, *The News People.*

86. David Pearce Demers, "Use of Polls in Reporting Changes Slightly Since 1978," *Journalism Quarterly,* 64:839-42 (1987).

87. Leonard Downie, Jr., *The New Muckrakers* (New York: Mentor, 1976) and Leonard Leslie Sellers, *Investigative Reporting: Methods and Barriers* (Ph.D. Diss., Stanford University, 1977).

88. James S. Ettema and Theodore L. Glasser, "Public Accountability or Public Relations? Newspaper Ombudsmen Define Their Role," *Journalism Quarterly,* 64:3-12 (1987).

89. Thimios Zaharopoulos and Ronald E. McIntosh, "Newspaper Pultizer Prizes and Their Relationship to Circulation," paper presented to the Association for Education in Journalism and Mass Communication (Kansas City, Mo., August 1993), and Meyer and Arant, "A Test of the Neuharth Conjecture." Meyer and Arant also found that newspapers that win Pulitzer Prizes make fewer spelling and editing errors.

90. Lee B. Becker, Randy Beam and John Russial, "Correlates of Daily Newspaper Performance in New England," *Journalism Quarterly,* 55:100-8 (1978).

91. Stephen Lacy, "The Effects of Group Ownership on Daily Newspaper Content," paper presented to the Midwest Association for Public Opinion Research (Chicago, November 1986).

92. Patrick R. Parsons, John Finnegan, Jr., and William Benham, "Editors and Their Roles," pp. 91-103 in Robert G. Picard, James P. Winter, Maxwell E. McCombs and Stephen Lacy (eds.), *Press Concentration and Monopoly: New Perspectives on Newspaper Ownership and Operation* (Norwood, N.J.: Ablex, 1988), p. 102.

93. Dean M. Flatt, "Managerial Incentives: Effects at a Chain Owned Daily," *Newspaper Research Journal,* 2(1):48-55 (1980).

94. See Barry R. Litman and J. Bridges, "An Economic Analysis of Daily Newspaper Performance," *Newspaper Research Journal,* 7(3):9-26 (1986).

95. Theodore L. Glasser, David S. Allen and S. Elizabeth Blanks, "The Influence of Chain Ownership On News Play: A Case Study," *Journalism Quarterly,* 66:607-14 (1989).

96. Litman and Bridges, "An Economic Analysis of Daily Newspaper Performance," and Dan Drew and G. Cleveland Wilhoit, "Newshole Allocation Policies of American Daily Newspapers," *Journalism Quarterly,* 53:434-40 (1976).

97. Gerald L. Grotta, "Consolidation of Newspapers: What Happens to the Consumer," *Journalism Quarterly,* 48:245-50 (1971).

98. Loren Ghiglione, *The Buying and Selling of America's Newspapers* (Indianapolis, Ind.: R. J. Berg, 1984).

99. David Bruce Daugherty, "Group-Owned Newspapers vs. Independently Owned Newspapers: An Analysis of the Difference and Similarities" (Ph.D. Diss., University of Texas, 1983).

100. Stephen Lacy and Frederick Fico, "Newspaper Quality and Ownership: Rating the Groups," *Newspaper Research Journal,* 11(2):42-56 (1990). The index was composed of the following: commitment to locally produced copy, amount of non-advertising copy, ratio of non-advertising to advertising space, number of interpretative and in-depth stories, amount of graphics, number of wire services, story length — more depth, and reporter workload.

101. David C. Coulson, "Impact of Ownership on Newspaper Quality," *Journalism Quarterly,* 71:403-10 (1994), p. 408.

102. Beam, "The Impact of Group Ownership Variables."

103. Demers, "Corporate Newspaper Structure and Emphasis on Profits and Product Quality."

104. Stephen Lacy and Daniel Riffe, "The Impact of Competition and Group Ownership on Radio News," *Journalism Quarterly,* 71:583-93 (1994), and Paul D. Baldridge, "Group and Non-Group Owner Programming: A Comparative Analysis," *Journal of Broadcasting,* 11:125-30 (1967).

105. Johnstone, Slawski and Bowman, *The News People,* and Daniel B. Wackman, Donald M. Gillmor, Cecile Gaziano and Everette E. Dennis, "Chain Newspaper Autonomy as Reflected in Presidential Campaign Endorsements," *Journalism Quarterly,* 52:411-20 (1975).

106. Peter M. Blau and Marshall W. Meyer, *Bureaucracy in Modern Society,* 3rd ed. (New York: Random House, 1987). See Chapter 5.

107. See, e.g., Weber, *The Theory of Social and Economic Organization,* and H. H. Gerth and C. Wright Mills (eds.), *From Max Weber* (New York: Oxford University Press, 1946).

108. Autonomy was often conceptualized as one dimension or component of professionalism. See Peter M. Blau, Wolf V. Heydebrand and Robert E. Stauffer, "The Structure of Small Bureaucracies," *American Sociological Review,* 31:179-91 (1966); Celia Davies, "Professionals in Bureaucracies: the Conflict Thesis Revisited," in Robert Dingwall and Philip Lewis (eds.), *The Sociology of the Professions* (New York: St. Martin's Press, 1983), pp. 177-220; Engel, "Professional Autonomy and Bureaucratic Organization," pp. 12-21; Jerald Hage, "An Axiomatic Theory of Organizations," *Administrative Science Quarterly* 10:289-320 (1965); and Richard H. Hall, "Professionalization and Bureaucratization," *American Sociological Review,* 33:92-104 (1968).

109. W. R. Scott, "Professionals in Bureaucracies: Areas of Conflict," in H. Vollmer and D. Mills (eds.), *Professionalism* (Englewood Cliffs, N.J.: Prentice Hall, 1966).

110. Hall, "Professionalization and Bureaucratization."

111. J. Kenneth Benson, "The Analysis of Bureaucratic-Professional Conflict: Functional Versus Dialectical Approaches," *The Sociological Quarterly,* 14:378-89 (1973), pp. 378-9.

112. Roger Mansfield, "Bureaucracy and Centralization: An Examination of Organizational Structure," *Administrative Science Quarterly,* 18:477-88 (1973).

113. Weber, *The Theory of Social and Economic Organization,* p. 197.

114. Weber, *The Theory of Social and Economic Organization,* p. 488.

115. Mansfield, "Bureaucracy and Centralization," p. 479.

116. Peter M. Blau and Richard A Schoenherr, *The Structure of Organizations* (New York: Basic Books, 1971); John Child, "Organization Structure and Strategies of Control: A Replication of the Aston Study," *Administrative Science Quarterly,* 17:163-77 (1972); and D. S. Pugh, D. J. Hickson, C. R. Hinings, and C. Turner, "Dimensions of Organizational Structure," *Administrative Science Quarterly,* 13:65-105 (1968).

117. Engel, "Professional Autonomy and Bureaucratic Organization," p. 19.

118. Blau and Meyer, *Bureaucracy in Modern Society,* p. 98. Also see Peter M. Blau, *The Organization of Academic Work* (New York: John Wiley and Sons, Inc., 1973).

119. Blau and Meyer, *Bureaucracy in Modern Society.*

120. Blau and Meyer, *Bureaucracy in Modern Society,* pp. 98-99.

121. David H. Weaver and G. Cleveland Wilhoit, *The American Journalist: A Portrait of U.S. News People and Their Work* (Bloomington: Indiana University Press, 1986).

122. David C. Coulson, "Journalists' Assessment of Group Ownership and Their Newspapers' Local News and Editorial Performance," paper presented to the Association for Education in Journalism and Mass Communication (Boston, August 1991).

123. American Society of Newspaper Editors, "News and Editorial Independence: A Survey of Group and Independent Editors" (April 1980).

124. Merrill Lindsay, "Lindsay-Schaub Newspapers," in "That Monopoly of Opinion," *The Masthead* (Fall 1974), pp. 21-23; "The Chain That Doesn't Bind," *Time* 17 (May 1968), pp. 71-72; and "Yeah, What About that Monopoly of Opinion?" *The Masthead* (Fall 1974), p. 12.

125. Wackman, Gillmor, Gaziano and Dennis, "Chain Newspaper Autonomy."

126. Wackman, Gillmor, Gaziano and Dennis, "Chain Newspaper Autonomy," p. 420.

127. Cecilie Gaziano, "Chain Newspaper Homogeneity and Presidential Endorsements, 1972-1980," *Journalism Quarterly*, 66:836-45 (1989), pp. 844-5.

128. John C. Busterna and Kathleen A. Hansen, "Presidential Endorsement Patterns by Chain-Owned Papers, 1976-84," *Journalism Quarterly*, 67:286-94 (1990).

129. Ronald H. Wagenberg and Walter C. Soderlund, "The Influence of Chain Ownership on Editorial Comment in Canada," *Journalism Quarterly*, 52:93-8 (1975).

130. G. A. Donohue, C. N. Olien and P. J. Tichenor, "Structure and Constraints on Community Newspaper Gatekeepers," *Journalism Quarterly*, 66:807-12, 845 (1989). Also see Olien, Tichenor and Donohue, "Relation Between Corporate Ownership and Editor Attitudes About Business."

131. G. Cleveland Wilhoit and Dan G. Drew, "Editorial Writers on American Daily Newspapers: A 20-Year Portrait," *Journalism Monographs*, vol. 129 (October 1991), p. 31.

132. David Pearce Demers, "Effect of Corporate Structure on Autonomy of Top Editors at U.S. Dailies," *Journalism Quarterly*, 70:499-508 (1993).

133. Gladney, "Newspaper Excellence," pp. 65, 67.

134. George A. Donohue, Clarice N. Olien and Phillip J. Tichenor, "Reporting Conflict by Pluralism, Newspaper Type and Ownership," *Journalism Quarterly*, 62:489-99, 507 (1985).

135. This argument is derived from my conversations with Phillip J. Tichenor.

136. Gladney, "Newspaper Excellence."

137. Parsons, Finnegan and Benham, "Editors and Their Roles."

138. Parsons, Finnegan and Benham, "Editors and Their Roles," p. 102.

139. Parsons, Finnegan and Benham, "Editors and Their Roles," p. 103.

140. Pellegrin and Coates, "Absentee-Owned Corporations and Community Power Structure."

141. James Worthy, "Organizational Structure and Employee Morale," *American Sociological Review*, 15:169-79 (1950).

142. Melvin L. Kohn, "Occupational Structure and Alienation," *American Journal of Sociology*, 82:111-30 (1976).

143. Kohn, "Occupational Structure and Alienation," pp. 127-8.

144. For a review, see Koya Azumi and Jerald Hage (eds.), *Organizational Systems* (Lexington, Mass.: D. C. Heath and Company, 1972), especially pp. 419-20.

145. He excluded newspaper executives. See Merrill Samuelson, "A Standardized Test to Measure Job Satisfaction in the Newsroom," *Journalism Quarterly*, 39:285-91 (1962).

146. George A. Donohue, Phillip J. Tichenor, and Clarice N. Olien, "Gatekeeping: Mass Media Systems and Information Control," pp. 41-69 in F. Gerald Kline and Phillip J. Tichenor (eds.), *Current Perspectives in Mass Communication Research* (Beverly Hills, Calif.: Sage Publications, 1972), p. 49.

147. For a summary, see Robert K. Merton, *Social Theory and Social Structure* (New York: Free Press, 1957 [1949]). See Chapter 8.

148. Merton, *Social Theory and Social Structure*, Chapter 8.

149. Johnstone, Slawski and Bowman, *The News People*, Chapter 8.

150. John W. C. Johnstone, "Organizational Constraints on Newswork," *Journalism Quarterly*, 53:5-13 (1976).

151. Johnstone, "Organizational Constraints on Newswork," p. 13.

152. Lee B. Becker, Idowu A. Sobowale and Robin E. Cobbey, "Reporters and Their Professional and Organizational Commitment," *Journalism Quarterly*, 56:753-63, 770 (1979).

153. For a discussion of the concept of organizational complexity and its relationship to size and ownership, see Demers, "Effect of Corporate Structure on Autonomy of Top Editors at U.S. Dailies," and "Corporate Structure and Emphasis on Profits and Product Quality at U.S. Daily Newspapers."

154. Weaver and Wilhoit, *The American Journalist*, pp. 88-92.

155. G. Cleveland Wilhoit and David Weaver, "U.S. Journalists at Work, 1971-1992," paper presented to the Association for Education in Journalism and Mass Communication (Atlanta, August 1994).

156. Lori A. Bergen and David Weaver, "Job Satisfaction of Daily Newspaper Journalists and Organizational Size," *Newspaper Research Journal*, 9:1-13 (1988).

157. Keith Stamm and Doug Underwood, "The Relationship of Job Satisfaction to Newsroom Policy Changes," paper presented to the Association for Education in Journalism and Mass Communication (Washington, D.C., August 1991), p. 16.

158. Betsy B. Cook, Steve R. Banks, and Ralph J. Turner, "The Effects of Work Environment on Job Burnout in Newspaper Reporters and Copy Editors," *Newspaper Research Journal*, 14:123-36 (1993).

159. Christina Maslach and Susan E. Jackson, *Maslach Burnout Inventory* (Palo Alto, Calif.: Consulting Psychologists Press, 1981).

160. Betsy B. Cook and Steven R. Banks, "Predictors of Job Burnout in Reporters and Copy Editors," *Journalism Quarterly*, 70:108-17 (1993).

161. Kristin McGrath, *Journalist Satisfaction Study* (Minneapolis: Associated Press Managing Editors Association, 1993), p. 6.

162. David Pearce Demers, "Effect of Organizational Size on Job Satisfaction of Top Editors at U.S. Dailies," *Journalism Quarterly*, 71:914-25 (1994).

163. A chain is usually defined as two or more newspapers in separate cities under the same ownership.

164. Some studies use more than two newspapers as a cut-off criteria, while others used size of chain.

165. Gerald H. Borstel, "Ownership, Competition and Comment," *Journalism Quarterly*, 33:220-2 (1956).

166. Grotta, "Consolidation of Newspapers: What Happens to the Consumer."

167. Wagenberg and Soderlund, "The Influence of Chain Ownership on Editorial Comment in Canada."

168. Wackman, Gillmor, Gaziano and Dennis, "Chain Newspaper Autonomy as Reflected in Presidential Campaign Endorsements."

169. Gaziano, "Chain Newspaper Homogeneity and Presidential Endorsements."

170. Busterna and Hansen, "Presidential Endorsement Patterns by Chain-Owned Papers."

171. Ralph Thrift, Jr., "How Chain Ownership Affects Editorial Vigor of Newspapers," *Journalism Quarterly*, 54:327-31 (1977).

172. Thrift, "How Chain Ownership Affects Editorial Vigor of Newspapers," p. 331.

173. American Society of Newspaper Editors, "News and Editorial Independence."

174. Mark Lee Goodman, "Newspaper Ownership and the Weekly Editorial in Illinois" (M.A. Thesis, South Dakota State University, 1982).

175. Daugherty, "Group-Owned Newspapers vs. Independently Owned Newspapers."

176. Byron St. Dizier, "Editorial Page Editors and Endorsements: Chain-Owned vs. Independent Newspapers," *Newspaper Research Journal,* 8:63-8 (1986). The finding that chain newspapers are more likely to support Republicans is interpreted here as providing support for the argument that corporate newspapers are less likely than entrepreneurial newspapers to promote social change, since Republicans, historically, have been more likely than Democrats to resist change and support traditional ways and value systems.

177. Kenneth Rystrom, "The Impact of Newspaper Endorsements," *Newspaper Research Journal,* 4:19-28 (1986).

178. F. Dennis Hale, "Editorial Diversity and Concentration," pp. 161-76 in Robert G. Picard, Maxwell E. McCombs, James P. Winter, and Stephen Lacy (eds.), *Press Concentration and Monopoly* (Norwood, N.J.: Ablex, 1988).

179. Hale, "Editorial Diversity and Concentration," p. 172.

180. Walter I. Romanow and Walter C. Soderlund, "Thomson Newspapers' Acquisition of 'The Globe and Mail': A Case Study of Content Change," *Gazette,* 41:5-17 (1988).

181. Roya Akhavan-Majid, Anita Rife, and Sheila Gopinath, "Chain Ownership and Editorial Independence: A Case Study of Gannett Newspapers," *Journalism Quarterly,* 68:59-66 (1991).

182. Roya Akhavan-Majid and Timothy Boudreau, "Chain Ownership, Organizational Prominence, and Editorial Role Perceptions," paper delivered to the Association for Education in Journalism and Mass Communication (Atlanta, August 1994).

183. Beam, "The Impact of Group Ownership Variables."

184. Wilhoit and Drew, "Editorial Writers on American Daily Newspapers," p. 31.

Chapter 9

A Theory of
Corporate Newspaper Effects

The empirical research reviewed in Chapter 8 provides some support for the critical model of corporate newspaper effects. Chain newspapers appear to place more emphasis on profits as an organizational goal than independently owned newspapers. Chains and large newspapers also are more profitable than independently owned newspapers and small newspapers, respectively. And the owners and managers of chain newspapers appear to be less involved in the local community and more oriented to their careers and their organizations.[1]

Additional research is necessary to clarify these effects. But even if it shows that chain or corporate newspapers are "greedier" or less concerned about product quality, at least one major theoretical problem would remain: *The critical model fails to account for social change.*[2] Taken to its logical extreme, the critical model implies that the content of corporate newspapers prevents or impedes any meaningful social change. Newspapers are assumed to be agents of economic or political elites, helping to maintain the status quo and repressing alternative voices and protest movements.[3]

There is little question that mainstream mass media provide broad-based support for dominant institutions and value systems. They cannot be called agents of radical change.[4] However, the view that mass media in general or corporate media in particular are incapable of generating any meaningful social change runs contrary to a large body of research which suggests that media have often played an important role in accelerating social movements during the 20th century. In particular, media coverage has helped usher in changes that have enhanced the rights of women, minorities, the working class, consumers, gays, the poor, and environmentalists.[5]

The alternative theory of effects presented in this chapter will contend that the corporate form of organization has contributed to these changes. In fact, it will be argued that as a newspaper acquires the characteristics of the corporate form of organization, it publishes more stories and editorials that are critical of dominant groups and ideas. Critical content does not automatically produce social change, but it does increase the probability of change because it often draws public and elite attention to the shortcomings and failings of existing social arrangements and, in some cases, legitimizes alternative ideas and challenging groups. Corporate newspapers are more critical of the status quo than entrepreneurial ones, it will be argued, primarily because of increasing role specialization. Specialization enhances the authority of journalists vis-à-vis the owners and external power groups, promotes the development of professional standards, and insulates the news production process from parochial political pressures.[6]

In addition to arguing that corporate newspapers are more critical of established authorities, the theory of effects presented here will contend that corporate newspapers pursue a much greater variety of goals than entrepreneurial newspapers. Contrary to the conventional wisdom, it will be argued that even though the corporate newspaper is more profitable, it places less emphasis on profits and more emphasis on product quality as organizational goals. Journalists at corporate newspapers also are expected to be more satisfied with their jobs and to be oriented more to the corporation than to the local community, and corporate editors are expected to have more autonomy. These hypotheses will be tested using a national probability survey of publishers and journalists and content analyses of editorial-page content.

A Theory of Effects

In mass communication research, the term "effects" is usually considered to be nearly synonymous with a large body of research that examines the impact of media messages on audiences, especially their attitudes, cognitions and behaviors. This is an important body of research.[7]

But in this study the term "effects" is used much more broadly — to encompass changes in organizational structure, attitudes or behaviors of organizational actors, and the products an organization produces. In particular, this study will examine the impact of corporate structure on five key topics or issues: profits, product quality and other nonprofit goals, community involvement, autonomy and job satisfaction, and editorial-page vigor.

Corporate Structure and Profits

As noted in previous chapters, the critical model of effects holds that corporate newspapers are more profit-oriented and more profitable. This approach does not distinguish between actual profitability and goal-seeking: It is assumed that because corporate newspapers are more profitable, they also place more emphasis on profits. The theory offered here diverges on this point. Corporate newspapers are expected to be more profitable *but to place less emphasis on profits.* This alternative perspective accepts the assumptions of the managerial revolution model, in that corporate organizations, which are more likely to be managed by professionals rather than the owners, do not maximize profits but seek to achieve other goals, including greater emphasis on product quality. However, corporate newspapers, like corporate organizations in general, are structurally organized to maximize profits.

• *Corporate Structure and Actual Profits.* Three major factors explain why corporate newspapers are more profitable. First, they have greater economies of scale.[8] The start-up or first-copy costs of a newspaper are the same regardless of whether the press run is 1, 100, or 1,000,000 copies. Larger newspapers benefit from economies of scale because the ratio of first-copy costs to the total number of copies is lower. As the quantity of output increases, the per-copy price declines. Economies of scale are also derived through product purchases and management efficiencies. Since larger newspapers and chains can buy raw materials in larger bulk, they usually can negotiate better prices than independently owned newspapers. Chains also may generate economies of scale through administrative and news-gathering practices. The span of control is wider in larger organizations — that is, one manager oversees more workers — and, thus, management costs per employee are lower.[9] Centralization and standardization of accounting procedures and printing plant facilities also can generate substantial savings. And in-house wire services and news bureaus that serve more than one newspaper lower news production costs.

Second, corporate newspapers would be expected to be more profitable because they have greater access than noncorporate newspapers to human and capital resources, which are crucial for adapting to changing market conditions. Chains and larger news organizations employ more highly educated and skilled employees because the work in them is more complex and specialized. They have the resources and knowledge, for example, to conduct sophisticated readership surveys. Larger, more complex organizations also have a greater capacity for adoption of innovations than smaller ones.[10] The innovative process in modern capitalism usually requires a substantial investment, which often exceeds the capital resources of smaller organizations. The argument here is not so much that family owned newspapers have inferior management but rather that corporate organizations have superior resources, both human and material, for making decisions.

And third, corporate newspapers are more profitable because they are insulated from many of the social and political pressures in the local community that inhibit maximization of profits. The owners of family owned enterprises usually live in the communities their newspapers serve and have close ties with local elites, who may very well expect the newspaper to put community well-being over maximization of profits.[11] In contrast, corporate newspaper owners are more likely to live in another community, and their managers have less commitment to the local community, since that newspaper is often a stopover on the corporate ladder. Thus, one might expect corporate newspapers to have weaker ties to the local community, even while the professionals in them have a stronger commitment to producing a high-quality product.

• *Corporate Structure and Profits as an Organizational Goal.* An organizational goal may be defined as a desired state of affairs which the organization attempts to realize.[12] Goals are not always formally or consciously created. But in modern organizations, creating goals is often one of the most important roles for organizational elites. Goals may be established by the owners or creators of the organization (e.g., stockholders, capitalists); by the managers or board of directors, who may or may not be owners or creators; by the members or employees; or by a combination of these three groups. The process of setting goals may involve democratic or centralized decision-making practices, but in large organizations consensus is rarely achieved. In practice, goals are often established through a complicated power struggle, with various individuals, groups or divisions within the organization seeking to promote their own interests or goals.

Although all organizations have goals, the degree to which they are achieved can vary considerably. Nearly all business organizations, for example, have profit as a goal, but competition, the conditions of the economy, access to and costs of raw materials or resources, and the cooperation of employees may enhance or inhibit goal achievement. In general, the leaders of most organizations want their members to identify with the goals, believing this will help the organizations accomplish them. However, this often is not a necessary condition for goal achievement. Prisons, for example, do not need the consent of their inmates to achieve their goal of restraining or punishing them.[13] The failure to turn a profit in the long run usually means the dissolution of the organization via bankruptcy or acquisition. Yet, even when goals are achieved, the organization may also change its goals or organizational structure.

Lavine and Wackman suggest that one of the most important goals sought by newspapers is seeking or maintaining profits.[14] Like all business organizations, newspapers must make a profit to remain viable as an organization. However, Lavine and Wackman argue that most newspapers, like most business organizations, pursue other goals as well. These include knowing and serving the market; producing a high quality product or service; attracting, training, challenging, promoting and keeping the best possible employees; positioning the organization to prosper in the future; and protecting the company's franchise. Lavine and Wackman also point out that various departments within the organization may pursue different goals. The news department may be concerned primarily with producing the highest quality news coverage, whereas the circulation department often focuses on boosting subscribership. These goals are not always compatible; however, the important question for the present study is not whether such conflict exists, but whether the types of goals emphasized or pursued changes as the structure of a newspaper organization changes.

The theoretical argument here is that even though corporate newspapers are structurally organized to maximize profits, they would be expected to place less emphasis on profits, because they are more likely to be managed on a day-to-day basis by professionals, who are less motivated by profits than owners, and because they are more financially stable and secure. During the 18th and early 19th centuries, most newspaper owners wore many hats. In addition to being the local postmaster and community printer, they were the publisher, editor, reporter, printer, typesetter, advertising manager, and circulation manager. Having multiple roles meant they made or were involved in virtually every decision affecting the organization. But as the newspaper grew and became more complex, more and more decisions had to be delegated to individuals who performed specialized roles. Today, most of the major decisions made at corporate newspapers are made by professional managers and technical experts. The owners may set general policy or budgets, but they depend very heavily on specialists and experts to operate the newspaper on a day-to-day basis.

Two factors are primarily responsible for the relative transfer of power to professional managers. The first is the dispersion of ownership. Historically, when an entrepreneurial publisher died, his or her holdings often were divided among two or more heirs, which tended to decentralize ownership. Today, dispersion through these means is becoming less common because the proportion of entrepreneurial or family owned newspapers is declining. But a new form of dispersion — public ownership — has replaced it. The sale of stock and securities to the public enables newspaper organizations to raise large amounts of capital in a relatively short period of time, but "going public" also tends to disperse ownership because as the number of owners (or shareholders) increases, the proportion of stock owned by any single individual decreases. The result is that the power of any single owner relative to other owners decreases, which in turn often enhances the relative power of professional managers.[15]

According to Kuczun, the first newspaper organization in the United States to offer public ownership was the Scripps-McRae chain.[16] By 1960, only 11 newspaper companies sold stocks or bonds to the public. Today, about one-third of all dailies are publicly owned.[17] Historically, the transition from private to public ownership has occurred more slowly in the newspaper industry than in other industries, partly because the difficulties of distributing a national newspaper have hindered centralization of ownership.[18] But the costs of operating a newspaper and keeping it competitive have risen dramatically during the 20th century, especially since the 1960s, and the newspaper industry is coming under the same kinds of pressures that other industries have faced. To purchase new technology, such as printing presses and computer systems, and to fund new ventures, such as mergers or buyouts, newspapers increasingly have turned to outside sources of capital.[19] As Kuczun put it:

> ... Who owns the mass media in the United States? On the surface, the answer to that question in the past decade increasingly has become the public through corporations that are publicly owned ... . However, control is vested in managers nominated by large minority holders of the stock.[20]

The growth of specialized knowledge also has contributed to the transfer of power from the owners to the managers. As an organization grows and becomes more complex, the technical knowledge required to operate it increases. As a consequence, the owners depend heavily on the expertise of professional managers and technical experts to run the organization on a day-to-day basis. Historically, this dependence has been particularly high at newspapers where ownership has been ceded to heirs who have little experience in managing a newspaper. But even publishers who have years of experience in the business have had difficulty keeping up with the expanding base of knowledge. Increasingly, workers are required to have advanced college degrees in journalism, advertising, marketing and finance.

The dependence on professional managers does not mean profit-making is not important in the corporate organization. To survive in any capitalist market system, a newspaper must be profitable. But professional managers and technical experts place less emphasis on profits than owners because they do not benefit directly or as directly from the profits. As Galbraith and others have pointed out, it is illogical and contradictory to argue that self-interest is a driving force behind human behavior but that professionals will set this aside to maximize profits for someone else. To the extent that performance is tied to profits, one might expect professional managers and corporate organizations to place greater emphasis on profits. But even if professionals' incomes were completely tied to profits, the argument here still would be that they place less emphasis on profits than owners. Why? Because most professionals, whether they have a business or journalism background, are not motivated solely by material rewards.[21]

As Schumpeter pointed out, professionals also seek respect and recognition from their peers.[22] Professionals define themselves by their work — i.e., they don't just have jobs, they have "careers." And in most professional occupations, obtaining respect and recognition depends to a large extent upon technical knowledge and skill — on "doing the job well." Profitability often may be taken as an indicator of high performance for top-level executives, who are expected to produce results for the owners. However, because profits can be affected by many factors other than managerial skill, such as poor market conditions,[23] profitability is not necessarily the best indicator of the worth of a professional. In fact, when top executives are fired for failing to turn a profit, they are often hired by other major companies in the field.

The types of goals pursued by professionals will vary from newspaper to newspaper, from occupation to occupation, and from manager to manager. However, since most professional groups seek to control their work, it is reasonable to expect that autonomy will be highly valued despite differences in social position. Managers on the business side also may be expected to place a high value on increasing circulation and acquiring other newspapers, since organizational growth can enhance the power and prestige of executives. Journalists, on the other hand, might be expected to place a high degree of emphasis on producing a high quality product. Winning reporting awards should also be important, with the Pulitzer Prize as the gold ring.[24] These nonprofit goals are discussed in more depth in the next section. The important point here is that professional managers, as opposed to the owners, are expected to place less emphasis on profits. More specifically, it could be argued that professionals will seek to obtain that minimum level of profit that satisfies owners and, at the same time, enables them to achieve their own personal goals.

The second major reason corporate newspapers would place less emphasis on profits as an organizational goal is that they are more stable and secure financially. They are less vulnerable to changes in the marketplace because, as noted above, they have greater access to human and capital resources and greater control over markets and prices.[25] Consequently, they have less need to be concerned about the bottom line and can turn their attention to other matters. In contrast, survival is a major concern in many entrepreneurial newspapers, particularly where there is a great deal of competition or unstable economic conditions. In small communities where the retail base is dwindling, the concern about profits at the local paper will be very high. A newspaper in such a community would be expected to place more emphasis on local economic development and to be a booster for local business and industry.[26] One advertiser also may represent a significant proportion of the total advertising budget and may play a more influential role in shaping news coverage.

The argument that corporate organizations place less emphasis on profits as an organizational goal is theoretically strong, but it needs to be reconciled with research which shows that chain newspapers place more emphasis on profits.[27] The explanation for this anomaly, it is argued here, can be found in communication patterns within the organization. The owner-manager of an independent newspaper generally shares little information about profits with nonowning managers. This is particularly true in a small town, where the newspaper is expected to put the informational needs of the community before the profit needs of the owners. At the entrepreneurial newspaper, information about profits is considered private and is closely guarded, since rumors of profit-gouging can bring strong social sanctions.

The chain newspaper, in contrast, is often publicly owned, which means profitability is a public matter and is often discussed at intraorganizational meetings. But even if the chain is nonpublic, the local publisher or individual in charge will often share such information with managers, in part to secure their loyalty and assistance in meeting profitability goals.[28] The local publisher's chances for promotion, salary increases and other rewards depends in part on the profitability of the local operation. Thus, managers and lower-level employees of chain newspapers would be expected to perceive their organizations as being more profit-oriented because their organizations are more open about the issue of profitability, whereas nonowning managers and employees at entrepreneurial newspapers know very little about the profitability of the company they work for because its owners do not talk about it. In sum, one would expect that:

H1: *The more a newspaper exhibits the characteristics of the corporate form of organization, the more profitable the newspaper.*

H2: *The more a newspaper exhibits the characteristics of the corporate form of organization, the less emphasis it will place on profits as an organizational goal or value.*

H3: *Chain newspapers will place more emphasis on profits than their respective counterparts at independently owned newspapers.*

Corporate Structure and Product Quality

The critical model assumes that corporate newspapers place less emphasis on product quality because they are more profit-oriented. The logic here is based on a zero-sum game: The more a newspaper maximizes profits, the less money it has to spend on collecting news, improving the product or serving the public (i.e., product quality).

Although this argument has a certain amount of intuitive appeal, theoretically it is more complicated than this. One important problem is the paradox of profitability: the more money a newspaper makes, the more it has to spend on improving the product. As noted in Chapter 8, some empirical research actually has shown that profitable newspapers spend a higher proportion and amount of money on the news production process.[29] Research also shows that emphasis on profits and product quality as organizational goals are not always inversely related.[30] Thus, the question is not just one of maximizing profits but also one of how much and what proportion of profits are spent on improving the news product.

In contrast to the traditional zero-sum position, the perspective here is that even though corporate newspapers are expected to be more profitable and to place less, not more, emphasis on profits as an organizational goal, they place more emphasis on product quality as an organizational goal. The main reason: Increasing role specialization promotes greater concern or emphasis on news and editorials and, at the same time, removes the influence of top management (i.e., publishers and owners) from the news production process.

Concern with profits would be expected to be higher at newspapers where the owner and editor roles are occupied by one person — i.e., where there is no role differentiation. One can still find multiple role positions at many weekly newspapers. The owner at such an organization often sells or manages the advertising department in addition to managing the editorial production. As an organization grows, however, these roles become differentiated, mainly because the amount of work increases for each role. In fact, at almost all dailies today, the publisher, advertising and editor roles are separated, and at most large newspapers or chain newspapers the owner and publisher roles are divorced. As the division of labor and role specialization expand, editors focus more and more on news production, while making money becomes the sole responsibility of the owner or publisher and advertising and circulation managers.

Increased focus on news production promotes the growth of specialized knowledge. Owners and publishers increasingly lose control over the news production process because they lack the specialized knowledge for performing that role. Making decisions about what stories to cover, what elements to include or exclude, and how to find the most efficient means for producing the news is much more complicated today than in the past. It usually requires an advanced college education[31] and extensive experience in the news room. The days of the editor who works his or her way up the ladder from a newsroom assistant position are virtually gone. Decision-making in modern corporate organizations increasingly requires formal training and education, and only journalists have the specialized knowledge to make those decisions that affect editorial content.

The growth of specialized knowledge means that journalists at corporate newspapers would be expected to place greater emphasis on producing a quality product, as well as such goals as winning reporting awards, acquiring the latest technology, and being innovative in news gathering. These are the goals that professionals revere most, and they — not profits — are the factors that lead to peer recognition, promotions, pay increases, better jobs, or greater power. The growth of specialized knowledge also means that other managers in the corporate news organization would be expected to place greater emphasis on other goals that will help them reach their personal goals. Maximizing growth of the organization, as noted earlier, has direct benefits for managers in all areas, especially top-level executives. As a manager's span of control increases, the power and salary of that manager generally increases. Corporate newspapers also would be expected to place greater emphasis on readership research because they are located in more pluralistic communities, where the diversity of lifestyles and interests is so complex that readers' needs cannot be effectively or efficiently measured through traditional methods, such as interpersonal contact.[32] Corporate newspapers also have the resources to conduct such research.

Another structural factor that explains why corporate newspapers place greater emphasis on product quality is competition, both internal and external. As shown in Chapter 7, corporate newspapers are located in markets that have more media competition. Competition for organizational resources (e.g., front-page space, promotions, pay, prestige) also is greater within the organization itself because they generally have more employees. For example, the competition for front-page space will be much greater at corporate newspapers because they have more reporters. It is acknowledged that competition can have adverse effects on quality, increasing the probability of sensational coverage for some stories.[33] But the weight of the evidence suggests that competition promotes a high quality news product.[34] Summing up the research, Stempel argues that:

> Chains have a distinct economic advantage derived from their experience and expertise in management, marketing and use of the economies of scale. Evidence is that this financial planning sophistication can make newspapers more profitable businesses without debasing the journalistic product.[35]

In sum:

H4: *The more a newspaper exhibits the characteristics of the corporate form of organization, the more emphasis that newspaper will* *place on product quality as an organizational goal or value.*

H5:   *The more a newspaper exhibits the characteristics of the corporate form of organization, the more emphasis that newspaper will place on other organizational goals, including maximizing growth of the organization, winning reporting awards, having the latest technology, beating the competition, conducting readership research, giving reporters more autonomy, being innovative, and increasing circulation.*

Corporate Structure and Community Involvement

The critical model's argument that the corporate newspaper reduces community identity and solidarity in the traditional sense seems logical. Owners and executives of chain organizations do not identify as strongly with the local community, and professional managers and editors are more oriented to the corporation and to their careers. One consequence is that the chain newspaper is likely to publish less local news.

However, this does not mean that the corporate newspaper is destroying community solidarity; rather, it is destroying traditional bases of solidarity, which tend to be rooted in local ties as opposed to a system-wide perspective. The chain newspaper's emphasis on nonlocal news represents, in part, an orientation to the larger social system. In an increasingly interdependent society, such an orientation may help local communities adapt to changing social and economic conditions. In fact, Gladney reported that small newspapers placed more emphasis on strong local news coverage and on news that focuses on common community values and helps give readers a sense of individual existence and worth, while large papers placed more emphasis on comprehensive coverage (i.e., "coverage of news from beyond the newspaper's immediate distribution area").[36] Increased commitment to the organization and the presence of codes of conduct also would be expected to insulate journalists at larger newspapers from parochial political pressures. Thus:

H6:   *The more a newspaper exhibits the characteristics of the corporate form of organization, the less involved and supportive it will be of the local community.*

Corporate Structure, Autonomy and Job Satisfaction

The critical model holds that the division of labor and role specialization lessen autonomy and job satisfaction. One reason for this is that job tasks become more mundane or tedious as tasks are broken down into more discrete and simple steps. Factory jobs are particularly susceptible to this process, as Smith and Marx pointed out. Another reason is that the number of rules and regulations generally increases as the division of labor expands. Such rules are often considered necessary for controlling and coordinating the actions of a large number of highly interdependent social actors, but they are seen as depersonalizing and infringing upon the freedom and autonomy of those workers. Research shows, in fact, that large newspapers have more rules and regulations, such as employee handbooks and codes of ethics,[37] and reporters' stories do receive more editing in larger organizations.[38]

Although the explanation above has a certain amount of intuitive appeal, it leaves two fundamental questions unresolved. First, if journalists at large newspapers are less satisfied with their jobs, then why are jobs at the largest newspapers the most coveted and prestigious?[39] Second, if journalists at large newspapers are less satisfied with their jobs, then why do large newspapers continue to thrive and prosper? Assuming satisfaction is related to job performance,[40] the loss-of-satisfaction argument means that large organizations should decay or become less efficient over time, but this has not been the case. In fact, larger organizations appear to be better equipped to adapt and survive in a changing environment.[41]

The theoretical position here acknowledges that the division of labor and role specialization may restrict autonomy and promote job dissatisfaction under the conditions mentioned above; however, these conditions do not apply to all employees under all circumstances. In fact, under most conditions, role specialization would be expected to enhance a journalist's autonomy and job satisfaction, because it creates the "expert" who has specialized knowledge on a topic. One of the most prominent specialized roles in the newspaper organization is the columnist, who usually is considered to be one of the best writers and reporters in the newsroom. Relative to other workers, the columnist has a great deal of freedom to do his or her job. The position also carries with it a great deal of power and prestige. Journalists who report on science, the environment, business and the arts also are often labeled "experts" and usually have a great deal of autonomy. In contrast, general assignment reporters and police beat reporters typically have the least amount of autonomy and are accorded the least amount of prestige. Most reporters begin on these beats, and editors monitor their work almost daily.

Thus, specialization and the presence of rules and more extensive copy editing should not be interpreted to mean that a loss of autonomy or job satisfaction occurs at all levels in the organization. Rather, the concept of relative deprivation suggests that the effect of newspaper structure on autonomy and job satisfaction depends upon the location of the job in the organizational hierarchy. For lower-level, nonmanagerial jobs, such as general assignment reporting positions, corporate newspaper structure very well may have a negative impact on autonomy and job satisfaction, since a reporter's activities are more highly regulated. But the opposite might be expected for higher-level jobs, such as top editor positions and specialized beats, for three major reasons.

First, editors at corporate newspapers have more social status and power and are more highly rewarded than editors at entrepreneurial newspapers, as a rule of thumb. Compared with editors at entrepreneurial newspapers, editors at corporate newspapers manage more people and control a larger budget, tasks that enhance their power and prestige. Editors at corporate newspapers also are paid better because their organizations are more profitable and can pay higher wages to draw better talent. Whether the primary reference group for a top editor at a corporate newspaper is other editors in the organization or editors at other newspapers,[42] the comparison leads to a positive assessment: Corporate editors have more prestige, status and rewards — factors that in turn would be expected to produce higher levels of autonomy and job satisfaction.

Although autonomy and job satisfaction are expected to be higher for top editors at corporate newspapers, this pattern may not hold for all lower-level positions. For instance, although reporters at corporate organizations generally enjoy higher social status and prestige than reporters at entrepreneurial organizations — and relative comparisons here would be expected to produce higher levels of autonomy and satisfaction — when reporters at corporate newspapers compare themselves to other reporters in their organization, the probability for dissatisfaction increases because, structurally, the probability also is greater that the reporter will know of a lesser qualified reporter who has been promoted or rewarded differentially. The number of reporters who will be dissatisfied when their story is not placed on the front page, for example, generally will be greater at corporate newspapers simply because there are more reporters competing for that limited space. This does not mean that reporters at corporate newspapers do not compare themselves to reporters at entrepreneurial newspapers — they do, and this comparison generally leads to a more satisfactory assessment. But this relative comparison is secondary — the primary reference group for reporters at corporate newspapers is other reporters on the same newspaper.

The second reason editors at corporate newspapers would be expected to be more satisfied than editors at entrepreneurial newspapers is that the social status disparity is greater in corporate organizations. The "satisfaction gap" hypothesis, as this has been called,[43] also is based on reference group theory and relative deprivation, but the relative comparison now is between roles (i.e., editor vs. reporter) rather than within (editor vs. editor). In other words, instead of comparing themselves to other editors, top editors are now comparing themselves to all other individuals in the organization, and in corporate organizations, the social distance between top-level managers and lower-level employees is much greater because the organization is more hierarchically organized. The editor of a corporate newspaper is insulated from the lower-level employees by a large number of managerial levels, and this accentuates social disparities. Top editors in such organizations rarely meet with or socialize outside of the office with reporters and other lower-level employees. This has the effect of increasing the perceived social status for top-level managers, which in turn can be expected to increase satisfaction. In contrast, the social distance between reporters and top-level editors at entrepreneurial newspapers is relatively small. Top editors meet frequently with reporters, and they may socialize outside of working hours. The organization is highly integrated and socially homogeneous, and relative comparisons here are less likely to produce a dissatisfied feeling.

The third reason corporate editors would be expected to have more autonomy and job satisfaction is that increasing role specialization increases the power of journalists relative to other top managers and the owners. As noted above, the editors *are* experts when it comes to news judgment and news production, and professional norms increasingly limit or constrain the authority of noneditorial personnel. In contrast, reporters and other lower-level employees may have less autonomy and job satisfaction as a newspaper becomes more "corporatized" because such organizations have a larger number of rules and procedures for controlling work routines. Organizations that employ a large number of people confront considerable problems in coordinating and controlling the news production process, and they attempt to overcome such problems through standardization and routinization of tasks and jobs. Formalized rules and procedures, including codes of ethics, are one mechanism for resolving such problems.

The impact of organizational structure on autonomy and satisfaction for top-level managers (i.e., publishers, general managers) would appear to be more complex. On the one hand, publishers and top-level managers at entrepreneurial newspapers should have more autonomy, because they are more likely to own the newspaper. On the other hand, their counterparts at corporate newspapers have more prestige and status in the system. These conflicting forces lead to the conclusion that little difference will exist between top-level managers in corporate versus entrepreneurial newspapers in terms of autonomy and satisfaction. However, as one moves down the newspaper hierarchy, the likelihood increases that a journalist will know of a lesser qualified journalist who has been promoted or rewarded. This relative comparison — along with the fact that higher rank brings more power, prestige and money — would be expected to contribute to greater autonomy and job satisfaction among editors than reporters at the same newspaper.

H7:   The more a newspaper exhibits the characteristics of the corporate form of organization, the greater the autonomy and job satisfaction of its top editors.

H8:   The more a newspaper exhibits the characteristics of the corporate form of organization, the more control it exerts over reporters' stories.

H9:   The more a newspaper exhibits the characteristics of the corporate form of organization, the lower the autonomy and job satisfaction of its lower-level reporters.

H10:   Corporate newspaper structure will have no impact on levels of autonomy or job satisfaction for publishers and top-level managers.

H11:   The higher the rank of an employee in the news organization, the greater the autonomy and job satisfaction.

Corporate Structure and Editorial-Page Vigor

To be sure, some newspapers that exhibit the characteristics of the corporate form of organization are less vigorous editorially than their entrepreneurial counterparts. Case studies can be produced to document such cases.[44] But, theoretically, the transition from the entrepreneurial to the corporate form of organization under most conditions would be expected to produce a more, not less, vigorous press. Two major reasons may be cited to support this proposition.

The first is that corporate newspapers themselves tend to be located in pluralistic communities, which contain more social conflict and criticism of dominant groups and value systems than homogeneous communities. A well-documented research finding is that newspapers in homogeneous communities contain less conflict and criticism.[45] The amount of social conflict and criticism of mainstream institutions and values in these community newspapers is low partly because the community contains a limited number of alternative or challenging groups and organizations. Small communities also do not encourage or tolerate a wide range of behaviors, opinions or values, at least openly. Elites in small, homogeneous systems share similar interests, values, goals and world views. Decision-making relies more heavily on consensus than debate.

In contrast, social conflict is a much more common feature of large, pluralistic communities because they contain a much greater variety of special interest groups competing for limited social, political and economic resources. Decision-making in such communities is expected to take into account a greater diversity of perspectives and views, and such communities are structurally organized to deal with conflict, having mechanisms such as boards of inquiry (e.g., racial discrimination commissions, civilian police review boards), formal labor-management negotiators, formalized grievance procedures, and administrative law judges. Although stories and editorials that contain conflict or criticism are often viewed as threatening to the social order, such stories often play a significant role in contributing to system stability because they introduce alternative ideas or innovations that enable organizations and institutions to adapt to changing conditions.

The second reason corporate newspapers would be expected to generate editorial content that is more critical of dominant institutions and values is that their publishers and editorial staffs are more insulated from special interests and political pressures. They are more insulated because (1) they are less likely to grow up in the community their newspaper serves, (2) they work at the newspaper for a shorter period of time, (3) they are oriented more to the corporation than to the local community, and (4) they are oriented more to the profession than to the local community.

Publishers and managers who have spent a lot of time in the community their newspaper serves often develop close personal ties to local elites and organizations. Such ties may foster a greater concern with the issues and problems facing the community; however, they also may lead to greater constraints on the editorial process. Friendships create obligations, and the ability of a newspaper to impartially report on controversial issues or matters, especially those that portray local elites in a negative way, may be compromised to the extent that a top-level manager is highly integrated into a community. The effect of such ties is particularly acute in a small town, because the local entrepreneurial newspaper depends on a smaller number of advertisers for its livelihood. While it is true that no newspaper can afford to alienate all or a substantial number of its advertisers and expect to be financially self-supporting over a long period of time, corporate newspapers are more financially stable, which means they are less dependent upon any single advertiser.

Top-level managers of corporate organizations also are more insulated from political pressures because they spend less time working at those newspapers and move more frequently from job to job. Many of these managers, including top-level editors, are interested in climbing the corporate ladder. This means they must be oriented to the larger corporate or chain organization, not the local community.[46] An orientation to the corporation may lead to less concern with local issues, but it also reduces the probability that local special interest groups will unduly influence the news production process, giving corporate newspapers a greater capacity to criticize local groups.

Perhaps more important than living in a community and climbing the corporate ladder, though, is the effect of professional norms and values on the editorial process. Professional codes of ethics define public conflict and criticism as newsworthy and condemn news that promotes local parochial interests over truth and the public good.[47] While professionalism exists to some degree at most newspapers, at corporate newspapers professionalism plays an even more prominent role.[48] Contrary to popular belief, the growth of corporate or bureaucratic institutions generally promotes — not retards — the development of professional norms and values.[49] The division of labor and role specialization that accompanies the growth of large-scale organization facilitates the development of professional norms and values in part because those organizations have a larger number of editorial employees who are structurally separated from workers in other functional areas. This separation facilitates the development of specialized skills and knowledge as well as professional codes of conduct. As noted above, large, complex corporate newspapers, in fact, are much more likely to have written ethical codes of conduct and to enforce them.

Professional codes of conduct are designed, of course, to control the behavior of professionals and, admittedly, they can, under certain circumstances, inhibit the diversity of ideas.[50] But they also can promote greater diversity by insulating journalists from special interest groups (e.g., advertisers, politicians, government) who seek to use the media to serve exclusively their own needs and interests.[51] Professional norms limit or constrain the authority of noneditorial personnel in the news production process. When it comes to producing the news, only the editors have the authority to make decisions that affect the editorial production process. Professional norms also help justify and legitimize the role of journalists in producing news for the broader society.

It is important to point out that the theoretical perspective presented here is partially at odds with the critical view that professionalism leads to homogeneity and standardization rather than diversity. For example, Glasser argues that professionalism

> means quite the opposite of diversity. Whereas the goal of diversity is to foster an appreciation for differences in experience and therefore differences in knowledge, the goal of a professional education is — in effect and usually by design — to unify knowledge by glossing over differences in experience. Professionalism implies standardization and homogeneity; it accounts not for differences among journalists but for what journalists have in common.[52]

Few scholars would disagree with the argument that professionalism can contribute to standardization and homogenization of behavior — codes of ethics, for example, are rules of conduct. However, viewing codes as an internal mechanism of social control (i.e., within the profession of journalism itself) is only half of the story. From a system perspective, professional norms and values also must be seen as helping to insulate journalists from groups or individuals who would like to manipulate the news to their own benefit. In fact, professional codes of ethics and norms account in large part for the ability of journalists to report legitimately news that occasionally criticizes the dominant ideologies and those in power.

In contrast to the critical model, the key strength of the structural model presented here is that it helps to account for social change and the role that mass media often play in promoting such change. As social systems (communities and the nation as a whole) become more pluralistic, news media become more critical of traditional ways and established institutions. Media reflect to some degree the diversity of the communities they serve, and increasing role specialization and professionalization, which are by-products of community growth, help to insulate journalists from parochial political pressures. And the increased level of criticism that emerges from these structural forces often contributes to a discourse that increases pressure on dominant institutions to respond to alternative ideas or the needs of groups.

Although corporate newspapers increase the probability that editorial content will be critical of established or mainstream groups, it is important to point out that the structural or cultural changes that sometimes result from these pressures are rarely radical. Social change comes slowly. Research shows, in fact, that mass media are highly responsive to political and economic centers of power and promote values generally consistent with capitalist ideals and elite interests.[53] The claims of challenging groups are circumscribed to a large extent by the opposing interests of those groups in power. The gains of the civil rights and women's movements of the 1960s, for example, have not eliminated economic, political and social disparities between the races and sexes. Nevertheless, it would be historically incorrect to claim that these movements have been ineffectual or that the mass media played no role in promoting their goals. Real structural change has occurred *within* the system during the 20th century (e.g., affirmative action standards, anti-discrimination laws), and media have played an important role in promoting and, later, legitimizing such changes. Therefore:

H12: *The more a newspaper exhibits the characteristics of the corporate form of organization, the greater the number of editorials and letters to the editor.*

H13: *The more a newspaper exhibits the characteristics of the corporate form of organization, the greater the frequency and proportion of editorials written by local staff.*

H14: *The more a newspaper exhibits the characteristics of the corporate form of organization, the greater the frequency and proportion of editorials and letters to the editor about local issues.*

H15: The more a newspaper exhibits the characteristics of the corporate form of organization, the greater the frequency and proportion of editorials and letters to the editor that will be critical of mainstream sources or institutions.

Shortcomings of the Corporate Effects Model

The theory of corporate effects presented above has a number of strengths, including the notion that it helps to account for social change. However, it also has at least two major weaknesses. One is that it fails to account for revolutionary or radical social change. Change is assumed to occur rather slowly, in part because dominant groups hold power and resist change. Media depend heavily on advertising to survive, and making a profit circumscribes the extent to which mainstream media may take radical stances. Dominant value systems, political elites and public opinion also limit change.

Another major shortcoming of the model presented here is that it cannot determine whether social change is occurring quickly enough to be of optimal benefit to society and/or challenging or alternative groups. Many critics would counter that even if corporate newspapers are more critical of mainstream groups than entrepreneurial newspapers, the editorial criticism they offer produces little in the way of meaningful social change. Such critics may be right. But if the theory presented here is correct, such arguments will need to depend more on value judgments about meaningful social change than on the notion that corporate newspaper structure diminishes editorial diversity. The theory here holds that the corporate newspaper will be critical of the status quo. Normative issues are explored in more depth in the concluding chapter of this book.

Summary

A theory of corporate newspaper effects was presented and empirically tested in this chapter. Five major effects or issues were examined:

1. Profits. Newspapers that exhibit the characteristics of the corporate form of organization were expected to be more profitable but, contrary to the critical model, it was expected that they would place less emphasis on profits and more emphasis on product quality as organizational goals.

Corporate newspapers are structurally organized to maximize profits, but role specialization decreases emphasis on profits as an organizational goal.

   2. Product Quality. Corporate newspapers were expected to place greater emphasis on producing a high quality product and on other, nonprofit goals, such as winning reporting awards, increasing circulation, giving reporters more autonomy, and maximizing growth of the organization. Role specialization and competition promote the pursuit of these nonprofit goals.

   3. Community Involvement. Consistent with the critical model, it was expected that corporate newspapers would be less involved in and supportive of the local community. Their owners and professional managers and editors tend to be more oriented to the corporation and to their careers than their counterparts at entrepreneurial newspapers. One consequence is that the chain newspaper is likely to publish less local news. However, the chain newspaper's orientation to the larger social system may help the local community to adapt to changing social conditions.

   4. Autonomy and Job Satisfaction. It was expected that self-reported autonomy and job satisfaction at corporate versus entrepreneurial daily newspapers in the United States would vary according to position in the organization. Top editors at corporate newspapers were expected to be more satisfied than top editors at entrepreneurial newspapers because (1) increased role specialization gives corporate editors greater autonomy, (2) corporate editors have more status, power and are more highly rewarded than editors at entrepreneurial newspapers as well as editors at their own newspapers, and (3) corporate editors have higher social status relative to most other employees in their organization (i.e., the social disparities between the top and bottom are greater). In contrast, it was expected that reporters at corporate newspapers would be less satisfied and would have less autonomy because (1) their organizations exert more formal control over reporters' stories and because (2) structurally the probability is greater that reporters will know of a lesser qualified reporter who has been promoted or rewarded differentially (i.e., the probability of relative deprivation increases). No differences in satisfaction and autonomy were expected for publishers, because even though entrepreneurial publishers might be expected to have higher levels of autonomy, any increased satisfaction here could be offset by the fact that those positions are less prestigious than comparable positions at corporate newspapers.

   5. Editorial-Page Vigor. Contrary to the critical model, the theoretical framework in this study posited that corporate newspapers would publish more staff-generated editorials, more editorials about local issues, and more editorials that are critical of mainstream groups than entrepreneurial newspapers. Corporate newspapers publish more staff-generated editorials and more editorials about local issues because they are larger, more structurally complex, and have more staff and resources. Corporate newspapers write more editorials that are critical of mainstream groups because they are more likely to be located in pluralistic communities that contain more criticism of dominant groups and value systems and because they are more insulated from local political pressures. On the latter point, the owners and managers of corporate newspapers are less likely to grow up in the community their newspaper serves, are more likely to work at the newspaper for a shorter period of time, are oriented to the larger corporation, not the local community, and are more likely to be guided by professional norms and values.

Notes

1. As noted in Chapter 8, however, most of the research does not support a critical model. In fact, the evidence strongly suggests that chain newspapers are more vigorous editorially.

2. Social change may be defined as the difference between current and antecedent conditions of any part of a social organization or social structure. See, e.g., Richard T. LaPiere, *Social Change* (New York: McGraw-Hill, 1965) and T. K. Oommen, *Protest and Change: Studies in Social Movements* (New Delhi, India: Sage, 1990).

3. The extent to which critics actually subscribe to this view varies considerably. Those with a more professional background tend to see corporate media as serving the economic needs of their owners to the detriment of the public (e.g., Ben H. Bagdikian, *The Media Monopoly*, 2nd ed. [Boston: Beacon Press, 1987]), whereas critics with a more neo-Marxist bent tend to to see corporate media as part of a larger hegemonic system of control, in which alternative radical ideas have little or no chance of emerging (e.g., Theodore Adorno and Max Horkheimer, *Dialectic of the Enlightenment* [London: Verso, 1979]). Most scholars steer a middle course (for review, see David Pearce Demers, "What Empirical Research Tells Us About the Dominant Ideology Thesis," unpublished paper [University of Wisconsin, River Falls, Wis., 1994]). In all cases, however, the critical model assumes that, as a newspaper acquires the characteristics of the corporate form of organization, the newspaper's content increasingly promotes the interests of economic and/or political elites to the detriment of other groups or classes.

4. One possible rare exception is the colonial press during the American Revolution, which helped mobilize and galvanize the colonists against the crown. See Michael Emery and Edwin Emery, *The Press in America,* 6th ed. (Englewood Cliffs, N.J.: Prentice-Hall, 1988), pp. 45-68.

5. See, e.g., Jeffrey C. Alexander, "The Mass Media in Systemic, Historical and Comparative Perspective," pp. 17-51 in Elihu Katz and Tamás Szecskö (eds.), *Mass Media and Social Change* (Beverly Hills, Calif.: Sage, 1981); Sandra J. Ball-Rokeach and Muriel G. Cantor (eds.), *Media, Audience and Social Structure* (Newbury Park, Calif.: Sage, 1986);

Fred J. Cook, *The Muckrakers: Crusading Journalists Who Changed America* (Garden City, N.Y.: Doubleday & Company, 1972); Julia Barton Corbett, *Media, Bureaucracy and the Success of Social Protest: Media Coverage of Environmental Movement Groups* (Ph.D. Diss., University of Minnesota, 1994); David Pearce Demers and Suzanne Nichols, *Precision Journalism: A Practical Guide* (Newbury Park, Calif.: Sage, 1987); Leonard Downie Jr., *The New Muckrakers* (New York: Mentor, 1976); David Halberstam, "The Education of a Journalist," *Columbia Journalism Review* (November/December 1994), pp. 29-34; Elihu Katz and Tamás Szecskö (eds), *Mass Media and Social Change*; Lauren Kessler, *The Dissident Press: Alternative Journalism in American History* (Beverly Hills, Calif.: Sage, 1984); Clarice N. Olien, Phillip J. Tichenor and George A. Donohue, "Media Coverage and Social Movements," pp. 139-63 in Charles T. Salmon (ed.), *Information Campaigns: Balancing Social Values and Social Change* (Newbury Park, Calif.: Sage, 1989); and David L. Protess, Fay Lomax Cook, Jack C. Doppelt, James S. Ettema, Margaret T. Gordon, Donna R. Leff, and Peter Miller, *The Journalism of Outrage: Investigative Reporting and Agenda Building in America* (New York: The Guilford Press, 1991).

6. While social change depends upon many factors others than media coverage itself — particularly the degree to which the proposed change can be accommodated without changing basic power relationships — from a system perspective, corporate media should be seen as social institutions that perform a feedback function, providing news and information that usually helps elite groups fight off challenges from alternative groups but, in some cases, legitimating the interests and goals of the latter (see Chapter 4).

7. See, e.g., Jennings Bryant and Dolf Zillman, *Media Effects: Advances in Theory and Research* (Hillsdale, N.J.: Lawrence Erlbaum Associates, 1994) and Richard M. Perloff, *The Dynamics of Persuasion* (Hillsdale, N.J.: Lawrence Erlbaum Associates, 1993).

8. For a general discussion of economies of scale, see Robert G. Picard, *Media Economics* (Newbury Park: Sage, 1989), pp. 62-5.

9. Peter M. Blau, "A Formal Theory of Differentiation in Organizations," *American Sociological Review,* 55:201-18 (1970).

10. However, larger organizations do not necessarily have a greater capacity for innovation; rather, they have the resources to adopt innovations.

11. Empirical support for these arguments may be found in Roland J. Pellegrin and Charles H. Coates, "Absentee-Owned Corporations and Community Power Structure," American Journal of Sociology, 61:413-9 (1956) and Patrick Parsons, John Finnegan Jr., and William Benham, "Editors and Their Roles," pp. 91-104 in Robert G. Picard, Maxwell E. McCombs, James P. Winter and Stephen Lacy (eds.), *Press Concentration and Monopoly* (Norwood, N.J.: Ablex, 1988).

12. Amitai Etzioni, *Modern Organizations* (Englewood Cliffs, N.J.: Prentice-Hall, 1964), p. 6.

13. Although criminologists have found that many prisons rely heavily on the cooperation of prisoners to function effectively.

14. John Lavine and Daniel Wackman, *Managing Media Organizations: Effective Leadership of the Media* (New York: Longman, 1988).

15. One of the reasons dispersion of stock ownership enhances the power of managers is that smaller stockholders often do not attend annual stockholder meetings and sign proxies which give the voting power of their stock to the managers. The managers seek to install directors who will support their policies. In extremely large corporations it is rare for even large banks, investment firms or pension funds to own more than 5 percent of the stock. See Chapter 8 for empirical support.

16. Sam Kuczun, "Ownership of Newspaper Increasingly Becoming Public," *Journalism Quarterly,* 55:342-4 (1978).

17. See Table 7.4 in Chapter 7.

18. See Chapter 2.

19. Kuczun, "Ownership of Newspapers Increasingly Becoming Public."

20. Kuczun, "Ownership of Newspaper Increasingly Becoming Public," p. 342.

21. However, one might expect that monetary rewards will be more important for professionals with a business background, given the high value that the professional business groups place on wealth as a measure of success.

22. Joseph A. Schumpeter, *The Theory of Economic Development* (Cambridge, Mass.: Harvard University Press, 1949). Prior to the 1970s, most sociologists emphasized the altruistic characteristics and traits of professions. Research by neo-Marxist scholars since the 1960s has focused more on the self-interested part. The view here is that most professions represent a blending of these two perspectives: They pursue goals that narrowly benefit their members but they also serve the public interest and are interested in producing a high-quality service or product. For contrasting views, see Talcott Parsons, "Professions," *International Encyclopedia of the Social Sciences,* vol. 12 (New York: Macmillan, 1968); Andrew Abbott, *The System of Professions: An Essay on the Division of Expert Labor* (Chicago: The University of Chicago Press, 1988); and Robert Dingwall and Philip Lewis (eds.), *The Sociology of the Professions: Lawyers, Doctors and Others* (New York: St. Martin's Press, 1983).

23. When a business fails to make a profit, top-level managers usually do all they can to place the blame on factors other than their decisions and actions. Because it is often difficult to determine the cause of poor profit-performance, top-level managers are often insulated from criticism.

24. Halberstam, "The Education of a Journalist," contains a good discussion of what it takes to be a respected journalist.

25. David Pearce Demers, "Effects of Competition and Structural Pluralism on Centralization of Ownership in the U.S. Newspaper Industry," paper presented to Association for Education in Journalism and Mass Communication (Minneapolis, August 1990).

26. C. N. Olien, P. J. Tichenor, G. A. Donohue, K. L. Sandstrom and D. M. McLeod, "Community Structure and Editor Opinions About Planning," *Journalism Quarterly,* 67:119-27 (1990).

27. See, e.g., David Pearce Demers, "Corporate Structure and Emphasis on Profits and Product Quality at U.S. Daily Newspapers," *Journalism Quarterly,* 68:15-26 (1991).

28. This proposition is based partly on my personal contacts with newspaper executives over the years.

29. William B. Blankenburg, "Newspaper Scale and Newspaper Expenditures," *Newspaper Research Journal,* 10(2):97-103 (1989).

30. Demers, "Corporate Structure and Emphasis on Profits and Product Quality at U.S. Daily Newspapers."

31. More than 7 of 10 dailies now require reporters to have a bachelor's degree. See Table 7.4 in Chapter 7.

32. A rationale and justification for using marketing research can be found in Philip Meyer, *The Newspaper Survival Book: An Editor's Guide to Marketing Research* (Bloomington, Ind.: Indiana University Press, 1985).

33. Gerald Stone, *Examining Newspapers: What Research Reveals About America's Newspapers* (Newbury Park, Calif.: Sage, 1987), p. 99.

34. Galen R. Rarick and Barrie Hartman, "The Effects of Competition on One Daily Newspaper's Content," *Journalism Quarterly,* 43:459-63 (1966) and Guido H. Stempel III, "Effects on Performance of a Cross-Media Monopoly," *Journalism Monographs,* vol. 29 (June 1973).

35. Stempel, *Examining Newspapers,* p. 104.

36. George A. Gladney, "Newspaper Excellence: How Editors of Small and Large Papers Judge Quality," *Newspaper Research Journal,* 11(2):58-72 (1990).

37. Douglas Anderson, "How Managing Editors View and Deal With Ethical Issues," *Journalism Quarterly,* 64:341-5 (1987) and David Pearce Demers, "Corporate Newspaper Structure and Organizational Goals," paper presented to the Association for Education in Journalism and Mass Communication (Atlanta, August 1994).

38. John W. C. Johnstone, Edward J. Slawski and William W. Bowman, *The News People* (Urbana, Ill.: University of Illinois Press, 1976) and David H. Weaver and G. Cleveland Wilhoit, *The American Journalists* (Bloomington, Ind.: Indiana University Press, 1986).

39. Johnstone, Slawski, and Bowman, *The News People,* p. 184, and Weaver and Wilhoit, *The American Journalists,* p. 163.

40. Research does not always support the notion that job satisfaction leads to better job performance. Structural constraints, such as production quotas, may play a more important role under some conditions. But, theoretically, the argument that satisfaction may affect productivity is very strong. For reviews of studies on the effects of job satisfaction, see Dean J. Champion, *The Sociology of Organizations* (New York: McGraw-Hill, 1975), Chapter 9, and Frank J. Landy, *Psychology of Work Behavior* (Chicago: The Dorsey Press, 1985), Chapter 11.

41. For a review of the literature, see David Pearce Demers, "Structural Pluralism, Intermedia Competition and the Growth of the Corporate Newspaper in the United States," *Journalism Monographs,* vol. 145 (June 1994). Research also shows that larger organizations are more profitable. See, e.g., Blankenburg, "Newspaper Scale and Newspaper Expenditures," and Marty Tharp and Linda R. Stanley, " A Time Series Analysis of Newspaper Profitability by Circulation Size," *Journal of Media Economics,* 5(1):3-12 (1992).

42. It is not entirely clear whether top editors view their relevant reference group as other editors on the same newspaper or top editors of other newspapers, but in either case the outcome is the same. This is not the case for lower-level positions.

43. This term was coined by mass communication professor Phillip J. Tichenor.

44. See, e.g., Andrew Kreig, *Spiked: How Chain Management Corrupted America's Oldest Newspaper* (Old Saybrook, Conn.: Peregrine Press, 1987).

45. Warren Breed, "Mass Communication and Sociocultural Integration," *Social Forces,* 37:109-16 (1958); George A. Donohue, Clarice N. Olien and Phillip J. Tichenor, "Reporting Conflict by Pluralism, Newspaper Type and Ownership," *Journalism Quarterly,* 62:489-99, 507 (1985); Morris Janowitz, *The Community Press in an Urban Setting* (New York: Free Press, 1952); and Arthur J. Vidich and Joseph Bensman, *Small Town in Mass Society* (Princeton, N.J.: Princeton University Press, 1968).

46. Pellegrin and Coates, "Absentee-Owned Corporations and Community Power Structure."

47. The American Society of Newspaper Editors' code of ethics contains the following dictum: "The American press was made free not just to inform or just to serve as a forum for debate but also to bring an independent scrutiny to bear on the forces of power in the society, including the conduct of official power at all levels of government." Quoted in Philip Meyer, *Ethical Journalism* (New York: Longman, 1987), p. 21.

48. Empirical support for this conclusion can be found in George Albert Gladney, "How Editors and Readers Rank and Rate the Importance of 18 Traditional Standards of Newspaper Excellence," paper presented to the Association for Education in Journalism and Mass Communication (Atlanta, August 1994). Gladney's study shows that editors at larger newspapers (size being one measure of complexity) are much more likely to say newspapers should be aggressive in their reporting and willing to hire top, professional staffers.

49. See J. Kenneth Benson, "The Analysis of Bureaucratic-Professional Conflict: Functional Versus Dialectical Approaches," *The Sociological Quarterly,* 14:378-9 (1973), and David Pearce Demers, "Effect of Corporate Structure on Autonomy of Top Editors at U.S. Dailies," *Journalism Quarterly,* 70:499-508 (1993).

50. For example, journalists could obtain a great deal more information from sources if they were allowed to use false identities in most situations, but this is deemed to be a violation of professional norms of conduct.

51. Meyer, *Ethical Journalism,* pp. 28-9, provides empirical support for this. He reports the results of a national ASNE survey which shows that journalists at large newspapers are much less likely than those at smaller newspapers to be restrained when reporting on controversial topics.

52. Theodore L. Glasser, "Professionalism and the Derision of Diversity: The Case of the Education of Journalists," *Journal of Communication,* 42:131-40 (1992), p. 134. Glasser's main argument is that higher education journalism programs reify professional standards and fail to teach their students how professionalism promotes social order, a point with which I wholeheartedly agree.

53. See, e.g., J. Herbert Altschull, *Agents of Power: The Role of the News Media in Human Affairs* (New York: Longman, 1984); W. Lance Bennett, *News: The Politics of Illusion,* 2nd ed. (New York: Longman, 1988); Stuart Ewen, *Captains of Consciousness: Advertising and the Social Roots of the Consumer Culture* (New York: McGraw-Hill, 1976); Mark Fishman, *Manufacturing the News* (Austin: University of Texas Press, 1980); Herbert J. Gans, *Deciding What's News* (New York: Vintage, 1979); Todd Gitlin, *The Whole World Is Watching: Mass Media in the Making and Unmaking of the New Left* (Berkeley: University of California Press, 1980); Janowitz, *The Community Press in an Urban Setting*; David L. Paletz and Robert M. Entman, *Media Power Politics* (New York: The Free Press, 1981); Phillip J. Tichenor, George A. Donohue and Clarice N. Olien, *Community Conflict and the Press* (Beverly Hills, Calif.: Sage, 1980); Gaye Tuchman, *Making News* (New York: Free Press, 1978); and Gaye Tuchman, "Mass Media Institutions," in Neil Smelser (ed.), *Handbook of Sociology* (Newbury Park, Calif.: Sage, 1988).

Chapter 10

Testing a Theory of Corporate Newspaper Effects

Previous empirical research on the effects of newspaper structure has suffered from two major problems. The first is that most studies have used relatively crude measures of organizational structure. As Chapter 8 showed, the two most widely used measures have been chain ownership and circulation. It was argued that, until recently, chain ownership was a good measure of the shift from the entrepreneurial to the corporate form of organization. Studies showed that it was strongly correlated with circulation, which is a good indicator of structural complexity (i.e., division of labor, hierarchy of authority, role specialization). However, the diffusion of chain ownership in the United States is now so widespread — nearly 80 percent of all dailies are owned by chains — that it no longer appears to be a good discriminator in cross-sectional studies.[1] Circulation is a much better measure, because it is a good measure of organizational complexity.[2] But circulation also measures consumer demand, and there appears to be no simple way to empirically separate the two.

The second problem is that some researchers have used case studies to make broad generalizations to the newspaper industry. Case studies of chain newspapers often conclude, for example, that they place a high degree of importance on profit-making.[3] Undoubtedly, chains place a great deal of emphasis on profits, but this finding cannot be interpreted as evidence that chains place more importance on profits than independently owned newspapers. Comparative analysis is necessary to draw such a conclusion, because profit-making is likely to be important in all forms of business organization. Thus, it would be unusual to find a case study of any newspaper where profit-making was not an important goal.[4]

The comparative analysis in this study is derived from quantitative survey research and content analyses using probabilistic samples of populations of newspapers and journalists. Although such methods usually cannot provide a great deal of in-depth analysis about a particular newspaper, they enable one to make generalizations to large populations of newspapers. A multiple-indicator measure of corporate structure also is employed.

Dataset

The data are derived from a national probability survey of top managers and journalists at daily newspapers in the United States in 1993. Questionnaires were mailed in September of that year to the highest ranking manager, the highest ranking editor, and a police reporter at 250 daily newspapers randomly selected from the *1993 Editor & Publisher International Yearbook*. Of the 750 questionnaires mailed, responses were obtained from 409 journalists at 223 newspapers, for a total response rate of 55 percent (90% of the newspapers responded). No significant differences in response rates were found for the three groups (top manager, 52%; top editor, 56%; and police reporter, 55%). There also was no significant correlation between the type of respondent (top manager, top editor, reporter) and newspaper circulation (r=.01). Additional information about the methodology is available in Chapter 7 (see Dataset #3).

In June 1994, another mailing was made to the 223 newspapers who responded to the mail survey discussed above, asking them to send tear sheets of the editorial and op-ed pages for the most recent Wednesday and Thursday editions of the newspaper (self-addressed, postage-paid envelopes were enclosed). Two consecutive days were sampled to reduce the burden of complying with the request and, hopefully, to increase the response rate. Two weekdays were selected because almost all newspapers that publish on weekends publish editorial pages in those editions but not weekday editions (i.e., sampling weekend dates may have led to an overestimate of the quantity of editorials in smaller newspapers). Newspapers that did not respond to the initial tearsheet mailing were then contacted by telephone.[5] Altogether, 198 newspapers, or 87 percent of the 223 newspapers in the sample, responded. The issues sent covered the period from early June to mid-August.

Although individuals responded to the mail questionnaire, the hypotheses dealing with profits, product quality, editorial content, and community involvement are tested using the newspaper as the unit of analysis. To conduct such an analysis, the findings were aggregated for each newspaper that had more than one respondent. For continuous measures (i.e., ordinal, interval and ratio level measures) and dichotomous nominal measures, the final value used in the analysis represented the mean of the ratings given. In cases where the values for one of the respondents were missing (e.g., failure to answer a question), the values of the other respondent(s) were substituted. No nominal variables containing more than three values were included in this analysis. Hypotheses for autonomy and job satisfaction are tested at the individual level of analysis.

The measures included:

• **Corporate Structure.** The 12-item corporate structure index and the five major dimensions or indicators composing that index are employed as the independent variables in this analysis. A complete discussion of these variables is contained in Chapter 7 (in particular, see Table 7.3).

• **Organizational Goals.** At least three ways to measure organizational goals have been suggested. One is to obtain copies of formal documents from the organizations. This has the advantage of clearly identifying the officially sanctioned goals of the organization. However, some organizations, especially smaller ones, do not develop formalized goals, and the absence of such documents cannot be taken to mean an organization has no goals. Another problem with this approach is that even though the organization may officially adopt one set of goals, actors within the organization may pursue other goals.

A second way to measure goals is through direct observation. If the observer is an outsider, this usually requires the cooperation of the organization, which may alter its behavior to please or obtain a favorable reaction from the observer. The observer may avoid this problem by becoming a covert participant. But in either case, the observer method of observation runs an increased risk of being undermined by preconceptions or biases of the observer.

To get around these problems, a third approach is to ask managers or employees to define the goals or rank-order them. The employees become, in essence, informants.[6] This approach does not guarantee that the responses obtained will accurately reflect the official goals of the organization. However, in many research projects, such as this one, the interest is not the official goals themselves but the perceived goals. This approach assumes that if workers in an organization believe maximizing profits is an organizational goal, for example, their behaviors or actions are likely to be influenced by such a perception.[7] When using the self-report approach to measuring goals, it is also important to distinguish clearly between organizational and individual goals. The organization may place a great deal of emphasis on profits as an organizational goal, whereas a manager may have the personal goal of being promoted. Although there is no necessary reason why organizational and individual goals should be at odds or contradictory, the important question from a public policy perspective is whether corporate organizations pursue goals that are different from noncorporate newspapers.[8]

This study employed the informant approach. Respondents were asked to rate 22 statements designed to measure emphasis that "top management at your newspaper" places on profits, product quality and other goals.[9] Responses were recorded on a seven-point scale ranging from "not very important" (1) to "extremely important" (7). All of the statements except one — conducting readership research — received a mean rating above 4.00, the midpoint. In order of importance, from highest to lowest, the mean ratings are shown in Figure 10.1. The results show that the typical newspaper places a high degree of importance on both profits and product quality. The most important goal identified was increasing circulation, which received nearly a 6 on the 7-point scale. This was followed closely by increasing profits, responding to readers' needs, improving the news product, doing the job well, reducing costs and maximizing profits. The least important goal was conducting readership research, but it still was considered important, scoring at the mid-point on the scale. Winning reporting awards and giving reporters more autonomy also received lower ratings relative to the other goals.

All of the items except "emphasis placed on finding the most efficient way to solve problems," which is a measure of corporate structure (see Chapter 7), were factor-analyzed (principal components, oblique rotation) using an eigenvalue of 1.0 as a minimum for defining a factor. This produced a four-factor solution, but several variables had strong multiple-factor loadings. Five- and six-factor solutions were extracted, the latter producing the most stable results, which are shown in Table 10.1. The first factor, defined as a quality index, contained eight items, but two of them — being innovative and beating the competition — had loadings less than

Figure 10.1
Importance of Organizational Goals

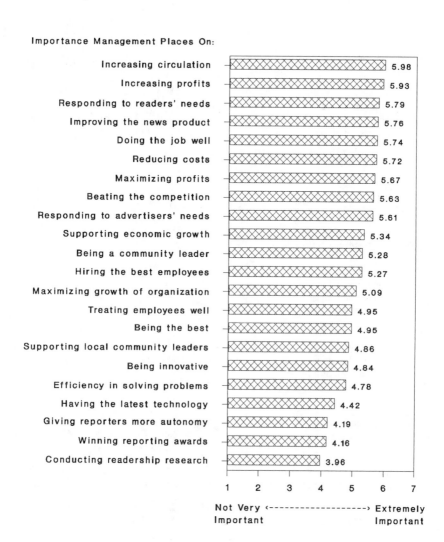

Importance Management Places On:

Increasing circulation	5.98
Increasing profits	5.93
Responding to readers' needs	5.79
Improving the news product	5.76
Doing the job well	5.74
Reducing costs	5.72
Maximizing profits	5.67
Beating the competition	5.63
Responding to advertisers' needs	5.61
Supporting economic growth	5.34
Being a community leader	5.28
Hiring the best employees	5.27
Maximizing growth of organization	5.09
Treating employees well	4.95
Being the best	4.95
Supporting local community leaders	4.86
Being innovative	4.84
Efficiency in solving problems	4.78
Having the latest technology	4.42
Giving reporters more autonomy	4.19
Winning reporting awards	4.16
Conducting readership research	3.96

1   2   3   4   5   6   7

Not Very <------------------> Extremely
Important   Important

.60 and also produced moderately high loadings on at least one other factor. These two items were excluded from the quality index, which included responding to readers' needs, doing the job well, improving the

Table 10.1
Profit and Quality Measures Factor-Analyzed[a]

	Factor Loadings						CE[b]
	F1	F2	F3	F4	F5	F6	
1. Quality Index (a+b+c+d+e+f)							
a. Responding to readers' needs	**.91**	.03	.01	.21	.05	.03	.76
b. Doing the job well	**.90**	-.02	.10	.02	-.08	-.11	.82
c. Improving the news product	**.89**	.01	-.11	-.05	-.05	.14	.79
d. Treating employees well	**.75**	-.12	.15	.10	.24	-.01	.77
e. Being the best	**.74**	-.08	-.00	-.23	.08	-.07	.78
f. Hiring the best employees	**.72**	.00	-.01	-.14	.17	.10	.75
g. Being innovative[c]	.55	.07	.11	-.22	.29	.08	.74
h. Beating the competition[c]	.42	.24	.17	-.34	.11	-.37	.66
2. Profit Index (a+b+c)							
a. Increasing profits	.01	**.91**	-.08	-.06	.02	.09	.86
b. Maximizing profits	-.15	**.90**	-.02	-.07	.04	.05	.84
c. Reducing costs	-.00	**.86**	.09	.17	.03	-.09	.72
3. Community Involvement (a+b+c)							
a. Supporting local community leadership	-.15	.06	**.85**	.12	.05	.24	.79
b. Supporting economic growth in the community	-.03	-.02	**.84**	-.17	-.08	-.03	.74
c. Being a community leader	.35	-.03	**.67**	.01	.10	-.18	.74
4. Unnamed Factor							
a. Winning reporting awards	-.11	-.01	.08	-.85	.02	-.05	.67
b. Conducting readership research	.40	-.11	-.03	-.43	.04	.22	.56
c. Maximizing growth of the organization	.15	.32	.04	-.42	.34	.15	.65
5. Unnamed Factor							
a. Giving reporters more autonomy	.17	.12	.02	-.03	.82	-.04	.80
b. Increasing circulation	.32	.33	.03	-.40	-.42	.12	.70
6. Unnamed Factor							
a. Responding to advertisers' needs	.08	.33	.19	.11	-.24	.64	.76
b. Having the latest technology	.19	-.03	.22	-.23	.20	.48	.60
EIGENVALUES	7.95	3.25	1.52	1.06	.88	.85	15.51
PERCENT OF VARIANCE	38%	16%	7%	5%	4%	4%	74%

[a]Principal components, oblique rotation (N=219).
[b]Communality estimates (i.e., total variance explained).
[c]Measure excluded from index because of low or mixed loadings.

news product, treating employees well, being the best, and hiring the best employees.

Three of the profit items — increasing profits, maximizing profits and reducing costs — loaded heavily on the second factor. It was expected that responding to advertisers' needs also would have loaded highly with these profit items, but it did not (.33); it had multiple loadings and was excluded from the analysis.[10] The third factor consisted of three community involvement measures. The rest of the items loaded on the remaining four factors, none of which was named because each contained multiple loadings or were conceptually mismatched. The analysis will examine each of these items separately (winning reporting awards, conducting readership research, maximizing growth of the organization, giving reporters more autonomy, increasing circulation, and having the latest technology). The six factors altogether explained 74 percent of the variance.

Four additional measures of emphasis on profits and product quality were included in the study. After rating the 22 importance measures, the respondents were asked to identify the first, second and third most important ones in that list. Table 10.2 provides descriptive statistics for these measures. One-fourth of the newspapers (25%) mentioned at least one of the three profit items as being the most important. The mean number of times profit was mentioned as one of the three most important goals was .61. Slightly more than half of the newspapers (53%) mentioned at least one of the six product quality items as the most important goal. The mean number of times quality was mentioned as one of the three most important goals was 1.29. In short, the analysis will include three "subjective" measures of profit and three "subjective" measures of product quality: one being a numerical index composed of the importance ratings, another being the percentage mentioning that goal as the most important, and the third being the mean number of times that goal was mentioned as one of the top three goals.

Three "objective" measures of profitability also were employed. The first one was based on a question which asked respondents to indicate whether their newspapers made a profit: "Which of the following best describes the 'bottom line' at your newspaper last year?" Responses were recorded on a four-point scale: (1) lost money, (2) broke even, (3) made up to 15 percent profit on revenues after taxes, (4) made over 15 percent profit on revenues after taxes. Table 10.2 shows that the mean value for this measure was 3.1; in other words, the average profit was between 0 and

Table 10.2
Descriptive Statistics for Profit and Quality Measures

	Mean	Std Dev	Minimum	Maximum	N
Subjective Profit Measures					
1. Profit Index (a+b+c)	17.33	2.99	3.00	21.00	222
a. Importance placed on increasing profits	5.93	1.06	1.00	7.00	222
b. Importance placed on maximizing profits	5.67	1.13	1.00	7.00	222
c. Importance placed on reducing costs	5.72	1.14	1.00	7.00	222
2. Proportion mentioning profit as most important goal in organization	.25	.34	.00	1.00	217
3. Number of times profit mentioned as 1st, 2nd or 3rd most important goal	.61	.68	.00	3.00	223
"Objective" Profit Measures					
1. Last year's profits	3.10	.79	1.00	4.00	181
2. Single-copy price	$.36	$.09	$.00	$.75	223
3. Open display advertising per inch rate	$30.51	$56.77	$3.00	$482.75	216
Quality Measures					
1. Quality Index (a+b+c+d+e+f)	32.91	6.20	11.00	42.00	221
a. Responding to readers' needs	5.79	1.03	2.00	7.00	222
b. Doing the job well	5.74	1.06	2.00	7.00	222
c. Improving the news product	5.76	1.19	1.00	7.00	223
d. Treating employees well	4.95	1.40	1.00	7.00	223
e. Being the best	5.41	1.28	1.00	7.00	221
f. Hiring the best employees	5.27	1.22	1.00	7.00	222
2. Proportion saying quality is most important goal	.53	.40	.00	1.00	217
3. Number of times quality mentioned as 1st, 2nd or 3rd most important goal	1.29	.80	.00	3.00	223
Community Involvement Measures					
1. Community Index (a+b+c)	15.46	3.18	4.00	21.00	221
a. Supporting local community leadership	4.86	1.39	1.00	7.00	221
b. Being a leader in the community	5.28	1.23	1.00	7.00	222
c. Supporting economic growth	5.34	1.24	1.00	7.00	221
Other Measures					
1. Being innovative	4.84	1.31	1.00	7.00	222
2. Giving reporters more autonomy	4.19	1.18	1.00	7.00	222
3. Conducting readership research	3.96	1.48	1.00	7.00	222
4. Winning reporting awards	4.16	1.26	1.00	7.00	223
5. Increasing circulation	5.98	1.10	1.00	7.00	223
6. Maximizing growth of the organization	5.09	1.31	1.00	7.00	219
7. Having the latest technology	4.42	1.34	1.00	7.00	223
8. Beating the competition	5.63	1.13	1.00	7.00	222

15 percent on revenues after taxes.[11] Only a fraction of the newspapers had lost money. Not unexpectedly, this measure produced the highest number of "don't know" responses and the smallest sample size of any measure (n=181). Many privately owned newspapers do not make their earnings public, even to their top-level employees. The second two measures were single-copy newsstand price and the open display advertising per inch rate. These measures also have the advantage of being independent of the honesty or knowledge of the respondents. They were coded from the *1993 Editor & Publisher International Yearbook*. The mean newsstand price was 36 cents, and the mean display ad rate was $30.51. These are not direct measures of profitability, but research shows that demand for newspapers and advertising is relatively inelastic.[12]

The zero-order correlations between the profit and product quality measures are shown in Table 10.3. Several patterns are evident. First, almost all of the "subjective" measures of profit are negatively correlated with the "subjective" measures of product quality. The one exception is the multiple indicator indices (r= -.00). This indicates that profits and product quality are important goals in all organizations, albeit a negative relationship emerges only when more sensitive (i.e., most important value) measures are used. Second, virtually none of the "objective" profit items are related to the "subjective" profit or product quality measures. And third, almost none of the "objective" measures are related to each other. The second and third findings support previous research which suggests that different measures of profit are often uncorrelated.[13]

• *Job Satisfaction.* Respondents were asked to indicate "on a scale from 1 to 7, where 1 means 'completely dissatisfied' and 7 means 'completely satisfied,' how satisfied are you with your job?" Forty-four percent selected a value of "6" or "7," and 75 percent selected a value of "5" or greater, indicating that most respondents are satisfied. The mean values are shown in Table 10.4.

• *Autonomy.* Five measures of autonomy were employed:

1. "Overall, how much freedom do you have to make important decisions about what you do and how you do it?" Responses were recorded on a five-point scale (values shown in brackets) — "no freedom [1], some freedom [2], a fair amount [3], a great deal [4], or complete freedom [5]."

2. "When it comes to making decisions about how to improve the quality of the editorial content in your newspaper, how much of a role do each of the following people (publisher/top editor/reporters) play — no

Table 10.3
Zero-Order Correlations Between Profit and Quality Measures

	2	3	4	5	6	7	8	9
"Subjective" Profit Measures								
1. Importance placed on profits (3-item index)	.37**	.44**	.01	.05	-.08	-.00	-.35**	-.37**
2. Profit most important value in organization	1.00	.74**	.08	-.03	-.12*	-.30**	-.63**	-.52**
3. Number of times profit mentioned as 1st, 2nd or 3rd most important value	.74**	1.00	.07	.09	-.06	-.35**	-.57**	-.57**
"Objective" Profit Measures								
4. Last year's profits	.08	.07	1.00	.11	-.07	.13*	.05	.05
5. Single-copy price	-.03	.09	.11	1.00	-.00	-.03	.06	.02
6. Open display ad rate per inch	-.12*	-.06	-.07	-.00	1.00	.13*	.10	.10
"Subjective" Quality Measures								
7. Importance placed on quality (6-item index)	-.29**	-.35**	.13*	-.03	.13*	1.00	.45**	.42**
8. Quality most important organizational value	-.63**	-.57**	.05	.06	.10	.45**	1.00	.73**
9. Number of times quality mentioned as 1st-3rd most important value	-.52**	-.57**	.05	.02	.10	.42**	.73**	1.00

*p<.05; **p<.01

role [1], some role [2], major role [3], or makes all decisions [4]?" Responses were recorded to match each sample group (i.e., the responses for reporters were based to the reporter sample, etc.).

3. "How much freedom do your reporters usually have in deciding which aspects of a story should be emphasized — none at all [1], some freedom [2], a great deal [3], or almost complete freedom [4]?"

4. "How much freedom do your reporters usually have in selecting the stories they work on — none at all [1], some freedom [2], a great deal [3], or almost complete freedom [4]?"

5. "How much editing do reporters' stories get from others in your organization — none at all [3], some [2], or a great deal [1]?" This measure was inversely coded to match other measures.[14]

The last three measures are identical to those used in the Johnstone, Slawski and Bowman study and Weaver and Wilhoit's replication.[15] The

Table 10.4
Descriptive Statistics for Autonomy, Job Satisfaction Measures

	Mean	Std Dev	Minimum	Maximum	N
Job satisfaction measure	5.10	1.35	1.00	7.00	401
Autonomy Measures					
1. Subjective autonomy index (a+b)†	0.00	1.00	-3.91	2.51	403
a. Freedom to make decisions	3.77	.85	1.00	5.00	408
b. Role top editors play in decisions about improving editorial content	3.00	.44	1.00	4.00	406
2. Objective autonomy index (a+b+c)†	0.00	1.00	-2.40	2.72	406
a. Freedom reporters have to decide which aspects of story to emphasize	2.91	.63	1.00	4.00	408
b. Freedom reporters have selecting stories	2.76	.63	1.00	4.00	408
c. Extent to which reporters' stories are edited (inversely coded)	1.75	.53	1.00	3.00	408
Control Variables					
1. Years worked in journalism	18.00	12.00	0.00	50.00	406
2. Gender (proportion male)	.80	.40	0.00	1.00	407
3. Age	42.00	12	22.00	74.00	407
4. Education (proportion with college degree)	.83	.38	0.00	1.00	408
5. Income (proportion earning over $50,000)	.42	.49	0.00	1.00	393
6. Title/Position					
a. Proportion who are publishers	.29	NA	NA	NA	409
b. Proportion who are editors	.47	NA	NA	NA	409
c. Proportion who are reporters	.23	NA	NA	NA	409

†Measures are standardized with mean=0 and SD=1.
NA=Not applicable.

five measures were factor-analyzed (principal components, varimax rotation). This produced a two-factor solution, with the first two measures loading highly on the first factor and the last three on the second factor. The first factor was defined as self-reported or "subjective" autonomy; the second was perceived control over reporters' stories, or "objective" autonomy (values were reversed so that high values mean more control and less autonomy). The items were standardized before creating the indices.

• *Job Title/Rank.* To test some of the autonomy and satisfaction hypotheses, it was necessary to include the title or rank of the respondents. This involved dividing the sample into three groups: publishers and top-level managers, editors, and reporters. The classification was made based on a question which asked respondents to provide their job title(s).[16]

Publishers, general managers and noneditorial managers comprised the first group (29% of the total sample; see Table 10.4); any respondent who held the title of "editor" was placed into the second group (47% of the sample); and reporters, most of whom covered the police beat, comprised the third group (23%).

• *Demographic Variables.* Several other demographic variables that in previous studies have been found to be correlated with autonomy or job satisfaction also were included in the analysis. They included years worked in journalism, gender, age, education and income (see Table 10.4). The last two were recorded on four-point and six-point scales, respectively.[17]

• *Editorial-Page Content Measures.* A research assistant who was unfamiliar with the theory and hypotheses in this study coded the content from the editorials and the letters to the editor. Three measures were coded. The first was focus of the editorial or letter:

> An editorial or letter to the editor or commentary is defined as **local** if the main topic of the article focuses primarily on issues, activities or matters that affect or concern the local community, which, for purposes here, is defined as the newspaper's primary market area. This includes the city and county in which the newspaper is located and, in the case of metropolitan dailies, the surrounding suburbs and urbanized areas. City hall, county government, and regional planning groups, for example, are local groups or organizations. However, state government, because its activities focus on the entire state and not just a local area, is defined as a **nonlocal** group, even if the statehouse is located in the community the newspaper serves. Any issue or matter associated with the federal government is nonlocal. If it is not clear whether the focus is local or nonlocal, choose local.

To assess the reliability of this measure, this researcher coded the content of 64 editorials and subjected the findings to a reliability statistical test. Intercoder reliability on this measure was 96%. The coefficient of reliability used was the ratio of coding agreements to the total number of coding decisions (CR=[Number of Agreements x 2] / [N1 +N2]).[18]

The second content item coded was critical evaluation:

> Is the main emphasis of the editorial or letter to the editor negative, positive or neutral in terms of the way it evaluates an action, rule, law, decision, position, value, idea, ideology, custom or practice **associated with a** *mainstream individual or group?*

> **Positive** is defined as content that is commending, applauding, approving or

admiring. **Negative** is defined as content that is faulting, blaming, censuring or disapproving. If a story contains content that is positive and negative toward the mainstream entity, the evaluation should be based on an overall assessment of the article (i.e., was it more positive than negative?). Stories, editorials, etc. that contain content that is neither positive nor negative or content that appears to be equally balanced should be coded **neutral**. If it does not deal with content that is critical or praiseworthy, then code it **neutral**. When a story contains no reference to a mainstream group, value, etc., it should be coded **not applicable**.

Mainstream is defined as an individual or group that is associated with **local, state or federal government** (e.g., city hall, police, schools, Congress, the president, courts, colleges, mayor, governor, state agencies, city council members, etc.), **the two main political parties** (Democrat and Republican), **private businesses and corporations**, or **mainstream churches** (mainstream protestant, Catholic or Jewish).

The vast majority of editorials dealt with issues surrounding the actions or activities of government. Intercoder reliability for the four-category measure of critical evaluation (positive, neutral, negative, not applicable) was not extremely high (64% agreement). To rectify this problem, the critical evaluation measure was dichotomized into critical vs. noncritical. This produced an intercoder reliability coefficient of 86 percent.

The source of the editorial was also coded:

Who wrote the editorial — someone from the local newspaper staff (usually identified as staff writer or in the case of editorials, no byline) or nonstaff, which includes content generated by wire services, syndicates, other newspapers, or special to the paper?

The reliability coefficient here was 100 percent.

Table 10.5 shows that the mean number of editorials produced over the two-day period was 2.64. Most of those are staff-generated (66%) but only a minority are about local issues (24%).[19] About 4 of 10 (40%) contain content that is critical of mainstream groups or authorities. The typical newspaper also published about five editorials over the two-day period, most of which were about local issues (70%). About 4 of 10 (37%) also contain content that is critical of mainstream groups or authorities. Descriptive statistics for other content measures are presented in Table 10.5.

Table 10.5
Descriptive Statistics for Editorial-Page Measures

	Mean	Std Dev	Minimum	Maximum	N
Editorial-Page Measures†					
1. Total number of editorials	2.64	1.84	0.00	8.00	198
2. Number of staff-generated editorials	2.16	1.92	0.00	8.00	198
3. Proportion of editorials staff-generated	.66	.43	0.00	1.00	198
4. Number of editorials about local issues	.72	.92	0.00	4.00	198
5. Proportion of editorials about local issues	.24	.31	0.00	1.00	198
6. Number of editorials critical of mainstream groups/institutions/sources	1.31	1.34	0.00	6.00	198
7. Proportion of editorials critical of mainstream groups/institutions/sources	.40	.36	0.00	1.00	198
8. Total number of letters to the editor	5.09	4.62	0.00	18.00	198
9. Total number of letters about local issues	4.22	3.84	0.00	15.00	198
10. Proportion of editorials about local issues	.70	.39	0.00	1.00	198
11. Number of editorials critical of mainstream groups/institutions/sources	2.34	2.53	0.00	12.00	198
12. Proportion of editorials critical of mainstream groups/institutions/sources	.37	.31	0.00	1.00	198

†Statistics are for two issues of the newspaper.

Findings

The data provide partial or full support for 12 of the 15 hypotheses. The findings did not support the expectation that corporate newspapers would be less involved in or supportive of the local community — no difference was found. The data also do not support the hypothesis that reporters at corporate newspapers have less autonomy or are less satisfied with their jobs. No differences were found in terms of autonomy, and reporters at corporate newspapers were actually more satisfied with their jobs. Contrary to expectations, publishers at corporate newspapers also were more satisfied with their jobs.

H1: Corporate Structure and Profitability

The data generally support the hypothesis that the more a newspaper exhibits the characteristics of the corporate form of organization, the more profitable it is. Table 10.6 shows that the corporate newspaper index is positively correlated with last year's reported profit margin and the amount

Table 10.6
Correlations Between Corporate, Profit and Quality Measures[a]

Independent Variables/Indices

Dependent Variables	Corporate Index	Structural Complexity	Ownership Structure	Rules & Procedures	Rational Decision Making	Hire College Grads
"Objective" Profit Items						
1. Last year's profits	.14*	.08	.09	.08	.06	.14*
2. Single-copy price[b]	.05	.09	-.01	.04	-.08	.03
3. Open display ad rate per inch[b]	.26**	.27**	.16**	.20**	.04	.14**
"Objective" Profit Items						
4. Importance placed on profits (3-item index)	-.01	-.14*	.05	-.02	.05	-.03
5. Profit most important value in organization	-.18**	-.19**	.08	-.13*	-.16**	-.10
6. Number of times profit mentioned as 1st-3rd most important value	-.18**	-.18**	.12*	-.12*	-.28**	-.09
"Subjective" Quality Items						
7. Importance placed on quality (6-item index)	.58**	.27**	.15*	.36**	.76**	.12*
8. Quality most important organizational value	.31**	.19**	.01	.21**	.32**	.12*
9. Number of times quality mentioned as 1st-3rd most important value	.34**	.24**	.06	.26**	.34**	.06

$*p<.05; **p<.01$
[a]All correlations below are zero-order except those contained in the rows for single-copy price and open display advertising rate per inch, which are first-order correlations after controlling for circulation.
[b]First-order correlations after controlling for circulation.

charged for open display advertising. There is no relationship between corporate structure and single-copy newsstand price. The zero-order correlation between the corporate index and last year's reported profit margin is .14 (p<.05). All five corporate dimensions are positively related to the profit margin measure, but only one — hiring college graduates — is significantly related (r=.14, p<.05).

The correlations for the other two "objective" profit measures are first-order correlations, taken after removing the effects of circulation. The logic here is to remove any spurious effects that may be a function of circulation (i.e., larger circulation newspapers generally have more content and, thus, could charge more per copy) as opposed to organizational structure.[20] In the case of newsstand price, the control made no difference — neither circulation nor corporate structure is a predictor. The single-copy cost of a newspaper appears to be driven more by convention, history or norms than by actual quantity or volume of the product itself. However, corporate structure is significantly related to advertising rates even when controlling for circulation (r=.26, p<.01). Every dimension of the corporate newspaper index except rationality is significantly related to advertising rates.

H2: Corporate Structure and Profits As Goal

The data generally support the second hypothesis: The more a newspaper exhibits the characteristics of the corporate form of organization, the less emphasis it places on profits. Table 10.6 shows that the correlation between the corporate index and two of the three "subjective" profit items — profit mentioned as most important value and number of times profit mentioned as one of the top three values — are significant (in both cases the correlation -.18, p<.01). The correlation between the corporate index and the 3-item profit index is negligible (r=-.01, p>.05). These findings suggest that making a profit is a goal that is important in all newspaper organizations, but only the rank-order measures were sensitive enough to detect differences between corporate and noncorporate organizations.

Analysis of the five individual corporate structure measures generally followed these trends. One exception is that structural complexity, in contrast to the other four measures, is negatively related to the 3-item profit index (r=-.14, p<.05). Three of the five measures — structural complexity, rules and procedures, and rational decision-making — are significantly related to emphasis placed on profits as the most important goal or as one of the top three goals, but ownership structure and requiring a college degree for reporters were not. Ownership, in fact, is positively related to the number of times profit was mentioned as the first, second or third most important value. This finding supports other studies which have found that chain ownership is significantly related to emphasis on profits.[21]

Table 10.7
Predictive Power of Corporate Measures Compared[a]

		Complexity Measures		Ownership Measures	
Dependent Variables	Corporate Index	Structural Complexity	Circulation	Ownership Structure	Chain Ownership
"Subjective" Profit Items					
1. Importance placed on profits (3-item index)	-.01	-.14*	-.09	.05	.02
2. Profit most important value in organization	-.18**	-.19**	-.12*	.08	.11*
3. Number of times profit mentioned as 1st, 2nd or 3rd most important value	-.18**	-.18**	-.06	.12*	.14*
"Objective" Profit Items					
4. Last year's profits	.14*	.08	-.10	.09	.12*
5. Single-copy price[b]	.05	.09	NA	-.01	-.03
6. Open display ad rate per inch[b]	.26**	.27**	NA	.16**	.02
"Subjective" Quality Items					
7. Importance placed on quality (6-item index)	.58**	.27**	.11*	.15*	.03
8. Quality most important organizational value	.31**	.19**	.08	.01	-.04
9. Number of times quality mentioned as 1st, 2nd or 3rd most important value	.34**	.24**	.10	.06	-.09

*$p < .05$; **$p < .01$
NA=Not applicable
[a]All correlations below are zero-order except those contained in the rows for single-copy price and open display advertising rate per inch, which are first-order correlations after controlling for circulation.
[b]First-order correlations after controlling for circulation.

H3: Chain Ownership and Profits

The data generally support the hypothesis that chain newspapers place more emphasis on profits than their respective counterparts at independently owned newspapers. Table 10.7 shows that chain ownership is significantly related to two of the three "subjective" profit measures — emphasis placed on profit as the most important value and number of times profit mentioned as one of the top three most important values (r=.11, p<.05, and r=.14, p<.05, respectively). Chain ownership also is positively related to last year's reported profit (r=.12, p<.05).

Table 10.7 also compares the predictive validity of the chain ownership and circulation measures to the multiple-indicator ownership and structural complexity variables used in this study. The results indicate that neither ownership variable is a strong predictor of the profit measures. The structural complexity index, however, is a much better predictor of the "subjective" profit measures than circulation.

H4: Corporate Structure and Product Quality

As expected, the more a newspaper exhibits the characteristics of the corporate form of organization, the more emphasis that newspaper places on product quality as an organizational goal or value. Table 10.6 shows that the correlations between the corporate index and the three product quality measures are moderately strong, ranging between .31 and .58. Structural complexity, rules and procedures, and rationality are moderately correlated with all three quality measures. The correlations for ownership structure and hiring college graduates are weaker and in several cases nonsignificant. Table 10.7 also shows that the structural complexity index is a much better predictor of the quality measures than raw circulation.

H5: Corporate Structure and Other Nonprofit Goals

The data support the fifth hypothesis, which expected that the more a newspaper exhibits the characteristics of the corporate form of organization, the more emphasis it places on other nonprofit organizational goals, including maximizing growth of the organization, winning reporting awards, having the latest technology, beating the competition, conducting readership research, giving reporters more autonomy, being innovative, and increasing circulation. Table 10.8 shows that the corporate index is significantly and positively related to every one of these measures. Once again, the three best predictors within the index are structural complexity, rules and rationality.

H6: Corporate Structure and Community Involvement

The data do not support the hypothesis that newspapers which exhibit the characteristics of the corporate form of organization would be less involved or supportive of the local community. In fact, some of the findings support the opposite conclusion. Table 10.8 shows that the correlation between the corporate index and the community involvement

Table 10.8
Correlations Between Corporate and Other Measures

Independent Variables/Indices

Dependent Variables	Corporate Index	Structural Complexity	Ownership Structure	Rules & Procedures	Rational Decision Making	Hire College Grads
1. Maximizing growth of the organization	.36**	.15*	.15*	.19*	.49**	.04
2. Winning reporting awards	.38**	.17**	.21**	.33**	.15*	.16**
3. Having the latest technology	.33**	.25**	-.01	.17**	.45**	.09
4. Beating the competition	.39**	.20**	.12*	.25**	.40**	.21**
5. Being innovative	.51**	.21**	.09	.33**	.68**	.04
6. Giving reporters more autonomy	.32**	.10*	.09	.15*	.61**	-.02
7. Conducting readership research	.51**	.31**	.15*	.35**	.48**	.15*
8. Increasing circulation	.22**	.14*	.16*	.14*	.20**	-.03
9. Community involve- ment (3-item index)	.10	-.10	.00	.13*	.39**	-.04

*p<.05; **p<.01

measure was not significant (r=.10, p>.05). However, two of the individual measures — rules and rationality — are positively correlated with the community involvement index (.13, p<.05, and .39, p<.01 respectively).

H7: Corporate Structure and Autonomy/Satisfaction of Top Editors

The data support the hypothesis that the more a newspaper exhibits the characteristics of the corporate form of organization, the greater the autonomy and job satisfaction of its top editors. Table 10.9 shows that the zero-order correlation between the corporate index and job satisfaction is .29 (p<.01) and between the corporate index and autonomy is .28 (p<.01). The structural complexity, rules and rationality dimensions are all significantly related to autonomy and satisfaction. Ownership structure is unrelated to both measures, which supports some of the findings above which show that ownership structure has limited effects on organizational goals. The measure which requires a bachelor's degree for a reporting position is significantly related to autonomy but not job satisfaction.

Table 10.9
Correlations Between Corporate,
Autonomy and Satisfaction Measures

Independent Variables/Indices

Dependent Variables	Corporate Index	Structural Complexity	Ownership Structure	Rules & Procedures	Rational Decision Making	Hire College Grads
Total Sample						
Job Satisfaction	.31**	.19**	.07	.17**	.42**	.03
Self-Reported Autonomy	.21**	.04	.05	.14**	.42**	-.01
Perceived Control Over						
Reporters' Stories	.27**	.27**	.06	.09*	.18**	.12**
Reporters						
Job Satisfaction	.22*	.16*	.14	.04	.35**	-.03
Self-Reported Autonomy	.06	-.10	.09	.11	.32**	-.09
Perceived Control Over						
Reporters' Stories	.03	.27**	-.05	-.01	-.17*	-.08
Editors						
Job Satisfaction	.29**	.30**	-.04	.22**	.32**	.06
Self-Reported Autonomy	.28**	.15*	-.06	.15*	.30**	.19*
Perceived Control Over						
Reporters' Stories	.33**	.29**	.14*	.11	.30**	.18*
Publishers/Top Managers						
Job Satisfaction	.25**	.15*	.03	.10	.28**	.10
Self-Reported Autonomy	-.02	.06	-.05	-.07	.10	-.10
Perceived Control Over						
Reporters' Stories	.27**	.28**	-.02	.08	-.01	.21**

*$p < .05$; **$p < .01$

H8: Corporate Structure and
Control Over Reporters' Stories

The data provide partial support for the hypothesis that corporate newspapers would exhibit more control over reporters' stories. Table 10.9 shows that publishers and editors at corporate newspapers are more likely than their counterparts at entrepreneurial newspapers to say that reporters' stories are more heavily edited and that reporters have less freedom to select stories and to decide what to emphasize (for publishers, r=.27, p<.01; and for editors, r=.33, p<.01). However, this finding does not hold for reporters (r=.03, p>.05). An examination of the individual corporate dimensions indicates that, as expected, reporters in larger, more complex newspapers (structural complexity dimension) do believe those organizations exert more control over their stories (r=.27); however, these effects are mostly neutralized by the rationality dimension, which is negatively correlated with control variable (r= -.17, p<.05). In other words, reporters who say their newspapers place a high degree of emphasis on finding the most efficient way to solve problems also tend to say their stories are more heavily edited and controlled.

H9: Corporate Structure and Autonomy/Satisfaction of Reporters

The data do not support the hypothesis that the more a newspaper exhibits the characteristics of the corporate form of organization, the lower the autonomy and job satisfaction of its reporters. In fact, Table 10.9 indicates that reporters at corporate newspapers are more satisfied with their jobs than reporters at entrepreneurial newspapers (r=.22, p<.05). Both the structural complexity and rationality dimensions are significantly related to satisfaction. The corporate index is not significantly related to reporters' self-reported autonomy (r=.06, p>.05).

H10: Corporate Structure and Autonomy/Satisfaction of Publishers

The data provide only partial support for the expectation that there would be no difference between corporate and entrepreneurial publishers in terms of autonomy and job satisfaction. In Table 10.9, corporate publishers report having the same amount of autonomy as entrepreneurial publishers (r= -.02, p>.05). However, contrary to expectations, corporate publishers are more satisfied with their jobs (r=.25, p<.01). Like the findings for reporters and editors, the key dimensions influencing this relationship are structural complexity and rationality.

H11: Rank and Autonomy/Satisfaction

As expected, the higher the rank of an employee in the news organization, the greater the autonomy and job satisfaction. Table 10.9 shows that the zero-order correlation between rank (reporter=1, editor=2;

and publisher=3) and self-reported autonomy is .38 (p<.01); that is, publishers report having the most autonomy and reporters the least (standardized means are +.67, -.12 and -.43, respectively). This relationship is nonlinear — autonomy increases exponentially as rank increases — but it is not extremely strong.

Additional regression analysis was conducted to examine the effect of corporate structure and autonomy on job satisfaction. A large body of research shows that autonomy is one of the best predictors of job satisfaction. A fundamental question is what impact this variable will have on job satisfaction while controlling for corporate structure. Table 10.10 shows the results of a two-step hierarchical regression. The first step for the entire sample shows that both the corporate index and rank are significantly related to job satisfaction (beta=.25, p<.01, and beta=.26, p<.01, respectively). Both of these predictors account for about 13 percent of the variance in job satisfaction. At step 2, the coefficient for the rank variable becomes nonsignificant (beta=.05, p>.05), and the coefficient for the corporate index declines (beta=.16, p<.05). Additional analysis shows that self-reported autonomy mediates virtually all of these effects — it is a significant and powerful predictor of satisfaction (beta=.40, p<.01).

Contrary to previous research, step 2 of the regression model shows that the number of years a respondent worked in journalism is negatively related to satisfaction, meaning those who have worked in the business longer are more dissatisfied. At a bivariate level, number of years is positively related to satisfaction (r=.16, p<.01). But this relationship becomes negative (r= -.16) when controlling for the other variables, especially income, which is strongly correlated with number of years (r=.67, p<.01; see Table 10.10).[22] These findings suggest that journalists whose incomes do not grow become less satisfied with their jobs over time. As might be expected, the relationship is strongest for reporters (beta= -.30, p<.01), who have lowest prestige and status of the three groups. In contrast to previous research, income was not a significant predictor of job satisfaction — autonomy plays the major role. Education and control over reporters' stories are not significantly related to satisfaction.

H12: Corporate Structure
and Number of Editorials/Letters

The data support the hypothesis which expected that the more a newspaper exhibits the characteristics of the corporate form of organization, the greater the number of editorials and letters to the editor. Table 10.11

Table 10.10
Hierarchical Regression of Job Satisfaction
on Corporate and Predictor Measures

Model/Independent Variables	Total Sample† (N=287)	Reporters (n=69)	Editors (n=107)	Publishers/ Managers (n=101)
Step 1				
Corporate Index	.25**	.20*	.28**	.24*
Job Title (rank)	.26**	NA	NA	NA
R²	.13**	.04*	.08**	.06*
Step 2				
Corporate Index	.16**	.12	.13	.20*
Job Title (rank)	.05	NA	NA	NA
Self-Reported Autonomy	.40**	.36**	.47**	.33**
Income	.13	.12	.11	.10
Years in Journalism	-.16**	-.30**	-.10	-.18*
Education	-.06	.02	-.12	-.08
Control Over Stories	.01	-.03	.03	.09
R² Change	.14**	.21**	.20**	.11**
Total R²	.27**	.25**	.28**	.17**

*p<.05; **p<.01
Standardized regression coefficients shown in table.
†Total sample size is greater than the sum of the three groups because of missing values.
NA=not applicable.

shows that the zero-order correlation between the corporate structure index and number of editorials is .42 (p<.01). The corresponding correlation for letters to the editor is .49 (p<.01). Three of the five corporate dimensions — structural complexity, rules and procedures, and hire college graduates — are significantly related to the corporate structure index. The correlation for the ownership structure dimension is positive but not statistically significant. All five dimensions are significantly related to the number of letters to the editor. Separate analysis shows that the correlations between chain ownership (0=independent; 1=chain), and these editorial-page measures are not significant (data not shown).

H13: Corporate Structure and Staff-Generated Editorials

The data support the hypothesis that the more a newspaper exhibits the characteristics of the corporate form of organization, the greater the number and proportion of staff-generated editorials. Table 10.11 shows that the

Table 10.11
Correlations Between Corporate and Editorial-Page Measures

Independent Variables/Indices

Dependent Variables	Corporate Index	Structural Complexity	Ownership Structure	Rules & Procedures	Rational Decision Making	Hire College Grads
Number of Editorials	.42**	.59**	.11	.24**	-.03	.27**
Number of Letters to Editor	.49**	.61**	.18*	.29**	.13*	.23**
Staff-Generated Editorials						
Number	.43**	.68**	.09	.30**	-.06	.24**
Proportion	.33**	.45**	.07	.23*	-.01	.23**
Editorials About Local Issues						
Number	.22*	.41**	.04	.10	-.09	.15*
Proportion	.09	.19**	.01	-.01	-.04	.11
Letters about Local Issues						
Number	.45**	.50**	.17**	.26**	-.17**	.22**
Proportion	.19**	.09	.05	.05	.13*	.30**
Editorials That Are Critical of Mainstream Groups						
Number	.33**	.46**	.16*	.17**	-.08	.16*
Proportion	.20**	.24**	.09	.10	-.02	.13*
Letters That Are Critical of Mainstream Groups						
Number	.52**	.61**	.20**	.29**	.18**	.21**
Proportion	.32**	.26**	.12*	.15*	.09	.27**

*p<.05; **p<.01

zero-order correlation between the corporate newspaper index and number of staff-generated editorials is .43 (p<.01); the correlation for proportion of staff-generated editorials is .33 (p<.01). Three of the five corporate dimensions — structural complexity, rules and procedures, and staff expertise (hire college graduates for reporting positions) — are significantly related to both of the staff-generated measures. The correlations for chain ownership show that it is not significantly related to either of the staff-generated measures (data not shown).

H14: Corporate Structure and Local Editorials/Letters

The data generally support the hypothesis that corporate organizations would publish a greater number and proportion of editorials and letters to the editor about local issues. Table 10.11 shows that the correlation between the corporate newspaper index and number of local editorials is .22 (p<.05). Two of the five dimensions — structural complexity and hire college graduates — are significantly related to the number of local editorials measured. The corporate index is not significantly related to the proportion of editorials (r=.09, p>.05), but the structural complexity dimension is (r=.19, p<.01) — i.e., larger, more complex organizations write more local editorials. The correlations between the corporate newspaper index and letters to the editor are statistically significant and consistent with expectations (r=.45 for number and r=.19 for proportion). Again, chain ownership is not significantly related to either of the local editorial measures (data not shown).

H15: Corporate Structure and Editorials Critical of Mainstream Groups

As expected, the more a newspaper exhibits the characteristics of the corporate form of organization, the greater the number and proportion of editorials critical of mainstream groups or sources. The correlation between the corporate index and number of critical editorials is moderately strong (r=.33, p<.01; see Table 10.11). Four of the five dimensions — structural complexity, ownership structure, rules, and staff expertise — are significantly related to this measure. The correlation between the corporate index and proportion of critical editorials also is statistically significant (r=.20, p<.01), but only structural complexity and staff expertise are related to this measure. The relationships between the corporate index and number of critical letters to the editor is quite strong (r=.52, p<.01). All five of the dimensions are significantly related to corporate structure. The correlation between the corporate index and proportion of critical letters is moderately strong (r=.32, p<.01). Four of the five corporate dimensions are related (the exception is rational decision-making). Again, the chain ownership measure by itself is not related to either of the critical editorial-page measures (data not shown).

Summary

A theory of corporate newspaper effects was empirically tested in this chapter using a national probability mail survey of 409 journalists at 223 newspapers. Data for the editorial-page propositions were obtained from a content analysis of two issues from 198 of those newspapers.

The findings support most of the hypotheses. The more a newspaper exhibits the characteristics of a corporate organization, the higher the profits, the less emphasis it places on profits as an organizational goal, and the more importance it places on product quality and other nonprofit goals (i.e., maximizing growth of the organization, winning reporting awards, using the latest technology, beating the competition, being innovative, giving reporters more autonomy, conducting readership research and increasing circulation). Contrary to expectations, corporate newspapers were no less involved in or less supportive of their communities. Top editors at corporate newspapers report having higher levels of autonomy and job satisfaction. In contrast to the conventional wisdom and the relative-deprivation hypothesis, the data show that reporters and publishers at corporate newspapers also are more satisfied with their jobs. And reporters at corporate newspapers do not report having lower levels of autonomy, even though editors and publishers widely agree that stories at corporate organizations are more highly controlled and edited. For reporters, any loss of autonomy here appears to be offset by the fact that their organizations are perceived to be more rational. Job satisfaction appears to flourish in a "rational" environment.

Findings support nearly all of the editorial-page hypotheses. Corporate newspapers publish a larger number and proportion of editorials and letters to the editor, a larger number and proportion of staff-generated editorials, a larger number of editorials that deal with local issues, a larger number and proportion of letters to the editor that deal with local issues, and — most importantly — a larger number and proportion of editorials and letters to the editor that are critical of mainstream groups and institutions. Consistent with much of the literature, this study found no relationship between editorial-page content and chain ownership. Chain ownership, it was argued in previous chapters, is too crude of a measure of organizational structure to be useful by itself.

The strength of the structural model presented here is that it helps to account for social change and the role that mass media often play in promoting such change. As social systems become more pluralistic, news media within those systems become more critical of traditional ways and established institutions. Media reflect to some degree the diversity of the communities they serve, and increasing role specialization and professionalization, by-products of community and organizational growth, insulate journalists from political pressures. The increased level of criticism that emerges from these structural forces contributes to discourse that places increased pressure on existing institutions to change.

Despite the strengths of the structural model tested here, one shortcoming is that it cannot determine whether social change is occurring quickly enough to be of optimal benefit to society and/or challenging or alternative groups. As noted in Chapter 9, many critics would counter that even if corporate newspapers are more critical of mainstream groups than entrepreneurial newspapers, the editorial criticism they offer produces little in the way of meaningful social change. But in light of the findings in this study, the validity of such arguments will need to depend more on value judgments about meaningful social change than on the notion that corporate newspaper structure produces less diversity on its editorial pages.

Notes

1. David Pearce Demers, "Corporate Structure and Emphasis on Profits and Product Quality at U.S. Daily Newspapers," *Journalism Quarterly,* 68:15-26 (1991). In macro-level longitudinal studies, however, chain ownership continues to be a good measure of corporate complexity. See David Pearce Demers, "Structural Pluralism, Intermedia Competition, and the Growth of the Corporate Newspaper in the United States," *Journalism Monographs,* vol. 145 (June 1994).

2. Lori A. Bergen and David Weaver, "Job Satisfaction of Daily Newspaper Journalists and Organizational Size," *Newspaper Research Journal,* 9(2):1-13 (1988); Paul J. Deutschmann, "Predicting Newspaper Staff Size from Circulation," *Journalism Quarterly,* 36:350-4 (1959); and John E. Polich, "Predicting Newspaper Staff Size from Circulation: A New Look," *Journalism Quarterly,* 51:515-7 (1977).

3. See, e.g., John Soloski, "Economics and Management: The Real Influence of Newspaper Groups," *Newspaper Research Journal,* 1:19-28 (1979) and James D. Squires, *Read All About It! The Corporate Takeover of America's Newspapers* (New York: Times Books, 1994). Also, the publisher of a weekly newspaper that I once worked for had little interest in editorial matters and saw the newspaper as primarily a source of income.

4. The lack of evidence showing that independently owned newspapers are profit-oriented may simply be a function of the fact that few case studies of them have been conducted.

5. In some cases, the newspapers would send tear sheets only after payment of a small charge.

6. Amitai Etzioni, *Modern Organizations* (Englewood Cliffs, N.J.: Prentice-Hall, 1964), p. 6.

7. As W. I. Thomas once remarked: "If men define situations as real, they are real in their consequences." Cited in David Jary and Julie Jary, *The HarperCollins Dictionary of Sociology* (New York: HarperCollins, 1991), p. 520.

8. The researcher who wishes to study organizational goals also faces a number of other measurement problems. For additional information, see Richard H. Hall, *Organizations: Structures, Processes and Outcomes* (Englewood Cliffs, N.J.: Prentice-Hall, 1987), pp. 261-97.

9. Exact wording of the question was: "How much importance does top management at your newspaper place on the following beliefs or values?"

10. The multiple loadings may stem from the fact that this measure produces mixed reactions from respondents. On the one hand, responding to advertisers' needs may be seen as serving a customer or a public; on the other, it may be seen as pursuing profits. Because of this ambiguity, the item is excluded from the analysis.

11. Percentages are not useful to report here because the responses are aggregated and averaged, creating in some cases fractional values.

12. For a review of the research, see Robert G. Picard, *Media Economics: Concepts and Issues* (Newbury Park, Calif.: Sage, 1989), pp. 48-51, and Regina Lewis, "Relation Between Newspaper Subscription Price and Circulation," *The Journal of Media Economics,* 8(1):25-41 (1995). I also personally observed a student newspaper at a Midwest university raise its advertising rates by 33 percent with no measurable loss in advertising inches.

13. See Hall, *Organizations: Structure, Processes & Outcomes,* pp. 261-97.

14. The questions in the reporter sample were tailored to that group, substituting "your reporters" or "reporters'" with "your" and "you," respectively.

15. John W. C. Johnstone, Edward J. Slawski and William W. Bowman, *The News People* (Urbana, Ill.: University of Illinois Press, 1976) and David H. Weaver and G. Cleveland Wilhoit, *The American Journalists* (Bloomington, Ind.: Indiana University Press, 1986).

16. Sample group was not used because some respondents in each group did not meet the original sampling criteria; that is, in some cases, the questionnaire was completed by someone other than the person or position identified in the original mailing.

17. Education: high school or less, two-year college degree or trade school degree, bachelor's degree, and graduate degree. Income: less than $20,000; $20,000 to $29,999; $30,000 to $49,999; $50,000 to $69,999; $70,000 to $89,999; and $90,000 or more.

18. O. R. Holsti, *Content Analysis for the Social Sciences and Humanities* (Reading, Mass.: Addison-Wesley), p. 140.

19. Note that in Table 10.5 the ratio of number of staff-generated editorials (the second item in the table) to the total number of editorials (first item) does not equal the proportion of editorials that are staff-generated (third item) (.82 vs. .66).

20. Log of circulation also was employed, but the results were nearly identical.

21. See, e.g., Demers, "Corporate Structure and Emphasis on Profits and Product Quality," and David Pearce Demers and Wackman, "Effect of Chain Ownership on Newspaper Management Goals," *Newspaper Research Journal,* 9(2):59-68 (1988).

22. The correlation was not strong enough to pose problems of multicollinearity in the model.

Part 5

CONCLUSION

Chapter 11

Is the Corporate Newspaper a Menace?

The growth of the corporate newspaper has been one of the most controversial trends in the U.S. daily newspaper industry during the 20th century. In 1900, the typical daily had a circulation of 7,500 and was owned and operated by a family or an individual who lived in the community their newspaper served. Today the typical daily is five times larger, managed by professionals rather than the owners, and owned by a chain or group whose headquarters is usually located in another city or state.

The growth of the corporate newspaper has been controversial because many critics believe it is destroying democracy and good journalism. They charge that the corporate newspaper emphasizes profits more than quality, restricts journalists' autonomy, alienates workers, fails to serve the informational needs of the community, supports the interests of big business over those of the public, and, most importantly, fails to produce a diversity of ideas. Diversity is believed to be important for discovering truth and reaching sound public policy decisions, as well as being a measure of personal freedom.

Is the corporate newspaper a menace, as most critics claim? Or can it play the role of messiah, promoting social change that lessens inequalities and injustices?

The primary objective of this book was to answer these questions by reviewing the theoretical and empirical literature on organizational structure and by creating and testing a theory that specifically attempts to explain the growth and consequences of the corporate newspaper. The results of this effort are summarized below. Conclusions and implications for public policy follow.

Summary

The origins of the corporate form of organization can be traced to the early guild groups and the joint-stock company, the latter of which was created in the 16th and 17th centuries to fund large public works projects. One of the key advantages of these social forms over traditional forms of organization (e.g., sole proprietorship form of business) is that they survived beyond the life of any individual member. The joint-stock company also enabled companies to raise large amounts of capital in a short period of time, greatly facilitating the growth and development of large-scale organization.

The typical newspaper in the United States during the 18th and 19th centuries was an individually or family-owned and managed enterprise. The organization was small, and the content focused heavily on national and international political and business events and commentary and was geared to meet the needs of a small number of political and business elites. The owner-publisher depended heavily on subscription fees and support from political parties and other groups to finance the operation. But the entrepreneurial newspaper has been in decline ever since. Consistent with changes taking place in other industries and businesses, the newspaper grew dramatically at the close of the 19th century and the beginning of the 20th century. Today the typical daily is owned by a chain or group and exhibits the characteristics of the corporate or bureaucratic form of organization: a professional style of management, a highly developed division of labor and role specialization, lots of rules and regulations, a hierarchy of authority, and rationality in decision-making (i.e., it seeks to be efficient). News is aimed at a mass audience and covers a wide variety of economic, political and social events and issues. Economically, today's newspaper depends heavily on revenues from classified and display advertising rather than subscriptions.

A number of factors have contributed to these changes, but historically the two most important are urbanization and industrialization. Both generated increased needs for information and news. Urban residents, then as now, depend heavily upon other individuals and organizations for food, clothing, shelter, public services, and other basic necessities of life. Newspapers provide information that helps people to achieve their goals in an increasingly interdependent society. Political elites also depend heavily upon the mass media for information to help them make policy decisions and to help generate support from other elites and the public for the decisions they make.

Industrialization also has promoted the growth of the corporate form of organization. During the 19th century, manufacturers needed access to large, heterogeneous markets, and one efficient method for reaching such markets was through advertising. The dramatic growth of the newspaper at the close of the 19th century is directly related to the growth of advertising in the private sector. Newspapers delivered consumers to manufacturers. At the same time, the managers and owners of industry and business have been voracious consumers of news and information. They read newspapers to monitor their economic and political environments and to help them make decisions that may affect their organization's chances of adapting to changing environment.

The review of the historical literature also found that the number of entities that own newspapers (sole proprietorships, partnerships and legal corporations) has declined dramatically during the 20th century. This decline is primarily a function of the growth of chain organizations. Household newspaper circulation, which generally grew throughout the 19th century and early 20th century, also has decreased since the late 1940s. Competition from television is often thought to be responsible for this, but the empirical evidence does not provide strong support for this relationship. Although chain ownership and the decline in newspaper penetration have led some scholars to argue that diversity in the marketplace is shrinking, empirical evidence for these claims is also lacking. Furthermore, the notion that diversity is declining is inconsistent with several other trends, including dispersion of ownership in the newspaper industry, increased control of newspaper organizations by managers, and the explosive growth in the number and variety of print and electronic media during the 20th century. The latter includes an explosion in the number of writings critical of capitalism (i.e., Marxist and post-modern).

Early writers on organizational development and change generally agreed that the division of labor increases the productive capacity of labor and that competition stimulates social and technological innovation. These factors, in turn, promote additional growth and organizational complexity. More specifically, Adam Smith's analysis of the division of labor suggests that larger, more complex newspapers are more efficient, productive and profitable, and that newspapers controlled by managers place less emphasis on profits. Karl Marx's analysis implies that competition promotes the growth of large-scale newspaper organizations (and vice versa) because it stimulates innovation, reduces prices and runs less efficient newspapers out of business. Herbert Spencer's concept of social differentiation suggests that the growth and development of the mass media is a consequence of social actions to integrate and coordinate complex social systems. Similarly, Emile Durkheim's analysis suggests that the corporate newspaper is the product of increasing growth in the population and the division of labor and a reduction of traditional ties. Durkheim's analysis also implies that as a social system becomes more complex, the diversity of ideas increases. Max Weber drew attention to three historical conditions — money economy, education, and capitalism — that have contributed to growth of the corporate form of organization. And Joseph Schumpeter's observation that professional managers and technocrats are the driving force behind modern capitalism implies that corporate newspapers will place more emphasis on quality and other nonprofit goals.

Modern social system theory builds on the ideas of these early theorists. This theory is distinguished from other perspectives by its emphasis on the totality of the whole, its notion of boundary maintenance, and its idea of interdependence of the parts. The general model of social change in system theory can be described as neo-evolutionary — as social systems become more differentiated, functionally specialized and interdependent, the number and variety of mass media increase. Mass media, like other major institutions, provide information that reduces social distance and helps social actors achieve their goals. In this capacity, the media play a system maintenance function: They are agents of social control. However, they, in turn, are controlled by other subsystems and by general system values. The diversity of content is constrained or shaped by dominant values, such as responsible capitalism and social order, and by the dependence that media have on elites as sources for news and advertisers for financial support. Mass media are not a necessary condition for social organization, but they are for complex social organization.

A review of the empirical literature supports a systems perspective: Media play an important role in explaining the persistence and stability of modern capitalism. They depend heavily on political and economic centers of power for the news, which means social problems usually are framed from the position of those in power and news content generally promotes values consistent with capitalist ideals and elite interests. Mainstream media rarely, if ever, facilitate or cause radical social change. The watchdog function of the press is largely a myth.

At the same time, however, the literature shows that it would be inaccurate to argue that media are lapdogs of the powerful, as some hegemonic models or Critical Theories contend. As a group, journalists are more liberal than elites and the public. Media content, especially in pluralistic systems, is much more critical of elites and dominant values than content in small, homogeneous systems. Investigative reporting and news coverage of social movements often promote change and reform, frequently to the displeasure of conservatives and sometimes to the benefit of underprivileged groups. And, depending in part on what they read and see in the media, ordinary citizens can develop highly critical views of those in power and the social system in general. Donohue, Tichenor and Olien's guard-dog metaphor is a more accurate description of the media's role in society. Media messages provide broad-based support for the "system" — its values, rules, institutions and leaders — but it often criticizes those in power, especially when elite groups disagree over fundamental questions of policy.

The notion that mass media can criticize those in power or promote social reform has not gone unnoticed in some studies of ideology. However, many neo-Marxist scholars have failed to identify the conditions in which alternative or challenging ideas and groups may emerge and gain access to media. As a consequence, many theories of ideology fail to explain the role that mass media have played in promoting social and political reforms during the 19th and early 20th centuries, including the expansion of women's and civil rights, the emergence of anti-trust laws, the rise of the middle class, and the growth of labor movements.

A review of the empirical literature on newspapers revealed that competition is widely believed to be an important factor promoting the growth of the corporate form of organization. Research provides some support for the intramedia hypothesis (competition between dailies) and the umbrella hypothesis, but it generally fails to support the intermedia competition hypothesis (that newspapers compete with broadcast media). In particular, there is little empirical evidence showing that television is responsible for the decline of newspaper penetration or the growth of the corporate newspaper, despite the intuitive appeal of that hypothesis.

Although structural pluralism is not widely recognized in mass communication research as a factor that promotes the development of the modern corporation, empirical research supports the argument that pluralistic communities are more likely to have newspapers with the characteristics of a modern corporation. Media in pluralistic communities are larger, have a greater division of labor and role specialization, and historically were more likely to be part of a chain organization. Empirical research suggests that competition between media increases as structural pluralism increases. Larger, heterogeneous communities have a greater number and variety of mass media.

A theory of origins was presented which attributed the rise of the corporate form of organization in the U.S. daily newspaper industry primarily to structural pluralism. Two major reasons were given to support this relationship. The first is need for information: As a social system becomes more complex, informational needs increase dramatically. Information is a necessary condition for coordinating and controlling social action in systems that are highly diversified and interdependent. The second reason structural pluralism promotes the growth of the corporate newspaper revolves around the effect of competition. As social systems grow and become more complex, competition between mass media for limited resources (e.g., advertising and audiences) increases, which intensifies social and technological innovations that eliminate competitors and promote the growth of corporate media organizations. A number of other factors help explain why pluralism promotes the growth of the corporate newspaper. Most notably, these include concentration of ownership in the retail industry, the decline in partisanship and the growth of objectivity as a professional norm, and changes in tax laws that favor large-scale organization. Capitalism is not a necessary condition for corporate organization, but capitalism is more effective at promoting growth of the corporate form of organization than other economic systems because competition is an institutionalized value.

From this perspective, the corporate newspaper may be viewed in part as an outgrowth of the need in a highly urbanized, industrialized society to coordinate and control complex, interdependent relationships in an industrialized, urbanized society. Organizational structure becomes more complex over time, primarily because of economies of scale, and the corporate form of organization, in turn, enhances the adaptive capacity of the newspaper organization.

This theory of origins was tested using data from two macro-level longitudinal studies during the 20th century and one recently conducted cross-sectional probability survey of 223 newspapers in the United States. The data show that pluralism is a significant and strong predictor of the corporate newspaper indices in all three datasets. The more complex the community, the more likely its newspapers exhibit the characteristics of the corporate form of organization. The data also show that competition from broadcast media increases as structural pluralism increases. Large, complex communities have a greater number of radio and television stations. The data provide only partial support, however, for the argument that intermedia broadcast competition mediates some of the effect of structural pluralism on corporate newspaper structure.

The latter finding may stem from weak measurement. The measures of competition in this study — number of competitive media, proportion of advertising obtained by alternative media and newspaper advertising rates — may not be sensitive enough to measure the effects of competition. The model tested also assumes that intermedia competition promotes organizational growth because it enhances the innovation process which, in turn, generates economies of scale. No empirical measures of innovation or economies of scale were included in this study, but such measures may be necessary to demonstrate an empirical relationship between competition and corporate newspaper structure.

However, the finding that intermedia competition has little or no direct effect on the growth of the corporate newspaper may reflect actual conditions. A number of other studies have failed to support the inter-media hypothesis. This body of literature suggests that even though television, radio, and newspapers offer information and news that is redundant in some ways, in most other aspects they cannot be considered functional substitutes. Radio's entertainment music format, television's entertainment theatrical format, and newspapers' in-depth coverage of political and business news have enabled them "to niche" and survive. Additional research on competition is necessary. But even if it shows that intermedia competition plays little or no role in the growth of the corporate newspaper, this does not mean competition is irrelevant. This study focused on intermedia competition — i.e., competition from broadcast media. Intracity daily newspaper competition, scholars widely agree, historically has played a major role in promoting the growth of the corporate newspaper through economies of scale and intracity mergers.

Most of the empirical research on the newspaper organization has focused on effects rather than origins. From a public policy perspective, the key question is whether the corporate form of organization is destroying or limiting diversity of ideas or perspectives. The conventional wisdom holds that the corporate newspaper is a menace to good journalism and democratic institutions. More specifically, the "critical model" claims that the corporate newspaper places more emphasis on profits because it has more market power, is more likely to be publicly owned, and is less concerned about the local community. A zero-sum assumption that follows from this proposition is that the corporate newspaper also places less emphasis on quality. Charges that the corporate newspaper restricts journalists' autonomy and produces less satisfied employees are based primarily on the argument that decision-making becomes more centralized as an organization grows and becomes more bureaucratized. The corporate newspaper is destroying community solidarity because its owners and managers care more about profits and their careers than the local community. And the corporate newspaper is said to be less vigorous editorially because it cannot afford to alienate advertisers, readers or sources and expect to maximize profits.

A review of the literature supports some of these arguments. Chain newspapers appear to place greater emphasis on profits, and larger newspapers and chains appear to be more profitable. Some evidence also suggests that chain newspapers devote less space to local news coverage and their editors are less oriented to the local community. However, when taken as whole, the evidence fails to provide strong support for the "critical model." Although corporate newspapers appear to be more profitable, there is little evidence to suggest that this has adversely impacted the editorial product or journalistic freedom and autonomy. In fact, the evidence overwhelmingly suggests that chain and large newspapers are more vigorous editorially and that large newspapers place much more emphasis on product quality. A large body of research in the social sciences indicates that as an organization grows in size, capitalists play less role in the day-to-day operations and decision-making, while managers and technocrats play a bigger role. And a content analysis of the *New York Times* during the 20th century supports the notion that power is shifting: attributions of capitalists and their spokespersons declined, while attributions of technocrats increased substantially. In short, the research provides more support for post-industrial theories than the critical model.

More formally, post-industrial theories contend that large, corporate organizations should place less value on profit maximization because they are controlled not by the owners (i.e., stockholders), who benefit directly from the profits, but by professional managers, who obtain most of their income through a fixed salary. Aside from earning a minimum level of profit, managers would be expected to place greater emphasis on autonomy, organizational growth, planning, knowledge and expertise. These factors are recognized as the basis of power and prestige among professionals, and they are essential for long-term survival of the organization. Post-industrial theories also contend that control of corporate organizations in modern societies is gradually being transferred from the owners to knowledge-based professional and scientific groups (or intellectuals). A post-industrial society is one in which knowledge is the primary source of innovation and social organization. In the economy, this is reflected in the decline of manufacturing and goods and the rise of service industries, especially health, education, social welfare services and professional/technical services. These changes are expected to foster a new class structure — one in which professional and technical occupations gradually replace the capitalists. Rewards in a post-industrial society are based primarily on achievement, as opposed to inheritance, property or ascribed characteristics.

Using this literature and social system theory as a foundation, a theory of corporate newspaper effects was developed and empirically tested. Five major sets of hypotheses were tested.

First, it was expected that newspapers which exhibit the characteristics of the corporate form of organization would be more profitable but, contrary to the critical model, it was expected that they would place less emphasis on profits and more emphasis on product quality as an organizational goal. Corporate newspapers are structurally organized to maximize profits, but role specialization decreases emphasis on profits.

Second, corporate newspapers were expected to place more emphasis on quality and on other nonprofit goals, such as maximizing growth of the organization, being innovative, having the latest technology, winning reporting awards, increasing circulation and giving reporters more autonomy. Role specialization, professional norms and competition between professionals promote the pursuit of these nonprofit goals.

Third, it was expected that corporate newspapers would be less involved in and supportive of the local community, since their owners and managers tend to be oriented more to the corporation and their careers. One consequence is that the chain newspaper would be expected to publish less local news. However, the chain newspaper's orientation to the larger social system may have the consequence of increasing interdependence, which may help the local community adapt to changing social conditions.

Fourth, it was expected that self-reported autonomy and job satisfaction at corporate versus entrepreneurial daily newspapers would vary according to position in the organization. Top editors at corporate newspapers were expected to be more satisfied than top editors at entrepreneurial newspapers because increased role specialization gives them greater autonomy and because they have more status and power and are more highly rewarded. In contrast, it was expected that reporters at corporate newspapers would be less satisfied and would have less autonomy, since their organizations exert more formal control over reporters' stories and, structurally, the probability is greater in those organizations that reporters will know of a lesser qualified reporter who has been promoted or rewarded differentially (i.e., the probability of relative deprivation increases).

And finally, contrary to the conventional wisdom, this study posited that as a newspaper acquires the characteristics of the corporate form of organization, it will publish more staff-generated editorials, more editorials and letters to the editor about local issues, and more editorials and letters that are critical of mainstream groups. Corporate newspapers are expected to publish more staff-generated editorials and more content about local issues because they are larger, more structurally complex, and have more staff and resources. Corporate newspapers also are more critical of mainstream groups, because they are more likely to be located in pluralistic communities, which contain more groups that are critical of established authorities, and because they are more insulated from parochial political pressures. Owners and journalists of corporate newspapers are more insulated because they are less likely to grow up in the community their newspaper serves, are usually employed at the newspaper for a shorter period of time, are more oriented to the larger corporation and their profession, and are working in an environment where professional norms and values play a more prominent role in day-to-day decision-making. Professional norms and values are mechanisms for regulating and controlling the behavior of journalists, but they also help to legitimate their authority to report the news and to insulate the news production process from groups that would use the news to advance their own interests at the expense of the public or other groups.

This theory of effects was empirically tested using a national probability mail survey of 409 journalists at 223 newspapers and a content analysis of 198 of those newspapers. The findings provide strong support for most of the hypotheses. The more a newspaper exhibits the characteristics of a corporate organization, the more profitable it is, the less emphasis it places on profits as an organizational goal, and the more importance it places on product quality and other non-profit goals. Contrary to expectations, corporate newspapers were no less involved in or less supportive of their communities, which suggests that corporate newspaper structure does not necessarily have an adverse impact on community solidarity. As expected, top editors at corporate newspapers report having higher levels of autonomy and job satisfaction. Even though the story-production process at corporate newspapers appears to be more heavily regulated, reporters at those newspapers did not report having lower levels of autonomy and actually were more satisfied with their jobs. The data suggest that any loss of autonomy in the news production process is more than offset by the fact that their organizations are perceived to be more rational. In other words, job satisfaction appears to flourish in an environment that places a premium on finding the most efficient means to solve problems. Contrary to the critical model, publishers at corporate newspapers also reported higher levels of job satisfaction.

The cross-sectional data in the study also show that corporate newspapers are much more vigorous editorially than entrepreneurial newspapers. Corporate newspapers publish a larger number and proportion of editorials and letters to the editor, a larger number and proportion of staff-generated editorials, a larger number of editorials that deal with local issues, a larger number and proportion of letters to the editor that deal with local issues, and — most importantly — a larger number and proportion of editorials and letters that are critical of mainstream groups and institutions. Consistent with much of the literature, this study found little or no relationship between editorial-page content and chain ownership or between organizational values and chain ownership. Chain ownership, the evidence suggests, is too crude of a measure of organizational structure in cross-sectional studies. This measurement problem may account for much of the mixed findings in the literature. The empirical results from the original research in this study are summarized in Table 11.1.

Conclusion

In conclusion, is the corporate newspaper a menace?

Table 11.1
Summary of Findings

Hypotheses On Origins	Outcome
H1: Structural pluralism ---> Corporate newspaper (+)	Supported
H2: Structural pluralism ---> Media competition (+)	Supported
H3: Intermedia competition ---> Corporate newspaper (+)	Weak support

Hypotheses On Effects	Outcome
H1: Corporate structure ---> Profits (+)	Supported
H2: Corporate structure ---> Profits as goal (-)	Supported
H3: Chain ownership ---> Profits as goal (+)	Supported
H4: Corporate structure ---> Product quality (+)	Supported
H5: Corporate structure ---> Nonprofit goals (+)	Supported
H6: Corporate structure ---> Community involvement (+)	No support
H7: Corporate structure ---> Autonomy and job satisfaction for top editors (+)	Supported
H8: Corporate structure ---> Control over stories (+)	Partial support
H9: Corporate structure ---> Autonomy and job satisfaction for lower-level reporters (-)	No support
H10: Corporate structure ---> Autonomy and job satisfaction for publishers and top-level managers (0)	Partial support
H11: Employee rank ---> Autonomy and job satisfaction (+)	Supported
H12: Corporate structure ---> Number of editorials and letters to the editor (+)	Supported
H13: Corporate structure ---> Number and proportion of locally produced editorials (+)	Supported
H14: Corporate structure ---> Number and proportion of editorials/letters about local issues (+)	Supported
H15: Corporate structure ---> Number and proportion of editorials/letters critical of mainstream groups (+)	Supported

Key: (+) positive relationship hypothesized; (-) negative relationship hypothesized; (0) no relationship hypothesized.

A definitive answer cannot be given, since the history of the corporate form of organization has yet to play itself out. But the theory and data in this study indicate that critics have vastly overstated the consequences and adverse effects of the corporate form of organization, as well as misunderstood its origins and development. The corporate newspaper provides broad-based support for dominant institutions and values, to be sure. But such support is not homogeneous or monolithic. As a social system becomes more pluralistic, newspapers become more "corporatized," and news and editorial content becomes more critical of traditional ways, mainstream groups and established authorities. In relative terms, the corporate newspaper has a much greater capacity than the entrepreneurial newspaper to promote social change. An increased level of criticism does not guarantee social change, but it does increase the probability of change. Historically, in fact, the corporate newspaper has played an important role in promoting many of the social changes that have benefited alternative and disenfranchised groups, reduced social conflict, contributed to social order and reduced the revolutionary potential of nonruling classes.

Although the corporate newspaper has a greater capacity to promote social change, the theory and data in this study cannot be used to call the the corporate newspaper a messiah. It often publishes news and information that has adverse consequences for disadvantaged, challenging or alternative groups, and for society as a whole. Like its entrepreneurial counterpart, the corporate newspaper generally marginalizes alternative points of view — rarely does its content promote radical social change. The ability of media to advance social change is highly circumscribed by the economic system (need to make a profit) and political systems (need for legitimacy from public and sources). The corporate newspaper is, indeed, an agent of social control.

Thus, this study concludes by taking the middle ground on the debate over whether the corporate newspaper is a menace. More accurately, the corporate newspaper should be seen as a social institution that *promotes controlled social change* — change that at times accommodates the needs and interests of challenging groups but that usually does not dramatically alter the power of dominant groups in the short term. This conclusion has important implications for mass media and public policy. But before turning to them, one other question needs to be answered: Why do so many professionals and social scientists continue to believe the corporate form of organization is destroying journalism and democracy?

As noted in Chapter 1, one of the major reasons, I believe, is that few researchers have focused on its social and historical origins and development. The corporate newspaper should be seen as the outcome of a complex series of instrumental and structural changes that can be traced to the Middle Ages. Some of these changes were not consciously planned or anticipated. Virtually no one, for example, anticipated the demand for information that industrialization and urbanization eventually generated. Almost no one (with the exception of Marx) anticipated the impact that market competition and economies of scale would have on centralization of ownership. Likewise, no one sought to create more social conflict as social systems became more structurally complex. But needs for information, competition and increasing structural pluralism — along with conscious decisions to hire more employees and expansion in the division of labor and role specialization — helped to create the structural conditions that have promoted the growth of the corporate form of organization.

Some scholars have argued that the increasing level of conflict between editors and noneditorial "MBAs" in the corporate organization is a sign that journalists are losing power. To the contrary, this is a sign that the owners are losing control over the professionals, who are now dealing more directly with questions related to profits. Historically, the entrepreneurial publisher-owner rarely shared in-depth information about profits with nonowning managers, even the editors. Such matters were deemed private, especially in a small-town setting. However, as owners lose control over day-to-day operations, profit-making is a topic of discussion for all managers, not just the owner-publisher and advertising managers. In some cases, this increases conflict between journalists and nonjournalist managers, since profit-making is not a major goal pursued by journalists. It is not surprising, then, to see increasing concern among many journalists and editors about the role of profits in the organization — they are now part of the power structure and are often asked to contribute directly to that goal.

Implications

No doubt many professionals and scholars will be skeptical of the conclusion that corporate newspapers have a greater capacity to promote social change. Critics, especially those on the radical left, will argue that even if corporate newspapers are more critical of mainstream groups, that criticism is too little and too late. To them, the amount and type of critical content is not meaningful enough to save society or emancipate the individual, even in the long run. Social change that accommodates the needs of disenfranchised groups occurs much too slowly. Moreover, many critics will continue to argue that newspapers exert greater hegemonic control as they become more corporatized.

Such critics may be correct on the question of whether newspapers and other mass media are destroying society and personal autonomy over the long run. This study could not address such a complex issue. However, my opinion is that even though mass media depend much too heavily on economic and political elites for the news and, consequently, are much too supportive of the status quo, there is little evidence to suggest that society is falling into decline or that people are more repressed. Furthermore, although I would personally like to see more content that criticizes social injustices and draws attention to the social and structural origins of them,[1] the data and theory presented in this book do not support the critics' claim that newspapers become less critical of the status quo as they become more corporatized. They become more responsive to social and political cleavages and, theoretically, have a greater capacity to stimulate social processes that lead to social change.

This conclusion has important implications for public policy and future research. First, it means that *calls for reform in the newspaper industry will need to depend more on value judgments about what kind of change is meaningful or desirable, rather than on empirical claims about the menacing aspects of corporate newspaper structure.* If social reform is desired, it should not be directed at destroying the corporate form of organization, per se. Rather, administrative, professional and legislative reform efforts should be aimed at protecting and promoting the First Amendment and professional standards that give journalists greater authority in the news organization and more autonomy from political and economic pressures, both external (e.g., sources) and internal (e.g., owners and nonjournalist managers).[2] In contrast, laws, policies or practices that aid and support the entrepreneurial form of organization are likely to inhibit the pace of social change. Some critics will argue that professionalism and codes of ethics decrease diversity because they standardize practices. This undoubtedly is true in some instances, but standardization does not necessarily diminish diversity.[3] From a systems perspective, professional standards need to be seen as empowering journalists — they help to insulate them from parochial political pressures in the community as well as from the self-serving interests of the owners.

Second, this study strongly suggests that *the diversity of ideas and thoughts in the marketplace will increase as long as a social system becomes more pluralistic.* Bagdikian and others are convinced that the diversity of ideas is shrinking because of the decline of newspaper owners. If one assumes that owners control the organization, then this **may** be true for the newspaper industry. However, if managers are gaining control or if the entire social system is taken into account, then diversity is clearly increasing.   Increasing pluralism generally means an increase, not a decrease, in diversity, because ideas and different points of view are themselves a social product — that is, they emerge primarily through the interaction of individuals in social settings.[4] More specifically, as social systems grow and become more structurally complex, the number and variety of media increases.   Many of these media outlets cater to specialized groups and audiences, and the ability of any single media outlet to attract viewers or followers from the population as a whole decreases. This may explain, in part, why network television and newspapers have lost viewers and readers.

As noted earlier, the number and variety of mass media increase as a social system becomes more structurally pluralistic, this does not mean that all forms of media will continue to grow as a system becomes more complex. The level of competition, changes in technology, war, economic crises, individual decision-making, and other phenomenon also affect the growth and life-span of media organizations.   Some media forms (e.g., the telegraph) will die off. However, when the social system as a whole is taken into account, these losses are offset by the growth in other media forms (e.g., wireless radio).

As noted earlier, the notion that diversity is increasing is partially at odds with many Marxist-inspired or post-modern theories about the mass media. Many critical and hegemonic theorists argue, for example, that even though the number of groups and media outlets may have increased substantially, this does not necessarily mean an increase in the diversity of ideas.[5]   In fact, many argue that mass media, because they are so ubiquitous, actually promote greater homogeneity of information and ideas, particularly ideas that support and maintain capitalism as the ideal economic system. Once again, there is no question that mainstream mass media generally support capitalism and other dominant institutions, but this does not mean they become less critical of those institutions.   A good example may be taken from the field of mass communication itself.[6]

Thirty years ago virtually no academic journals in the field of mass communication catered to Marxist scholarship. Many book publishers also were reluctant to publish such works.   Today, however, at least four journals provide regular access to alternative and critical points of view,[7] and hundreds of books critical of the mainstream mass media are published each year.[8] Many publishers now specialize in critical works. In fact, neo-

Marxist and postmodern scholars produce much of the academic research on the mass media today, especially in Europe.[9] Scholarship that addresses the nonmainstream concerns of feminists, minorities and gay groups has also become much more widely available. While scholarly publications generally reach highly specialized audiences, their political and social impact should not be underestimated, given the historical role that academic institutions have played in controlling knowledge in a social system. In fact, many scholars believe neo-Marxist and postmodern perspectives are becoming the dominant force in the field.[10]

Third, *newspapers that acquire the characteristics of the corporate form of organization will be in a better position to survive in the post-industrial age.* The reason is relatively straightforward: Those are the organizations that are more profitable and have greater access to capital and human resources. It is the highly educated and trained professional managers who have the expertise to help newspapers adapt to changing economic and social conditions, and corporate newspapers rely more heavily on such managers.

Fourth, *the findings in this study may be interpreted as supporting post-industrial theories, which hold that knowledge, rather than capital, is becoming the axial principle in modern society.* The coming of the post-industrial society is expected to foster a new class structure — one based on the supremacy of professional and technical occupations — that gradually displaces the capitalists.[11] The data in this study suggest that corporate newspapers simultaneously reflect and promote this shift of power in the system. At the organizational level, they reflect it because they rely more heavily on trained experts and technocrats to produce the newspaper. At the societal level, corporate newspapers rely more heavily on professionals and technocrats to collect the news. Over time, such dependence may be expected to promote social change that gradually breaks down traditional authority structures.

Future Research

The findings in this study also have a number of implications for future research on media. In particular, the crucial question should not be whether the corporate newspaper is a mechanism of social control — since all mainstream media perform that function — but, rather: How is that control effectuated and who benefits from it? If the scientific goal is to find ways to promote social change that lessens inequalities or injustices, then research needs to focus heavily on identifying the mechanisms and processes that explain why media may impede social change in one context and, alternatively, enhance it in another.

More studies are needed, for example, that (1) identify the mechanisms or contingent conditions in which newspapers undertake investigative projects and the structural impact of those projects;[12] (2) examine why and how media cover social movements and contribute to enhancing or detracting from the legitimacy of those movements; (3) explore how editors may enhance or maintain their power relative to other managers in the organization who would prefer to place less emphasis on news or quality; (4) examine more closely the impact of corporate structure on autonomy and satisfaction for other roles in the organization and on news content itself; in particular, a key question will be whether the findings for editors may be generalized to reporters who have specialized roles at newspapers; and (5) research more closely the impact of corporate structure on decision-making processes. On this latter point, the managerial revolution does not mean that society is moving inexorably toward greater democracy. The very nature of the corporate form of organization itself seems to limit, for the sake of efficiency, the amount of democratic rule that is possible. Nevertheless, the extent to which democratic decision-making can exist in a corporate organization depends in part on how it is structured — i.e., whether top management seeks the input of the lower levels — and research needs to examine the mechanisms that help to support democratic decision-making in the newsroom.

Empirical research also needs to move beyond simple chain or public ownership variables. Chain ownership needs to be understood within the context of broader changes in organizational structure. It is only one indicator of a more complex construct, and it is a very crude measure with limited conceptual and empirical usefulness when used as a stand-alone.

Finally, a fundamental question will be the extent to which the findings in this study can be generalized to other media subsystems, such as television and radio. The answer would seem to depend on three factors: (1) the amount of government regulation, (2) economies of scale achieved in a particular form of media, and (3) changes in technology. FCC regulations currently limit the number of radio and television stations that can be owned by a single individual or company,[13] and this can prevent or inhibit concentration of ownership and the development of large-scale organizations in these and other industries. This, of course, has not been the case in the newspaper industry. Economies of scale also promote concentration of ownership and the development of large-scale organization, as is evident in the newspaper industry. Television and radio may benefit even more than newspapers from such economies, since boosting a broadcast signal is relatively inexpensive and can dramatically increase the size of an audience.

The growth of corporate organization in other media systems will depend considerably on new developments in technology, which may render existing media technologies obsolete. New technology does not necessarily mean the demise of contemporary media organizations, since they may adapt and change to such technology. The possibility always exists that future innovations may render an existing media form obsolete. However, this study demonstrates that newspapers which exhibit the corporate form of organization will be better equipped to adapt to changes in a post-industrial world.

Notes

1. But I cannot, at this point in time, support calls for revolutionary change. One problem that has always plagued revolutionary theories is how to implement change without great suffering and hardship. Social and economic conditions are almost always worse after than before a revolution.

2. For example, Donald M. Gillmor, *Power, Publicity and the Abuse of Libel Law* (New York: Oxford University Press, 1992), argues that the libel law should be changed to make it impossible for policy makers and celebrities to sue for libel in exchange for the voluntary opportunity to respond in the media.

3. For example, if a rule required all reporters to double the number of sources they include in their stories, ceteris paribus, diversity would increase.

4. This is not to deny that ideas have origins in individuals, but all ideas and perspectives are shaped by historical, social and cultural forces.

5. For review, see Denis McQuail, *Mass Communication Theory: An Introduction,* 3rd ed. (London: Sage, 1994), pp. 61-118. Also see Chapter 4 in this book for a comparison of neo-Marxist models with the more pluralistic one advanced in this book.

6. The process of increasing diversity also can be illustrated with this book, which is itself the product of many other ideas that have accumulated over time and through interactions with other scholars in the field and, in turn, is likely to generate many other opinions and ideas from other scholars and professionals, some of which will be highly critical of its conclusions. The radical left will claim I am an apologist for the system, while the right will see me as a left-leaning critic.

7. They include *Critical Studies in Mass Communication, Journal of Communication, Journal of Communication Inquiry,* and *Communication Theory.* Many "mainstream" journals, such as *Journalism and Mass Communication Monographs* and *Journalism and Mass Communication Quarterly,* also are publishing works by neo-Marxists.

8. This statement is based on my personal observation of the promotional literature that I receive from book publishers and from my own book collection, which I estimate is about three-fourths critical, the rest being mostly descriptive treatises of how media function (e.g., introductory texts).

9. McQuail, *Mass Communication Theory*, pp. 61-118.

10. This point is discussed in W. James Potter, Roger Cooper and Michel Dupagne, "The Three Paradigms of Mass Media Research in Mainstream Communication Journals," *Communication Theory*, 3:317-35 (1993).

11. Daniel Bell, *The Coming of the Post-Industrial Society* (New York: Basic Books, 1976 [1973]).

12. The Northwestern project is a good example. See David L. Protess, Fay Lomax Cook, Jack C. Doppelt, James S. Ettema, Margaret T. Gordon, Donna R. Leff and Peter Miller, *The Journalism of Outrage: Investigative Reporting and Agenda-Building in America* (New York: Guilford Press, 1991).

13. For example, FCC rules limit the number of radio stations a broadcaster may own to 20 FM and 20 AM radio stations. See Joe Flint and Peter Viles, "Hill Squeezes the FCC's Radio Rules," *Broadcasting* (Aug. 10, 1992), pp. 4, 12, and *Broadcasting and Cable Yearbook* (New Providence, N.J.: R.R. Bowker, 1995).

Bibliography

Aaronovitch, Sam and Malcolm C. Sawyer, *Big Business: Theoretical and Empirical Aspects of Concentration and Mergers in the United Kingdom* (London: Macmillan, 1975).

Abbott, Andrew, *The System of Professions: An Essay on the Division of Expert Labor* (Chicago: The University of Chicago Press, 1988).

Abercrombie, Nicholas, Stephen Hill and Bryan S. Turner, *Dictionary of Sociology*, 2nd ed. (London: Penguin Books, 1988).

Abraham, M. Francis, *Modern Sociological Theory* (Delhi, India: Oxford University Press, 1982).

Adorno, Theodore and Max Horkheimer, *Dialectic of the Enlightenment* (London: Verso, 1979).

Akhavan-Majid, Roya and Timothy Boudreau, "Chain Ownership, Organizational Prominence, and Editorial Role Perceptions," paper delivered to the Association for Education in Journalism and Mass Communication (Atlanta, August 1994).

Akhavan-Majid, Roya, Anita Rife, and Sheila Gopinath, "Chain Ownership and Editorial Independence: A Case Study of Gannett Newspapers," *Journalism Quarterly,* 68:59-66 (1991).

Aldrich, Howard E. and Peter V. Marsden, "Environments and Organizations," pp. 361-92 in Neil J. Smelser (ed.), *Handbook of Sociology* (Newbury Park, Calif.: Sage, 1988).

Alexander, Jeffrey C., "The Mass News Media in Systemic, Historical and Comparative Perspective," pp. 17-51 in Elihu Katz and Tomás Szecskö (eds.), *Mass Media and Social Change* (Beverly Hills, Calif.: Sage, 1981).

Alexander, Jeffrey C. (ed.), *Neofunctionalism* (Beverly Hills, Calif.: Sage, 1985).

Alexander, Jeffrey C., "The New Theoretical Movement," pp. 77-101 in Neil J. Smelser (ed.), *Handbook of Sociology* (Newbury Park, Calif.: Sage, 1988).

Altheide, David L., *Media Power* (Beverly Hills, Calif.: Sage, 1985).

Altman, "Consuming Ideology: The Better Homes in America Campaign," *Critical Studies in Mass Communication,* 7:286-307 (1990).

Altschull, J. Herbert, *Agents of Power* (New York: Longman, 1984).

American Society of Newspaper Editors, "News and Editorial Independence: A Survey of Group and Independent Editors" (April 1980).

Anderson, Douglas, "How Managing Editors View and Deal With Ethical Issues," *Journalism Quarterly,* 64:341-5 (1987).

Angell, Robert Cooley, *The Integration of American Society* (New York: Russell & Russell, 1975 [1941]).

Applebaum, Richard P., *Theories of Social Change* (Chicago: Markham, 1970).

Asch, Peter, *Industrial Organization and Antitrust Policy* (New York: John Wiley and Sons, 1983).

Atkinson, Dick, *Orthodox Consensus and Radical Alternative: A Study in Sociological Theory* (New York: Basic Books, 1972).

Azumi, Koya and Jerald Hage (eds.), *Organizational Systems* (Lexington, Mass.: D. C. Heath and Company, 1972).

Bagdikian, Ben H., *The Information Machines* (New York: Harper & Row, 1971).

Bagdikian, Ben H., "Conglomeration, Concentration, and the Media," *Journal of Communication,* 30(2):59-64 (1980).

Bagdikian, Ben H., *The Media Monopoly,* 2nd ed. (Boston: Beacon Press, 1987).

Bailey, Kenneth D., *Sociology and the New Systems Theory* (Albany, N.Y.: State University of New York Press, 1992).

Baker, C. Edwin, *Ownership of Newspapers: The View From Positivist Social Science* (Cambridge, Mass.: The Joan Shorenstein Center at Harvard University, September 1994).

Baldridge, Paul D., "Group and Non-Group Owner Programming: A Comparative Analysis," *Journal of Broadcasting,* 11:125-30 (1967).

Ballinger, Jane R., "Media Coverage of Social Protest: An Examination of Media Hegemony," paper presented to the Association for Education in Journalism and Mass Communication (Kansas City, Mo., August 1993).

Ball-Rokeach, Sandra J., "The Origins of Individual Media System Dependency: A Sociological Framework," *Communication Research,* 12:485-510 (1985).

Ball-Rokeach, Sandra J. and Muriel G. Cantor (eds.), *Media, Audience and Social Structure* (Newbury Park, Calif.: Sage, 1986).

Ball-Rokeach, Sandra J. and Melvin L. DeFleur, "A Dependency Model of Mass Media Effects," *Communication Research,* 3:3-21 (1976).

Ball-Rokeach, Sandra J., Melvin Rokeach and Joel W. Grube, *The Great American Values Test: Influencing Behavior and Belief Through Television* (New York: Free Press, 1984).

Ball-Rokeach, Sandra J., Melvin Rokeach and Joel W. Grube, "Changing and Stabilizing Political Behavior and Beliefs," pp. 280-90 in Sandra J. Ball-Rokeach and Muriel G. Cantor (eds.), *Media Audience and Social Structure* (Newbury Park, Calif.: Sage, 1986).

Barron, Jerome A., "Access to the Press: A New Concept of the First Amendment," pp. 9-15 in Michael C. Emery and Ted Curtis Smythe (eds.), *Readings in Mass Communications: Concepts and Issues in the Mass Media,* 2nd ed. (Dubuque: William C. Brown Co., 1974).

Beam, Randal A., "The Impact of Group Ownership Variables on Organizational Professionalism at Daily Newspapers," *Journalism Quarterly,* 70:907-18 (1993).

Becker, Lee B., Randy Beam and John Russial, "Correlates of Daily Newspaper Performance in New England," *Journalism Quarterly,* 55:100-8 (1978).

Becker, Lee B., Idowu A. Sobowale and Robin E. Cobbey, "Reporters and Their Professional and Organizational Commitment," *Journalism Quarterly,* 56:753-63, 770 (1979).

Bell, Daniel, *The Coming of the Post-Industrial Society* (New York: Basic Books, 1976 [1973]).

Bell, Daniel, *The End of Ideology* (Cambridge, Mass.: Harvard University Press, 1988 [1960]).

Belson, William A., "The Effects of Television on the Reading and the Buying of Newspapers and Magazines," *The Public Opinion Quarterly,* 25:366-81 (1961).

Bennett, W. Lance, *News: The Politics of Illusion,* 2nd ed. (New York: Longman, 1988).

Benson, J. Kenneth, "The Analysis of Bureaucratic-Professional Conflict: Functional Versus Dialectical Approaches," *The Sociological Quarterly* 14:378-89 (1973).

Bergen, Lori A. and David Weaver, "Job Satisfaction of Daily Newspaper Journalists and Organizational Size," *Newspaper Research Journal*, 9(2):1-13 (1988).

Berger, Peter L. and Thomas Luckmann, *The Social Construction of Reality* (New York: Anchor Books, 1966).

Berle, Adolf A., Jr., and Gardiner C. Means, *The Modern Corporation and Private Property* (New York: Macmillan, 1932).

Bernstein, Eduard, *Evolutionary Socialism* (New York: Schocken, 1961 [1899]).

Bertalanffy, Ludwig von, "General System Theory," pp. 6-21 in Brent D. Rubin and John Y. Kim (eds.), *General Systems Theory and Human Communication* (Rochelle Park, N.J.: Hayden Book Company, 1975).

Biagi, Shirley, *Media/Impact: An Introduction to Mass Media* (Belmont, Calif.: Wadsworth, 1994).

Blair, John Malcolm, *Economic Concentration, Structure, Behavior and Public Policy* (New York: Harcourt-Brace, 1972).

Blalock, Herbert M., "Causal Inferences, Closed Populations, and Measures of Association," *American Political Science Review*, 61:130-6 (1967).

Blankenburg, William B., "Determinants of Pricing of Advertising in Weeklies," *Journalism Quarterly*, 57:663-6 (1980).

Blankenburg, William B., "Structural Determination of Circulation," *Journalism Quarterly*, 58:543-51 (1981).

Blankenburg, William B., "A Newspaper Chain's Pricing Behavior," *Journalism Quarterly*, 60:275-80 (1983).

Blankenburg, William B., "Newspaper Scale and Newspaper Expenditures," *Newspaper Research Journal*, 10(2):97-103 (1989).

Blankenburg, William B. and Gary W. Ozanich, "Public Ownership of Newspaper Corporations: A Cause in Search of Effects," paper delivered at Midwest Association for Public Opinion Research annual meeting (Chicago, November 1990).

Blankenburg, William B. and Gary W. Ozanich, "The Effect of Public Ownership on the Financial Performance of Newspaper Corporations," *Journalism Quarterly* 70:68-75 (1993).

Blau, Peter M., "A Formal Theory of Differentiation in Organizations," *American Sociological Review,* 55:201-18 (April 1970).

Blau, Peter M., *The Organization of Academic Work* (New York: John Wiley and Sons, Inc., 1973).

Blau, Peter M. and Marshall W. Meyer, *Bureaucracy in Modern Society*, 3rd ed. (New York: Random House, 1987).

Blau, Peter M. and Richard A Schoenherr, *The Structure of Organizations* (New York: Basic Books, 1971).

Blau, Peter M., Wolf V. Heydebrand and Robert E. Stauffer, "The Structure of Small Bureaucracies," *American Sociological Review*, 31:179-91 (1966).

Bleyer, Willard Grosvenor, *Main Currents in the History of Journalism* (New York: Houghton Mifflin, 1927).

Bogart, Leo, "How the Challenge of Television News Affects the Prosperity of Daily Newspapers," *Journalism Quarterly*, 52:403-10 (1975).

Bogart, Leo, *Press and Public*, 2nd ed. (Hillsdale, N.J.: Lawrence Erlbaum Associates, 1989).

Bohrnstedt, George W., "Observations on the Measurement of Change," in E. F. Borgotta (ed.), *Sociological Methodology* (San Francisco: Jossey-Bass, 1969).

Borgatta, Edgar F. and George W. Bohrnstedt (eds.), *Sociological Methodology* (San Francisco, Jossey-Bass, 1969).

Borstel, Gerald H., "Ownership, Competition and Comment," *Journalism Quarterly*, 33:220-2 (1956).

Boulding, Kenneth E., *The World as a Total System* (Beverly Hills, Calif.: Sage, 1985).

Breed, Warren, "Social Control in the Newsroom: A Functional Analysis," *Social Forces*, 33:326-55 (1955).

Breed, Warren, "Mass Communication and Sociocultural Integration," *Social Forces*, 37:109-16 (1958).

Brigham, Clarence S., *History and Bibliography of American Newspapers 1690-1820* (Worcester, Mass.: American Antiquarian Society, 1947).

Broadcasting Publications, *The Broadcasting Yearbook* (Washington, D.C.: Broadcasting Publications, 1991).

Brozen, Yale, *Concentration, Mergers, and Public Policy* (New York: Macmillan, 1982).

Bruck, Peter, "Strategies for Peace, Strategies for News Research," *Journal of Communication*, 39(1):108-29 (1989).

Bryant, Jennings and Dolf Zillman, *Media Effects: Advances in Theory and Research* (Hillsdale, N.J.: Lawrence Erlbaum Associates, 1994).

Buckley, Walter, *Sociology and Modern Systems Theory* (Englewood Cliffs, N.J.: Prentice-Hall, 1967).

Burch, Philip H., *The Managerial Revolution Reassessed* (Lexington, Mass.: D.C. Heath and Company, 1972).

Burnham, James, *The Managerial Revolution* (New York: John Day, 1941).

Burrowes, Carl P., "The Functionalist Tradition and Communication Theory," paper presented to the Association for Education in Journalism and Mass Communication (Kansas City, Mo., August 1993).

Busterna, John C., "The Cross-Elasticity of Demand for National Newspaper Advertising," *Journalism Quarterly*, 64:346-51 (1987).

Busterna, John C., "Commentary: Competitive Effects of Newspaper Chain 'Deep Pockets,'" *Newspaper Research Journal*, 10(4):61-72 (1988).

Busterna, John C., "Trends in Daily Newspaper Ownership," *Journalism Quarterly*, 65:831-8 (1988).

Busterna, John C., "How Managerial Ownership Affects Profit Maximization in Newspaper Firms," *Journalism Quarterly*, 66:302-7, 358 (1989).

Busterna, John C. and Kathleen A. Hansen, "Presidential Endorsement Patterns by Chain-Owned Papers, 1976-84," *Journalism Quarterly*, 67:286-94 (1990).

Champion, Dean J., *The Sociology of Organizations* (New York: McGraw-Hill, 1975).

Chester, Giraud, "The Press-Radio War: 1933-1935," *Public Opinion Quarterly*, 13:252-64 (1949).

Child, John, "Organization Structure and Strategies of Control: A Replication of the Aston Study," *Administrative Science Quarterly*, 17:163-77 (1972).

Cirino, Robert, *Power to Persuade* (New York: Bantam Books, 1974).

Coen, Robert J., "Estimated Annual U.S. Advertising Expenditures 1935-1985," unpublished report (New York: McCann-Erickson Advertising, Inc., 1986).

Coen, Robert J., "Estimated Annual U.S. Advertising Expenditures 1935-1987," unpublished report (New York: McCann-Erickson Advertising, Inc., 1987).

Cohen, Percy S., *Modern Social Theory* (New York: Basic Books, 1968).

Cohen, Stanley and Jock Young (eds.), *The Manufacture of News* (London: Constable, 1981).

Coleman, James S. *Community Conflict* (New York: The Free Press, 1957).

Comanor, William S., "Conglomerate Mergers: Considerations for Public Policy," in R. Blair and R. F. Lanzillotti (eds.), *The Conglomerate Corporation: A Public Problem?* (Cambridge: Oelgeschlager, Gunn and Hain, 1981).

Commission on Freedom of the Press, *A Free and Responsible Press* (Chicago: University of Chicago Press, 1947).

Compaine, Benjamin M., "Newspapers," pp. 27-93 in Benjamin M. Compaine, Christopher H. Sterling, Thomas Guback and J. Kendrick Noble, Jr., *Who Owns the Media: Concentration of Ownership in the Mass Communications Industry* (White Plains, N.Y.: Knowledge Industry, 1982).

Compaine, Benjamin M., "The Expanding Base of Media Competition," *Journal of Communication,* 35(3):81-96 (1985).

Compaine, Benjamin M., Christopher H. Sterling, Thomas Guback and J. Kendrick Noble, Jr., *Who Owns the Media? Concentration of Ownership in the Mass Communications Industry* (White Plains, N.Y.: Knowledge Industry, 1982).

Comte, August, "The Progress of Civilization Through Three States," in A. Etzioni and E. Etzioni-Halevy (eds.), *Social Change* (New York: Basic Books, 1973).

Cook, Betsy B. and Steven R. Banks, "Predictors of Job Burnout in Reporters and Copy Editors," *Journalism Quarterly,* 70:108-17 (1993).

Cook, Betsy B., Steve R. Banks, and Ralph J. Turner, "The Effects of Work Environment on Job Burnout in Newspaper Reporters and Copy Editors," *Newspaper Research Journal,* 14(3/4):123-36 (1993).

Cook, Fred J., *The Muckrakers: Crusading Journalists Who Changed America* (Garden City, N.Y.: Doubleday & Company, 1972).

Corbett, Julia Barton, *Media, Bureaucracy and the Success of Social Protest: Media Coverage of Environmental Movement Groups* (Ph.D. Diss., University of Minnesota, 1994).

Coser, Lewis, *The Functions of Social Conflict* (New York: Free Press, 1956).

Coulson, David C., "Journalists' Assessment of Group Ownership and Their Newspapers' Local News and Editorial Performance," paper presented to the Association for Education in Journalism and Mass Communication (Boston, August 1991).

Coulson, David C., "Impact of Ownership on Newspaper Quality," *Journalism Quarterly,* 71:403-10 (1994).

Crozier, Michael, *The Bureaucratic Phenomenon* (Chicago: The University of Chicago Press, 1964).

Dahrendorf, Ralf, *Class and Class Conflict in Industrial Society* (Stanford, Calif.: Stanford University Press, 1959 [1957 German version]).

Daugherty, David Bruce, "Group-Owned Newspapers vs. Independently Owned Newspapers: An Analysis of the Difference and Similarities" (Ph.D. Diss., University of Texas, 1983).

Davie, W. R. and J. Lee, "Television News Technology: Do More Sources Mean Less Diversity?" *Journal of Broadcasting & Electronic Media,* 37:453-64 (1993).

Davies, Celia, "Professionals in Bureaucracies: the Conflict Thesis Revisited," in Robert Dingwall and Philip Lewis (eds.), *The Sociology of the Professions* (New York: St. Martin's Press, 1983).

DeFleur, Margaret H., "Foundations of Job Satisfaction in the Media Industries," *Journalism Educator,* 47(1):3-15 (1992).

DeFleur, Melvin L., "Mass Media as Social Systems," pp. 63-83 in Wilbur Schramm and Donald F. Roberts, *The Process of Effects of Mass Communication* (Urbana, Ill.: University of Illinois Press, 1971).

DeFleur, Melvin L. and Sandra Ball-Rokeach, *Theories of Mass Communication*, 5th ed. (New York: Longman, 1989).

Demers, David Pearce, "Use of Polls in Reporting Changes Slightly Since 1978," *Journalism Quarterly,* 64:839-42 (1987).

Demers, David Pearce, "Crime News and the Rise of the Modern Police Department," paper presented to the Midwest Association for Journalism and Mass Communication Historians (Evanston, Ill., April 1990).

Demers, David Pearce, "Effects of Competition and Structural Pluralism on Centralization of Ownership in the U.S. Newspaper Industry," paper presented to the Association for Education in Journalism (Minneapolis, August 1990).

Demers, David Pearce, "Corporate Structure and Emphasis on Profits and Product Quality at U.S. Daily Newspapers," *Journalism Quarterly,* 68:15-26 (1991).

Demers, David Pearce, *Structural Pluralism, Competition and the Growth of the Corporate Newspaper in the United States* (Ph.D. Diss., University of Minnesota, 1992).

Demers, David Pearce, "Effect of Corporate Structure on Autonomy of Top Editors at U.S. Dailies," *Journalism Quarterly,* 70:499-508 (1993).

Demers, David Pearce, "Media Use and Beliefs About Economic Equality: An Empirical Test of the Dominant Ideology Thesis," presented to the Midwest Association for Public Opinion Research (Chicago, November 1993).

Demers, David Pearce, "Corporate Newspaper Structure and Organizational Goals," paper presented to Association for Education in Journalism and Mass Communication (Atlanta, August 1994).

Demers, David Pearce, "Effect of Organizational Size on Job Satisfaction of Top Editors at U.S. Dailies," *Journalism Quarterly,* 71:914-25 (1994).

Demers, David Pearce, "Front-Page News Story Attribution and the Managerial Revolution," unpublished paper (University of Wisconsin—River Falls, Wis., October 1994).

Demers, David Pearce, "The Relative Constancy Hypothesis, Structural Pluralism and National Advertising Expenditures," *Journal of Media Economics,* 7(4):31-48 (1994).

Demers, David Pearce, "Structural Pluralism, Intermedia Competition and the Growth of the Corporate Newspaper in the United States," *Journalism Monographs,* vol. 145 (June 1994).

Demers, David Pearce, "What Empirical Research Tells Us About the Dominant Ideology Thesis," unpublished paper (University of Wisconsin—River Falls, Wis., 1994).

Demers, David Pearce, "Corporate Newspaper Structure and Editorial Page Vigor," paper presented to the International Communication Association (Albuquerque, N.M., May 1995).

Demers, David Pearce, "Does Personal Experience in a Community Increase or Decrease Newspaper Reading?" *Journalism Quarterly* (in press).

Demers, David Pearce and Suzanne Nichols, *Precision Journalism: A Practical Guide* (Newbury Park, Calif.: Sage, 1987).

Demers, David Pearce and Daniel B. Wackman, "Effect of Chain Ownership on Newspaper Management Goals," *Newspaper Research Journal,* 9(2):59-68 (1988).

Demers, David Pearce, Dennis Craff, Yang-Ho Choi, and Beth M. Pessin, "Issue Obtrusiveness and the Agenda-Setting Effects of National Network News," *Communication Research,* 16:793-812 (1989).

Dertouzos, James N. and K. E. Thorpe, *Newspaper Groups: Economies of Scale, Tax Laws, and Merger Incentives* (Santa Monica, Calif.: Rand, 1985).

Deutschmann, Paul J., "Predicting Newspaper Staff Size from Circulation," *Journalism Quarterly,* 36:350-4 (1959).

Devey, Susan M., "Umbrella Competition for Circulation in the Boston Metro Area," *Journal of Media Economics*, 2(1):31-40 (1989).

Dicken-Garcia, Hazel, *Journalistic Standards in Nineteenth-Century America* (Madison, Wis.: University of Wisconsin Press, 1989).

Dimmick, John and Eric Rothenbuhler, "The Theory of the Niche: Quantifying Competition Among Media Industries," *Journal of Communication*, 34(1):103-19 (1984).

Dingwall, Robert and Philip Lewis (eds.), *The Sociology of the Professions: Lawyers, Doctors and Others* (New York: St. Martin's Press, 1983).

Donohue, George A., "Adaptation Isn't Enough: Rural Communities Need Mutation," *Sociology of Rural Life*, 11(1):1-2, 7 (1990).

Donohue, George A., Phillip J. Tichenor and Clarice N. Olien, "Mass Media Functions, Knowledge and Social Control," *Journalism Quarterly*, 50:652-9 (1973).

Donohue, G. A., C. N. Olien and P. J. Tichenor, "Structure and Constraints on Community Newspaper Gatekeepers," *Journalism Quarterly* 66:807-12, 845 (1989).

Donohue, G. A., C. N. Olien and P. J. Tichenor, "A Changing Media Environment in the U.S.," paper presented to the Association for Education in Journalism and Mass Communication (Boston, August 1991).

Donohue, George A., Phillip J. Tichenor, and Clarice N. Olien, "Gatekeeping: Mass Media Systems and Information Control," pp. 41-69 in F. Gerald Kline and Phillip J. Tichenor (eds.), *Current Perspectives in Mass Communication Research* (Beverly Hills, Calif.: Sage Publications, 1972).

Donohue, George A., Clarice N. Olien and Phillip J. Tichenor, "Reporting Conflict by Pluralism, Newspaper Type and Ownership," *Journalism Quarterly*, 62:489-99, 507 (1985).

Donohue, G. A., P. J. Tichenor and C. N. Olien, "Metro Daily Pullback and Knowledge Gaps Within and Between Communities," *Communication Research*, 13:453-71 (1986).

Donohue, G. A., C. N. Olien, P. J. Tichenor and D. P. Demers, "Community Structure, News Judgments and Newspaper Content," paper presented to the Association for Education in Journalism and Mass Communication (Minneapolis, August 1990).

Donohue, George A., Phillip J. Tichenor, and Clarice N. Olien, "A Guard Dog Perspective on the Role of Media," *Journal of Communication*, 45(2):115-32 (1995).

Downie, Leonard, Jr., *The New Muckrakers* (New York: Mentor, 1976).

Downing, John, "Alternative Media and the Boston Tea Party, " pp. 180-91 in John Downing, Ali Mohammadi and Annabelle Sreberny-Mohammadi (eds.), *Questioning the Media* (Newbury Park, Calif.: Sage, 1990).

Dreier, Peter and Steven Weinberg, "Interlocking Directorates," *Columbia Journalism Review* (November/December 1979).

Dun & Bradstreet, *Dun & Bradstreet Reference Book of Corporate Managements* (New York: Dun & Bradstreet, 1968-1980).

Durkheim, Emile, *The Division of Labor in Society,* trans. W. D. Halls (New York: Free Press, 1984 [1893]).

Dyer, Carolyn Stewart, "Economic Dependence and Concentration of Ownership Among Antebellum Wisconsin Newspapers," *Journalism History*, 7(2):42-6 (1980).

Editor & Publisher, *Editor & Publisher International Yearbook* (New York: Editor & Publisher, 1991).

Edwards, Richard, *Contested Terrain* (New York: Basic Books, 1979).

Eisenstadt, S. N., "Macro-Societal Analysis — Background, Development and Indications," pp. 7-24 in S. N. Eisenstadt and H. J. Helle, *Macro-Sociological Theory: Perspectives on Sociological Theory* (Newbury Park, Calif.: Sage Publications, 1985).

Eliasoph, N., "Routines and the Making of Oppositional News," *Critical Studies in Mass Communication,* 5:313-34 (1988).

Eltis, W. A., "Adam Smith's Theory of Economic Growth," in Andrew S. Skinner and Thomas Wilson (eds.), *Essays on Adam Smith* (Oxford: Clarendon Press, 1975).

Emery, Edwin, *History of the American Newspaper Publishers Association* (Minneapolis: University of Minnesota Press, 1950).

Emery, Michael and Edwin Emery, *The Press and America* (Englewood Cliffs, N.J.: Prentice-Hall, 1988).

Engel, Gloria V., "Professional Autonomy and Bureaucratic Organization," *Administrative Science Quarterly,* 15:12-21 (1970).

Entman, Robert M., *Democracy Without Citizens: Media and the Decay of American Politics* (New York: Oxford University Press, 1989).

Epstein, Edward Jay, *News From Nowhere* (New York: Random House, 1973).

Ettema, James S. and Theodore L. Glasser, "Public Accountability or Public Relations? Newspaper Ombudsmen Define Their Role," *Journalism Quarterly,* 64:3-12 (1987).

Etzioni, Amitai, *Modern Organizations* (Englewood Cliffs, N.J.: Prentice-Hall, 1964).

Ewin, Stuart, *Captains of Consciousness: Advertising and the Social Roots of the Consumer Culture* (New York: McGraw Hill, 1976).

Ferguson, James M., "Daily Newspaper Advertising Rates, Local Media Cross-Ownership, Newspaper Chains, and Media Competition," *The Journal of Law & Economics*, 26:635-54 (1983).

Finnegan, John R., Jr., and Kasisomayajula Viswanath, "Community Ties and Use of Cable TV and Newspapers in a Midwest Suburb," *Journalism Quarterly,* 65:456-63 (1988).

Fishman, Mark, *Manufacturing the News* (Austin, Texas: University of Texas Press, 1980).

Flatt, Dean M., "Managerial Incentives: Effects at a Chain Owned Daily," *Newspaper Research Journal,* 2(1):48-55 (1980).

Fligstein, Neil and Peter Brantley, "Bank Control, Owner Control, or Organizational Dynamics: Who Controls the Large Modern Corporation," *American Journal of Sociology,* 98:280-307 (1992).

Flint, Joe and Peter Viles, "Hill Squeezes the FCC's Radio Rules," *Broadcasting* (Aug. 10, 1992), pp. 4, 12.

Folkerts, Jean and Dwight L. Tweeter, Jr., *Voices of a Nation: A History of the Media in the United States* (New York: Macmillan, 1989).

Galbraith, John Kenneth, *The New Industrial State,* 3rd ed. (New York: Mentor, 1978).

Gamson, William A., *Talking Politics* (Cambridge, Mass.: Cambridge University Press, 1992).

Gans, Herbert J., *Deciding What's News* (New York: Vintage, 1979).

Gaziano, Cecilie, "Chain Newspaper Homogeneity and Presidential Endorsements, 1972-1980," *Journalism Quarterly,* 66:836-45 (1989)

Gellhorn, Ernest, *Antitrust Law and Economics* (St. Paul, Minn.: West, 1986).

Gerbner, George and Larry Gross, "Living With Television: The Violence Profile," *Journal of Communication,* 26(2):173-99 (1976).

Gerbner, George, Larry Gross, Michael Morgan and Nancy Signorielli, "Growing Up With Television: The Cultivation Perspective," pp. 17-41 in Jennings Bryant and Dolf Zillman (eds.), *Media Effects: Advances in Theory and Research* (Hillsdale, N.J.: Lawrence Erlbaum Associates, 1994).

Gerth, H. H. and C. Wright Mills (eds.), *From Max Weber: Essays in Sociology* (New York: Oxford University Press, 1946).

Ghiglione, Loren, *The Buying and Selling of America's Newspapers* (Indianapolis, Ind.: R. J. Berg, 1984).

Giddens, Anthony and Jonathan H. Turner (eds.), *Social Theory Today* (Stanford, Calif.: Stanford University Press, 1987).

Gieber, Walter and Walter Johnson, "The City Hall Beat: A Study of Reporter and Source Roles," *Journalism Quarterly,* 38:289-97 (1961).

Gillmor, Donald M., *Power, Publicity and the Abuse of Libel Law* (New York: Oxford University Press, 1992).

Gitlin, Todd, "Media Sociology: The Dominant Paradigm," *Theory and Society,* 6:205-53 (1978).

Gitlin, Todd, *The Whole World Is Watching: Mass Media in the Making and Unmaking of the New Left* (Berkeley, Calif.: University of California Press, 1980).

Gladney, George A., "Newspaper Excellence: How Editors of Small and Large Papers Judge Quality," *Newspaper Research Journal,* 11(2):58-72 (1990).

Gladney, George Albert, "How Editors and Readers Rank and Rate the Importance of 18 Traditional Standards of Newspaper Excellence," paper presented to the Association for Education in Journalism and Mass Communication (Atlanta, August 1994).

Glasser, Theodore L., "Professionalism and the Derision of Diversity: The Case of the Education of Journalists," *Journal of Communication,* 42:131-40 (1992).

Glasser, Ted L., Dave S. Allen and Sue Elizabeth Blanks, "The Influence of Chain Ownership on News Play: A Case Study," *Journalism Quarterly,* 66:607-14 (1989).

Glasgow University Media Group, *Bad News* (London: Routledge & Kegan Paul, 1976).

Goode, William J., "A Theory of Role Strain," *American Sociological Review,* 25:483-96 (1960).

Goodman, Mark Lee, "Newspaper Ownership and the Weekly Editorial in Illinois" (M.A. Thesis, South Dakota State University, 1982).

Gordon, Robert Aaron, *Business Leadership in the Large Corporation* (Berkeley, Calif.: University of California Press, 1961 [1945]).

Gouldner, Alvin W., "The Norm of Reciprocity," *American Sociological Review,* 25:161-78 (1960).

Graber, Doris A., *Mass Media and American Politics,* 3rd ed. (Washington, D.C.: Congressional Quarterly Press, 1989).

Griswold, Rufus Wilmot (ed.), *The Prose Works of John Milton,* vol. I (Philadelphia: J. W. Moore, 1856).

Griswold, William Floyd, Jr., *Community Structure, Reporter Specialization and Content Diversity Among Midwest Daily Newspapers* (Ph.D. Diss., University of Minnesota, 1990).

Grotta, Gerald L., "Consolidation of Newspapers: What Happens to the Consumer," *Journalism Quarterly,* 48:245-50 (1971).

Hage, Jerald, "An Axiomatic Theory of Organizations," *Administrative Science Quarterly* 10:289-320 (1965).

Hagner, Paul R., "Newspaper Competition: Isolating Related Market Characteristics," *Journalism Quarterly,* 60:281-7.

Halberstam, David, "The Education of a Journalist," *Columbia Journalism Review* (November/December 1994).

Hale, F. Dennis, "Editorial Diversity and Concentration," pp. 161-76 in Robert G. Picard, Maxwell E. McCombs, James P. Winter, and Stephen Lacy (eds.), *Press Concentration and Monopoly* (Norwood, N.J.: Ablex, 1988).

Hall, A. D. and R. E. Fagen, "Definition of Systems," *General Systems,* 1:18-28 (1956).

Hall, Richard H., "Professionalization and Bureaucratization," *American Sociological Review*, 33:92-104 (1968).

Hall, Richard H., *Organizations: Structures, Processes & Outcomes* (Englewood Cliffs, N.J.: Prentice-Hall, 1987).

Hall, Stuart, "Culture, the Media and the Ideological Effect," pp. 315-48 in James Curran, Michael Gurevitch and Janet Woollacott (eds.), *Mass Communication and Society* (London: Edward Arnold, 1977).

Hannah, Leslie, *The Rise of the Corporate Economy* (London: Methuen, 1976).

Hannan, Michael T. and John H. Freeman, "The Population Ecology of Organizations," *American Journal of Sociology*, 82:929-64 (1977).

Hartley, John, *Understanding News* (London: Methuen, 1982).

Hartmann, Paul and Charles Husband, "The Mass Media and Racial Conflict," pp. 288-302 in Stanley Cohen and Jock Young (eds.), *The Manufacture of News* (London: Constable, 1981).

Hawley, Amos Henry, *Human Ecology: A Theory of Community Structure* (New York: Ronald Press, 1950).

Heilbroner, Robert L., *The Worldly Philosophers,* 6th ed. (New York: Simon & Schuster, 1986).

Herman, Edward S., "Diversity of News: 'Marginalizing' the Opposition," *Journal of Communication*, 35(3):135-46 (1985).

Herman, Edward, "Media in the U.S. Political Economy," pp. 75-87 in John Downing, Ali Mohammadi, and Annabelle Sreberny-Mohammadi (eds.), *Questioning the Media: A Critical Introduction* (Newbury Park, Calif.: Sage, 1990).

Herman, Edward S. and Noam Chomsky, *Manufacturing Consent: The Political Economy of the Mass Media* (New York: Pantheon, 1988).

Hiebert, Ray Eldon, Donald F. Ungurait and Thomas W. Bohn, *Mass Media II: An Introduction to Modern Communication* (New York: Longman, 1979).

Hindley, Brian V., "Separation of Ownership and Control in the Modern Corporation," *The Journal of Law and Economics,* 13:185-221 (1970).

Hirsch, Paul M., "The 'Scary World' of the Nonviewer and Other Anomalies: A Reanalysis of Gerbner et al.'s Findings on Cultivation Analysis, Part I," *Communication Research,* 7:403-56 (1980).

Hirsch, Paul M., "On Not Learning From One's Own Mistakes: A Reanalysis of Gerbner et al.'s Findings on Cultivation Analysis, Part II," *Communication Research,* 8:3-37 (1981).

Hirsch, Paul M. and Tracy A. Thompson, "The Stock Market as Audience: The Impact of Public Ownership on Newspapers," pp. 142-58 in James S. Ettema and D. Charles Whitney (eds.), *Audiencemaking: How the Media Create the Audience* (Thousand Oaks, Calif.: Sage, 1994).

Holsti, Ole R., *Content Analysis for the Social Sciences and Humanities* (Reading, Mass.: Addison-Wesley, 1969).

Homans, George C., *Social Behavior: Its Elementary Forms* (New York: Harcourt Brace Jovanovich, Inc., 1974).

Hudson, Frederick, *Journalism in the United States: 1690 to 1872* (New York: Harper & Brothers, Publishers, 1873).

Hughes, M., "The Fruits of Cultivation Analysis: A Re-Examination of Some Effects of Television Watching," *Public Opinion Quarterly,* 44:287-302 (1980).

Hurd, G., "The Television Presentation of the Police," in Tony Bennett et al. (eds.), *Popular Television and Film* (London: BFI/Open University Press, 1981).

James, David R. and Michael Soref, "Profit Constraints on Managerial Autonomy: Managerial Theory and the Unmaking of the Corporate President," *American Sociological Review,* 46:1-18 (1981).

Janowitz, Morris, *Community Press in an Urban Setting,* 2nd ed. (Chicago: University of Chicago Press, 1967 [1952]).

Janowitz, Morris, "Communication, Mass: The Study of Mass Communication," pp. 41-53 in David L. Sills (ed.), *International Encyclopedia of the Social Sciences,* vol. 3 (New York: Macmillan, 1968).

Jary, David and Julia Jary, *The HarperCollins Dictionary of Sociology* (New York: HarperCollins, 1991).

Johnstone, John W. C., "Organizational Constraints on Newswork," *Journalism Quarterly,* 53:5-13 (1976).

Johnstone, John W. C., Edward Slawski and William Bowman, *The News People: A Sociological Portrait of American Journalists and Their Work* (Urbana, Ill.: University of Illinois Press, 1976).

Kamerschen, David R., "The Influence of Ownership and Control on Profit Rates," *American Economic Review,* 58:432-47 (1968).

Katz, Elihu and Tamás Szecskö (eds.), *Mass Media and Social Change* (Beverly Hills, Calif.: Sage, 1981).

Kaul, Arthur J. and Joseph P. McKerns, "The Dialectic Ecology of the Newspaper," *Critical Studies in Mass Communication,* 2:217-33 (1985).

Kellner, Douglas, *Television and the Crisis of Democracy* (Boulder: Westview Press, 1990).

Kessler, Lauren, *The Dissident Press: Alternative Journalism in American History* (Beverly Hills, Calif.: Sage, 1984).

Kim, Jae-On and Charles W. Mueller, *Factor Analysis: Statistical Methods and Practical Issues* (Beverly Hills, Calif.: Sage, 1978).

Kim, Jae-On and Charles W. Mueller, *Introduction to Factor Analysis* (Beverly Hills, Calif.: Sage, 1978).

Klapper, Joseph T., *The Effects of Mass Communication* (New York: The Free Press, 1960).

Kmenta, J., *Elements of Econometrics* (New York: Macmillan, 1986).

Kobre, Sidney, "The First American Newspaper: A Product of Environment," *Journalism Quarterly,* 17:335-45 (1940).

Kobre, Sidney, *Development of American Journalism* (Dubuque, Iowa: Wm. C. Brown Company Publishers, 1969).

Kohn, Melvin L., "Occupational Structure and Alienation," *American Journal of Sociology,* 82:111-30 (1976).

Kosicki, Gerald M., "Problems and Opportunities in Agenda-Setting Research," *Journal of Communication,* 43(2):100-28 (1993).

Kramer, Joel, "Beats Open a Window Onto How a Paper Sees the News," *Star Tribune* (February 28, 1994), p. A29.

Kraus, Sidney and Dennis Davis, *The Effect of Mass Communication on Political Behavior* (University Park, Penn.: Pennsylvania State University Press, 1976).

Kreig, Andrew, *Spiked: How Chain Management Corrupted America's Oldest Newspaper* (Old Saybrook, Conn.: Peregrine Press, 1987).

Kuczun, Sam, "Ownership of Newspaper Increasingly Becoming Public," *Journalism Quarterly,* 55:342-4 (1978).

Kuhn, Thomas, *The Structure of Scientific Revolutions* (Chicago: University of Chicago Press, 1962).

Kwitney, Jonathan, "The High Cost of High Profits," *Washington Journalism Review* (June 1990).

Lacy, Stephen, "Competition Among Metropolitan Daily, Small Daily and Weekly Newspapers," *Journalism Quarterly*, 61:640-4, 742 (1984).

Lacy, Stephen, "Monopoly Metropolitan Dailies and Inter-City Competition," *Journalism Quarterly*, 62:640-4 (1985).

Lacy, Stephen, "The Effects of Group Ownership on Daily Newspaper Content," paper presented to the Midwest Association for Public Opinion Research (Chicago, November 1986).

Lacy, Stephen, "The Effect of Growth of Radio on Newspaper Competition, 1929-1948," *Journalism Quarterly*, 64:775-81 (1987).

Lacy, Stephen, "The Impact of Intercity Competition on Daily Newspaper Competition," *Journalism Quarterly*, 65:399-406 (1988).

Lacy, Stephen and Shikha Dalmia, "The Relationship Between Daily and Weekly Newspaper Penetration in Non-Metropolitan Areas," paper presented to the Association for Education in Journalism and Mass Communication (Montreal, August 1992).

Lacy, Stephen and Frederick Fico, "Newspaper Quality and Ownership: Rating the Groups," *Newspaper Research Journal*, 11(2):42-56 (1990).

Lacy, Stephen and Robert G. Picard, "Interactive Monopoly Power in the Daily Newspaper Industry," *The Journal of Media Economics*, 3(2):27-38 (1990).

Lacy, Stephen and Daniel Riffe, "The Impact of Competition and Group Ownership on Radio News," *Journalism Quarterly*, 71:583-93 (1994).

Lakatos, Imre, "Falsification and the Methodology of Research Programmes," pp. 91-196 in Imre Lakatos and A. Musgrave (eds.), *Criticism and the Growth of Knowledge* (Cambridge, England: Cambridge University Press, 1970).

Land, Kenneth C., "Mathematical Formalization of Durkheim's Theory of the Division of Labor," pp. 257-82 in Edgar F. Borgatta and George W. Bohrnstedt (eds.), *Sociological Methodology* (San Francisco: Jossey-Bass, 1969).

Landy, Frank J., *Psychology of Work Behavior* (Chicago: The Dorsey Press, 1985).

Lane, Roger, "Policing the City: Boston 1822-1885," in Jerome Skolnick and Thomas C. Gray (eds.), *Police in America* (Boston: Little, Brown & Co., 1975).

LaPiere, Richard T., *Social Change* (New York: McGraw-Hill, 1965).

Larner, Robert J., *Management Control in the Large Corporation* (Cambridge, Mass.: Dunellen, 1970).

Lasswell, Harold D., "The Structure and Function of Communication in Society," pp. 84-99 in Wilbur Schramm and Donald F. Roberts (eds.), *The Process and Effects of Mass Communication* (Urbana, Ill.: University of Illinois Press, 1971).

Lavine, John and Daniel Wackman, *Managing Media Organizations: Effective Leadership of the Media* (New York: Longman, 1988).

Lazarsfeld, Paul F. and Patricia Kendall, *Radio Listening in America* (New York: Prentice-Hall, 1948).

Lazarsfeld, Paul and Robert Merton, "Mass Communication, Popular Taste and Organized Social Action," pp. 95-118 in L. Bryson (ed.), *The Communication of Ideas* (New York: Harper and Brothers, 1948).

Lee, Alfred McClung, *The Daily Newspaper in America: The Evolution of a Social Instrument* (New York: Macmillan, 1937).

Lee, Chin-Chuan, *Media Imperialism Reconsidered* (Beverly Hills, Calif.: Sage, 1980).

Lerner, Daniel, *The Passing of Traditional Society* (New York: Macmillan, 1958).

Levi-Strauss, Claude, *Totemism* (Boston: Beacon Press, 1963).

Levy, Marion J., Jr., *The Structure of Society* (Princeton, N.J.: Princeton University Press, 1952).

Lewis, Regina, "Relation Between Newspaper Subscription Price and Circulation," *The Journal of Media Economics,* 8(1):25-41 (1995).

Lewis-Beck, Michael S., *Applied Regression: An Introduction* (Beverly Hills, Calif.: Sage, 1980).

Lichter, S. Robert and Stanley Rothman, "Media and Business Elites," *Public Opinion Quarterly,* 4:42-6 (1981).

Lindsay, Merrill, "Lindsay-Schaub Newspapers," in "That Monopoly of Opinion," *The Masthead* (Fall 1974).

Litman, Barry R., "Microeconomic Foundations," pp. 3-34 in Robert G. Picard, James P. Winter, Maxwell E. McCombs and Stephen Lacy (eds.), *Press Concentration and Monopoly* (Norwood, N.J.: Ablex, 1988).

Litman, Barry R. and Janet Bridges, "An Economic Analysis of Daily Newspaper Performance," *Newspaper Research Journal,* 7(3):9-26 (1986).

Littlejohn, Stephen W., *Theories of Human Communication* (Belmont, Calif.: Wadsworth, 1983).

Locke, John, *The Second Treatise of Civil Government and A Letter Concerning Toleration* (Oxford: B. Blackwell, 1946 [1690]).

Lowe, A., "Adam Smith's System of Equilibrium Growth," in Andrew S. Skinner and Thomas Wilson (eds.), *Essays on Adam Smith* (Oxford: Clarendon Press, 1975).

Lowery, Shearon T. and Melvin L. DeFleur, *Milestones in Mass Communication* (New York: Longman, 1989).

Luhmann, Niklas, *The Differentiation of Society* (New York: Columbia University Press, 1982).

Mansfield, Roger, "Bureaucracy and Centralization: An Examination of Organizational Structure," *Administrative Science Quarterly,* 18:477-88 (1973).

Marcuse, Herbert, *One-Dimensional Man* (Boston: Beacon Press, 1964).

Marger, Martin N., *Elites and Masses* (New York: D. Van Nostrand Company, 1981).

Markus, Gregory B., *Analyzing Panel Data* (Beverly Hills, Calif.: Sage, 1979).

Marx, Karl, "Economic and Philosophic Manuscripts of 1844," pp. 66-125 in Robert C. Tucker (ed.), *The Marx-Engles Reader,* 2nd ed. (New York: W. W. Norton & Company, 1978).

Marx, Karl, *Capital: A Critique of Political Economy,* vol. 1, trans. by Samuel Moore and Edward Aveling (New York: International Publishers, 1987 [1867]).

Maslach, Christina and Susan E. Jackson, *Maslach Burnout Inventory* (Palo Alto, Calif.: Consulting Psychologists Press, 1981).

Matthews, Donald R. and James W. Protho, *Negroes and the New Southern Politics* (New York: Harcourt, Brace & World, 1966).

McCarthy, Mayer N. and John D. Zald, "Resource Mobilization and Social Movements: A Partial Theory," *American Journal of Sociology,* 82:1212-41 (1977).

McCarthy, Mayer N. and John D. Zald (eds.), *The Dynamics of Social Movements: Resource Mobilization, Social Control and Tactics* (Cambridge, Mass.: Winthrop Publishers, 1979).

McCombs, Maxwell, "Mass Media in the Marketplace," *Journalism Monographs,* vol. 24 (August 1972).

McCombs, Maxwell, "Effect of Monopoly in Cleveland on Diversity of Newspaper Content," *Journalism Quarterly,* 64:740-4, 792 (1987).

McCombs, Maxwell, "News Influence on Our Pictures of the World," pp. 1-16 in Jennings Bryant and Dolf Zillmann (eds.), *Media Effects: Advances in Theory and Research* (Hillsdale, N.J.: Lawrence Erlbaum Associates, 1994).

McCombs, Maxwell E. and Donald L. Shaw, "The Agenda-Setting Function of the Mass Media," *Public Opinion Quarterly,* 36:176-87 (1972).

McConnell, Campbell R., *Economics: Principles, Problems, and Policies,* 10th ed. (New York: McGraw-Hill, 1987).

McGrath, Kristin, *Journalist Satisfaction Study* (Minneapolis: Associated Press Managing Editors Association, 1993)

McLeod, Douglas M. and James K. Hertog, "The Manufacture of 'Public Opinion' by Reporters: Informal Cues for Public Perceptions of Protest Groups," *Discourse and Society,* 3(3):259-75 (1992).

McManus, John H., *Market-Driven Journalism: Let the Citizen Beware?* (Thousand Oaks, Calif.: Sage, 1994).

McNeill, William H., *History of Western Civilization,* 6th ed. (Chicago: The University of Chicago Press, 1986).

McQuail, Denis, *Mass Communication Theory: An Introduction,* 3rd ed. (London: Sage, 1994).

Merton, Robert K., *Social Theory and Social Structure,* 2nd ed. (London: The Free Press, 1957 [1949]).

Merton, Robert K., *Social Theory and Social Structure,* 3rd ed. (New York: The Free Press, 1968 [1949]).

Meyer, Marshall W., William Stevenson and Stephen Webster, *Limits to Bureaucratic Growth* (New York: De Gruyter, 1985).

Meyer, Philip, *The Newspaper Survival Book: An Editor's Guide to Marketing Research* (Bloomington, Ind.: Indiana University Press, 1985).

Meyer, Philip, *Ethical Journalism* (New York: Longman, 1987).

Meyer, Philip and David Arant, "A Test of the Neuharth Conjecture: Searching an Electronic Database to Evaluate Newspaper Quality," paper delivered at Association for Education in Journalism and Mass Communication (Kansas City, Mo., August 1993).

Meyers, Marion, "Reporters and Beats: The Making of Oppositional News," *Critical Studies in Mass Communication,* 9:75-90 (1992).

Michels, Robert, "Oligarchy," pp. 48-67 in Frank Fischer and Carmen Sirianni, *Critical Studies in Organization and Bureaucracy* (Philadelphia: Temple University Press, 1984).

Mill, John Stuart, *Principles of Political Economy* (New York: Appleton, 1887).

Mills, C. Wright, *White Collar* (New York: Oxford University Press, 1953).

Mills, C. Wright, *The Power Elite* (New York: Oxford University Press, 1956).

Moch, Michael K. and Edward V. Morse, "Size, Centralization and Organizational Adoption of Innovations," *American Sociological Review,* 42:716-25 (1977).

Molotch, Harvey and Marílyn Lester, "Accidental News: The Great Oil Spill as Local Occurrence and National Event," *American Journal of Sociology,* 81:235-60 (1975).

Monge, Peter, "The Systems Perspective as a Theoretical Basis for the Study of Human Communication," *Communication Quarterly,* 25:19-29 (1977).

Monsen, Joseph R., Jr., John S. Chiu and David E. Cooley, "The Effect of Separation of Ownership and Control on the Performance of the Large Firm," *Quarterly Journal of Economics,* 82:435-51 (1968).

Morales, W. Q., "Revolutions, Earthquakes, and Latin America: The Networks Look at Allende's Chile and Somoza's Nicaragua," pp. 79-116 in W. C. Adams (ed.), *Television Coverage of International Affairs* (Norwood, N.J.: Ablex, 1982).

Mott, Frank Luther, *American Journalism: A History 1690-1960*, 3rd ed. (New York: The Macmillan Company, 1962).

Münch, Richard, "Parsonian Theory Today: In Search of a New Synthesis," pp. 116-55 in Anthony Giddens and Jonathan H. Turner (eds.), *Social Theory Today* (Stanford, Calif.: Stanford University Press, 1987).

Murdock, Graham and Peter Golding, "For a Political Economy of Mass Communications," *The Socialist Register*, 205-34 (1973).

Murdock, Graham and Peter Golding, "Capitalism, Communication and Class Relations," pp. 12-43 in James Curran, Michael Gurevitch and Janet Woollacott (eds.), *Mass Communication and Society* (Beverly Hills, Calif: Sage, 1977).

Nadel, S. F., *The Theory of Social Structure* (New York: The Free Press, 1957).

National Research Bureau, *The Working Press of the Nation: TV & Radio Directory*, vol. 3 (Chicago: National Research Bureau, 1993).

Newfield, Jack, "Journalism: Old, New and Corporate," in Ronald Weber (ed.), *The Reporter as Artist: A Look at the New Journalism* (New York: Hastings House, 1974).

Niebauer, Walter E., Jr., Stephen Lacy, James M. Bernstein, and Tuen-yu Lau, "Central City Market Structure's Impact on Suburban Newspaper Circulation," *Journalism Quarterly*, 65:726-32 (1988).

Nixon, Raymond B., "Trends in Daily Newspaper Ownership Since 1945," *Journalism Quarterly*, 31:3-14 (1954).

Nixon, Raymond B. and Jean Ward, "Trends in Newspaper Ownership and Inter-Media Competition," *Journalism Quarterly*, 38:3-14 (1961).

Nord, David Paul and Harold L. Nelson, "The Logic of Historical Research," pp. 278-304 in Guido H. Stempel III and Bruce H. Westley (eds.), *Research Methods in Mass Communication* (Englewood Cliffs, N.J.: Prentice-Hall, 1981).

Norton, Mary Beth, David M. Katzman, Paul D. Escott, Howard P. Chudacoff, Thomas G. Paterson and William M. Tuttle, Jr., *A People and A Nation: A History of the United States* (Boston: Houghton Mifflin, 1982).

Nutter, G. Warren and Henry Adler Einhorn, *Enterprise Monopoly in the United States: 1899-1958* (New York: Columbia University Press, 1969).

O'Brien, Frank M., *The Story of the Sun* (New York: George H. Doran Company, 1918).

Olien, Clarice N., George A. Donohue and Phillip J. Tichenor, "The Community Editor's Power and the Reporting of Conflict," *Journalism Quarterly*, 45:243-52 (1968).

Olien, C. N., G. A. Donohue and P. J. Tichenor, "Media Competition and Community Structure," report to the American Newspaper Publishers Association (March 1981).

Olien, C. N., G. A. Donohue and P. J. Tichenor, "Media and Stages of Social Conflict," *Journalism Monographs*, vol. 90 (November 1984).

Olien, C. N., G. A. Donohue and P. J. Tichenor, "Metropolitan Dominance and Media Use," *American Newspaper Publishers Association News Research Report*, no. 36 (1986).

Olien, C. N., G. A. Donohue and P. J. Tichenor, "Media Mix and the Metro-Nonmetro Knowledge Gap: Information Deprivation in an Information Age?" paper presented to the Midwest Association for Public Opinion Research (Chicago, November 1990).

Olien, C. N., P. J. Tichenor and G. A. Donohue, "Relation Between Corporate Ownership and Editor Attitudes Toward Business," *Journalism Quarterly* 65:259-66 (1988).

Olien, Clarice N., Phillip J. Tichenor and George A. Donohue, "Media Coverage and Social Movements," pp. 139-63 in Charles T. Salmon (ed.), *Information Campaigns: Balancing Social Values and Social Change* (Newbury Park, Calif.: Sage, 1989).

Olien, Clarice N., Phillip J. Tichenor and George A. Donohue, "Media Redistribution in the U.S.: A Growing Information Gap Between Metro and Nonmetro Areas?" paper presented to the American Association for Public Opinion Research (Phoenix, May 1991).

Olien, C. N., P. J. Tichenor, G. A. Donohue, K. L. Sandstrom and D. M. McLeod, "Community Structure and Editor Opinions About Planning," *Journalism Quarterly,* 67:119-27 (1990).

Olsen, Marvin E. *The Process of Social Organization* (New York: Holt, Rinehart and Winston, 1968).

Oommen, T. K., *Protest and Change: Studies in Social Movements* (New Delhi, India: Sage, 1990).

Ostrom, Charles W., Jr., *Time Series Analysis: Regression Techniques,* 2nd ed. (Beverly Hills, Calif.: Sage, 1990).

Paletz, David L. and Robert M. Entman, *Media Power Politics* (New York: The Free Press, 1981).

Paletz, David L., P. Reichert and B. McIntyre, "How the Media Support Local Government Authority, *Public Opinion Quarterly,* 35:808-92 (1971).

Palmer, John, "The Profit-Performance Effect of the Separation of Ownership from Control in Large U.S. Industrial Corporations," *Bell Journal of Economics and Management Science,* 4:299-303 (1973).

Papendreou, Andreas G., "Some Basic Problems in the Theory of the Firm," pp. 183-219 in Bernard F. Haley (ed.), *A Survey of Contemporary Economics,* vol. II (Homewood, Ill.: Irwin, 1952).

Pareto, Vilfredo, *The Mind and Society: A Treatise on General Sociology* (New York: Dover, 1973).

Park, Robert E., *The Immigrant Press and Its Control* (New York: Harper, 1922).

Park, Robert E., "The Natural History of the Newspaper," *American Journal of Sociology,* 29:273-89 (1923).

Park, Robert E., "News as a Form of Knowledge," *American Journal of Sociology,* 45:669-86 (1940).

Park, Robert E. and E. W. Burgess, *Introduction to the Science of Sociology* (Chicago: The University of Chicago Press, 1921).

Parsons, Patrick, John Finnegan, Jr. and William Benham, "Editors and Their Roles," pp. 91-104 in Robert G. Picard, Maxwell E. McCombs, James P. Winter and Stephen Lacy (eds.), *Press Concentration and Monopoly* (Norwood, N.J.: Ablex, 1988).

Parsons, Talcott, *The Social System* (New York: The Free Press, 1951).

Parsons, Talcott, "A Revised Analytical Approach to the Theory of Social Stratification," in Richard Bendix and Seymour Martin Lipset (eds.), *Class, Status, and Power* (Glencoe, Ill.: Free Press, 1953).

Parsons, Talcott, "Professions," *International Encyclopedia of the Social Sciences,* vol. 12 (New York: Macmillan, 1968).

Pellegrin, Roland J. and Charles H. Coates, "Absentee-Owned Corporations and Community Power Structure," *American Journal of Sociology,* 61:413-9 (March 1956).

Pember, Don R., *Mass Media in America* (Chicago: Science Research, 1974).

Perloff, Richard M., *The Dynamics of Persuasion* (Hillsdale, N.J.: Lawrence Erlbaum Associates, 1993).

Peterson, Robert A., Gerald Albaum, George Kozmetsky and Isabella C. M. Cunningham, "Attitudes of Newspaper Business Editors and General Public Toward Capitalism," *Journalism Quarterly,* 61:56-65 (1984).

Pfeffer, Jeffrey, *Power in Organizations* (Marshfield, Mass.: Pitman, 1981).

Pfeffer, Jeffrey and Gerald R. Salancik, *The External Control of Organizations* (New York: Harper & Row, 1978).

Picard, Robert G., *Media Economics* (Newbury Park, Calif.: Sage, 1989).

Picard, Robert G., James P. Winter, Maxwell E. McCombs and Stephen Lacy (eds.), *Press Concentration and Monopoly* (Norwood, N.J.: Ablex, 1988).

Polich, John E., "Predicting Newspaper Staff Size from Circulation: A New Look," *Journalism Quarterly,* 51:515-7 (1974).

Potter, W. James, Roger Cooper and Michel Dupagne, "The Three Paradigms of Mass Media Research in Mainstream Communication Journals," *Communication Theory,* 3:317-35 (1993).

Powell, W., "The Blockbuster Decade: The Media as Big Business," *Working Papers for a New Society* (July/August 1979), pp. 26-36.

Powledge, Fred, *The Engineering of Restraint* (Washington, D.C.: Public Affairs Press, 1971).

Pritchard, David, "Homicide and Bargained Justice: The Agenda-Setting Effect of Crime News on Prosecutors," *Public Opinion Quarterly,* 50:143-59 (1986).

Protess, David L., Fay Lomax Cook, Jack C. Doppelt, James S. Ettema, Margaret T. Gordon, Donna R. Leff, and Peter Miller, *The Journalism of Outrage: Investigative Reporting and Agenda-Building in America* (New York: Guilford Press, 1991).

Pugh, D. S., D. J. Hickson, C. R. Hinings, and C. Turner, "Dimensions of Organizational Structure," *Administrative Science Quarterly,* 13:65-105 (1968).

Pusateri, C. Joseph, *Big Business in America: Attack and Defense* (Itasca, Ill.: F. E. Peacock Publishers, 1975).

Rarick, Galen R. and Barrie Hartman, "The Effects of Competition on One Daily Newspaper's Content," *Journalism Quarterly,* 43:459-63 (1966).

Ray, Royal H., "Economic Forces as Factors in Daily Newspaper Concentration," *Journalism Quarterly,* 29:31-42 (1952).

Riffe, Daniel, Charles F. Aust, and Stephen R. Lacy, "The Effectiveness of Random, Consecutive Day and Constructed Week Sampling in Newspaper Content Analysis," *Journalism Quarterly,* 70:133-9 (1993).

Robinson, John P. and Leo W. Jeffries, "The Changing Role of Newspapers in the Age of Television," *Journalism Monographs,* vol. 63 (September 1979).

Rodden, John, "Ma Bell, Big Brother and the Information Services Family Feud," *Media Studies Journal,* 6(2):1-16 (1992).

Rogers, Everette M., *Diffusion of Innovations,* 3rd ed. (New York: The Free Press, 1983).

Rogers, Everett M. and Steven H. Chaffee, "Communication and Journalism from 'Daddy' Bleyer to Wilbur Schramm," *Journalism Monographs,* vol. 148 (December 1994).

Romanow, Walter I. and Walter C. Soderlund, "Thomson Newspapers' Acquisition of 'The Globe and Mail': A Case Study of Content Change," *Gazette,* 41:5-17 (1988).

Rosse, James N., "The Evolution of One Newspaper Cities," paper prepared for the Federal Trade Commission Media Symposium in Washington, D.C. (December 14-15, 1978).

Rosse, James N. and James N. Dertouzos, "An Economist's Description of the 'Media Industry,'" pp. 40-192 in *Proceedings of the Symposium on Media Concentration, December 14-15, 1978,* vol. 1 (Washington, D.C.: Bureau of Competition, Federal Trade Commission, 1979).

Rosse, James N., James N. Dertouzos, Michael Robinson and Steven Wildman, "Economic Issues in Mass Communication Industries," paper prepared for the Federal Trade Commission Media Symposium (Washington, D.C., December 14-15, 1978),

Rothenbuhler, Eric W., "Neofunctionalism for Mass Communication Theory," *Mass Communication Yearbook,* vol. 6 (Newbury Park, Calif.: Sage, 1987).

Rule, James B., *Theories of Civil Violence* (Berkeley, Calif.: University of California Press, 1988).

Rystrom, Kenneth, "The Impact of Newspaper Endorsements," *Newspaper Research Journal,* 4:19-28 (1986).

Samuelson, Merrill, "A Standardized Test to Measure Job Satisfaction in the Newsroom," *Journalism Quarterly,* 39:285-91 (1962).

Scherer, F. M., "Technological Change and the Modern Corporation," pp. 270-95 in B. Bock, H. J. Goldschmid, I. M. Millstein and F. M. Scherer (eds.), *The Impact of the Modern Corporation* (New York: Columbia University Press, 1984).

Schiller, Dan, "An Historical Approach to Objectivity and Professionalism in American News Reporting," *Journal of Communication,* 29(4):46-57 (1979).

Schudson, Michael, *Discovering the News* (New York: Basic Books, 1978).

Schudson, Michael, "The Politics of Narrative Form: The Emergence of News Conventions in Print and Television," *Daedalus,* 11:97-112 (1982).

Schumpeter, Joseph A., *The Theory of Economic Development* (Cambridge, Mass.: Harvard University Press, 1949).

Scott, John, "Managerial Revolution," pp. 353-5 in William Outhwaite and Tom Bottomore (eds.), *The Blackwell Dictionary of Twentieth-Century Social Thought* (Oxford, England: Blackwell, 1994).

Scott, Paul T., "The Mass Media in Los Angeles Since the Rise of Television," *Journalism Quarterly,* 31:161-6, 192 (1954).

Scott, W. R., "Professionals in Bureaucracies: Areas of Conflict," in H. Vollmer and D. Mills (eds.), *Professionalism* (Englewood Cliffs, N.J.: Prentice Hall, 1966).

Seldes, George, *Freedom of the Press* (Indianapolis: Bobbs-Merrill, 1935).

Seldes, George, *Lords of the Press* (New York: J. Messner, 1938).

Sellers, Leonard Leslie, *Investigative Reporting: Methods and Barriers* (Ph.D. Diss., Stanford University, 1977).

Sethi, S. Prakash, "Corporation," in *Academic American Encyclopedia,* electronic version (Danbury, Conn.: Grolier, 1992).

Severin, Werner J. and James W. Tankard, Jr., *Communication Theories: Origins, Methods, Uses* (New York: Hastings House, 1979).

Shah, Hemant, "News and the "Self-Production of Society," *Journalism Monographs,* vol. 144 (April 1994).

Shaw, David, "Public and Press — Two Viewpoints," *Los Angeles Times* (August 11, 1985).

Shaw, Donald L., "News Bias and the Telegraph: A Study of Historical Change," *Journalism Quarterly,* 44:3-12, 31 (1967).

Sheehan, Robert, "There's Plenty of Privacy Left in Private Enterprise," *Fortune* (July 15, 1966).

Shoemaker, Pamela, "Media Treatment of Deviant Political Groups," *Journalism Quarterly,* 61:66-75, 82 (1984).

Small, Albion W., *General Sociology* (Chicago: University of Chicago Press, 1905).

Smelser, Neil J., *The Sociology of Economic Life* (Englewood Cliffs, N.J.: Prentice-Hall, 1963).

Smith, Adam, *The Wealth of Nations* (New York: Modern Library, 1937 [1776]).

Smith, Adam, *An Inquiry Into the Nature and Causes of the Wealth of Nations* (Chicago: William Benton, Encyclopedia Britannica, Inc., 1952 [1776]).

So, Alvin Y., *Social Change and Development: Modernization, Dependency and World-System Theories* (Newbury Park, Calif.: Sage, 1990).

Sobel, Judith and Edwin Emery, "U.S. Dailies' Competition in Relation to Circulation Size: A Newspaper Data Update," *Journalism Quarterly*, 55:145-9 (1978).

Soley, Lawrence C., "Pundits in Print: 'Experts' and Their Use in Newspaper Stories," *Newspaper Research Journal*, 15(2):65-75 (1994).

Soley, Lawrence C. and Robert L. Craig, "Advertising Pressures on Newspapers: A Survey," *Journal of Advertising*, 21(4):1-9 (1992).

Soloski, John, "Economics and Management: The Real Influence of Newspaper Groups," *Newspaper Research Journal*, 1:19-28 (1979).

Spencer, Herbert, *First Principles*, vol. 1 (New York: De Witt Revolving Fund, 1958 [1862]).

Spencer, Herbert, *Principles of Sociology*, 3rd ed. (New York: D. Appleton, 1910 [1888]).

Spencer, Herbert, *The Principles of Sociology*, vol. III (New York: D. Appleton, 1897).

Spencer, Herbert, "The Evolution of Societies," in A. Etzioni and E. Etzioni-Halevy (eds.), *Social Change* (New York: Basic Books, 1973).

SPSS Inc., *SPSS/PC+ Trends* (Chicago: SPSS, Inc., 1990).

Squires, James D., *Read All About It! The Corporate Takeover of America's Newspapers* (New York: Times Books, 1994).

St. Dizier, Byron, "Editorial Page Editors and Endorsements: Chain-Owned vs. Independent Newspapers," *Newspaper Research Journal*, 8:63-8 (1986).

Stamm, Keith R. and Avery M. Guest, "Communication and Community Integration: An Analysis of the Communication Behavior of Newcomers," *Journalism Quarterly*, 68:644-56 [1991]).

Stamm, Keith and Doug Underwood, "The Relationship of Job Satisfaction to Newsroom Policy Changes," paper presented to the Association for Education in Journalism and Mass Communication (Washington, D.C., August 1991).

Stempel, Guido H. III, "Effects on Performance of a Cross-Media Monopoly," *Journalism Monographs*, vol. 29 (June 1973).

Stinchcombe, Arthur L., *Constructing Social Theories* (Chicago: University of Chicago Press, 1968).

Stone, Gerald, "A Mellow Appraisal of Media Monopoly Mania," pp. 44-60 in Michael C. Emery and Ted Curtis Smythe, *Mass Communication: Concepts and Issues in the Mass Media* (Dubuque, Iowa: Wm. C. Brown Company, 1980).

Stone, Gerald, *Examining Newspapers: What Research Reveals About America's Newspapers* (Newbury Park, Calif.: Sage, 1987).

Sweezy, Paul M., *The Theory of Capitalist Development* (New York: Modern Reader, 1970).

Sweezy, Paul M. and H. Magdoff, *The Dynamics of U.S. Capitalism* (New York: Modern Reader, 1972).

Taylor, Frederick, *Scientific Management* (New York: Harper & Row, 1964 [1947]).

Tharp, Marty and Linda R. Stanley, "Trends in Profitability of Daily U.S. Newspapers by Circulation Size, 1978-1988," paper presented to the Association for Education in Journalism and Mass Communication (Minneapolis, August 1990).

Tharp, Marty and Linda R. Stanley, "A Time Series Analysis of Newspaper Profitability by Circulation Size," *Journal of Media Economics*, 5(1):3-12 (1992).

Theodorson, G. A. and A. G. Theodorson, *A Modern Dictionary of Sociology* (New York: Crowell, 1969).

Thrift, Ralph, Jr., "How Chain Ownership Affects Editorial Vigor of Newspapers," *Journalism Quarterly*, 54:327-31 (1977).

Tichenor, Phillip J., "The Logic of Social and Behavioral Science," pp. 10-28 in Guido H. Stempel III and Bruce H. Westley (eds.), *Research Methods in Mass Communication* (Englewood Cliffs, N.J.: Prentice-Hall, 1981).

Tichenor, Phillip J., George A. Donohue and Clarice N. Olien, "Mass Communication Research: Evolution of a Structural Model," *Journalism Quarterly*, 50:419-25 (1973).

Tichenor, Phillip J., George A. Donohue and Clarice N. Olien, *Community Conflict and The Press* (Beverly Hills, Calif.: Sage, 1980).

Tijmstra, L. F., "The Challenge of TV to the Press," *Journal of Broadcasting*, 4(1):3-13 (1959-60).

Tillinghast, Diana Stover, "Limits of Competition," pp. 71-87 in Robert G. Picard, James P. Winter, Maxwell E. McCombs and Stephen Lacy (eds.), *Press Concentration and Monopoly* (Norwood, N.J.: Ablex, 1988).

Tillinghast, William A., "Declining Newspaper Readership: Impact of Region and Urbanization," *Journalism Quarterly*, 58:14-23, 50 (1981).

Tiryakian, Edward A., "On the Significance of De-Differentiation," pp. 118-34 in S. N. Eisenstadt and H. J. Helle (eds.), *Macro-Sociological Theory* (Beverly Hills, Calif.: Sage Publications, 1985).

Toulmin, S. and J. Goodfield, *The Architecture of Matter* (New York: Harper & Row, 1962).

Touraine, Alaine, *The Post-Industrial Society* (New York: Random House, 1971).

Tuchman, Gaye, *Making News* (New York: Free Press, 1978).

Tuchman, Gaye, "Mass Media Institutions," pp. 601-26 in Neil J. Smelser (ed.), *Handbook of Sociology* (Beverly Hills, Calif.: Sage, 1988).

Tucker, Robert C. (ed.), *The Marx-Engles Reader*, 2nd ed. (New York: W. W. Norton & Company, 1978).

Tunstall, Jeremy, *Journalists at Work* (London: The Anchor Press, 1971).

Turner, Jonathan H., *The Structure of Sociological Theory* (Homewood, Ill.: The Dorsey Press, 1978).

Turner, Jonathan H., *Herbert Spencer: A Renewed Appreciation* (Beverly Hills, Calif.: Sage Publications, 1985).

Turner, Jonathan H. and David Musick, *American Dilemmas: A Sociological Interpretation of Enduring Social Issues* (New York: Columbia University Press, 1985).

Underwood, Doug, "When MBAs Rule the Newsroom," *Columbia Journalism Review* (March/April 1988), pp. 23-30.

Underwood, Doug, *When MBAs Rule the Newsroom: How the Marketers and Managers Are Reshaping Today's Media* (New York: Columbia University Press, 1993).

U.S. Bureau of the Census, *County and City Data Book: 1994* (Washington, D.C.: U.S. Government Printing Office, 1994).

U.S. Bureau of Census, *Historical Statistics of the United States, Colonial Times to 1970* (Washington, D.C.: U.S. Government Printing Office, 1975).

U.S. Bureau of the Census, *Statistical Abstract of the United States: 1989* (Washington, D.C.: U.S. Government Printing Office, 1989).

U.S. Bureau of Census, *Statistical Abstract of the United States: 1990* (Washington, D.C.: U.S. Government Printing Office, 1990).

U.S. Bureau of Census, *Statistical Abstract of the United States, 1991* (Washington, D.C.: U.S. Government Printing Office, 1991).

U.S. Department of Commerce, *Historical Statistics of the United States, 1789-1945* (Washington, D.C.: U.S. Government Printing Office, 1949).

U.S. Temporary National Economic Committee, *The Distribution of Ownership in the 200 Largest Nonfinancial Corporations,* Monograph 29 (Washington, D.C.: U.S. Government Printing Office, 1940).

van den Berghe, Pierre L., "Dialectic and Functionalism," in R. Serge Denisoff et al. (eds.), *Theories and Paradigms in Contemporary Sociology* (Itasca: F. E. Peacock Publishers, 1974).

Vidich, Arthur J. and Joseph Bensman, *Small Town in Mass Society* (Princeton, N.J.: Princeton University Press, 1968).

Villard, Oswald Garrison, "The Press Today: The Chain Daily," *The Nation* (May 21, 1930), pp. 597-8.

Viswanath, K., Emily Kahn, John R. Finnegan, Jr., James Hertog and John D. Potter, "Motivation and the Knowledge Gap: Effects of a Campaign to Reduce Diet-Related Cancer Risk," *Communication Research,* 20:546-63 (1993).

Wackman, Daniel B., Donald M. Gillmor, Cecilie Gaziano and Everette E. Dennis, "Chain Newspaper Autonomy as Reflected in Presidential Campaign Endorsements," *Journalism Quarterly,* 52:411-20 (1975).

Wacquant, Loïc J. D., "Positivism," pp. 495-98 in William Outhwaite and Tom Bottomore (eds.), *The Blackwell Dictionary of Twentieth-Century Social Thought* (Oxford, England: Blackwell, 1994).

Wagenberg, Ronald H. and Walter C. Soderlund, "The Influence of Chain Ownership on Editorial Comment in Canada," *Journalism Quarterly,* 52:93-8 (1975).

Wallace, Ruth A. and Alison Wolf, *Contemporary Sociological Theory* (Englewood Cliffs, N.J.: Prentice-Hall, 1986).

Wallerstein, Immanuel, *The Modern World-System I: Capitalist Agriculture and the Origins of the European World-Economy in the Sixteenth Century* (New York: Academic Press, 1974).

Wallerstein, Immanuel, *The Modern World-System II: Mercantilism and the Consolidation of the European World-Economy, 1600-1750* (New York: Academic Press, 1980).

Wanta, Wayne, Mary Ann Stephenson, Judy VanSlyke Turk and Maxwell E. McCombs, "How President's State of Union Talk Influenced News Media Agendas," *Journalism Quarterly,* 66:537-41 (1989).

Waterman, David, "A New Look at Media Chains and Groups: 1977-1989," *Journal of Broadcasting & Electronic Media,* 35:167-78 (1991).

Weaver, David H. and G. Cleveland Wilhoit, *The American Journalists: A Portrait of U.S. News People and Their Work* (Bloomington, Ind.: Indiana University Press, 1986).

Weber, Max, *Economy and Society: An Outline of Interpretive Sociology* (New York: Bedminster Press, 1922).

Weber, Max, *The Theory of Social and Economic Organization,* trans. A. M. Henderson and Talcott Parsons (New York: The Free Press, 1964 [1947]).

White, William Allen, (Editorial), *Emporia (Kansas) Gazette* (December 23, 1925).

Wilhoit, G. Cleveland and Dan G. Drew, "Editorial Writers on American Daily Newspapers: A 20-Year Portrait," *Journalism Monographs,* vol. 129 (October 1991).

Wilhoit, G. Cleveland and David Weaver, "U.S. Journalists at Work, 1971-1992," paper presented to the Association for Education in Journalism and Mass Communication (Atlanta, August 1994).

Wilson, Thomas C., "Community Population Size and Social Heterogeneity: An Empirical Test," *American Journal of Sociology,* 91:1154-69 (1986).

Wood, William C. and Sharon L. O'Hare, "Paying for the Video Revolution: Consumer Spending on the Mass Media," *Journal of Communication,* 41(1):24-30 (1991).

Worthy, James, "Organizational Structure and Employee Morale," *American Sociological Review,* 15:169-79 (1950).

Wright, Charles R., *Mass Communication: A Sociological Perspective* (New York: Random House, 1959).

Wright, Charles R., "Functional Analysis and Mass Communication," *Public Opinion Quarterly,* 24:605-20 (1960).

Wright, Charles R., *Mass Communication: A Sociological Perspective,* 3rd ed. (New York: Random House, 1986).

Wright, B. E. and John M. Lavine, *The Constant Dollar Newspaper: An Economic Analysis Covering the Last Two Decades* (Chicago: Inland Daily Press Association, 1982).

Wrong, Dennis H., "The Oversocialized Conception of Man in Modern Sociology," *American Sociological Review,* 26:183-93 (1961).

Zaharopoulos, Thimios and Ronald E. McIntosh, "Newspaper Pulitzer Prizes and Their Relationship to Circulation," paper presented to the Association for Education in Journalism and Mass Communication (Kansas City, Mo., August 1993).

Zeitlin, Maurice, "Corporate Ownership and Control: The Large Corporation and the Capitalist Class," *American Journal of Sociology,* 79:1073-119 (1974).

Index

ISBN 0-8138-2269-6